Also by Colin Fletcher

The Secret Worlds of Colin Fletcher (1989)

The Complete Walker III (1984)

The Man from the Cave (1981)

The New Complete Walker (1974)

The Winds of Mara (1973)

The Man Who Walked Through Time (1968)

The Complete Walker (1968)

The Thousand-Mile Summer (1964)

RIVER

RIVER

One Man's Journey Down the Colorado, Source to Sea

by Colin Fletcher

 Alfred A. Knopf   New York   1997

THIS IS A BORZOI BOOK
PUBLISHED BY ALFRED A. KNOPF, INC.

http://www.randomhouse.com/

Grateful acknowledgment is made to the following for
permission to reprint previously published material:
Cambridge University Press: Excerpt of Elizabeth Loftus
interview with Jack Hamilton, from *Affect and Accuracy in Recall:
Studies of "Flashbulb" Memories,* edited by Eugene Winograd
and Ulric Neisser (New York: Cambridge University Press, 1992).
Reprinted by permission of Cambridge University Press.
Harcourt Brace & Company and *Faber and Faber Limited:*
Excerpt from "The Hollow Men," from *Collected Poems 1909–1962*
by T. S. Eliot, copyright © 1936 by Harcourt Brace & Company,
copyright © 1963, 1964 by T. S. Eliot. Rights outside
the United States administered by Faber and Faber Limited,
London. Reprinted by permission of Harcourt Brace & Company
and Faber and Faber Limited.
Houghton Mifflin Company: Excerpt from "What Any Lover Learns,"
from *Collected Poems 1917–1982* by Archibald MacLeish, copyright
© 1985 by The Estate of Archibald MacLeish. All rights
reserved. Reprinted by permission of Houghton Mifflin Company.
Sterling Lord Literistic, Inc.: Excerpt from *Desert Notes*
by Barry Lopez (New York: Avon Books), copyright © 1976
by Barry Holstun Lopez. Reprinted by permission of
Sterling Lord Literistic, Inc.

Library of Congress Cataloging-in-Publication Data
Fletcher, Colin.
River: one man's journey down the Colorado, source
to sea / by Colin Fletcher.—1st ed.
p.   cm.
ISBN 0-394-57421-4 (alk. paper)
1. Colorado River (Wyo.–Mexico)—Description and travel.
2. Rafting (Sports)—Colorado River (Wyo.–Mexico)
3. Fletcher, Colin—Journeys—Colorado River (Wyo.–
Mexico)   I. Title.
F788.F56   1997
917.91'30453—dc20   96-13220   CIP

Manufactured in the United States of America
First Edition

river:

A copious stream of water flowing in a channel towards the sea . . .
A copious stream or flow *of* (something) . . .
. . . the boundary between life and death.

—*The Oxford English Dictionary*

Contents

RIVER

SOURCES

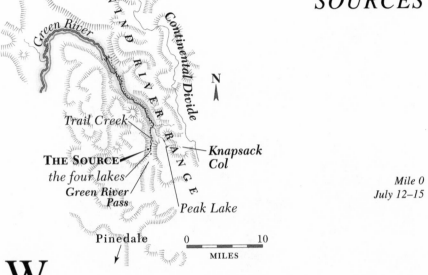

THE SOURCE
the four lakes
Green River
Pass

Trail Creek

Knapsack
Col

Peak Lake

Pinedale

0   10
MILES

N

Mile 0
July 12–15

Well, see you in six months," said John. We shook hands. Then I turned and began to walk out across the almost level floor of the mountain pass, toward the lakes.

At first, easy going: firm glacial moraine. Even with my heavy pack, I could stride out. But soon I was laboring across sodden, tussocky grassland that enveloped the lakes.

The four lakes—no more than ponds, really—lay out in the middle of the pass. The first three drained south, the way we had come. So the fourth and farthest was the one. The map said it drained north, and if it did so then it would mark the beginning of the river. *The* river.

I slogged slowly on. Gusts of wind funneled past. Overhead, along snow-marbled peaks, clouds hung gray and low.

Underfoot, the grass grew even soggier, rougher. I moved slowly but steadily across it, eyes riveted on puddle and beehive tussock, mind preoccupied with decisions about where next to put a boot down. Then I looked up and found myself facing an abrupt green bank, shoulder high.

Beyond the bank I could see, almost at eye level, a water surface whipped by wind gusts. It was both dull and shining, like hammered pewter. I began to climb the bank—knife-edge and nervously aware that the water was the fourth lake, and that it probably marked the true beginning of my journey.

I reached the top of the bank. A brief impression of a little lake, indeed no more than a pond; beyond it, a gentle slope mottled with snow patches

*The start. Green River Pass. I walk toward
the four lakes and, I hope, the river's source.*

and bare rock but softened by grass and dark spruce trees. Off to my right, a hint of an outlet. So the lake almost certainly drained north. I began turning to wave a final goodbye to John.

Because of my pack's inertia, I turned slowly. And I had hardly begun to pivot when I saw, bearing down on us from the south, a vast, swirling wall of grayness. The racing cloud wall filled the pass. It blotted out the flanking peaks.

My arm, poised to wave, stabbed southward in warning. The tiny figure on the far side of the pass turned to face the approaching storm. For a moment we both stood staring. Then we were waving hurried farewells.

I waited barely long enough to see John shoulder his pack and begin striding back the way we had come. Then I turned and began to skirt the lake, left-handed and lickety-split. The lake margin was windswept and soggy but on the slope beyond it the spruces and outcrops whispered "campsite."

As I hurried around the lake I passed a snowbank nestling among boulders and wondered briefly if it might be the river's ultimate birthplace. Then I was at the foot of the slope. A small rivulet cascaded down it, into the lake. If permanent, it must lead to the true source. I began to climb the slope, following the rivulet.

Off to my left, the massive cloud wall loomed closer now, blacker.

Fifty paces up the slope, trees and rock cradled a shallow natural cup or dell. The floor of the dell might turn soggy in a downpour, but it would do at a pinch. I dumped my pack there, beside a fallen tree, then hurried on up the rivulet until I could see the beginnings of an open grassy place through which it flowed. This sloping, rock-girt meadow somehow looked as if it might lead to the real source, to my kind of source; but it offered no hint of a better campsite.

I half-ran back down to my pack.

The trees and rocks that sheltered the little dell hid all but the top of the approaching cloud wall, but it looked very close now. As I pulled the tent out of its bag my bare arm reported big, cold raindrops. I put on my rain-jacket.

By the time I had the tent laid out flat and the fly sheet spread over it for protection, rain was falling steadily, heavily. But the thin skewer pegs and even the four bigger snow pegs for the fly-sheet corners went easily into the soft wet ground, and a boulder and a sapling and the fallen tree trunk provided additional quick, safe anchors. Within minutes I had the tent up, pack safely inside, rainjacket off and a groundsheet covering the floor. The floor was only mildly damp.

For a moment I paused and listened to rain pounding on taut fly sheet. The bright orange tent with its dark blue fly was an old friend. I trusted it. We understood each other, too, and that had helped. An unfamiliar tent might have been hell to pitch quickly.

I pulled off my boots and unpacked the bedroom; inflated the mattress pad, unfurled my sleeping bag, then stretched out on it. The rain was getting heavier. There'd be little to do for a while except sleep, and that suited me fine: sleeping is one of my fields of competence.

I could do with a breathing spell, anyway. It was always like that at the start: you needed time to readjust to the wilderness world. Time to get back in touch with solitude. The three-day approach march with John had been good; we'd meshed well. But now I could begin to wrap myself in the richness of being alone.

The rain pounded on, just above my head. I stirred, unpacked the kitchen. Outside the part-open door flap, under the fly sheet's sheltering alcove, I set up the stove and cooked a late lunch of couscous-in-tomato-sauce soup. When it was ready I transferred half of it from the pot into my Lexan cup. Then I lay back, propped on one elbow, slowly spooning soup from the cup and staring out through the still part-open door flap. All I could see was slanting rain, blurred shapes, oppressive grayness. But a July storm, here in the Wyoming Rockies, would with luck last no more than a day. Maybe two. Then the skies would clear. I smiled to myself. There was a fitness to the journey's beginning this way. It echoed the pattern of the long-drawn-out preparations.

Three years earlier, the groundwork had begun almost serenely. But then had come a cloud wall of obstacles and frustrations that at times raised doubts about whether the project would ever get launched. At the eleventh hour, though, the last hurdle had fallen—had melted away, really—and John and I had set out from roadhead, virtually on schedule, for our approach march to the source. And now, sipping soup in my little tent, I felt curiously confident that the echo I'd detected would resonate true: that the journey would also surmount its stormy start, and would soon shine.

I smiled again. If you are going to attempt long solo journeys you had better, for safety's sake, be a realist; but at root you must also be an unreasoning optimist. It occurred to me that I'd been applying optimism in headlong doses ever since I conceived the notion of making this source-to-sea journey.

I poured the last of the soup from pot into cup.

Looking back, the moment of conception wasn't easy to determine. But the journey had been no sudden, quirky brainstorm. If you took the long view you could detect a configuration that had been building for a lifetime.

The earliest stratum was probably laid down half a century earlier in England, during my youthful Devonian period. Early one morning I'd begun to walk up a Dartmoor river from the road nearest its source. I'd followed it, mile after wild mile, to the source, then struck across open moor to the source of another river and followed that river down to the place it, in turn, first crossed a road. That river journey had occupied only one day in my life but a lasting niche in my memory. And variations on its pilgrimage theme had persisted down the decades.

War had consumed my early twenties, but afterward, during five years in Africa, some small safari springs had welled up. Then, in my late thirties and early forties, many minor rivulets had coalesced. A clear pattern emerged. I was, it seemed, a sucker for bright-colored dreams that involved traveling under my own steam, preferably on foot, from a well-defined A to a well-defined B—not in order to get from one of these points to the other but to discover and relish what lay between. It turned out that I had a complementary weakness, or strength, for turning such dreams into deeds. Three times within five years I shucked off "civilized" entanglements and made backpack journeys that lasted several months. Two of these walks—the two that had been truly successful—took place in the

U.S.; and each of them happened to follow, in part or whole, the lower Colorado River.

Through my late forties and early fifties, the pattern continued, in miniature. I made countless shorter backpack trips, and several took me along further stretches of the lower Colorado. As I approached my sixties, the germ of the idea for this journey had come close to surfacing: I wrote that "sometime in the next hundred and fifty years I plan to complete a piecemeal walk along the entire Colorado River." Then, one spring morning in my mid-sixties, I was taking a shower when it came to me that what I most wanted to do with my life just then was to follow a major river, under my own power, from its source to its mouth.

As far as I could now discern, lying in my tent three years later, echoes from the two long American walks had helped recrystallize the old pattern.

I had for years seen those walks as highlights of my life, and that spring morning in the shower I'd recognized that if I wanted to make another such journey, time was running out. At sixty, if you command even median powers of self-delusion, you can still kid yourself you're young; at seventy, I suspected, it might be more difficult.

I also realized that I'd grown soft. Things had been going too well lately. Too easily. I needed something to pare the fat off my soul, to scare the shit out of me, to make me grateful, again, for being alive. And I knew, deep and safe, beyond mere intellect, that there is nothing like a wilderness journey for rekindling the fires of life. Simplicity is part of it. Cutting the cackle. Transportation reduced to leg- or arm-power, eating irons to one spoon. Such simplicity, together with sweat and silence, amplify the rhythms of any long journey, especially through unknown, untattered territory. And in the end such a journey can restore an understanding of how insignificant you are—and thereby set you free.

From the first, there was precious little doubt about whether this particular dream was the one I had been waiting for, and I think I knew almost at once that I would go. It was probably the idea of traveling on instead of alongside the river that clinched it: here was a journey consistent with the old pattern yet also new. There'd have to be some backpacking at the start, when the river was still a mountain creek, and perhaps again near the end; but mostly I'd travel by raft or some other vessel.

As usual, intellectual reasons hardly seemed to feature in my decision. After all, following a river from its source to its mouth was so natural and whole and round a notion that it called for no dry intellectual explanation. And I had long known one important thing: any river is more than just a river. Much more. It can stand, easily and naturally, for many things.

Anyway, the dream held up. And now, lying in my tent at the river's source and reviewing the journey's genesis, I saw more clearly than ever that it had emerged from the confluence of a lifetime's rivulets and tributaries—and therefore made profound sense.

Once you've dreamed of making such a journey you face whole hives of reasons that keep swarming in to demonstrate why you should not transmute dream into reality. Good, sensible, weighty reasons. Fortunately, I'd managed to sidestep them all.

From the start, I was clear about certain basic things. I wanted the journey to be substantially uninterrupted, so that it flowed like the river. I wanted to travel not just solo but slowly, with time to stand and stare. A year would be perfect. And I wanted a quiet, unostentatious journey. A genuine journey, free from the artificiality and distortion that the presence of any outside observers, let alone the media, is bound to impose. A journey, not an exploit.

At the time the idea burst on me I was fully occupied with other matters, and for months all I could do was let things simmer. I don't think there was ever much doubt in my mind, but almost a year passed before I brought the project up for open debate. I promptly ratified it by a landslide 1–0 vote, and began planning.

Now, some people seem to imagine that once you've decided to make a journey of this kind, all you do is pick up your hat and walk out the door. Or something like that. T. S. Eliot, for one, knew differently: *"Between the idea / And the reality / Between the motion / And the act / Falls the Shadow."* I knew all about the Shadow that falls during the jigs you dance as preludes to wilderness journeys. In theory, what you're doing is simply striving, by meticulous planning, to minimize Murphy; to shoot him down with foresight. But in practice, eventually, the Shadow always falls. When it did, this time, it was a doozy. And it had left its imprint.

At the start, though, my planning had for a longish spell proceeded slowly and sensibly enough, with preliminary research sandwiched in, as opportunity arose, between more pressing affairs.

First, I'd had to clarify and refine.

Although my early and natural choice of a river had been the Colorado, I didn't want to accept that decision blindly, without proper deliberation. So I considered several other candidates, far and near. But none of them really stood a chance. Thirty years of intermittent walking beside the Colorado's lower reaches, between Marble Canyon and the Mexican border, had in a sense made it "my" river (a ridiculous claim when viewed from outside, but a solid conviction when felt in the gut). On the other hand, the upper 1000 miles of river would, with one minuscule exception, be new territory for me. Besides, the Colorado is no ordinary river. Although it is, at 1700 miles, the second-longest in the United States, its banks are not, like those of most big American rivers, heavily populated. No big city stands on them, and in the first 1300 miles I'd pass only three places that might qualify as towns. The river flows through an astonishing diversity of terrain, including the most dramatic canyon country in America. Except near the end, it flows largely through federal land, protected from private development. Its Grand Canyon provides not only a visual wonder of the world but also perhaps the country's toughest whitewater challenge.

Yet this wildness coin has an anomalous flip side. Because all but the headwaters flow through desert, and the river is the area's prime source of water—that lifeblood of existence on this planet—it has attracted prodigious attention, both political and engineering. We humans now control its flow so iron-fistedly that my friend Philip L. Fradkin called his book about the Colorado *A River No More*. He reports that we divert more water to points outside its basin than we do from any other American river. And he calls it "the most dramatic, and the most highly litigated and politicized river in this country." In other ways, too, the Colorado is unlike most rivers. It does not grow steadily bigger: after an early maturity it receives no major permanent tributaries. In its final stages—largely but not entirely because of human interference—it tends to taper away. For years on end it may never reach the ocean.

One way and another, the Colorado seemed an irresistible choice for my journey. Anyway, I chose it.

That done, I had to define "the Colorado." The name originally applied only to the waterway below the junction of the Green and Grand Rivers. Then, in 1921—the year of my conception—under pressure from booster politicians in the state of Colorado, the Grand was renamed: the main river and the former Grand became, together, "the Colorado." But because the Green is 300 miles longer than the former Grand (it also drains a larger area), geographers regard it as the "master stream," and its headwaters in Wyoming as the source of the Colorado. I was happy to go along with the geographers—especially as all reports had the Green wilder and less spoiled, with a source more befitting a major river.

Next question: just where is the source of the Green? The Green's longest branch, and therefore its master stream, drains out of Peak Lake, at 10,500 feet in Wyoming's Wind River Range, and the lake's main feeder is considered to originate at Knapsack Col, 1700 feet higher. So at first I thought of Knapsack Col as the starting point of my journey. But problems surfaced. Deep snow and avalanche threats normally prevented you from footslogging in to Peak Lake, let alone Knapsack Col, until late August. For me, that was too late. By now I'd reluctantly decided to cut my journey to six months: unless I yearned to chip ice off riverside boulders I should aim to be out of Grand Canyon by mid-November. Experience and expert advice also suggested that if I had to backpack at all down in Mexico, as seemed likely (because a long stretch of river just below the border is often drained dry by irrigation ditches), I'd be wise to do so in midwinter; otherwise, even if the river did not finally fade away into the sand, I might. Unless I hurried—the way I was determined not to—I could meet these target dates only by starting no later than mid-July.

I therefore decided to accept as "my" source a small, unnamed lake at the head of Trail Creek, four straight-line miles from Knapsack Col. Most years, it seemed, you could walk in there by mid-July. Naturally, I disliked even this minor fudge. But the lake lies only 150 vertical feet lower than Peak Lake; and Trail Creek is barely two miles shorter than the master stream, which it soon joins. Besides, there was something about the lie of the land on the map—perhaps the way Trail Creek formed a logical, straight-line extension of the main river—that made it seem the right kind of place to start. It had become important to me, this business of feeling right about the place the journey began, and most of the misgivings about choice of source vanished when Philip Fradkin, who had been to both the Trail Creek lake and Knapsack Col while researching *A River No More*, told me, "Frankly, it's a lot better place. That's where the river *ought* to start."

By this time I'd managed to do some preparatory reading, and in the course of it learned to my surprise that no one seemed to have traveled the entire length of the river. Only three had come close. When John Wesley Powell led his pioneering boat party through the canyons in 1869, most of the group stopped as soon as they cleared Grand Canyon, but two of the men, Hall and Hawkins, apparently went on down to the sea. The Powell party started, though, 225 miles below the source—at the town of Green River, Wyoming (sometimes called Green River City). Ellsworth Kolb and his brother Emery (whom I met briefly before my walk through Grand Canyon in 1963, when he was over eighty), had in 1911 run the same stretch of river and taken the first movies of such a trip, and Ellsworth later went on down to the sea, alone. But the Kolbs had also launched at Green River City. There seemed to be no other candidates for a source-to-sea journey, and the prospect of becoming the first, if I succeeded, added an undeniable piquancy to my project.

External demands on my time at last slackened and the real planning started. At first, things went smoothly. When I consulted a river-running expert, he confirmed my intuition that an inflatable raft was the proper choice of vessel—and arranged a thirteen-day practice trip for me on the Idaho Salmon. Then, just as the planning began to gain momentum, it was braked by the first in what would turn out to be a series of body-blow obstacles and frustrations. Literal body blows: one-two, recurring.

Now, few things are drearier than a relentless litany of personal ailments. What's more, an informed preacher only makes things worse—and I've been known to claim the presidency of Local 1 of ABSH, the Amalgamated Brotherhood of Suffering Hypochondriacs. In this case, though, I think the facts can stand alone. First, a heavyweight flu bug moved in— and lingered and went on lingering (I have a history of such nonsense). Next, angina attacks triggered angiograms, then an angioplasty. A second and mercifully fleeting flu bug came and went—but persistent and increasing pain in my right wrist began to raise doubts about whether I could row, steadily and sometimes fiercely, for six straight months.

Meanwhile, in between these preliminary medical hurdles, I hacked away at the list of things that had to be done. Deciding on make and model of raft and of tubular metal frame to hold it rigid. Choosing among kitchensful of freeze-dried foods for convenience, toxicity and, above all, nutritional value. Amassing maps. Wading through whitewater equipment catalogues that listed every item you could imagine and some you couldn't. Getting National Park Service permits, notably for passage through Grand Canyon. Selecting pickup points for food, extra equipment and mail—at dams, ranger stations, post offices and other waypoints—then contacting the right people at each of them. Making arrangements for getting around dams. And setting up cast-iron, trustable plans with an outfitter in Pinedale, Wyoming, for a rendezvous with the raft at the highest feasible point. To fine-tune some of these matters I made a 4000-mile, seven-state reconnaissance swing—taking pains, with one exception, to avoid seeing the Green or Colorado. On this hurried drive I managed to fit in two days on an Idaho river learning how to line a raft around a rapid single-handed, then refreshing and improving such skills at reading rapids as I'd learned on the earlier practice trip.

For a spell, things went well. I decided on the small outboard motor I would buy. (I planned, of course, to run the living river under my own steam. That is, with my own oars. But rowing a bulbous inflatable raft several hundred miles down the reservoirs created behind major dams would probably be impossible, at least in headwinds, so I'd decided that where engineers had obliterated the river I could legitimately use one of their products to move me forward.) I began to assemble smaller gear, too: technical whitewater equipment, from oars, pumps and a pressure gauge to dry bags, river sandals and a semi-dry suit; ropes, watertight ammunition boxes and a padded, watertight container for photographic equipment; also such ancillary items as a water filter, film and biodegradable soap. Meanwhile, I tried to discover whether I could bypass the reported dry stretch of river below the Mexican border by rafting through irrigation canals; but my assault against the twin barriers of language and bureaucratic inertia were limping toward stalemate when more body-blows fell.

The artery cleared by the first angioplasty reclogged. A second operation, promptly performed, levied a six-month wait before doctors could give me the go-ahead. Side glances from friends now began to imply a new question: "Can the old buzzard make it? Or will he keel over with a heart attack in the middle of some god-awful rapid?" But I rather think my logical and calculating sectors—insofar as they were engaged—saw the heart problem as just another and somewhat minor hazard among many, and my surface response was, "What better way to go?" Deeper down, of course, I knew the journey posed very real dangers. I even suffered occasional qualms about them. But I did not believe they'd sink me.

Before long, an orthopedist advised that with a prompt fix to my wrist I'd be ready to row by the following July. Ten days before Christmas I had carpal tunnel surgery. At this point the planning process would have moved into higher gear—but in late January yet another flu bug hit. A blockbuster.

This third bug three-quarter clobbered me. And it lingered, in repeated big-league relapses, even longer than the first. (Virus infection relapses are a phenomenon still laughed out of court by most doctors; but, it seems to me, affirmed by a growing list of patients.) About this time a friend looked me in the eye and said, "You don't think somebody is trying to tell you something?" I even began to consider postponement for a year. Well into April, the flu Shadow kept surging over me, in waves. But during a promising ebb tide I made my decision: go flat-out for a July start.

In May the planning moved to its inevitable, madhouse crescendo. My living room disappeared under a blizzard of food and supplies. Minefields of last-minute glitches appeared. I mine-swept. Days dawned and died, dawned and died. Flu relapses waxed, waned. One last-minute alarm: a minor skin cancer. It went the way of all such flesh.

The outboard motor arrived; then the raft and its custom-made tubular interior frame, with detachable transom for the motor. In mid-June I tried out raft and motor on a local lake, had the transom modified, then carried out another trial.

That the trials took place at all was largely due to my near neighbors, the Sextons: John, a bulky, bearded and beamish photographer with a growing national reputation; and Victoria, his quiet, coiled-but-controlled wife and business manager. For months they'd given me zesty support and by now were enmeshed in the project. They would meet me in Pinedale, Wyoming, before the start, and John would come on the approach march to the source, backpacking extra gear and sparing me a ruinous load. Victoria would drive my rented van back to California, where she'd handle back-home logistical support throughout the trip. At its end the Sextons would, if possible, drive down to Mexico and bear me home.

After the raft trials, time to zip things down. I began to pack food and supplies into labeled cardboard boxes. My living room floor reemerged. I loaded raft and gear into the rented van and at last, on July 1, headed for Pinedale.

During the long drive, perhaps because of overenthusiastic backpack trials at roadside camps, the flu came back: in Salt Lake City, a brief hospital visit. Next day I managed to drop off some supplies at Fontenelle Dam (Victoria Sexton would UPS the rest, at appropriate intervals, to successive pickup points), but by the time I reached Pinedale the flu relapse had zombied me.

John and Victoria arrived. I remained zomboid. (Later, John told me that with two days to go before he must either start the approach march or go home to meet other commitments, he said to Victoria, "Judging by how he looks right now, no way we can go!") Then the malaise began to ebb, fast. On July 10, John and I heaved heavy packs onto our backs, left Victoria at roadhead and headed up into the Bridger Wilderness. I still seemed to be spread pretty thin along the backbone, but we took it slowly. Two and a half days later, John said, "Well, see you in six months," and we shook hands.

And now here I was, lying in my tent holding an empty cup, listening to a storm drumming the tent fly. Out through the part-open door flap I could still see only slanting rain, blurred shapes and oppressive grayness. But the optimist in me still felt confident the journey would echo and extend the trajectory of its prologue: would surmount this stormy start and, before long, glitter.

I put down the cup, lay back on my sleeping bag, dozed. When I awoke, rain was still lashing down and the wedge of view was still gray, oppressive. The day seeped dozily away. The night thundered and lightninged, but by daylight the storm had tapered off into tiptoe tappings. All morning the clouds hung low and gray. Then, a little before noon, they began to break up. I crawled outdoors. In one of the protecting spruces, a robin was fluttering his plumage dry. I stood up. Down the emerging, deep-cut V of Trail Creek Canyon, mists still clung to a line of sheer black cliffs. Rock and mist blocked the downriver view, but my mind's eye could see far beyond them. Could discern, whole and clear, the shape of the journey that lay ahead.

For two or three days I would stay in this camp, try to find the source I wanted and, if I succeeded, linger long enough to fix the feel of it on the emulsion of memory. Within seven days I had to rendezvous with my raft, twenty-five miles downriver. In the following month I'd run 350 miles of fast water, free of serious rapids, that would offer, among fuller things, a breaking-in time for raft and techniques. During this month I'd emerge from the mountains into desert. Then the Gates of Lodore would lead me into canyon country and the first challenging rapids—where John Wesley Powell had lost a boat and left such names as Disaster Falls and Hell's Half Mile. Next came 400 miles of canyons—Desolation, Labyrinth, Stillwater—each magnificent but none with major rapids. Immediately below the Green's confluence with the Colorado I'd face the bigger, more testing rapids of Cataract Canyon; then, beyond Lake Powell and Glen Canyon Dam, the journey's prime physical challenge—the Grand Canyon rapids. Below Lake Mead and Hoover Dam should come a time for reflection, down 300 miles of river that I'd already traveled on foot, much of it on my first long walk, thirty years before; and I hoped that down this stretch my memories would turn out to be a mirror that enriched rather than a screen that obscured. Beyond the Mexican border, the only thing I felt sure I'd face was uncertainty. Philip Fradkin had told me, "Down there in the delta, everything's a mirage—physically and emotionally. Nothing is what it seems to be." Sometimes, south of the border, the river continued to run. Sometimes irrigation ditches sucked it dry. So I might have to walk for a spell. But after sixty miles the residues of the irrigation water came together again. When Philip last saw this reconstituted river it eventually sank away into the sand or into a saline lake, but now rumor had it following a new course and running, at least intermittently, clear out to the Gulf of California, or Sea of Cortez. Only one thing about the delta seemed certain: somewhere down there, in sand or sea, after 1700 miles of life, the river would die.

Standing now at its birthplace, looking down the deep V of Trail Creek Canyon, I felt confident that what my mind's eye saw stretching out far beyond the mists and black cliffs was indeed the shape my journey would take. But experience had also taught me that the only sure thing about your expectations in such matters is that nothing will pan out quite the way you expect.

Down Trail Creek Canyon, the mists were lifting. Soon I could see snow patches capping the black cliffs. I turned back toward my tent. Up in the spruce trees, a redheaded finch was mounting his dowdy lover.

It was time to seek out the source. My kind of source.

That morning I investigated the lake. The time had not yet come for a walk up the rivulet to find out what lay at the head of its sloping, rock-girt meadow.

It turned out that in addition to the single lake I'd seen as I hurried past with my mind on the approaching storm, five others drained north. Connected by a network of channels and seepages, they clustered together on the flat green floor of the pass, just before it dropped away down Trail Creek. They looked permanent. And close up, their plain grassy shores revealed pleasing intricacies. A natural courtyard of delicate pale pink cups, invisible from a distance, covered a space half as big as a tennis court. A granite boulder sheltered a miniature English garden, yellow and blue and riotous. But in the end the lakes lacked. They were all right in their way, I decided, but they wouldn't do; were not a fit birthplace for a mighty river. As I reached this conclusion, rain began to fall. I hurried back to camp.

It rained all afternoon. I put in more doze time.

Around five o'clock the clouds abruptly cleared. I went outside. Sunlight. A bustling breeze, full of promise. Down in the V of Trail Creek Canyon, mist streamers rising from the black cliffs like ghostly ballerinas. Above me, in the spruces, a bird rally: a robin, a junco, a yellowish warbler, a woodpecker and two currently uncarnal finches—each bird bedraggled but fluttering itself back into flyability, and the assembly thereby shaking from the dark spruces a cascade of glistening raindrops. All the place lacked was a Clark's nutcracker—a gray, inquisitive, raucous-voiced jay that I count among my friends, and whose debut on each mountain trip I choose to see as an almost ceremonial welcome back into the high country.

The warbler flickered downward, began to butterfly about its yellow business. I changed back from camp shoes into boots, grabbed a spare roll of film, set off up the rivulet, came to the foot of the sloping, rock-girt meadow.

The rivulet ran down the center of the meadow. I began to walk up beside it, past miniature waterfalls and riffles and pools that curled and angled around white boulders. Soon, up ahead, protruding above a low hump, the tips of a line of spruces. The light sharp now. Electric. The treetops standing out like black arrow tips.

I walked on. The line of spruce trees lifted slowly into view. Then I was around the hump that had obscured them and the rivulet was angling in from my right front, quicksilver in the sunlight, and I could see that it ended—or, rather, began—at a little dell nestling at the base of a steep, rock-strewn slope. Even in that first moment, the dell glittered.

I walked on up and stood at its foot.

The dell was, I suppose, nothing more than a small triangular hollow scooped out at the foot of the slope. An echo, in sharper focus, of my camp dell. But in its way it was almost perfect. Not really beautiful, perhaps— not in any intrinsic, pinnable sense—but compact and integrated. A steep grassy bank, rich with embedded boulders. Torrents tumbling down between the boulders and converging into instant rivulet. Behind, dark spruces and rock-strewn slope.

But then, doubt. The dell's shape suggested that a spring, or springs, should well up from its foot. Perhaps they did; but if so, the torrents tumbling down between its boulders concealed them. The torrents, in fact, now seemed to create the rivulet. I began to scramble up the jumble of rocks, seeking the source of the main torrent. Almost at once, I stopped. Torrents flowed all around me. It was impossible to say which was the main one. And then I saw that they might all be temporary. Mere storm-children. Not until the storm-water drained away would I know if the dell source was indeed spring-fed and permanent.

The sun sank behind the slope and shadow snuffed out the magic. I walked slowly back down to camp.

Next morning I went back. The torrents had vanished. But from the base of the sloping bank two strong springs welled up, ran separately for a dozen feet, then converged to form the rivulet.

I sat down on the bank's most çomfortable-looking boulder.

So the river began the way most things begin. You could look deep and say that it had been in utero ever since storm clouds inseminated the earth with snow or rain and performed an act of conception. Or you could consider only what you saw on the surface and regard the two wellsprings as father and mother, commingling to generate the source of the river. It was still possible, of course, that the springs might not be permanent. But for the moment, anyway, I could choose to see the dell as the source of the Green River, and therefore of the true Colorado.

The sun beat warm on my skin. Its beams now shone directly into the dell and robbed it of the evening magic, but they made the place warm, accessible. My eyes explored the ground just beyond my boots. As always happened when you looked closely at the earth, it offered messages both ancient and ephemeral: a granite boulder seamed with intruded rivers of quartz; a patch of lichen—one of our earliest land-living antecedents; red

Indian paintbrushes and smaller flowers; dead pine needles; a splashed bird dropping. There were other things I'd missed at first, too: a certain symmetry to the dell's near-circular floor—half water, half land; the water itself—pure and unsullied, innocent as a newborn babe. The harmonies of the place were coalescing in my mind, joyously, when I glimpsed, above and to my left, a flash of gray, and down from one of the spruce trees shafted the raucous caw of a Clark's nutcracker.

I lifted my eyes. Beyond the meadow, beyond green spruce wedges, down in the V of Trail Creek Canyon, stood the line of cliffs. Beneath the radiant morning sun, they were no longer black. Like the whole gleaming world of rock and snow and trees and grassland and birdlife around me, with its scudding frieze of white clouds, they shone warm and welcoming.

I sat still, there on the boulder.

The dell was the place all right. It had what the lakes lacked. Connected, converging harmonies, perhaps. Or the possibility of romance. It was the sort of place in which, given the right tilt of mind, anything could happen—though given the wrong tilt, of course, nothing would happen. Geographers or no, it was my kind of source. Was a fit place for the birth of the Colorado.

I stood up and stretched and began walking back to camp.

*The source dell and the way ahead. "Beyond the
meadow, beyond green spruce wedges, down in the
V of Trail Canyon, stood the line of cliffs . . ."*

You might reasonably assume that at this point I struck camp and started my walk downriver. But from the earliest planning I'd seen myself staying at the source for several days. What I had in mind, I think, was making sure I carried the feel of the place down the miles and months of the journey. Carried it sharp and vivid. Beginnings are things that tend to hang in our memories, ready for unexpected recall, down all our years. Beginnings of almost any kind: the awakening of love, the unfolding of an idea, the first hours of a war, even of a new job; more broadly and certainly, the earliest years of our lives. So I wanted to imprint the river's source indelibly on my mind. It seemed important, for some reason, that I be able to look back in retrospect—even from far beyond the journey—and remember the details of how it all started.

Anyway, I lingered. For two more days I tried to absorb deep into my bones the quintessences of the river's birthplace. Not just the source dell but the whole stage.

Mostly I sat around doing nothing, doing everything.

Slowly, as I gave the place time, I came to see how, only a hundred centuries back, ice had created the bones and sinews of the current landscape. Those low banks that surrounded some of the lakes, for example—such as the one I'd found myself facing after I walked away from John and came to the fourth lake—had been bulldozed by the tongues of small side-canyon glaciers as they receded and then advanced again during a few decades or centuries of a cold snap, just before they melted away as the world warmed up at the end of that last ice age. It seemed fitting, somehow, that dying glaciers had created the hollows for the lakes that were now, perhaps, the birthplace of the Colorado.

My camp remained delightfully private. No one intruded. A few backpackers passed in the distance, traveling alone or in twos and threes, along a trail that was a continuation of the one John and I had followed. Once, a group on horseback. But all were silent toy figures, safely over on the far side of the pass. Still, they reminded me of something I'd forgotten. The trail must have been the one I walked along for a few miles, thirty years earlier, on my only other trip into these mountains. The memory of those overlapping miles was faint, though, and did not intrude.

The evening of my second day of lingering, I walked back up to the source. If anything, it looked even more attractive, more fitting. I climbed the rock-strewn slope behind it and from its crest, at 10,800 feet, surveyed the panorama that spread in every direction. Down in the V of Trail Creek Canyon, at the base of the cliffs, I could now see trees, even meadows. And beyond them, from this higher place, I seemed able not only to see the lineaments of my journey but also to look down the length and life span of the mighty Colorado.

Next morning I was ready to leave. But I continued to linger over my lingering.

I breakfasted late, in sunshine. Below, a duck foraged for its own breakfast and sent circles dilating across the shining, glassy lake. A breeze shattered the glass, gained sinew, graduated to wind. A raven flapped by, slow and serene, upwind, up the pass; then came back downwind, fast and focused. I watched it dwindle to a speck, vanish.

And all morning I went on taking my time. I did all the cleanup chores that needed to be done. I did some that didn't really need doing. I found a photograph that demanded to be taken, and then another and another. Watched birds with extravagant care. Tried to ruminate profoundly over the fact that I had seen no mammals except backpackers and horses. And when I ran out of such pretexts I just sat and savored—reluctant, now, to leave this place that was in theory the same gray and hostile one I had arrived at three days earlier.

In the end I ran out of excuses. The tent had been struck and dried, everything was stowed inside the pack, the pack stood propped up by my walking staff and I had extracted every possible titillation of pleasure from seeing how sunlight was already sending life and health surging back into the rectangle of grass and small plants that for three days had been crushed beneath my tent floor.

I turned away from the pack at last and walked up my rivulet. I followed it through the meadow and around the edge of the low grassy hump and came to the source dell. Its twin springs still welled up strong, confident, reassuring.

For a while I stood looking at the dell, striving to banish any bogus, obligatory sense of significance and to focus such genuine elements of it as I could muster. Instead, I began to feel a hint of the numbness that always seems to envelop me at the start of something potentially momentous. As antidote, I busied myself with finding a flat place to put the camera so that I could take a self-portrait, here at the source, at the beginning. For a moment I found myself wishing I'd worn the pack: a photograph with it on my back would have looked more impressive, more representative, more symbolic. Almost at once, I unwished. Even such a mild, internal "performance" would have distorted reality. Would have injected an element of artificiality.

With curious semidetachment, I shot several self-portraits. Then, for a minute or two, I just stood there, waiting. The thought came to me: the man who takes the last step of a journey is not the same man as the one who took the first. Then, at seven minutes past noon on July 15, almost dead on schedule, I took the first step of my journey down the Colorado, toward Mexico and perhaps the sea.

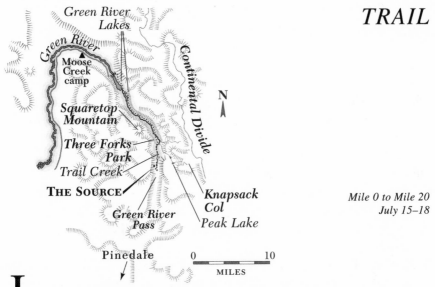

2

Mile 0 to Mile 20
July 15–18

Ipaused beside the grassy hump for a last glimpse of the source dell, then walked on down the meadow. The incipient numbness began to ebb. By the time I reached camp and swung the pack onto my back it was fading.

A silent but sweeping farewell to the camp dell. Turn, walk down to the lakes. Skirt them left-handed as far as the little creek—still just a rivulet, really—that seemed to be the main outlet. There, a pause—to hedge my bet. Summer might possibly cancel "my" source springs, but the lakes were surely permanent. At a guess, several springs welled within them. And by pausing at their outlet I'd made sure that, one way or another, I had "started" at the river's source. I began to walk down the creek, out into new territory. The numbness had finally vanished.

At first I walked slowly, following each twist and turn of the infant river. I wanted these formative stages of the river's life, like the source, fixed firmly in memory. Fond parents, to help them remember budding junior, tend to take copious snaps; and I snapped.

For a hundred yards the land sloped only gently. At first the creek was so narrow that grass occasionally thatched it over and it gurgled through brief tunnels. Soon, feeders nourished it. Before long it averaged a couple of feet across—still an infant, but one that had learned to bawl. Then, just before the pass fell away into Trail Creek Canyon, the land flattened out for a few yards and the creek widened into broad, shallow, grass-rimmed pools in which the water did not visibly move. One pool must have been thirty feet across.

Then the creek had gathered itself and plunged over the lip of the pass and was cascading down a bouldered slope in half a dozen ill-defined torrents. I clambered down beside them. The torrents funneled into a boulder-strewn gully. I scrambled on. Then the slope had slackened and the boulders had thinned and the channels had converged into a creek again and it was once more tinkling baby talk as it squirmed down a shallow miniature valley. The valley was swathed in grass and polka-dotted with white boulders.

We moved on down, the river and I, both of us more relaxed now. For the river, the slope had slackened; for me, the tension—the worst of the straining to register each pinpoint early detail. Besides, I feel at home in valleys of this kind. They have been part of my life since childhood, when I used to build dams in small streams very like this one, and do other childish, important things. You could say, no doubt, that such places and such games had helped form me. In recent years, come to think of it, I seemed to say things like that more and more often.

A quarter of a mile, and the little valley flattened out into the first place that could by any stretch of imagination be called a park. ("Park" is the name given in this part of the world to a level, open area surrounded by

The infant river plunges over the lip of the pass, begins
its journey toward Mexico and perhaps the sea.

mountains or forest. It is likely to be grassy but may or may not be a river meadow. It can be of almost any size.) Once in the park, I dawdled. After all, there was no hurry: only twenty-five miles to my raft rendezvous and almost five days left.

A trail angled down from the right and crossed the river. The trail had been there all the time, out of sight, somewhere up the slope, but I had forgotten about it. I was glad about the forgetting: it had let me walk this vital first stretch of river free from even a reminder of other people. Had let me walk wrapped in solitude, with receptors keen, unclogged.

The trail was there, though, and I used it. It offered easier walking. Now, convenience is an insidious temptation; to deflect it you must apply sterling resolve. But I no longer felt any pressing need for such resolve. This backpacking stretch, though very much a part of the journey, was in a sense only its prelude: you could say with some truth that the real journey would start when I pushed my raft out into the river. But during these first miles—certainly down to Three Forks Park, where the river's character clearly changed—I wanted to continue relishing things. The newness. The familiarity, too. For although I remembered almost nothing of this country from thirty years earlier, I had down my decades walked through much magnificent mountain scenery, and I didn't know how much more I had left. Judging by a few remarkable acquaintances, there might be twenty more years of it. Still, you never know.

The trail recrossed the creek. Feeder streams had been tumbling in, and it was now ten or twelve feet wide, so there were stepping-stones and you could picture backpackers with wet feet. Could also begin to think of trout. I'd still not seen any, though. Perhaps the racing, rockbound water was too nutrient-poor to nourish the insects that nourish trout.

The trail plunged into forest. I paused for lunch beside the creek, tucked in between two boulders, below a waterfall. The creek was no longer mere infant but a brawling, obstreperous young child, and I sat enveloped in its bellowing. It was comforting, I found, to know that the rivulet from my source formed part of that rampaging torrent—even though so intermingled now with water from other sources that it could no longer form a discrete thread. I checked the map: 9,900 feet. For me, it was the first time below 10,000 feet in four days; for the river, the first time ever.

After lunch we meandered on down through the forest. In among the trees there were no vistas, only a string of cameos. A tiered gallery of red Indian paintbrushes. In a clearing, a day rally of pale brown moths. High in a spruce tree, pecking and fussing, a sparrow that sported a black eyestripe. Once, I heard a hummingbird zoom in and buzz me, then decamp so promptly that I failed to see even a blur. But still no mammals.

The trail switchbacked down into the first map-designated park: Trail Creek Park. The map showed that I had already passed, without knowing it, a side trail to Peak Lake and the geographers' source. It dawned on me that I'd probably come down that trail thirty years earlier before turning back up toward the pass. That day, I remembered, I'd felt sub-par and my pack was riding my back like a bear, and I was going out after ten days with a large group of people in dramatic peak country and so, one way and another, had not fully registered the world around me. That—and my having walked uphill rather than down—was why the two miles of trail common to both journeys had seemed totally unfamiliar. Still, it was good to know that ahead, now, the country would be new in every conceivable sense.

Once I moved out into the open park I could see black clouds building. Soon, thunder reverberated up the canyon. I lengthened my stride. The map showed that less than a mile ahead a 1000-foot escarpment dropped off into a cliff-girt gorge; and this gorge debouched into Three Forks Park—much bigger, and promising sheltered campsites.

The creek tumbled on. A few drops of rain fell. By now the creek had outgrown stepping-stones. I crossed a three-log bridge, came to the lip of the escarpment. Below, the creek cascaded away in a long white ladder of waterfalls. I was standing looking at this cataract when a man came down the trail. He stopped beside me.

He was young. Late thirties, maybe. Long and lean, whipcord and disheveled. On his back he carried a very small pack.

"Just bivouac stuff," he said. He had a fenced-off, self-sufficient air. Some people might call it arrogance, but I knew all about that, from the inside.

The man's lean face pleated into a smile. "Suddenly felt I had to get away and sweat it all out of me. So this morning I headed for Peak Lake. Want to get back to roadhead today if I can, but if I don't . . . well, I can tuck in somewhere for the night."

Yes, he'd made it to Peak Lake. No, there was precious little snow there. And at Knapsack Col? He wasn't sure.

"Well, if I'm to make it down today, gotta be on my way."

I watched him stride off down the trail. Yes, probably late thirties. And fit. A spasm of envy. For the first time, I found myself understanding up and clear, and accepting resignedly, that the time had passed—was at last back behind some gentle and unperceived corner—when, flu aside, I had the bounce and stamina to do, as I'd always done, the sudden, mad, intensely sane sort of thing he was doing.

I swung my own pack onto my back. It felt heavier now.

There were compensations, of course. Age is the price we pay for experience. As the years rolled by, many things in life became more difficult but more rewarding. Backpacking, for example, you found yourself caring less about miles, more about delight. (True, you sometimes had difficulty deciding whether you were genuinely less interested in covering the miles or simply unable to.) Every now and again the thought would surface that your current trip might be your last, and this whetted appreciation. You looked more; thought more. Eventually came an acceptance that beauty, which you once considered icing, was maybe the whole cake.

I cinched my pack belt tight, followed the young man down the trail.

Half an hour later I stepped out of the trees at the foot of the escarpment, into Three Forks Park.

Everything had changed. In front of me, within a ring of dark conifers, spread a long, lush meadow. Through it meandered not a creek but a river. A river that flowed not limpid clear but milky blue.

The color transformation was something I should have expected. The two feeders that joined Trail Creek here and gave Three Forks Park its name—one of them the Green River master stream that drained Knapsack Col—would collect runoff from glaciers up near the Continental Divide, barely four miles east. And silt from these glaciers, held in suspension, made the river milky blue.

I found a flat enough place to camp, back among spindly trees, above the meadow. Not a clearing, really. Just a small tree-free patch. But it offered both privacy and shelter from any wind that might funnel through the canyon. Before setting up camp I went down to the meadow, carrying all three plastic canteens and the water filter.

The meadow's tall, lush grass turned out to be largely waterlogged, and I had to pick a circuitous route to the river. Downstream, I could now see, granite cliffs soon gave way to buttressed red bluffs of the layered kind best known from Grand Canyon but that also form the theme of bluffs and canyons clear across the Southwest's desert canyonlands. Upstream, the snow-flecked peaks were a flat, uniform gray beneath a flat, uniformly gray sky. All around me, even in the somber light that filled it, the park stretched green and luminously beautiful.

I came to the water's edge. The river was now thirty or forty feet wide. It flowed deep and powerful. No white water, but its surface roiled in contorted swirls and spinning eddies. Close up, the glacial silt looked only a nuance less thick, but I found one eddy where the milky blueness thinned out a little. I knelt beside this eddy and set my canteens down on the grass, and as I began to pull the water filter from its blue canvas case, the corner of my eye caught a blur of movement.

I turned my head. Over on the far side of the river, at the edge of dark green conifers, a large animal was moving away from me with the sort of tentative, throttled-down urgency that said it had been mildly disturbed. I barely had time to distinguish its pale rump and decide it was almost certainly an elk—no time, even, to see if it carried a rack—before it vanished into the trees.

Almost at once, farther left, another, darker blur of movement. As I looked, the animal turned broadside: a cow moose. I lifted my binoculars. For a moment the moose stood still, barely a hundred yards away, brown and muscular against a green conifer. Then she started to move toward the trees. I slipped from my shirt pocket the tiny camera that was the only one I carried on this backpacking leg of my journey. Through its wide-angle lens the moose would look like a poodle, but better a poodle than nothing. I took one shot. Then the moose, too, had vanished into the trees. I knelt motionless for a spell, waiting, hoping. At last I began to fill my canteens. But as I pumped the filter I kept glancing across the river at the line of dark trees. And at one check, sure enough, she was there again.

This time she was closer, and easing toward me. I took another picture. She kept coming. At first she traveled parallel to the river; but when she came opposite, perhaps twenty yards beyond the far bank, she hesitated, then turned and moved directly toward me. Now, instinct kept overriding curiosity. Her legs would stop; then her head would turn and she was half-hurrying away. But within a few strides she would halt, pause—and move back toward me. During one of her pauses I took a third picture. At the faint camera click she half-cantered away. Only a short distance, though; then back toward the river. This time, she came almost to the bank and stood there, stock-still, neck slightly extended, eyes fixed on me. Slowly, I lifted my binoculars. Her coat was dark and damp. The dewlap, oddly small. Above the flat, paler face-front, her ears stood erect. The eyes, and every muscle, radiated curiosity. For a long time we inspected each other across the swirling blue river. Then the moose seemed to lose interest. She began to move away. I went back to pump-filtering water into my canteens. Once, when I looked up, she stood half-concealed behind a small tree, reassessing me. Next time I checked, nothing.

I finished filling the canteens. Compared with Alaskan moose I'd seen, she was small. And our meeting had been low-key, undramatic. But as I wended back toward camp across the meadow I found myself looking around with new appreciation at this rich and beautiful park, already flagged as a landmark in my young journey.

Back at camp, the mosquitoes ruled. I pitched my tent, fast.

After dinner I checked the map. The oval pool of my flashlight confirmed that river and I were now at 8400 feet. In the course of 4½ miles we'd lost 2000 feet of elevation—almost 20 percent of the total we'd lose in our full 1700 miles.

That night I had a dream. Next morning, as rarely happens, it hung vivid in my mind. I was camped in that same place among the spindly trees, so tucked away that even another backpacker was unlikely to find me. But when I awoke in the morning (in my dream), the tent stood at the edge of a town. It was in the same place, that is, but the trees had gone and people were streaming along a sidewalk in solid phalanx. They surged silently past, seeming to ignore me yet at the same time to exude disapproval. I got up and crouched outside the tent, watching the horde flow past. I was terrified.

"Is this P—— ?" I eventually asked one passerby. I think the word that emerged was "Princeton," but its meaning was "Pinedale."

"Yes," said the passerby. Or perhaps he just nodded.

Crouching there beside the tent, I fumbled at an explanation for the overnight metamorphosis. At last I found something dream-sensible, crawled back into the tent, slid down into my sleeping bag, willed a reversion to the original forest site—and was safely back.

When I awoke—perhaps immediately after willing the reversion, but perhaps much later—it was daylight. I sat up and peered through the mosquito netting that covered the tent's doorway. All around me stood trees—the same spindly but precious trees that had stood there the night before.

I zipped the netting open. A squirrel tiptoed along a fallen tree trunk, inspected me, then retreated without complaining, as most squirrels would have done, at my unwarranted intrusion.

Almost noon, after a late start. At the foot of the meadow I stopped, turned, looked back.

Sunlight now filled the park. The place glowed. I let my eyes run over it all: dark conifers fencing lush green meadow; steep, encompassing granite cliffs; the distant, gray, snow-streaked peaks. Then I turned and walked on down the trail.

Below the park, the river boiled into turmoil. In the meadow it had looked raftable, but although it was possible in some stretches to picture an expert maneuvering a raft through the raging and constricted white water, mostly it was not. At one log-jammed chute, even a kayaker would have had to portage.

All day the river gained stature. It was like watching an infant grow in caliber as experiences flood in and broaden its mind, or a family unfold as more children are born. Soon, the river averaged fifty or sixty feet across.

It rarely looked fordable, and before long I recrossed it over a long log bridge: two single logs, barkless and not extravagantly wide, met end to end in midriver and rested there on a big boulder. A few feet below them, the river raced past, white and talkative. I was glad of my staff as a stabilizing third leg.

I lunched on the far side of the bridge, beside a granite slab. In front of me, the river cascaded seaward.

It was more than a mountain torrent now. Not yet, of course, the river it would become. But undeniably a fledgling river.

I ran my eye along the narrow log bridge.

· How did the saying go? "You can never cross the same river twice, the flow of things being what they are." True, of course. In a sense. You could never recross the same molecules of water. What persisted was the pattern. The pattern was what gave the river an entity. The same with other living entities, really. That was how things flowed.

I leaned back against the granite boulder. Beyond the river, the forest stretched green and silent.

This was one of the rewards of wilderness solitude: you found it easier to connect. Easier to see what you mostly knew only in an intermittent and unfocused way. For example, that many "things" other than rivers were not really things but patterns that persisted. In an individual, if you . . .

Off to my right, movement: a man and a woman with a dog coming up the trail. They turned out to be pleasant folk and we exchanged pleasantries. Then all three crossed the log bridge, very competently, and vanished upstream.

I leaned back once more against the rough granite. Now that they'd gone, the forest was once again, except for the river, green and silent. It occurred to me that earlier in the day when I'd met another couple I had found myself thinking, "Dammit! The place is crowding up." This is the flip side of solitude. The sour side. A few days out and alone, and you're in danger of wrapping its cloak so tightly that it constricts. Self-protection can leak over into something embarrassingly close to paranoia.

That afternoon I ambled down another two or three miles—with a sense of traveling in two worlds. Up to my left, asserting the gray granite firmament, soared Squaretop Mountain, its huge bulk indeed squared emphatically off, molar-tooth fashion. To my right, though, cliffs now rose canyonland red. And downriver they seemed to be falling back and hinting at open country.

The narrow, discreet trail—traveled but not overused—threaded on down through spindly conifers. From time to time, more cameos: a grassy clearing yellowed by sunflowers; once, a small open space bisected by a

After 10 miles the river slows to swirl-and-eddy, no longer swashbuckles. Snow-flecked Squaretop Mountain presides.

dead tree trunk rotting back to new life, and a pink rose already blooming beside it.

The river's milky blueness had now faded to a pale residual tinge. Still no sign of trout. But two consumers of small aquatic lifeforms demonstrated by their presence that the larder was no longer bare. A slate-gray dipper double-dipped near both banks, reconnoitering and then diving through a series of side pools. Later, just after the river had ceased to swashbuckle past boulders and had slowed to swirl-and-eddy, much as in Three Forks Park but more sedately, I paused to watch through binoculars a merganser and her brood. The ducklings—probably totaling eight or ten, but too perpetually mobile for a trustworthy census—mostly swam as a compact band in mother's wake; but all at once they would dash off en masse, dive in an eddy, surface somewhat scattered—and then, apparently comprehending the awful immensity of the wide, wide world, scutter back into disciplined phalanx.

By the time I camped, the river's glacial blue had waned to trace memory. Downstream, hints of a widening valley confirmed the map bulletin: Upper Green River Lake.

My camp, on a hillock overlooking the river, was sylvan but insectual.

All evening, mosquitoes controlled the territory. As protection I drank my penultimate snoot of Wild Turkey—but before falling asleep discovered that it had failed, fundamentally, to deter an invading tick.

Next morning, a few minutes below camp I could for the first time see, as backdrop to the valley's cleavage, not rock walls but a green and rolling ridge. Soon I was walking along the eastern shore of Upper Green River Lake. A glacier had no doubt scooped out the hollow in which the lake lay, and when it receded there had been time for all local elements—topography, vegetation, animal life—to evolve slowly, naturally. So the lake now nestled neatly and harmoniously into the landscape.

It was about a mile long. Dark conifer forest sloped down to the water's edge. Behind me, Squaretop presided benignly, photogenically. Fleecy white clouds drifted across deep blue sky. You could not have asked for a better mountain lake or a finer day. But my living, flowing river was in abeyance and I felt the loss.

Near the foot of the lake I found a trailside spring and stopped for lunch. After my customary twenty-minute siesta I began to brew tea. I was looking across the lake at the line of red canyonland cliffs that rose above the trees and thinking in a clouded, pre-caffeine-fix sort of way that the geological transition was over and I had now moved out beyond the mountain granite, when I saw two backpackers coming down the trail. I am not over-prone to initiating wilderness conversations, but as this pair came close I saw that they both carried ice axes.

"Greetings!" I called out. "You've been up high?"

"Yeah," said the man. "Followed the crest quite a ways." He was tall and greyhound, approaching my age.

"Just come down this morning," said the woman. She was blonde and had some years of catching up to do.

"Did you by any chance pass Knapsack Col?"

"Sure," said the man.

"Much snow there?"

"Surprisingly little."

"So little that I could have climbed up to it from Peak Lake?"

"Well, we didn't actually look, but I'd say it's very possible."

By this time the couple had moved off the trail and now stood beside me. They were cordial people. We chatted, eventually exchanged names: Dale and Frandee Johnson. Twenty years earlier, when Dale had been running his successful company offering premarked do-it-yourself kits of lightweight backpacking gear, we'd exchanged correspondence. We now shared, we discovered, recent angioplasty experience.

"I wonder if you'd do me a favor?" I asked him.

"Of course."

"Last night I found a tick in my backside. A greasy antibiotic failed to make the damned thing back out, and when I tried to pull it out this morning I may have left the head behind. Could you possibly check for me?"

"No problem," said Dale. "Just let me get my other glasses out." He began to take off his pack.

"Oh, it'll take you ages to find them," said Frandee. "Besides, I'm so nearsighted that for this job I can see better than you, even when you've got your glasses on. And I'm sure Colin won't mind."

Moments later she pronounced me tick-free. As I pulled my shorts back up I asked about Lyme disease and Rocky Mountain spotted fever. They'd not heard reports of either in this part of the Rockies.

After the Johnsons had gone I brooded briefly on the perfidy of Knapsack Col, decided it was no use crying over unspilt snow, packed my gear and went on down the trail.

A narrow strip of flat and open land separated the first and second lakes. Passing through, I learned that even in such a seemingly candid place three large moose that have been languidly feeding and entirely visible as you fiddle your camera ready can moments later, when you're ready to take a photograph, have melted mysteriously away.

The second lake was an elongated replica of the first. At its foot, the wilderness would end. I was beginning to look for a campsite short of the boundary when I saw, out on the lake, a green canoe paralleling my progress. The canoe was heavily laden, and its two life-jacketed paddlers stroked away with a slow, easy, synchronized rhythm. I halted, watched. It was good, I found, to see these canoeists moving so serenely through the water. The river might be in abeyance but they were in harmony with its substance—and at present I was not. To my surprise, I found myself, as a landlubber, envying them. Then feeling empathy. Very soon now, things would change.

The campsite I chose, just above the wilderness boundary, at first seemed a mere place of convenience. Its prime attraction was a spring. The water bubbled up, virgin, from the ground, so it could hardly be contaminated with *Giardia* or any allied evil and I could fill my canteens without the hassle of filtering.

The place I rolled out mattress pad and sleeping bag was the only dry and flat and tolerably level one near the spring. Some years earlier, the shallow hollow in which it lay had been burned over, and the place was now, though fairly open, studded with tree stumps and skewed snags, all mildly blackened. But aspen stands, above and below, helped soften the prevailing scruffiness, and there was a view out over the lake, 100 vertical feet below. The map showed that down at the end of the lake, on the opposite shore, a road ended in a campground and a few scattered buildings; but the lip of my hollow hid these first outposts of civilization.

There were few mosquitoes, and I did not put up the tent. Once I'd unpacked I sat quietly, resting body and mind. Time passed. Afternoon filtered toward evening. The light crystallized. Far up the lake, still standing benign guard over the canyon, over the world, Squaretop jutted up clear and keen, a majestic monolith that Hollywood might have found fit for *Close Encounters* or even *2001*. The lower stand of aspens, stark in sunlit silhouette against the black slope beyond the lake, now gleamed potent green and silver. Behind me, a faint sound: a young buck wandered by, unaware of my presence, or perhaps just unafraid.

A silver-and-green, high-wing, fixed-undercarriage plane cruised slowly past, low and noisy. Except for a couple of jets several days earlier, it was the first plane I'd seen; and the jets had been high and unreal, in another world, so this was the first motor I had really heard since John and I left Victoria and our vans at roadhead.

After the plane had gone I sat listening to the silence.

A powerboat roared up the lake. (Although I was still inside the wilderness, the powerboat was not: the boundary followed the near shoreline.) Slowly, the boat's roar faded. Silence flowed back, healing the wound. Then, a new and different noise. Up from the lake—faint at first, but building—floated the chatter of shrill young voices. Soon I could see a red canoe steering a capricious course as its three occupants flailed their paddles at erratic whim. The hubbub reached a peak. Then the canoe had veered away and was weaving its fickle path out across the lake. The voices began to subside. But when the canoe swung close under a curving line of gray cliffs on the far shore the voices rose in delighted experiment as its owners discovered the cliffs' echo power. A radio joined their game. For a number or two, rock 'n' roll backed yell 'n' holler. Then the canoe was moving downlake again, toward the campground.

Back in my world, another passing deer stomped in surprise before cantering off in a wide downhill detour—not really alarmed, just disturbed. It disappeared into the aspens. The aspens now stood in subtle shadow: diaphanous, elusive.

I started to cook dinner. The powerboat came roaring back, lights on: first, green for starboard; then the white stern light. Except for the beam of my small and sparingly used flashlight, they were the first artificial lights of the trip. The lights vanished, the roar died away. But soon, from down at the campground, across a mile of lake, floated a cacophony of shouts and whoops. I sat looking out into the blackness. Over in the campground, a car honked. Then silence fell once more. I sat on. At fifteen miles, it seemed, the river had lost its innocence.

I began to eat. Eventually, of course, everything suffered a loss of innocence. Well, almost everything. The loss tended to be seen as a landmark in an entity's evolution, and to be recorded in both myth and history. Take the specific entity *Homo sapiens*. We had both the serpent offering Eve the apple in Eden and Neolithic man developing agriculture beside the Euphrates.

A burst of campground laughter floated across the lake.

Loss of innocence could be seen as a rite of passage, of course—and therefore by no means a bad thing. Looking back now, you could say that the development of agriculture had made possible our rapid population increase—which had helped us emerge as the most extraordinary animal so far; a remarkable species, rich in unique potential. But you could also say that a toxin had been hoed into those first productive fields. Could say that they had triggered our rapid early population growth—which now, extended far beyond usefulness, threatened our very existence. The paradox might not please you, but that was how things flowed.

I finished dinner, lay back in my sleeping bag.

Or take the individual entity "me." Now that I considered the matter, it was difficult to decide just when I had lost my innocence. The first shock of boarding school seemed a prime candidate. Ditto World War II. But there was a moment at the edge of an English resort town when I sat on the upper deck of a bus, waiting for it to start, and found myself looking down at an expanse of tarmac stretching flat and gray in pools of dim light cast by street lamps (they may have been shrouded wartime street lamps, or perhaps it was peacetime and foggy); found myself looking down and understanding with a wave of revulsion the bleak dreadfulness of it all, the desolate and deadening wrongness. Of course, none of these candidates might be valid. Some people said I was still an innocent. What else, they asked, could you call someone who persisted in believing he could whenever he felt like it just slough off civilization and hightail away on long and lonesome journeys, often through remote wilderness? I didn't necessarily agree, but if they were by any chance right then maybe seasoned innocence wasn't such a bad thing.

I raised myself on one elbow.

Moonlight now flooded the hollow. The burned snags had become stage puppets in arrested motion, rich with potential for secret and antic night dances. Down against the lake's blackness, the aspens were barely substantial, almost ethereal.

As I lay back into my sleeping bag I became conscious of my feet, down at its foot. They felt sweaty, still tired. I began to think, "I really ought to rinse them." Then I was asleep.

About noon next day, after another late start, I passed out of the Bridger Wilderness—and crossed a second boundary, too.

The trail, suddenly bright red with detritus from nearby cliffs, climbed a rise dotted with sagebrush—that signature plant of the high desert—and I found myself in Big Sky country. Rolling sagebrushed plain. Curving sagebrushed hills. Dark conifer wedges. A wooden bridge across the river. Post-and-rail fencing. Then the first buildings of my journey: two rustic, tin-roofed wooden structures. And overhanging it all, a very big sky indeed.

I walked on out into this new and open world.

On my left the lake had narrowed and its water had begun, just visibly, to move. But it was still a lake. I came to the bridge. Beneath it the water accelerated and lake abruptly became river—a transformed river swirling limpid clear past boulders and slicing through deep, dark channels in patterns that melded into a perfect ensemble for the Trout Quintet. At once, two fishers. Overhead, an osprey planed whitely past, scoping. Downstream, a mammal waded deep, sunlight glinting on his fly rod.

I crossed the bridge, walked on. A dirt road now paralleled the river. Occasionally, more mammals passed along it, and their vehicles trailed ephemeral lenses of dust. But the sagebrush ruled.

I camped early, on a low hump between road and river. It was a perfect place for the kind of languid evening I wanted. The week of wilderness solitude had now built an envelope of peace around me, but I knew this would be my last assuredly tranquil backpacking camp. By next evening my mind would no doubt be buzzing with preparations for the raft rendezvous—at seven o'clock the following morning—with Rex Paulson, the Pinedale sports store owner who had fostered all my local arrangements.

I ate an early dinner, then sat and watched evening shadows reach out across bare and rolling sagebrush, across swirling river, across more sagebrush. Upriver, beyond sagebrush and conifers, Squaretop Mountain still molar-thrust, granitic yet semi-Hollywood. Behind it ranged gray peaks, distant and toylike, no longer quite real. Below me, fish sipped insects and printed a steady pattern of rings on the river's burnished surface. Three ravens flapped past, low.

I sat quiet and happy within my protective envelope.

All at once I became aware that the day's last sunbeams, skimming the sage crowns, had revealed an astonishing world. A world hidden until then by the coarseness of my vision.

The valley's whole airspace now palpitated with a restless, barely transparent tapestry woven from tiny dustspecks of insect life, all whirling and spinning in a mad, ceaseless dance. And below this near-abstract mural I could now see, laid thick and almost unbroken over the bare and empty sagebrush, a silver carpet of spider webs. For lingering minutes, the carpet looked solid enough for a man to walk on. Then the sunbeams had gone and the evening shadow had reached out and my eyes once more reported only empty air and bare, commonplace sagebrush.

Before I fell asleep, the journey's first coyote yowls came floating across the river.

3

RAFT

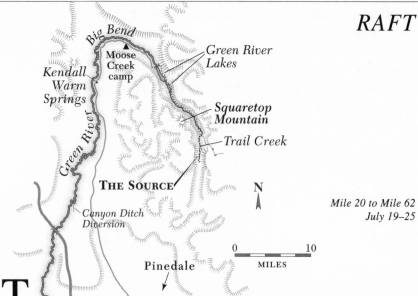

Mile 20 to Mile 62
July 19–25

Two mornings later I was waiting in the rendezvous camp just below Moose Creek when, a few minutes after seven, Rex Paulson turned off the road and came bumping down toward me in his white Subaru station wagon. On a trailer behind it rode my raft, blue and bulbous and beautiful.

Almost three days passed before I left Moose Creek Camp. Three days that buzzed with administrative detail. But finally, conversion complete. Everything raft-shape. Then, the moment of departure turned out to be so undramatic, so low-key, that it slid by almost unnoticed.

What happened was that the launching got submerged in the wake of a rehearsal.

Moving the loaded raft from its safe anchorage in a side-channel— easing it through a narrow riffle and out into the main river—offered a chance to practice a technique for lining the raft around unrunnable rapids of the kind I'd eventually face. I'd tried the operation once, in Idaho, under an expert's watchful eye. But solo would be different. And long before the raft was ready I'd decided to conduct a trial, under meek conditions, as a prelude to the launch proper.

Everything went flawlessly. The raft, at the end of a long nylon climbing rope, came gently to rest at exactly the place I'd planned, alongside a low grassy bank. And as I walked down the bank, holding the raft in place with the red climbing rope I'd now untied from its upriver point of attachment, coiling it as I went, I felt exuberant, almost festive. When I reached the raft I stepped aboard to stow the coiled rope; then, no doubt swept along by the sudden and unexpected elation, I let us drift away from the bank.

We quickly gained speed, pirouetted. Not until I'd picked up the oars and swung the raft around so that we faced downstream did I register that the moment of drifting away from the bank had marked what could be called, with at least some truth, the real start of my journey. By then it was too late to mount even a muted celebration. But I did register that the time was just after four o'clock, that afternoon of July 22.

I maneuvered the raft out into midstream, began to float down the gleaming river—and discovered that not only had we reestablished contact but that by traveling *on* the river rather than *beside* it I'd transformed our relationship.

Here on the river, the world spread wider, brighter, softer. All around me, beyond the raft's bulging blue flanks, swirling water gleamed and glinted and glittered. Molten silver, miraculously burnished. Above and beyond it, green willow-fringed banks and rolling emerald hills and dark wedges of forest slid slowly past.

The water honed the high-country light to an even keener edge. Clear across the shimmering river, beneath the shifting shadows of fleecy white clouds that drifted unhurriedly by, the rings of feeding fish widened, waned. A beaver nosed up a back eddy, upperworks low and long and

Trying out the raft, ready at last, in a small
side channel at Moose Creek Camp.

wetly glistening, and paid no attention to me. Over us all lay a beautiful silence.

I gave myself up to delight in this new world. This world that should not have been unexpected. For a spell I simply sat and let its harmonies wash over me. Allowed them to muffle, then hush, the lingering dissonances of Moose Creek Camp.

Messages from this new and wider world reached me in a curious, split-level fashion.

At first the river ran swift and swirly: no real hazards, but a need for almost continual maneuvering through run and riffle, past eddy and back-water. Up at this surface level, my mind delighted in the way the raft handled. It had impressed me on the lake trials; but then it carried no load, and the water stood still. Now, with a heavy load, in fast water, I soon found I could correct course with the nudge of an oar, could pivot on a handkerchief.

In a raft you normally travel down fast-moving water—unless it's white and big—broadside to the current. Technical considerations prescribe this crab approach—so contrary to right practice in any other vessel—but it generates big aesthetic dividends. Whenever pilot duties permit, you're not only free to look up or down or across the river but also, if you want to enjoy the opposite sector of river and bank and landscape, to pivot the raft, bow for stern, and float on. I made full use of this freedom. And during that first hour, although the surface of my mind busied itself with reading the river and reacting, I could respond to the broader world in a curiously aware yet unaware mode that let me almost consciously revel in my unconsciousness of what was happening.

After a couple of miles the swirls and runs and riffles died away. Perfect. As I floated down the now-placid river I could sometimes ship the oars and do things other than row. The waterproof camera box, strapped to the raft frame at my right side, held a small tape recorder, and as soon as my hands were free I took it out and spoke my mind. "Already, I feel almost like Toad of Toad Hall," I said. " 'This is the life for me! . . . Boats, beautiful boats!' Except that for me it's 'Raft, beautiful raft!' " On reflection, I felt unsure whether Toad actually used these words in *The Wind in the Willows*. But that was all right: they reflected his exuberance, and mine.

There was one element in my appreciation of the new travel mode that I disliked having to acknowledge.

At the end of each day's backpacking I'd been glad to stop. Sometimes I couldn't have gone much farther. Yet each day's journey had been short. I'd suffered no more actual flu relapses, but had to admit now that the bug had probably been aftermathing me—and that cruising downriver with no load on my back, sitting at comparative ease, currently suited me a great deal better.

The clothing left me freer, too. I still wore my broad-brimmed back-packing hat and short-sleeved shirt, but otherwise only thin quick-dry shorts and open rubber-soled river-runner's sandals—except that aboard the raft I added, most of the time, my brand-new, bright orange life jacket.

I floated on downriver, enjoying the new freedom.

By this time we'd begun to move through a strip of country that had for months been fluttering around my mind. The topo map showed a six- or seven-mile stretch of meandering river bordered by fenland: a blue ribbon contorted into sinuous curves and flanked by green swaths of marsh and a blue jumble of eel-like sloughs and off-crescent lakes that spoke eloquently of old, discarded channels. An authentic map junkie finds such cartographic images irresistible. From the moment I saw this one, months earlier, I'd waited with impatience for the reality. My mind's eye had conjured up and retained, almost without my knowing it, a picture of a secret and mysterious place rich in trees and hanging moss and wallowing moose.

At the start, what I found was a wide-open place in which you could rarely see a damned thing beyond a low fringe of greenery or a raised alluvial bank. Distant hills, yes. Even mountains. Sometimes, gently sloping conifer stands. But mostly the middle distance had died. All I now had was the river. The river and its wildlife.

The most insistent lifeforms were the mosquitoes. They pounced the moment I penetrated the marsh, and only liberal sloshings-on of repellent blunted the onslaught enough for me to appreciate other fauna.

They were there, though.

A mother duck scuttered out to midriver and flapped and flapdoodled in a diversion ploy any politician would have appreciated; but as soon as I was safely past she stopped bluffing—and when I looked back and saw her swimming quietly toward the far bank I could imagine her heart beginning to beat a little more slowly as she rounded up her scattered brood. Two beavers inspected me, and I inspected several of their waterside, inter-leaved-stick lodges. A mini-flock of redwing blackbirds flutter-clustered on limber green reeds. Twice, big flocks of sandhill cranes sailed majestically southward, high and gray and indistinct, and both times their loud and continuous do-do-do-do-DOO call seemed to trigger prolonged bouts of lowing from herds of invisible cattle, somewhere out in invisible hinterlands. Slowly, I followed the cranes southward.

I was traveling south now because I had rounded what the map called Big Bend. At the start, down Trail Creek Canyon, the river and I had headed due north. As the days passed, we began to angle westward. By the time we reached Green River Lakes our course was northwest; at Moose Creek Camp, due west. There, Big Bend began: as we approached the marsh, the river swung abruptly left; a couple of miles, and we were traveling due south. And that made a difference. Even in the planning stages it had seemed fitting that I should switch from backpacking to rafting at the river's pivot, at the point it switched from northering to the southering that would be its general bearing for the rest of its life. And now, with my plan realized, sailing south and seaward, I felt that I had at last shucked the preludes; had set firm and final course.

There still seemed no need to hurry. Twice, I fly-fished briefly. No trout, only two small whitefish; but my festive mood still reigned. About halfway through the marsh I passed the entrance to a slough. In spite of the many shown on the map, it was the first I'd actually noticed, and it looked just the sort of place I would have liked to explore; but before that thought had fully jelled I was past the entrance. By that time, anyway, a mild sense of pressure had begun to build. Because of the late start I'd meant to camp fairly quickly. But the marsh promised few campsites. The map did suggest one likely candidate, and when I got there, around seven o'clock, it looked ideal—until massed squadrons of mosquitoes bombed me into quick and precipitous retreat. Even out on the river they'd now become baleful. I decided to push on.

A little after eight o'clock, with dark clouds building ahead, I at last emerged from the marsh. The mosquito attacks eased. A mile downriver they'd almost ceased. And on the right bank there was a grassy flat, dry and inviting.

As I finished tying the raft, fore and aft, I looked back upriver. Still nothing much to see. No trees with hanging moss. No wallowing moose. No secrets of any kind. No mystery at all. The marsh had fulfilled its dismal start. It had been like one of those long-looked-forward-to childhood vacations that you imagine is going to be perfect; and when you get there there's some pestilence in the form of poisonous other kids or iron-handed grown-ups or something else. Yet the marsh disappointment had failed to tarnish the day. All in all, it had been a good rebeginning. For one thing, I had in spite of the late start come almost ten miles. There was more to it than that, though.

I set up camp on the grassy strip, close beside the river.

During the night, heavy rain fell. But I woke to find the sun rising into a clear sky and the river still lying there alongside me. I sat up. The murmurings of gentle water had been with me all night, soft but sure. And that had changed our relationship. We had slept together, and now I could begin to understand her. There was no hurry, though. Anything worth doing is worth doing slowly.

All morning, I took my time. I took my time over breakfast. I took my time over readying food and maps for the day, and over washing clothes and self. I took my time over such minor chores as lubricating oarlocks and the scissors on my Swiss Army knife. Then I took my time over filtering water from the river into canteens—a major hassle on the backpacking leg because to save weight I'd left behind the little brush for cleaning the filter's ceramic element. With the brush, filtering became less of a hassle but remained a minor pain. That relaxed morning it generated only the subdued but warm pleasure I felt at doing all the other chores.

Now, at root there is little difference between camping routines for backpacking and for rafting. Cooking, for example, is essentially the same. So is pitching and living in a tent (though I now had a new tent, because my old and trusted one had demonstrated on the approach march that its floor was no longer waterproof—which was why I'd had to spread a groundsheet over it that first stormy night at the source—and John had bought a new one for me in Pinedale and sent it out with Rex Paulson). But technique distinctions do exist. And camping as a solo river-runner, rather than in a group, was new to me. For example, dry bags in the complexity I needed were unexplored territory.

Dry bags are large, rugged, waterproof sacks in which you carry the bulk of your gear that must be protected from the spray and even deluges that cascade over the raft in white water—and from total immersion if you flip. Because a river-runner is free to carry much more gear than a backpacker, and indeed must carry more, loading and unloading camp gear at the start and end of each day become big and almost dominating deals, and your efficiency revolves to a surprising degree around the way you organize things in the dry bags—at least some of which you unload at every camp. So that second morning on the river I second-thought my dry-bag organization. I had three easily distinguishable bags—one red, one yellow and one pale blue—and I carefully rethought just which items should go into which bag, in what order. I took my time over it, too.

I not only took my time, I took pleasure in taking my time. Before long, daily chores would be just that: mere chores. But for the moment I was actually enjoying them. And wallowing in the luxury of being able to be inefficient. Whenever I felt like it, I just sat or stood and contemplated.

Sometimes I mulled hardscrabble matters. The ten miles traveled the previous day was the statistical norm I'd set for the whole journey. Ten miles a day, 1700 miles: 170 days; six months. Some days I'd go zero

First riverside camp: time to pause, contemplate.

miles, of course, so on others I'd have to cover twenty or thirty. It was good to know, now, that even on short travel days I could make ten.

During one interlude of contemplation—a.k.a. wool-gathering—I sat in front of the tent and let my eye follow the broad line of the river as it curved away downstream and vanished below a bulbous green hill be-spiked with conifers. I refocused, close. Just beyond my tent, at the water's edge, stood one of the stalwart and curiously architectural thistles I'd been admiring ever since Three Forks Park. A dozen feet inland, beyond a strip of smooth green grass, grew the pair of low but sturdy bushes to which I'd tied the raft's bow and stern lines. I let my eye wander idly back along the yellow lines to the blue raft with its silver-bright steel frame and dry boxes. Sometimes, now, it seemed as if a raft—even this particular raft—had from the start been an integral part of the plan for my journey. My mind switched back to the "normal" outside world; a world that already seemed distant and tenuous and marginally real, the way it always does when you've been "out" for a week or so.

Looking back into that world, I remembered the way I had early in my planning felt the need for advice from a river-running expert about the proper choice of vessel—and had had the wit and luck to write to Martin

Litton. I knew him only by reputation as, among other things, the doyen of modern whitewater-running in Grand Canyon. Though now around seventy, he was said to be chipper as a chipmunk.

The day he got my letter, he phoned.

"I'll be happy," I told him, "to drive up to see you and talk. Anytime it's convenient."

"Oh, don't bother," said Martin. "I'll fly down."

A week later he landed his elegant radial-engined Cessna on our village airstrip and I drove him to my house. There, I outlined my plan and we discussed some tentative choices.

"You say you want to go the whole way in the same craft?"

"Yes. Seems to me that's the only way I can achieve continuity. Switching would destroy something. And I want a boat that could become my 'home' for six months."

Martin nodded, smiled. "Obviously, my first thought is a dory."

It quickly became clear that he lavished even more passion on the beautiful dories he'd pioneered on the Colorado than he did on his immaculate vintage Cessna. "But it takes years to learn how to handle a dory," he said. "And in the worst of the water you'll be running, a canoe's not really practical. A kayak is—but even if you learned how to handle one, you couldn't carry enough gear. One of these new inflatable catamarans might be good, technically—but that wouldn't give you much of a home, either. Which leaves us with . . . you know, to be honest, I loathe rafts. Clumsy damned things. Ugly, too. Not like dories at all. But they're certainly more forgiving. Yes . . . I think you're right. For this trip, a raft looks like the only practical answer."

After that, the only question was the size and make of inflatable whitewater raft. My final choice between two reputable brands hinged largely on weight. Manhandling a raft alone, especially if I needed to portage, would be less of a brute if the vessel were as light as was consistent with ruggedness. In the end, I decided on a self-bailing "New Wave" by Maravia, 13½ feet long, 6¼ feet wide, its tubular hull constructed with a tough, no-seam, sprayed-on outer layer. This seamless-urethane-outer-layer system, not yet fully proven in prolonged use (though that would soon change), promised to be a revolutionary advance—and largely because of it, the raft weighed only seventy-five pounds. The rigid tubular steel frame I had custom-made for the raft, and the two large waterproof steel storage boxes that fitted snugly into this frame, were rather heavy as a unit but broke down into manageable pieces. On top of one storage box was fixed a padded and extraordinarily comfortable seat that I had fallen in love with on contact. And as I sat in front of my tent that second morning on the river, it occurred to me that I had yet to suffer even a twinge of regret at any major equipment decision.

But the finest equipment won't do you much good unless you know how to use it.

When I met Martin Litton I had never sat in an inflatable raft, let alone piloted one through white water. But Martin—who that first day and later poured out a stream of river information—proved to be generous with more than advice. He invited me to go along on one of his commercial trips on the main Idaho Salmon, the River of No Return. An additional small raft could accompany the dories, and a spare boatman would instruct me. We launched in late August. For two days I floundered through rapids with my instructor aboard. Then I began to get the hang of it, and run solo. The river was low but technically demanding. By the time we pulled out on the Snake River, thirteen days later, I felt surprisingly competent.

My mind flicked back into the present. All in all, it seemed as if I'd done everything that could have been done in the way of preparation, and I felt ready for whatever lay ahead. Eager, too. But for now it seemed enough just to sit there beside the river, taking my time, and feel the sun strike warm on bare forearms.

Once more I let my eye run over the raft riding blue and quiet at the water's edge—and found myself thinking with pleasure that already I felt the beginnings of affection for this little vessel that would for six months be my home. I registered, individually and ensemble, the gleaming steel frame and dry boxes, the thick black foam on the box lids, the padded white seat on the after box, the yellow dry bag behind it, the spare oars strapped red and ready along each side tube, between the silvery oarlock stands and the blue and white safety rope that encircled the raft. I noted the long red lining rope coiled neatly at the bow, and the yellow bow and stern lines reaching out straight and vivid across green grass to the bushes that held the raft tethered. I turned my head and took in, one by one, the architectural thistle, the broad river flowing by, the bulbous green hill bespiked with conifers and, finally, overhead, the flat-bottomed white clouds drifting slowly eastward. Yes, I said to them all. Yes.

At 1:30, that second day on the river, I at last stopped taking my time.

A mile south and seaward, I eased the raft cautiously toward a long, broken run. Rex Paulson had said that in all the hundred or so miles above Fontenelle Reservoir, this was the one place that might give me trouble. "I'm not sure there'll be enough water for you to go through without having to get out and pull."

From above, the run looked straightforward. I selected what seemed to be the deepest route, aimed us down it, bow-first. We went through without even grazing a rock. At the foot I pulled left into an eddy, just above Kendall Warm Springs.

I'd read about the Springs. They promised a living biology lesson, and duty drove me ashore.

The Springs, I was able to confirm, emerged from several sources in a low hillside. And they converged to form a wide but shallow stream that meandered for about three hundred yards, then tumbled into the river down miniature falls, a dozen feet high. This barrier, built by travertine deposits from the mineral-rich stream, had long ago cut off from their mother stock in the main river a population of small fish, now considered distinct and officially labeled Kendall Warm Springs Dace. A neat sign elaborated: *"The largest fish grow to be two inches long. During spawning, the male turns purple, the female a light green. These tiny dace are rare and endangered. . . ."*

Dutifully, I wandered up and down the stream's banks. Sure enough, minuscule fish darted through its clear and shallow water, but to my eye they looked a dull uniform gray. I kept at it, trying to feel zealous. Perhaps it was the pedagogical signs. Or the lurking knowledge of long-standing proposals for a dam that would flood this stretch of river; the plans currently stood thwarted, but you should trust dam builders the way you trust rattlesnakes. Or perhaps it was just the dark clouds that had built up and now began to decant an intermittent drizzle. Anyway, whatever the reason, zeal eluded me.

Back at the raft I felt vaguely cheated—and a shade guilty because I'd failed to absorb what should have been a vivid lesson in evolutionary divergence. Overhead, the clouds still hung somber, still dripped rain. I cast off—and almost at once found myself racing into a "rock garden."

It turned out to be a long and stirring run. For three miles the river barreled through a maze of protruding rocks that demanded almost continuous maneuvering. The raft responded, pivoting and deflecting deftly at every command. My feet, braced on a crossbar, could feel the living river. My hands knew its pulse through the smooth wooden oar handles. It was all great fun. And though never a really taxing test, it was also a vivid lesson in evolutionary progress. Progress, that is, in a minor branch of cultural evolution.

One of the two basic techniques of whitewater rafting that run directly and disconcertingly counter to those used with orthodox vessels is, as I've said, traveling beam-on to the current. This practice, calculated to capsize any traditional boatman's stomach, becomes essential in fast-moving water that is not white and big, especially when it's punctuated by boulders or other obstacles. So most of the way down that long rock garden below Kendall Warm Springs we traveled beam-on, broadside.

The prime reason for the beam-on technique is maneuverability. A raft traveling bow-first at the same speed as the water responds to your steering efforts sluggishly if at all. But turn broadside in water that's neither too white nor too big and you can avoid any obstacle fairly easily. Well, almost any obstacle, and sometimes fairly easily. You simply push or pull on the oars. If you heed a basic fast-water rule, "Face the danger," it works remarkably well. On my Idaho training trip I had found it worked too well: approaching an obstacle, I tended to overcorrect. This failing, apparently par for the beginner's course, had persisted all through the previous day. But when I emerged from the Kendall rock garden I felt I'd achieved a quantum nudge toward controlled dexterity.

The broadside technique is known as "ferrying": the raft moves much like a cross-river ferry. And in practice you tend to travel not squarely broadside but angled to some degree, just as a fast-water ferry does. In this ferrying mode you can pivot very quickly, with sharp counter-pulls on the oars, to a facing-downstream stance. And that brings us to the second fundamental technique of rafting that runs counter to boating orthodoxy.

When you row a boat you face your wake. In a raft you normally, though not always, face the way you are going. In big white water you cannot travel broadside: you would soon capsize or "flip." So you go either bow- or stern-first. (In whitewater rafts, bow and stern are physically identical; it's solely a matter of which way you face, though you establish that when you fit frame and seating.) You face downstream in white water because only that way can you see what lies ahead and so make the split-second decisions the river will at times demand almost continuously. Should I pass left of this boulder, or right? Ferry beam-on or pivot bow-first? Push hard through that gap—or pull hard to hold almost stationary for a quick reassessment of the miniature white maelstrom below it? Career full speed ahead to give us the best chance of cresting that huge next wave—or hold back a little longer for a better chance of correcting course? Hold straight now or correct a touch right—so that we'll hit the wave absolutely head-on, as we must if we're not to spin sideways and flip? The Kendall rock garden, though a paltry challenge compared with the rapids I knew lay ahead, had provided valuable practice in all these maneuvers except hitting waves head-on. It had clearly helped sharpen my technique. Unlike Kendall Warm Springs, it had provided a vivid lesson in evolutionary progress. In a minor branch of cultural evolution. Very minor, no doubt. But consequential progress of a kind that can slide past unnoticed in the unfolding story of a journey—or of a river, a life or a community. In bigger stories, too.

Below the rock garden, the river still ran fast. I sped on down. The dark clouds had now lifted, but the rock-garden run had been so absorbing that I had no idea just when the drizzle had stopped.

By six o'clock I'd run only five river miles, but I pulled in to the right bank. A mile downstream, the national forest ended. Beyond, for a hundred miles, the river ran mostly through private property, and I'd been warned that local ranchers did not treat trespassers gently. Public-land parcels—administered by either the Bureau of Land Management or the Wyoming Game and Fish Department—were few and widely separated. Their spacing would more or less dictate where I could camp, and therefore how far downriver I must go each day; and when I pulled in to the right bank that evening I knew that beyond it there were no more public parcels for at least a dozen miles.

I set up camp in a beautiful, green, conifer-fringed cup. That night it again rained, hard. At dawn a soft and tactile mist blanketed the river. But by 10:30, when I at last completed the still-unfamiliar morning chores and cast off, the mist had lifted to reveal sky washed limpid blue and a burnished sun that promised heat.

Crossing the forest boundary brought no drastic change of scene. At first the river looped through fenland that the map reported as a subdued reprise of the intriguing stretch below Big Bend; and once again I found an enclosed, reed-fringed reality—pleasant enough yet dull. But this time I'd built no expectancy barrier and I floated contentedly on. Contentedly and slowly: after a brisk start, the current had slackened to a dawdle.

Soon, on a strip of dry bank, a weathered log cabin. Before long, another—with two young fellows building a rather more pretentious edifice beside it. One of them stopped hammering to watch me drift past. His voice floated amiable and clear across naked new rafters, ancient reeds and timeless river.

"Hi! Been catching many?"

"Well, I'm not really fishing—just floating."

"Uh-huh. Where d'you start?"

"Just below Green River Lakes."

"Heh, that's quite a trip!"

"Oh, this is only the begi—"

The second builder interrupted. "That's a pretty fancy rig you got there."

"Yeah, made for running white water, down in the canyons."

The second young man ran the back of a hand across his mouth. "The canyons? How far you floating?"

"Just to the ocean."

Polite laughter. "If they hadn't put dams in the way, you could have done it too."

"Oh, I've got ways around 'em."

The builders clearly didn't believe me. I rowed on, content and relaxed. Newly relaxed.

There is always, I guess, a certain tension about beginnings. The beginning of anything. Once the initial tightness has passed you think you're already good and relaxed. But later—a few minutes or hours or days later, depending on what that particular beginning begins—you consciously register that *now* you're relaxed. And you know that until then you therefore cannot have been.

This river journey had turned out to be riddled with beginnings. Even this first rafting leg was both the journey proper and yet at the same time another prelude: not exactly a shakedown cruise—if something serious needs fixing on a shakedown cruise you can turn around and go home— but an interval of on-the-job training during which I must get used to equipment and hone embryonic river skills. At a guess, this transitional pseudo-prelude would last about a dozen days. It would probably end when I'd passed my first port of administrative call—the village of La Barge, a hundred miles downriver—and reached the head of Fontenelle Reservoir. That first artificial impoundment would by its nature form a break in the flow of river and journey—and promised to mark the end of this final, transitional beginning.

Meanwhile, the other beginnings seemed over. As I drifted on, beyond the skeleton of the raw new cabin, the young men's hammer beats grew fainter, faded. Out there on the gleaming river, the sun beat down warm and sweet. The raft bulged blue around me. The oars spoke softly to their oarlocks, tactfully to my hands. I rowed on southward. Time and the river, I felt sure, would soon smooth away any lingering tensions.

Dry stretches of bank now became more common. Occasionally they supported buildings. But the buildings all looked old and weathered. Some were rotting away. And the change from public to private land seemed to have produced little impact on the river.

Or on its wildlife.

A riverbank movement focused just long enough to become a big brown deerlike mammal, then dissolved into dense willows before I could be sure the pale butt really signaled "elk."

Duck families of several species kept echoing, with variations, the maternal display I'd seen up in the fenland. Mostly, the gambit clicked. But when Mama went into her diversion routine—splashing wildly, perhaps dragging a wing in mock injury—the kids often wasted her altruism. They would scutter away but fail to take cover. Sometimes they'd even follow her into open water—and she'd look as frustrated as any human mother facing analogous snafus.

Downstream, river right, a large dark bird alit in a treetop. Its mate joined it and they exchanged what I took to be brief bowing greetings. Then, side by side, taut with distrust, they watched me slide by under the far bank, two-hundred-odd feet away. Just as it became clear that I no longer threatened them, and they had begun to relax, a fish rose upstream of us and they both snapped alert. Tentative identification: black-crowned night herons.

The most conspicuous wildlife were beaver and moose.

Stick lodges built in varying styles at various heights above water level were apparently the beavers' winter residences and summer cabins, and intermittently the inhabitants made their presence known. The double-drumbeat "ker-*ploosh*" of a tail slap. A small wet nose gliding along the river's surface. Or a stationary head with bright black eyes, clearly people-watching and doubtless wondering what the hell this big blue foreign thing could possibly be.

Soon, briefly, my first seen-from-the-raft moose: a cow drinking placidly in a side slough. Several times, big brown bodies crashing off through willows. Once, a young bull statuesque and safely distant, just watching me pass.

Then, an unhurried private picture show.

Noon. After a floating, on-the-move lunch I was looking for a bankside siesta berth when I saw, beneath already drooping eyelids, well ahead on the grassy right bank, a cow moose and calf, browsing. They vanished, reappeared. I let myself drift in to the left bank, made fast. Directly across the river, in bright sunlight, mother and child willow-browsed on. I took pictures. The zoom and rewind mechanisms of my new automatic camera whirred like minor whirlybirds, and at first the moose kept glancing over. Soon they were ignoring the sound.

Mama was almost black; the calf, milk-chocolate. Big shoulder-humps made both animals look swaybacked. Through binoculars I could see the odd little tassel hanging down from Mama's neck—the tassel all adults seem to grow. When she faced me head-on the sunlight italicized a peculiar puckering of the skin between her ears, as if a single horn wanted to burst forth and convert her into a rather bovine unicorn.

The big brown beasts moved down into the water, into dappled shade;

browsed placidly on. Half an hour passed. Then they climbed back up onto the bank and began to scythe down standing willows like hippopotamuses beside the upper Nile. Eventually they browsed their way out of sight. At last I could take my siesta.

Post siesta, that third rafting day, the river kept switching character.

It would change from fast and rocky—typical trout water—to slow and unbroken. Then, within that more placid role, its bed kept making abrupt and radical wardrobe changes. First, the plain unassuming peasant garb of open, barren sand. Then fine green weeds suitable for a demure but lively coquette. Back to plain sand. Soon, a return to rich, sinuously waving weed beds. The shifts succeeded each other almost metronomically, as if the river were leading two contrasting lives, the way a young human lives his or her days switching almost metronomically from school to home— or later, from work to home—each life separate, counter-balancing.

I rowed on downriver. By now I'd learned that although the fast water was fun, these slow reaches were what gave me time to savor.

During the planning I'd said to one river-runner, "Oh, but mostly I don't want to row. I just want to drift down with the river, flowing with it."

The expert had smiled. "I know," he said. "And so you will, sometimes. But I think you'll find that most of the time you row. Even in calm water. You won't always row *hard*, but mostly you'll row."

Now I was learning what he meant. Mostly I rowed. Not always hard. But as a rule I found myself rowing fairly steadily and studying the water ahead.

The spur was not simply my ten-miles-a-day target.

Even in slow-moving water a rafter needs to look ahead, so that he can make full use of the current—as he must if he wants to conserve energy and achieve any sort of steady progress. In fast, swirling water, the contrast between main current and slack water or eddy is obvious enough, but even there the difference between the speed you go when dead center in the main flow and when a foot or so to one side is, though less evident, often substantial. In slow water the difference widens. And in slack water, even without an upstream wind—virtually guaranteed by Murphy's Law—such current as there is becomes crucially important. What's more, indicators of just where the current will help and where subvert your progress are often veiled. A few flecks of foam may be the only clues. You therefore travel bow-first, facing downstream—as you more or less must, anyway, because of the almost perpetual need to watch for obstacles—and you control your progress with the oars. If you just drift you're sure to lose the current's assistance and likely to find yourself moving back upstream in an eddy. You may even hit the bank.

By now I knew that keeping a forward watch and rowing fairly steadily involved an ongoing technical barrier.

Because you're facing forward, you do not pull on the oars as in normal rowing. You must "push." That is, you force the oar handles away from you. Now you can pull more strongly than you can push, but the advantages that accrue from facing forward mean that when you push you tend to move downriver faster than when you pull. At first, though, prolonged pushing feels awkward and inefficient. By now I'd recognized that one major gulf between expert and beginner rafters, on the mundane level, lies in competence at pushing: the expert can push almost as efficiently as he pulls. I was still very much a beginner; but that third rafting afternoon whetted my competence.

Not that technical concerns swamped my sense of enjoyment. Far from it. Although I drifted less often than I'd hoped, my downriver progress that relaxed afternoon was a long, slow pageant. Squadrons of white galleon-clouds sailed majestically overhead—and, by reflection, up the river. Their shifting shadows kaleidoscoped the open sagescape.

Far to my left, a line of gray mountains now paralleled the river. The cloud shadows enriched them, too. The map maintained that the mountains were those along whose far flank I'd northered on foot, and one molar-tooth peak certainly looked like Squaretop.

Time, though, hung anything but heavy on my hands. Almost always, too much to do. Piloting, at some level, virtually every yard. Catching up, at this early stage of the journey, on a stream of rafty chores. World-watching. And map reading.

From the start, map reading had been a big deal. I have a maply mind. When I'm traveling, almost anywhere, I tend to feel vaguely uncomfortable if I can't pinpoint my location, and this stretch of river abetted my instincts. The leapfrogging from one public-land camp to the next meant I always needed to know where I was; and when you're running a river that loops repetitively through flattish country routinely screened by tall bankside vegetation, map reading consumes a lot of time. You have to rely on very small bits of information that demand close scrutiny. If you lose track and have to start over from something close to scratch, you soon find yourself all at sea or river. So I had to keep checking the map.

Watching the world pass by also consumed a lot of time.

At noon, drier and more open country ahead had suggested heavier human impact. Just beyond the cow-moose-and-calf siesta site, sure enough, a cluster of farm buildings. Soon, the first modern riverside house—solidly built, mildly elegant in its suburboid fashion, starkly out of place.

But the river continued to present cameos from wilder lives.

People-watching beavers. A deer pausing to peer at me from bankside willows before melting away. A motionless brown hawk imitating one of the small brown conical rock turrets that capped the bank on which it had perched. Just as motionless, on a cable that crossed the river, an osprey, black and white and splendid. Once, crawling across the raft's pale blue floor, an elegant gray-green caterpillar, unfurry overall but sprouting odd tufts of hair and flaunting eight bright orange blotches. It looked very lost, and I rehabilitated it to a grassy bank.

Next day the pageant continued.

Silhouetted on a low horizon, a mini-convention of pronghorns. A rabbit nibbling his grassy bank. At lunch, in the eddy beside the raft, a dense and elongated shoal of trout fry that stretched upstream, black and writhing, for fifty yards. The one wildlife element notably absent: mosquitoes.

Although man's hand lay less heavily than I'd expected, that fourth day's big event turned out to be a human artifact that, while minor in itself, carried heavy freight.

I was floating down a swift but smooth glide, controlling the raft with occasional oar nudges and looking lazily ahead, when I saw an unnaturally straight line reaching out across the river. At the line's left edge a track angled down a sagebrush slope. Where track met river, the bank had been bulldozed out into a rough soil-and-stone buttress. I floated on down. The unnatural line focused into a barrier of boulders and white water. Then, more clearly, into a man-banked shallow that angled across the river and thereby diverted part of its flow leftward, into a bypass ditch. A low concrete structure suggested headgates, to control water flow. I found and negotiated a route through the barrier, pulled in left and walked over to the ditch below the headgates.

The ditch was barely fifteen feet wide, three feet deep. But the map labeled it "Canyon Ditch," and the name rang a bell. This was, I knew, only the first of many such irrigation ditches—a puny harbinger of multitudinous man-made structures designed to harness and inhibit the river. Some, like this ditch, bled it for irrigation. Others, immeasurably more massive, sought power.

I stood for a long time beside Canyon Ditch. It flowed peacefully past. Sunlight burnished its surface. Trout darted for shelter beneath its banks. Grass overhung the banks, gave way to sagebrush. Cloud shadows painted their brief and beautifying daubs across the sagebrush, raced on. In spite of what I knew about the modern river's story, it was difficult to grasp that this small and innocent-looking little conduit predicted the shape of things to come.

Below Canyon Ditch Diversion the river swirled through another rock garden. By the time I emerged into calmer water the afternoon clouds had built into a black and threatening rampart. Rain began to fall. At first, tentatively. Soon, gaining confidence, heavily. Before long, lashing down in torrential sheets that whipped the river's surface into a mercurial network of tiny, ephemeral stalagmites.

I rowed on. Peering ahead from within my rainjacket's battened hood, I watched the miniature stalagmites erupting from the surface of the rain-flogged river. I listened to nearby thunder and caught glimpses of lightning, off in the wings. After a while I found myself inquiring whether I was at that moment really enjoying what I was doing. The answer: Yes, provided it doesn't happen too often.

Then the lightning moved in from the wings. Moved center-stage. Bolt lightning. I don't think I saw any bolts actually strike, but all at once I was asking a different question: was it sensible to float down the middle of the river, soaking wet, in a raft fitted with a steel frame? After all, I was the tallest local object—in fact, the only raised one between the riverbanks—and therefore an impeccable lightning conductor. But by the time I'd taken my feet off the steel frame and then off a rubber-covered board attached to the frame and had placed them on the raft floor and had begun to doubt whether these precautions really made me as safe as when sitting in my car in a thunderstorm, especially with the rain streaming off my rainjacket and bare legs, the lightning had moved on.

As the storm drifted northward, sunlight began to shaft down between rifts in the lingering, still-black clouds. The shafts sent wanton patterns of glowing green brilliance and profound charcoal shadow racing across the landscape. A chiaroscurist movie director would have been in eight-and-a-halfth heaven.

By the time I camped, a double rainbow was arcing across sunlit sagebrush, and before dinner I caught two fat rainbow trout. They were my first fresh food in a fortnight and they tasted sublime.

After dinner I sat for a while, watching and listening to the night, then crawled into my tent. Before sliding down into my sleeping bag I began to study maps by flashlight.

But the pageant now staged a curtain call.

*Tranquillity. After rain, cloudshadows race across river
and landscape. "A chiaroscuroist movie director would
have been in eight-and-a-halfth heaven."*

Because there were no mosquitoes I had left the tent-door netting unzipped. And before long I became sharply aware that my flashlight had attracted an army corps of flying insects. They were nonbiting, but they
swarmed. To reverse the invasion I set the flashlight outside, base down—
and found myself in a ringside seat at a soundless *lumière* display.

The inverted cone of the flashlight beam had become, almost instantly,
a sovereign world in which tiny bodies of a thousand colors and conformations seethed and milled and surged and eddied and spun and gyrated
and pirouetted and whirligigged in floodlit dervish dance. I knelt and
stared. For a brief, interminable interlude I knew, or thought I knew, something of what it was like to be a nocturnal insect on a warm and humid
riverside evening, pulsing in glorious airborne congregation with my fellows within a sudden, irresistible, miraculous shaft of brilliance. Then I
turned off the flashlight—and canceled that vivid world.

4

SHAKEDOWN

Canyon Ditch Diversion

OLD FORT BONNEVILLE SITE

• Pinedale

Green R.

New Fork R.

Big Piney

"sick bay"

La Barge

OREGON TRAIL (SUBLETTE CUTOFF)

Fontenelle Reservoir

0 10
MILES

Mile 62 to Mile 146
July 26–August 2

Next day I went only seven miles. Deliberately.

From the earliest planning I'd known that on the river my progress would reflect, almost always, a tension between the urge to linger and the need to hold more or less on schedule. The way most journeys flow. And during the shakedown cruise I needed to show I could handle this tension.

So far, I'd leaned toward lingering—and the schedule had suffered. The pause at Moose Creek Camp had put me behind the three ball, and although I'd hoped to extricate myself with several day-runs longer than the ten-mile statistical norm, my best since then had been a dozen miles.

Time to catch up.

Long-term concerns about ice on Grand Canyon boulders and melt-down into Mexican sand were not the only issues generating schedule pressures. I'd told several people I'd reach certain places by certain dates, and although I'd stressed that the dates were mere targets I knew that by presenting them I'd hardened expectations. Specifically and immediately, on this inaugural leg, John and Victoria Sexton would be expecting me to phone from La Barge, my first checkpoint. So would the superintendent at Fontenelle Dam. If I failed to call on time they'd all start worrying.

In my tent the night before, studying maps by flashlight, I'd seen that the next thirty-five miles of river offered only two public-land campsites. The first, a state Game and Fish parcel, lay barely seven miles ahead. And even with an early start I couldn't hope to reach the second before dark.

Hobson's choice. So that day, only seven miles.

Next morning, camped on the Game and Fish parcel, I breakfasted at sunrise and by 9:15 was rowing determinedly south.

If all went well I would in thirty-six hours be around fifty miles downriver. This first day I'd have to make almost thirty miles, to the next publicland campsite; so it was the make-or-break day—and it promised to be a rather grim affair. My haste would no doubt seal off the passing show.

But as soon as I pulled out onto the river—earlier than on any other day—I was at once aware of the air's coolness, of the wide morning light's new brilliance. Pleasing green meadows slid by. And the river flowed fast and helpfully enough for me to travel three and a half miles in the first hour. Fast and quirkily enough to buoy my spirits.

During that hour the river had swung westward and begun to wriggle so schizophrenically across a stretch of broad alluvial valley that I did not always know which of several reed-fringed channels to take. In some of them there was barely room between the reeds for me to work both oars. The water swirled and vortexed along, rustling the reeds into soft music. It was as if, after easing into a rather solemn adolescence, the river had regained its childhood sparkle.

We were now deep in ranch country. Signs warned "Private Property— No Trespassing, Beaching Boats." More unnatural lines across the river signaled more diversion ditches, and downstream of them, discreet outflows refunded the unconsumed part of their borrowings. The recycled water looked clear and clean, without hint of the alkali it had leached from the land.

There were other signs, too. We began to pass more farm buildings. The old ones had character, the new ones did not. But then, age endows most things with character. Upriver, the banks had mostly been green and natural. Now, more and more often, riprap and other artifacts protected them against erosion—and disrupted harmonies. There was more fencing, too, much of it new. You couldn't call the country despoiled, but it had begun to look tarnished. The ex-farmer in me understood and condoned. Newer layers fretted.

Once, I passed two men stringing wire through a line of freshly implanted fence posts. They paused in their work and one of them took off his hat and wiped his brow.

"Say, looks like you're having a good time."

"Sure am."

The man waved his hat, put it back on, went back to work.

Naturally, more livestock now. Because cattle remain tied to the apron strings of the species that has bred them into their present configuration, they lack autonomy. They are . . . well, bovine. But they have curiosity. As I floated past they would stand and stare, sometimes suspend cud-chewing, even follow me down the bank to the next fence line and stand watching this strange blue object taper away out of their lives.

More signs of human life, too. I passed the first other watercraft—a small inflatable raft crewed by two men who were fishing rather than rafting. Minor and little-traveled roads had ever since Moose Creek Camp kept passing close to or even paralleling the river, but their impact had remained so marginal that by slow degrees I'd wrapped myself in a cocoon of silence and solitude and harmony of the kind that not merely cuts you off from the works of man but wipes from your memory a true recollection of what they are like. That morning, the cocoon survived, intact. Then I came to the first major highway bridge—major, that is, by sagebrush standards—and watched with a blend of awe and shock and derision the way cars beetled across it at the ridiculous speeds that I, too, beetled at when I was a resident of their world.

In spite of the human impact, wilder life still flourished. Mourning doves mourned, magpies pieballed by. A kingfisher flashed green and white and low, sending a fan of small fry hop-skip-and-jumping ahead of it in terror. Great blue herons stood fishing their shallows in statuesque solitude, solemn monuments to wisdom. Deer strolled onstage, made sauntering or skedaddling exits.

There were still beavers, too, in person and in gnawing memory.

By noon I'd come a dozen miles and the broad alluvial valley had begun to narrow. Ahead rose brown bluffs. The river was slowing down now and so was I. I pulled into the shallows for lunch, in the shade of cottonwood trees fringing a meadow. Among the living cottonwoods stood a scattering of conical-domed, freshly gnawed stumps.

As I ate lunch and drifted pleasantly toward siesta, it occurred to me that these pencil-pointed stumps, along with many others I'd already passed, wrote a colorful footnote to the day's live beaver appearances.

A couple of hours earlier I'd floated past what the map said was "Old Fort Bonneville Site." I did not stop to explore. And time pressure was not the only reason. I knew there was essentially nothing to see.

Things were not always so.

In the 1830s, General William Ashley, a leader in trapping the beavers of Green River, organized a series of annual rendezvous for pelt trading, and some of the most famous were held at Fort Bonneville. More than trading took place. In her book *Run, River, Run*, Ann Zwinger says that *"As many as 200 whites and 2000 Indians bargained and bartered . . . it was a medieval fair, a gambling spree, a squaw exchange and courting, an In-*

dian trade fair, a time to refurbish worn-out buckskins and to show off marksmanship, and for many, one long hangover." But by 1840, the year of the last rendezvous, the beaver—and therefore the fur trade—were "finished." General Ashley and his revelers faded away.

The years rolled by.

Today, it seems, only a plaque in open sagebrush marks the site of Fort Bonneville. But the beaver are back. Back in force. They build summer and winter residences all along the river, swim peacefully about their business with small heads awash, and occasionally slap tails with the distinctive double-beat ker-*plooshes* said to be danger warnings to colleagues. After dark they move ashore to gnaw-fell the living trees—and leave distinctive, pencil-pointed stumps.

Yes, we humans might now be moving back in—but the beavers had done so long ago. That's the way our planetary clock ticks. As I let myself slide down into siesta I seemed to hear, slightly distorted, a ticking echo from the courts of ancient Persia:

> *They say the Beaver and the Bull Moose keep*
> *The Banks where Ashley fur-trapped and drank deep.*

The siesta's aftermists began to disperse.

Omar . . . Ashley . . . the beaver . . . yes, that was the way things flowed. I sat up. Out in the meadow, the gnawed stumps still pencil-pointed. I brewed tea. But after all, it was hardly news that our world tends to flow in cycles, back on itself. Like water. No matter what clock is ticking. I rowed on southward. Some time during the next hour I passed within six straight-line miles of Pinedale, within thirteen of the roadhead from which John Sexton and I had headed north into the wilderness almost three weeks earlier.

I moved beyond the broad alluvial valley, past bluffs the river had sculpted from a pale alluvial mesa.

The word "alluvial" is properly applicable to both valley and mesa: both were created by waterborne particles. But the word is ticking to two different clocks. Used to describe the valley, "alluvial" means that the valley's floor was built in relatively recent times—is probably still building—from sediment washed down by the present river; sediment that's still soil, not rock. But the mesa is a geologic bulletin. The sediment that formed it was laid down millions of years ago and there has been plenty of time for heat and pressure to convert sand into rock. Into sandstone.

I had read the story of that sandstone and could remember the raw facts. But it always takes me time to move back even partway into the reality of geologic news. What immediately concerned me that afternoon, anyway, was the broken line of pale brown bluffs that the river had created from the mesa's flank.

The river had picked up speed again, and curved in sinuous loops, so the raft and I kept swinging in under the bluffs that lined its left bank. A bluff would tower over us, sheer, dominating. Then the current would sweep us out and away and I could see the whole huge, brooding cliff. Another loop would carry us back, close under another bluff. Soon we'd swing out again. Then back. And this pattern persisted. It went on mile after mile, rhythmically, delightfully. Theme and variations.

The first set of bluffs ended. The alluvial hills were still there but they lay back from the river and their lower slopes melded smoothly into the edges of the once-again-flat valley floor. The river still ran swift and its curves still swung from bank to bank, rhythmically, almost metronomically.

That long afternoon and evening they carried me along on more than my physical way.

Inflatable rafts do not look like delicately controllable vehicles, and most of them are not. I already knew mine definitely was. But in the course of that day my respect for it soared. My affection, too. Also confidence in my expertise. And I had a ball.

What set the ball rolling, oddly enough, was the pressure to forge ahead. All day I'd been striving to hold the raft precisely in the fastest threads of current and so waste none of their benefit. The outer bulges of swift-water loops imposed the most stringent demands for accuracy. There, for a few feet or a couple of hundred yards, the current would hug the bank like a lover. The vital thread of fast current was often only a foot or two wide, and in order to stay in it I had to travel broadside and maneuver so that the raft's bow almost grazed the greenery or pale sandstone. Often, I felt I could reach out and touch the soft green overhanging grass or run a finger over the coarse brown grain of the sun-shadowed sandstone. But whenever I saw a protruding obstacle ahead I had to be able to make an adjustment—often just a few inches—out into the river. Repeated minicorrections of this kind, invoked by delicate pressure on the oar handles— pull, push, then pull on one oar and push on the other—seemed to fill the long afternoon and evening of that day.

Then there was the wind.

An inflatable raft rides high and draws remarkably little water. It's therefore very sensitive to wind. In my "self-bailer" raft, the inflatable, six-inch-thick floor was a separate and detachable unit, lashed around its entire circumference to a flap that was fused to the main tube near its base.

The thin strap that lashed floor to tube passed through nearly a hundred brass grommets on both units, and these sizable grommets did the self-bailing: water that poured into the raft in big rapids could drain quickly away through them (the floor's top rides above the water surface). That was the system's prime function. But with it you could also control the raft's responsiveness and stability. Inflate the floor hard, and you floated high and maneuverable. Keep it soft or empty and you rode low and stable. To make the raft responsive—and keep my feet unwaterlogged—I'd pumped the floor hard. So we rode high and mighty sail-like—and that intermittently windy afternoon I learned a lot about operating in wind: When to hug lee shores. How to cut resistance in a strong upstream wind by rowing bow- or stern-first. How to ride downstream winds broadside and let the raft act as a sail. More subtly, how to allow for a quartering wind in swift water while maneuvering past obstacles or following precise routes down narrow currents.

One way and another, I had to be alert almost every moment of that long afternoon and evening. And although the river still presented only pale problems, I knew they were swirling good practice for the challenge that lay ahead: the big rapids that would begin once I passed through the Gates of Lodore.

But technique formed only the shell of what I learned that make-or-break day.

As the afternoon wore on, the current oscillated more and more regularly from bank to bank. At least, I'm not sure this was so, but it's how my mind recorded it. Hour after hour, I seemed to be swinging in close to one bank, then swinging back out and gliding toward the other—and a mirror-reprise. A modified reprise. For although the day had by now developed a specific and meticulous rhythm, details were always changing. Only patterns persisted. The river, as usual, was playing theme and variations.

Now, such repetitive music can in time lull you into a dreamlike, almost hallucinatory state of timelessness.

Theme and variations. The current swings in toward a left-bank meadow and I push gently on the right oar and pull gently on the left and the raft pivots broadside so that we move down with the bulging blue bow riding close herd on the meadow's fringing grasses—which are all I can now see, except for the background strip of pale blue sky and sailing white galleon-clouds—and then I adjust our position with soft forward pressure on both oars and the bow is brushing the longest of the drooping grass stems and I am admiring a daisy that pushes up pink and delicate between green tussocks; and then I see a dead bush hanging out over the water a dozen yards downstream and I pull softly on both oars and the bow eases away from the bank and we pass the dead bush and its outermost fringe is brushing the top of the bow and I can hear the faint ping as brittle twigs flick the taut tube, and then the current is swinging away from the bank and so are we, and out there the river and my world are wider and brighter and we are moving down toward a tongue that lips over a bar in a channel so narrow that once I've positioned us accurately above it I pivot us with a flick of the oars and float through bow-first with a narrow strip of smooth water on either side gleaming in the sunlight and broken water glittering beyond it and also out beyond the blue bow, and then the broken water is tapping messages on the taut drum of the raft floor and I am swinging us around to face the right bank, where the current is already heading, and this time the bank is green and dark with overhanging trees and bushes and I ease us to within a foot of their outer branches and the light is soft and muted but the swirling water keeps drum-talking to us and back in the trees and bushes the birds are talking too—deep inside the huge silence that envelops us all—and then we are swinging out and away once more and this time the river is ready to relax into a long pool and the tongue that leads into it is deep and smooth and we move through it broadside and I can look back and see the whole big, beautiful cottonwood grove that we have unknowingly skirted, and then the tongue begins to swirl and break and I let it swing the raft around until we are facing the left bank, which this time is a brown bluff that curves so evenly, with the current rippling serenely by, that I can hold the raft's smooth blue bow within inches of the rough brown rock and let my eye run along a pockmarked ledge and fol-low the escape route of a small and terrified lizard that scurries into deep shadow below the ledge and vanishes, and then we are once more swing-ing out and away and this time the tongue is two tongues with white water dividing them and I choose the nearer one and we glide smoothly through it and as we begin to swing toward the new right bank I detect a whisper of a breeze bearing news from the south, from the sea—and find myself, out there in the middle of the wide river, the wide world, relishing and rolling around my palate and striving to grasp and fix in memory the cadence of the river's rhythm with its themes and variations that are echoes of wider themes and variations.

A little before 7:30 I arrived at the parcel of public land that had been my daylong target. Arrived tired but content, with close to thirty miles un-der my gunwales. The make-or-break day had made it—without imposing any real sense of haste.

The only place to camp was an open bank, barren and desolate, dusty and cowpatted and mosquito-ridden; but during dinner a skein of twenty-two Canada geese flew low over camp in two air-brushing flotillas, black and magical against a red, red sunset.

In bed, I found myself lying with eyes closed, wishing the tent would stop turning in the current. I must have lain there, awake, for all of four minutes.

The second make-mileage day began by echoing themes from the first; then broke free.

By 8:30 I was back on the river. It still curved in wide loops, bank to bank, and I swung rhythmically on southward in fresh morning sunlight. The current still ran swift and swirling, too—through ranches that mostly lay light on land and river. Exceptions ranged from gross to comic.

Once, as I ferried around the cutting curl of a wide loop—the raft's bow brushing past grass, then bushes—my field of view changed radically. No more soft greenery. Instead, harsh cubist motley. Riprap: the bank reinforced with old automobile bodies. They stretched hood to trunk, hood to trunk, for two hundred yards or more—white skeletons, red skeletons, blue skeletons, two-tone brown skeletons, all peeling and rusting away. Gliding past them was like driving down the slow lane beside a ten-year-old traffic pileup.

Soon, river left, a scattering of Angus-Hereford cows grazed a green meadow. Beyond them ran a fence. Beyond it, on the crest of a low rise, a red tractor with an enclosed cab and white roof was pulling a roto-baler. Inside the cab, barely visible, sat a small dark figure. Nearby stood two hayricks, one complete, one still building. That was all—and I'm not sure what it was about the simple scene that touched me. Perhaps just a certain balance and cohesion to the tableau. Or perhaps a twinge of nostalgia for the years I'd managed a farm in the Kenya highlands. But I know that as I floated on down I felt a new awareness, prodded by old memories, of the human life going on around me, out in the flat valley.

Then there was the gadding bull. A furlong downstream, in bright seductive sunlight, already two-thirds of his way across the broad river, a very large and very masculine Charlais, pale almost to whiteness, was heading with Promethean intensity toward the right bank—clearly focused on the desperate and mildly mad lowing of a cow in heat. By the time the bull's one-track mind had registered my approach, we were less than fifty paces apart. For a long moment the huge beast stood there in midriver, belly awash, staring at the raft. Then he pivoted and plunged back toward the meadow in which grazed his rightful harem. He raised an arching bow wave and left a long white wake.

The wildlife equally raft-distrustful.

Two does and a spotted fawn, bambi-ing along the edge of a slough, panicked at the passing raft and blunderbussed into dense reeds. I swung past a sloping sandstone bluff, and half a dozen furry brown shapes—beaver-size but with bushy tails, and looking remarkably like marmots, which they were not—scrambled up the slope, vanished down black holes. Great blue herons now seemed to be posted every couple of hundred yards: they stood tall and silent and motionless and apparently unflappable—until we drew close and they flapped away downriver.

All morning, despite the passing show, we made good time. By eleven o'clock we'd reached the only riverbank parcel of public land in the next ten miles. I pulled in for lunch—and stayed, to my surprise, for five hours.

Because the back of the day's run was already broken, I took the chance to catch up with chores. A thirty-six-hour backlog of dreary water-filtering. Labeling rolls of used film. Relashing to the raft frame the water-proof camera box that always sat instant-ready at my right hand but had begun to work loose. Switching the yellow oars, which had bare wooden handles, with the red ones, which had been strapped along the gunwales as spares and which had foam rubber covers over the handles so that I'd be able to grip them securely when they got soaked in rapids: I wanted to try them out for feel, now, while the going was sweet. The chores dragged on, the way they always do. But I aided and abetted. For I also took the chance to look around.

Now, I had a wider view out over the landscape. When I faced back north I saw with a jolt of surprise that the mountains there looked very, very far away. And turning south, I saw that the Uinta Mountains, which until then had been a low line along the horizon, had lifted into a dark escarpment. We would not reach the foot of the 12,000-foot Uintas for another 250 river-miles; but when we did it would be at the river's improbable breach of the range through the Gates of Lodore.

What I really looked at, though, during that long midday pause was the undulating and slightly raised plain out beyond the sunken river valley.

Almost without my noticing it, the plain had begun to ease over into semi-desert. Any desert, because its thin vegetation reveals rock formations, tends to be geologically eloquent, and I found I could, almost without effort, read the geologic story of that pale landscape. By now I had lived long enough with the story to grasp tendrils of its reality, and I began to let my imagination roam back fifty million years.

The river and I were now winding our way southward over the dry bed of a lake that once covered this stretch of country. At times, inundated 15,000 square miles of it. Lake Gosiute, as geologists call it, seethed with life. According to Ann Zwinger in *Run, River, Run*:

Plants grew profusely and luxuriantly . . . turtles and crocodiles crawled along the shore. . . . Small camels and tiny four-toed horses grazed the meadows. Birds stalked the mud flats and left tined footprints of sand-piper-like wanderings. There were cypress swamps and relatives of japonica and fig, palm and grape, that gave way to forests of oak and maple and other hardwoods, and pine, spruce, and fir in the higher elevations. . . . The climate resembled that of the present-day Gulf Coast states, warm and humid with an annual rainfall between thirty and forty-three inches—today it is less than ten.

The desiccated plain out beyond the present river valley was the dried-out bed of this ancient lake. It was no longer flat but broken by uplifted ridges and mesas—the soft alluvial uplifts that the Green had sliced through, along with harder underlying sandstone, to create the riverside bluffs. Hills in the middle distance—alluvial hills with cream and pale pink strata—had once formed the rim of Lake Gosiute.

I sat watching cloud shadows scud across the pale desert basin that once cupped the lake. But by the end of my protracted lunch stop I'd barely begun to slip into reveries about that time fifty million years ago when crocodiles and camels and tiny four-toed horses roamed its steamy cypress swamps and hilltop forests. And the images were still faint, tenuous, provisional. There'd be time, though, later on. Plenty of time for me to pin down and round out the ghost of this ancient landscape. Lake Gosiute had stretched all the way to the present Uinta Mountains and, at the peak of its wide fluctuations, beyond them into what was now the Uinta Basin.

By the time we got moving again it was late afternoon. Yet I felt no great urgency. I even fished a little. Afternoon eased into evening. The clouds built into solid gray overcast. I floated on down. For a while, time slowed, almost petered out. But the day plodded on—and before it was over generated the last of its three landmarks.

The first landmark had been merely statistical. Some time during the morning I passed the journey's hundred-mile mark.

The second landmark was cartographic. And elusive. Reported, it may, on the outside, sound trivial. Experienced, deep in a travel cocoon, it was one of those elements that weave a wilderness journey. That stand out as authentic landmarks.

For a hundred miles now, each time I came to the end of a map and switched to another, the change had brought a sharp reminder of forward progress. It had always been like that, backpacking. But river-running is a more linear business than walking, and I'd already discovered that map changes now carried even heavier freight. Then, in early evening of that second long-mileage day, I switched to the last of my thirteen large-scale

USGS topo maps—and this transfer carried two extra loads of significance. Next day I'd have to rely entirely on a smaller-scale BLM series—and when you're living off maps any such change carries significance.

But the end of the topo maps also generated a puff of surprise; reminded me of something I'd forgotten. I'd bought the maps a year earlier, when my plan had been to backpack the river's first hundred miles—partly because I was at that time unsure of where river-running became possible and partly because years of experience had convinced me that walking would "keep me in closer touch with the country." When I'd shared this sentiment with river-runners it had raised eyebrows. Now it raised mine. I'd learned that if you want to move in touch with the land, walking is indeed the way to go; but if you want an affair with a river, the place to be is on it.

The day's third landmark was physical.

The map had prepared me for the Green's confluence with New Fork River—by far the biggest tributary to this point—and I was both eager and reluctant to get there. Almost without my noticing it, the Green had grown steadily in stature. Once or twice it had reverted briefly to something not unlike the intimate little river I'd launched into at Moose Creek Camp, but such reversions had become increasingly rare. As I floated on down toward the junction with New Fork River, beneath an overcast that hung thicker and more evenly than had previous afternoon gatherings, I didn't relish the prospect of leaving behind for good those faint, echoing intimations of youth.

Then, just above the junction, without warning, I found myself in a narrow channel, confined between tall reeds. The water ran fast, and probably deep. It roiled and swirled within manageable, intimate reach. And on either side, just beyond my oar tips, the reeds stood tall and thick and green and specific and comforting. I am not quite sure what I mean by that, but I know I felt suddenly happy.

It did not last. Hardly had I sampled this echo of youth before the river emerged from the reeds and was again running broader and less intimately between open banks. Almost at once the still-swift current was sweeping me past the junction.

The place turned out to be a letdown. On the map, the New Fork looked as big as, if not bigger than, the Green; but as far as I could make out in fading evening light it was much smaller. And the streams' combined flow at first seemed no greater than the Green's had been a mile or two upriver. This puzzled me.

Then I saw from the map that, just above the junction, major irrigation ditches bled both rivers. This tentative explanation for their reduced flow soon gained support. Within half a mile I found myself floating down an undeniably wider and stronger river—and side-ditches kept feeding the river, no doubt refunding the unconsumed portion of their borrowings.

The river continued to put on muscle. Now the runs carried new weight. Inspired respect.

I rowed on down the suddenly more mature river, taking stock of the widening waterway. It wasn't easy to accept that somewhere out there flowed a few molecules of water from "my" source. But then it occurred to me that if you broadened the definition of "my source," the odds halved. If a snowflake or raindrop fell a few inches south of my source dell—or of the uppermost lake in the cluster that formed my alternate source—it would drain southward, feeding the New Fork River; and here at the junction would join neighboring flakes and drops that had drained north. I found this daydream warm and comforting. Please do not ask me why.

A couple of miles below the junction I pulled in at the day's target-parcel of BLM land.

It was almost eight o'clock. The sky hung dark and a south wind had begun to blow. By the time my first-choice camp back in some bushes had proved mosquito-ridden beyond endurance, the wind was howling across my alternate site, out on an open bar. I reconnoitered for substitutes: none. A quick recheck of the bushes: despite the rising wind, still mosquito-ruled. Back out onto the pebbly bar. The wind now flirting with galedom. And still no alternatives. Without joy, I lugged the two essential dry bags from the raft to the bar's only patch of sand. Quickly, leaning into the wind, I collected driftwood and boulders. I'd just managed to get the tent up and finish anchoring everything with driftwood and boulders and oars when the wind, without warning, dropped. By the time I was safely indoors and beginning to cook dinner in the tent's alcove it was barely a breeze. I leaned forward, beyond the alcove's flap: a pair of stars already blinking down.

During dinner I reviewed the logistics. Exactly as planned, I had in two days come almost fifty miles. In two curiously unhurried days. So I knew that when necessary I could always, if the river was right, make up for lost time, fast. And now only twenty-seven miles to La Barge, my first port of call. Three easy days' travel. If all went well I'd reach there dead on schedule.

This reassurance made a difference. The catching-up had peeled off another onion skin of tension—another skin I'd not even known existed—and I felt more relaxed than at any time since walking away from the source. From the outside, such nebulous shifts of mood may seem trivial, but they lie at the core of any wilderness journey.

After dinner I went outdoors and stood in the darkness, looking up at a widening dome of stars. Now, I told myself, you can start enjoying the kind of trip you wanted. Across the river, coyotes yowled assent.

I went on standing there in the darkness. Clouds kept disclosing and deleting stars. Had the wind signaled a weather front? If so, was it still passing through? The afternoon had not followed the normal daily pattern: thunderstorms gathering around the Uinta's peaks, then spinning off galleon-clouds that drifted north and west. My weather radio had yet to emit a forecast—we were still beyond the range of any NOAA (National Oceanic and Atmospheric Administration) broadcasts—and I kept chewing away at the front-no-front question.

Weather always looms large on a wilderness trip—and fulfills an unexpected function.

Our remarkable success in providing ourselves with protection from the elements is one hallmark of our progress as a species. Up to a point. Modern life insulates us, with roofs and heaters and air-conditioning and sedans, against weather's more passionate effects; but we now tend to accept the protection so routinely and totally that we assume it's "the way things are." The protection has become mere convenience. A convenience we have not individually earned. And such a mind-set tends to generate squish, outside and in.

That is where the weather's unexpected function comes in. The rediscovery that it can pervade and often control your life turns out to be one of the hidden pleasures of a back-to-basics existence. The interludes of inconvenience should not go on too long. They can pall. But if applied in doses fitting to your temperament they stiffen sinew and soul, help keep you alive. Wholly squished citizens, of course, respond with a muttered "Sheer masochism!" But that night on the river bar, standing outside my battened-down tent with the wind only a memory but its meaning and aftermath intriguingly uncertain, standing there listening to a fresh chorus of coyote yowls float in over the river, I knew better.

Everyone, I guess, has mornings that get away from them.

I woke with the comfortable knowledge there was no need to hurry—and took it from there. A long, slow, comprehensive wash. Pleasurable lingering over sundry backed-up chores. A little laid-back fishing in the run that swept past camp. And an ongoing weather eye on a so-far cloudless sky. Other things, too. Somehow, past noon before I experienced even a pinprick urge to move on.

But mornings that get away from you can conceal pearls. They give your mind room to ramble. And all that forenoon on the open, sunlit pebble bar beside the shining river, while the surface of my mind loafed, deeper currents kept spinning off into eddies.

Mostly, these currents swirled in and around and over the river. Once, a little after midday, when I had struck and folded the tent and was about to stow it in its duffel bag, I wandered over to the foot of the run that flowed past the pebble bar and stood looking down at the shallow water, watching it curl around stones, pause momentarily behind them, then rush on toward the sea. This was the way all fast water flowed, of course. Slow things down a bit, in fact, and it was the way all rivers flowed.

I glanced out across my wide and restless river.

Once again I remembered the adage "You can never cross the same river twice, the flow of things being what it is." Yes, true all right. In a sense. You could never encounter the same molecules twice. We tend to think of a river as an entity, but it does not really exist. Not as a thing. It is a pattern. I'd known that for a long time.

I turned and began to walk back toward camp.

But then, that was how all things flowed. I knew that, too. It was strange, though, the way you needed constant reminders. Every living organism exists in a state of flux—is always changing the molecules that form it. In our present state of knowledge we do not seem to know for sure whether all our molecules change, but most of them certainly do. Those in our bone material, for example, change every few years. That's why you can never really meet the same person twice. Or, in the same sense, cannot visit the same country twice. For us to perceive this reality, though, our meetings with the person or country must be separated by long intervals.

I reached the already folded tent lying on the pebble bar; stood looking down at it.

You could sometimes feel the truth of the pattern business deep inside yourself. And also the falseness of it. The person you occasionally glimpsed, far back down the years, might not be fully recognizable as "you"; was sometimes hardly recognizable at all. Yet you harbored no real doubts that you were the same person you had always been. Patterns persisted.

Maybe you could never, in one sense, cross the same river twice; but its pattern persisted. In that sense it like hell had an ongoing entity. Like every living system, it was a confusing, infuriating, fascinating affair. That was how things flowed. No plots, just patterns.

I glanced upstream, toward the junction. I could no longer see it but I could remember the way the Green had changed, after that confusing hiatus of the irrigation draw-offs, from a temporarily narrow and intimate stream that seemed to have recaptured its youth into a broad and mature river. If you were in the right frame of mind you could think of it as an adolescent striving to reach out and explore emerging possibilities. After all, this kind of reaching out lies at the heart of healthy adolescence in any unit of "life"—that label we've given our maverick, anti-entropic side show on the wider, apparently entropic stage. (Or *is* it a side show?)

My eyes came back down to the run that flowed past camp. They followed the irregular line of its shore.

Exploring possibilities was one way you could think of the thrust that drove the first animals to colonize dry land. Complex, invertebrate, scorpionlike creatures had apparently crawled up onto ancient shores and begun a new life. What was it Loren Eiseley called them? "The failures of the sea"? Something like that. But you could also call those pioneers the sea's ultimate explorers. Much later, certain tree-dwelling lemurs may have descended from their traditional penthouses (though this story remains in dispute) to explore the possibilities of life down at grass level— and so initiate a lineage that would lead to primates, including man. You could also say (though some people might not) that a long way down the primate line, after Neolithic man's loss of innocence—begotten by his breakthrough into agriculture and the domestication of animals, perhaps around 4000 B.C.—he was exploring the new possibilities that these advances had opened up when he began to develop increasingly complex and fruitful societies: the Sumerian and Babylonian beside the Tigris and Euphrates Rivers, the Egyptian beside the Nile. Again, you could (and also could decline to) see the United States as reaching out beyond its new, adolescent western boundary along the Mississippi when, in 1803, it made the Louisiana Purchase, and the following year dispatched Lewis and Clark on their explorations.

As I've said, you must be in the right frame of mind before you can fully accept, let alone initiate, such a view of living patterns. But few modern parents would deny that exploration of limits is a salient feature of individual human adolescence. Most of us can summon up personal examples. One that stood out in my own mind took place beside that same Dartmoor river I'd followed to its source in my youthful Devonian period. . . .

A moving shadow flowed over me, broke the train of thought. I looked up. The day's first small cloud was floating by—and I was once more standing beside my folded tent, out on the open pebble bar. Cloud and shadow passed. I checked my watch. Almost one o'clock.

By 1:35 I was once more floating south.

Out on the sunlit river, a breeze brought soothing coolness and mingled dry desert aromas with the rich and sweeter river scents. Overhead, now, sailed the day's first galleon-flotillas. Their shadows chased each other across swirling river and pale alluvial plain. The raft's small talk—oars consulting oarlocks, floor debating ripples—intensified the wide and liquid silence. I floated on.

The river flowed wide and steady and free of obstacles, and it promised to offer little distracting excitement. After an hour or so I'd pass Big Piney. It lay a couple of miles back from the right bank—the first human community within eyeshot of the river that was big enough to have earned an official name. (On how many U.S. rivers, I wondered, could you travel a hundred miles before even seeing such a place?) But its presence suggested that the hand of man would lie heavy on the local landscape. Heavily enough to discourage wildlife, anyway.

Within minutes of launch, I found myself floating down toward the biggest bull moose I had yet seen. He was standing close to the right bank, fetlock-deep, rump toward me, feeding with rapt attention on overhanging willows. I had come level with him, out in midriver, before he turned his head. He stood motionless, head pivoted, legs planted wide, pale brown face aligned directly at me. His big black ears were cocked. But the dark eyes signaled no fear and only mild interest. The powerful body—dark brown, almost black—glistened. The rack—not large, but richly velveted—spread black against sunlit green foliage. The bull watched me float slowly by. Only when I'd passed and the breeze wafted my scent to him did he lift his head and come fully alert. But before I turned the next corner he was back to browsing on the riverside willows. Behind him rose a faintly sagebrushed slope, pale brown and desert dry.

But that afternoon belonged to the birds.

A lone osprey on a riverside cottonwood branch stuck to its post, rigidly vigilant, until I'd floated almost underneath, then took off—and as it flapped upstream a single white feather floated down, spinning and circling above the raft, pure as snow, airy as air, before sideslipping out of sight just beyond the bulging blue bow.

A streaking, churring, gray-and-white quartet of kingfishers belted it out across the sunlit river.

I swung touching-close past pale brown bluffs with abandoned swallows' nests clustered under the eaves of overhanging ledges. Each small gray nest was a rough hemisphere furnished with a protruding pipe-entrance. They reminded me of those swiveling fixtures on rest-room dryers that let you direct hot air to either face or hands. Each little cluster of nests blended exquisitely with the angles of the cliff face—beautiful as well as practical, like the most exquisite Indian cliff dwellings.

Time after time, I watched replays of a now-familiar scene. Every hundred yards or so, still, I'd see a statuesque great blue heron, a solemn monument to wisdom. Yet when I floated close it invariably seemed to demonstrate bird-brain judgment: it would take off, flap slowly downstream like a ragged gray duster, land after a couple of hundred yards in another shallow, wait until I was back within discomfort range, then flap off downstream once more—and repeat the process again and again for as much as a mile before it would at last swing in a big circle, left or right, and head back upstream, presumably to its rightful, lonely post.

Once, though, five great blue herons rendezvoused on a midriver sandbar, unfishing, unexplained.

Along the shallower shallows, busy with vital bill-probing affairs, waded small shorebirds in all their customary and confusing shapes, sizes and variations. (No matter how often I consult bird books I seem unable to remember for more than an hour how to individualize the copious crew of curlews and phalaropes and plovers and stilts and turnstones and avocets and dowitchers and godwits and killdeer and knots and sanderlings and whimbrels and willets and yellowlegs—not to mention the firmament of sandpipers.) Along this stretch of river they all seemed remarkably tame. In defiance of common sense, I found myself thinking of them as direct descendants of the birds that left three-tined fossil imprints around the shores of Lake Gosiute, fifty million seasons earlier.

I floated on, past pale brown bluffs and dark green cottonwood groves, through the river's liquid themes and variations: rippling run; smooth, sliding tongue; slow, resting pool.

At the head of one pool I saw, clustered around a tree-root obstruction, a congregation of large white shapes. "Swans!" I thought. Then the stately birds began to move warily downriver and my altered angle of view disclosed long yellow bills with yellow skin folded below. Then the congregation took off and I could see the wings' boldly black tips. And there swept over me the nostalgic affection I had felt for white pelicans ever since a Colorado morning, 1500 river-miles below that point and thirty years behind it, when I opened my eyes to find the blue sky filled with huge white birds, tinged pink by the rising sun. They had soared and circled in solid phalanx, lifting and eddying with the wind, gliding on immense, black-tipped wings. Faintly, I heard the music of air rushing through feathers. In that huge formation there was nearly always at least one bird beating its wings to hold position. But from time to time came a moment when every wing was stilled and the phalanx swept across the sky in majestic unity. Each interval of stillness and soaring movement was so simple and beautiful that I found my muscles tensing as I tried to grasp the moment and force it to endure. Now, I knew that it *had* endured.

The handprints man had left on river and local landscape turned out to be few and faint.

Even Big Piney lurked low and modest, well back from the river—just a few roofs and one water tower, far out in flat plain. Around six o'clock I passed under a minor bridge over the main river. Half an hour later, just above the BLM parcel on which I planned to camp, stood two long-abandoned log cabins—crumbling now, but with sturdy lines that still spoke of a stalwart past. As far as I could remember, they were the first riverside human dwellings I'd seen all day.

Just below the cabins, it occurred to me that in spite of the late start and leisurely day I'd already covered more than my statutory ten miles. Almost without trying. It looked as if I had indeed resolved—or at least learned to handle—the tension between my urge to linger and the need to meet my schedule.

I rowed on down toward the BLM parcel.

I'd honed my rafting techniques, too. As much as was possible at this stage, anyway. And with only two days' easy travel left before I reached La Barge, on schedule, it looked, one way and another, as if I could regard my shakedown cruise as over.

Ahead, the river forked. The main channel thrust directly ahead. A smaller, more indolent branch wandered off right. The map showed that before rejoining the mainstream it looped for half a mile along the edge of my target BLM parcel.

I eased us down the right fork.

The BLM parcel was perfect. Along its edge stretched one of the dark, richly inviting cottonwood groves. I found a good campsite among tall trees, then explored.

In one corner of the grove, a rough track dead-ended at a rusty oil drum shot recreationally full of holes. In another corner I stumbled on a faint trail, followed it to the top of a bluff.

Below, upstream and down, stretched the river's rich and winding world of willows and gravel bars and cottonwood groves—the world that for more than a week had, I now saw, segregated me. When I turned my back on this river world I looked out across almost featureless desert—prostrate, desiccated plain barely able to support a sickly-looking membrane of stunted sagebrush. Not even the scattered prickly pears truly thrived. Gray evening light lay leaden on the land.

For some time I lingered on the edge of the bluff, surveying first one world, then the other. When I turned at last and began to walk back down into the cottonwood grove, my legs suddenly felt as leaden as the lowering sky. A week with little or no walking hardly seemed an adequate explanation.

Next morning I woke drained of all urge to travel. An hour later, no longer any doubt. One by one, the familiar symptoms had sprouted; above all, more than my legs now felt leaden, and the world kept sliding away behind a miasma. But this time, I told myself, I was at least free: could apply the only sensible response to what I knew, doctors' denials or no, had to be a flu relapse.

Most of the day, I slept.

During waking interludes I lay in the shade of the tall trees and gazed idly up into green leaves trembling against a sky-blue background. At intervals, when the miasma waves receded, I became muzzily aware of how beautiful a place I'd chosen for my sick bay. All around, roughly ribbed tree trunks rose straight and clean. Between them, sunlight transformed lush grass into soft and luminous green pools. Mourning doves and humming bees deepened the silence.

Above the tree canopy, the sun swung slowly by. My thermometer registered ninety-something. I dozed, undozed.

In beautiful places, even when you're whole, mere thought can become an impediment. Can contaminate pleasure. But not always. Once that day, when the miasma half-lifted, I found myself wondering what meaning might lie behind the beauty that enveloped me—and concluded that there was only the beauty but that it was enough, was plenty.

The second morning I focused enough to notice my neighbors.

A red-shafted flicker flickered by. A pair of downy woodpeckers pecked wood. A raven reconnoitered. A flycatcher, a sparrow, a house wren and a kinglet visited. I began to recognize universal life cycles. My most constant companions were a pair of mountain bluebirds that made a livelihood by perching vigilantly on low cottonwood branches then pouncing like blue lightning bolts on unknown goodies down in the long grass; but the male—decked in wonderfully delicate aquamarine plumage—had to keep chasing away a now-unwelcome adolescent offspring that apparently fluttered on the brink of independence but remained unwilling to move out and explore wider possibilities. From time to time, violet-green swallows swooped and swerved and sideslipped with conventional swallow ecstasy in pursuit of insect-meals; because they mostly hunted and perched in pairs, and because some perched partners exhibited a familiar coquettishness, I assumed they were also in pursuit of other rapturous goals.

In late morning I felt strong enough to attack a few chores. Around noon

I luxuriated under my plastic-pouch solar shower, wrote several postcards. Then, stretched out in the shade of the green canopy—or, for a couple of midday hours, the shade of my blue tarpaulin—I began to read.

Sensitive Chaos, a book by Theodor Schwenk, examined water. *"Man's relationship to water has changed completely during the last few centuries,"* it began. *". . . The more man learned to know the physical nature of water and to use it technically, the more his knowledge of the soul and spirit of this element faded. . . . Wherever water occurs it tends to take on a spherical form. . . ."* Yes, I thought. That's the way it flows—like the rest of our world, with cyclical tendencies. *". . . Together earth, plant world and atmosphere form a single great organism, in which water streams like living blood."*

I read on: *"The meandering flow of water is woven through with a play of finer movements. These result in manifold inner currents which belong intimately to the life and rhythm of a river. As well as the movement downstream there is a revolving movement in the cross-section of the river. Contrary to a first impression the water not only flows downwards but also revolves about the axis of the river."* I suspected that a hydrologist might respond, "Sure, take out the whimsical stuff, and we all know that." But there was also a lot about the nature of waves, and of the vortices that appear when the speed differences between layers of moving water, such as a river, reach a certain point. There were discussions of other possibilities, too, such as *"the spiralling forms of muscles and bones [that] bear witness to the living world of water."*

I put the book down. A passing cloud shadow veiled the grove's brilliance.

If the book was right, then the river held possibilities I had yet to explore. Like all living entities, it . . .

The shadow passed on. Sunlight flooded back—restoring a line of thought that had been broken that morning on the pebbly bar.

The urge to reach out and explore new possibilities seemed latent in all living entities—proto-scorpions, lemurs, Neolithic man. Most of us can summon up personal examples. The one that had sprung into my mind at Pebbly Bar Camp, and been curtailed, took place beside the same Dartmoor river I had followed to its source in my youth. But the episode I now saw as a quintessential adolescent exploration of possibilities took place far downstream.

The episode must have occurred not too long after my walk to the source. I was probably about sixteen. At that time—and for another fifteen or twenty years—I might, if challenged to define the universe, have called it a place created for boys or young men to fish in. At a confident guess, I had walked to the source rather than fish the upper river only because it was closed season for trout. But that later summer, during the trout season, I for some reason made up my mind to walk southward down the river to the farthest point I had so far ventured, then fish my way downstream all through the night.

My ostensible targets were not the resident trout I normally fished for but the much bigger migratory sea trout, the equivalent of Pacific steelhead. The sea trout, along with salmon, ran far up the river. I think fishing for them at night was legal. Anyway, I went. (My mother, who loved me dearly, had the wit to know she must allow me a degree of freedom, and the courage to practice what she believed—just as she'd recognized that I needed discipline, and had steeled her tender heart and sent me away to boarding school. She'd taken full possession of my reins when my father had, in my fourth year and a deepening Depression, emigrated to Canada with the never-fulfilled idea that we should follow.)

Although I can no longer recall the events of that long night of fishing as a complete and flowing whole, certain elements still stand out. I know the moon shone brightly and I was able to make my way slowly southward along the river, through and around and over meadows and trees and rocks, fishing all promising pools. I am almost sure it was this night that generated a memory that still hangs in my mind of three otters—the only ones I remember seeing in England—cavorting across a moonlit meadow on the far side of the river. I know that at the beginning of the long night a huge excitement filled me and hung over everything; excitement at the newness of it all and at the venturing out into new territory, both physical and otherwise. I know that I fished steadily, hour after hour, but raised no sign of a fish. I know that as the stark moon shadows shortened and then lengthened and the night eased imperceptibly past its pit and crept on toward another day, the excitement began to wane. But it was still there in a tired and attenuated way when, as the first pale hints of dawn at last began to flatten out the moon shadows, I came to a long narrow pool—fast and swirling and rockgirt—and from its head cast across and downstream. At the end of my line was a plug—a bulky, jointed wooden lure that wriggles through the water like a live fish—and the wriggling transmitted constant vibrations through line and rod to my hand. In the powerful current that swept through that pool it also transmitted a strong and steady resistance. By now I'd grown used to the resistance and the vibrations, and I doubt that I still expected to feel anything else. And then both resistance and vibrations had been canceled, annulled, wiped away by an immense, shuddering pull that

was incomparably more monstrous than anything I had ever felt on a fishing line before, and almost before I'd comprehended what that meant the
shuddering pull had become an impossible freight-train of a downstream
run that appalled and enthralled me for the whole breathtaking eternity
that went on and on for what was probably at least four seconds until I felt
the fish turn back upstream. The huge bow in my rod weakened. For another brief eternity I reeled in, frantically—with an attenuated sense, transmitted through a line left halfway slack because the returning freight train
plain outran my reeling, of an irresistible force moving up without check
against the powerful current. Then the line went dead. I reeled in, more
slowly now, knowing what had happened. There was no longer any resistance at all. And when the end of the line came up out of the water, where
the plug had been there was only a frayed end of gut.

The tingling double eternity that lasted from the first gargantuan tug until the terrible moment my line went slack has survived almost unscathed
the erosion of more than fifty years. And has gained overtones. But at the
time, I'm sure, I saw that whole long night only as a great fishing adventure, not as a fitting adolescent exploration beyond known boundaries.

Another cloud shadow veiled my sick-bay grove, passed on. I stirred.

Lately, I seemed to have done an uncharacteristic amount of recalling
such early and formative daubs in the pattern that was me. But that growing tendency could be seen as part of another pattern. Those of us launched
before the Freudian flood tend to ignore the significance of such daubs until late in the sensitive chaos of life; typically, at the tag end of it, when we
and our generation are tottering toward extinction.

A dozen feet to my left, a chipmunk climbed slowly up a rough-ribbed
cottonwood trunk. I wondered if his toothmarks might indict him for the
recent gnawing theft of some plastic-bagged chocolate. Above him, a yellow warbler butterflied among dappled leaves. The leaves began to flutter.
Out in a clearing, the feeble tag end of a dust devil, a failure of the desert,
swirled dustless through the grove, leaving on green leaves the temporary
imprint of its invisible vortex.

I picked up the book again, went back to studying another sensitive
chaos.

Next morning I woke feeling almost wholly whole. At 8:49 I cast off—
with an unexpected sense that my two days tucked back in the sick bay,
away from the river, had cut me off from it. Had divorced us. But by
8:55, floating down a sunlit run with the silver water flickering and whispering and the blue raft already talking back, it was as if we'd never been
separated.

Twenty-five hours later I reached La Barge.

I went ashore, taking my waterproof "wallet"—a ziplock bag encapsulating both basic plastic and backup green currency—did all necessary phoning and shopping, stifled my disappointment at finding no hint that the village had been renamed La Raft for the day, sampled its main and almost only street—a broad, automobile-age thoroughfare of the well-Honey-I-guess-we'd-better-slow-down-a-tad-for-a-half-mile-'cause-of-the-local-cops brand—then walked back the hundred yards or so to the edge of town, where my raft was tethered.

A few yards beyond it three young girls were splashing about in the shallows and throwing sand at each other and playing games of the unstructured and utterly engrossing kind that make your days when you're around double-digit old. Although they'd left their shoes close to the raft, they barely seemed to notice my return. But as I rowed away a few minutes later they stopped playing, stood watching me go. All three waved goodbye. I waved back. They returned to more important matters. And as I let the river carry our lives apart again it occurred to me that they would in later years look back occasionally at childhood and remember the river flowing endlessly past but always waiting, ready, right in the backyard. Something you didn't think about, really. Something that was just there, a part of your life.

To my surprise, the clearing up of all outstanding administrative questions at La Barge had peeled away yet another unrecognized onion skin of tension. Now, I felt even freer to do the unstructured and utterly engrossing things that I had all along meant to do. I looked more closely at the water, for example, and detected new themes and variations in the way currents rolled and in the vortices they spun.

But freedom of the mind is not a neat and manageable commodity.

A dotted line on the map, angling across the river near the place I planned to camp, was marked "EMIGRANT TRAIL—SUBLETTE CUTOFF." I had read something about this cutoff or bypass on the Overland branch of the Oregon Trail that the emigrants followed a hundred and fifty years earlier, sometimes with their wagons streaming by in almost interminable lines, and as I approached it I could see from the lie of the land—the way broad gaps fed down to the river, east and west—why they had chosen this crossing place. The river ran shallow for a spell, too, and the Trail actually branched over two fords, a couple of miles apart. As I floated over the first ford it occurred to me that it was the sort of place at which any conscientious traveler pauses and rummages around and lets his imagination swoon off into the past on a lilting obbligato—if it's his day for that sort of thing. It was not my day.

I camped at the edge of a cottonwood grove, on the line of the invisible Trail's lower branch. Hardly had I set up camp on an open bank when I saw floating down the river toward me a scattered armada: eight or nine kids in big black auto tires, shepherded by three or four adults in small yellow rafts. Soon I could hear snatches of conversation. They seemed to be local people. Everyone was having a ball, and although none of the kids wore life jackets they'd been well briefed. As they approached my camp they saw that the current swirled against the bank in a dangerous undertow and kept yelling to each other, "Keep away from that bank! Keep away from that bank!" They passed safely by, a few yards offshore, and we all waved. I watched the armada drift on down. Even if it wasn't really your day for peering into the future you knew what the river would mean to them all, in retrospect, for the rest of their lives.

The way you first look at a river makes a difference. Makes a difference to the way you will see it in the future. Will see other things, too.

I'd long ago recognized that there's a remarkable richness in the ways different people look at rivers. And in the ways their disparate angles of vision can be almost endlessly subdivided. I'd probably first become conscious of rivers as discrete entities at about eleven, when I began fishing for the kinds of fish that in England are called "coarse," in America, "rough." When I graduated to fly-fishing my angle of vision shifted. Later, war opened my eyes to rivers as barriers to cross or to defend. (Once, in Germany, there'd been a momentary but vivid cross-pollination. We had crossed the River Weser and were moving upstream along its shoreline. An unknown number of enemy infantry were dug in just over the high bank. It was an uncomfortable world: occasional bullets and grenades, a few corpses and, once, a pair of German fighter-bombers zooming overhead, low. At that moment I happened to glance out over the river. Just offshore, its silvery, gently swirling surface was dimpled by the rings of fish sucking down invisible insects. They fed steadily, imperturbably. I stared. I think I smiled. Then eyes and mind went back to war.)

Most of my life I had from time to time rowed or paddled small boats. So I knew that angle of vision, too. Knew the things fishermen and boaters shared and did not share. And I recognized some of the subdivisions: sailing boats, houseboats, dinghies, dories, rafts, canoes, kayaks. Despite the differences, even apparently disparate views are far from mutually exclusive. At the start of my rafting lessons in Idaho, one instructor had asked if I was a fly fisherman. "Good," he said. "That helps. It means you know how to read the water."

Down the years I'd come to recognize other perspectives. Farmer or flood-control engineer, bridge builder or dam builder, hydrologist or health worker, photographer or poet: each saw different things when his eyes scanned a river, scanned the world. But your initial childhood experience probably refracted each adult angle of vision.

The kids' armada vanished around a bend.

At my feet, the river flowed on. I had unrolled my sleeping pad at its very brink, and after a while it occurred to me that I had never felt so intimately in touch with the Green River. Familiarity had something to do with it, of course. Out in the main current, on its surface, the river chuckled. Just below camp, where current and bank created the undertow, it muttered surly warnings. There were also occasional rumblings—though I couldn't decide whether they came from stones being rolled along the bottom or from dark doings under the bank. I could catch undertones, too, some constant and almost unnoticed, some sudden and insistent. But all these utterances were familiar now and therefore more easily understood, and richer.

After dinner I sat watching the day fade. A beaver materialized in an upstream eddy and squatted there in silent solitude, sometimes barely visible, sometimes humped up dark and dinosaurial. Closer, killdeer and their sandpiper cousins bill-probed silvery shallows. Offshore, a trout sucked down a surface insect, left a widening, telltale ring.

Of course, the disparate angles of vision didn't end with our species. Far from it. Mayfly or mosquito, trout or whitefish, kingfisher or killdeer, heron or beaver, moose or coyote: each had its specific view of the river, of existence.

The sun set. The last breeze died. I sat on, looking out over the river. Perfect, cloudless evening slid toward night. A bat flickered by.

My eye watched the bat cross open sky, followed it down into pale alluvial background, lost it in dark foliage.

The twilight deepened. I scanned the river, upstream and down, across—and realized that what I saw was a fitting and perfectly timed sample of the world I'd grown used to. And a perfect sample of the river at its present stage of growth. I let my eye wander over the constituent elements. At my feet, a lush grassy bank on the edge of a cottonwood grove—yet somehow not part of it. A few yards downstream, a single juniper tree, heralding the desert. Beyond the far bank's strip of green riverine richness, the pale desert. And back upriver, out in the desert, oil tanks.

Even the tanks were a valid sample. Just above La Barge my river world had suffered its first industrial intrusions. In the middle distance, several huge yellow machines had roared and lumbered obscurely as they scribbled modern industry's signature. Out across the flats, a swarm of oil-pumping units had nodded their grasshopper heads, methodically, endlessly. And now, peering into the twilight, I could still make out a few of them grasshoppering away, up there among the tanks.

Bare arms reported cold air. I put on a down jacket.

The oil invasion hardly delighted me, but it was probably the least offensive form of industrialization. If you were going to suffer a cancer, you could do worse. Within a few years the scars would with luck have healed. After a hundred and fifty miles traveling with the patient, I was beginning to have faith in her vitality. So far, in spite of the oil tanks and pumps and other infections, she remained essentially undamaged. Spoiled in places, true; but still not despoiled. Certainly not tamed. But both river and journey now stood on the brink of change. Were approaching milestones in their lives.

Fingertips reported a sharpening of the cold. I slid into my sleeping bag, lay looking up at emerging stars.

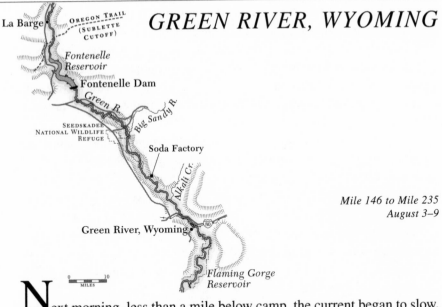

5

La Barge ◆ ORDON TRAIL
(SUBLETTE
CUTOFF)

Fontenelle
Reservoir

Fontenelle Dam

Green R.

Big Sandy R.

SEEDSKADEE
NATIONAL WILDLIFE
REFUGE

Soda Factory

Alkali Cr.

Green River, Wyoming

Flaming Gorge
Reservoir

0   10
MILES

GREEN RIVER, WYOMING

Mile 146 to Mile 235
August 3–9

Next morning, less than a mile below camp, the current began to slow, and a little before noon the living river petered out in the dead water of Fontenelle Reservoir. For the moment, it had surrendered, been tamed. At almost a hundred and fifty miles, it had lost its virginity.

Out on the reservoir, with the river once more in abeyance, I rafted to new rules. King Current had abdicated. Wind had stepped up to regent. And I rowed at his mercy.

Rowed, not motored. I'd decided against using the outboard on this first reservoir because storing it at La Barge would have been administratively jagged, because the reservoir was only twenty miles long, because the dam supervisor had virtually promised a north wind and because I felt that the challenge of crossing one stretch of dead water under my own steam should be met. So when the current died I knew the wind would rule.

At first, only a mild breeze. But southerly. Angling from the left, across my bow. I hugged the eastern, lee shore.

For an hour, all pleasant enough: a low bluff screened off the wind; and the reservoir was full, its shoreline therefore free from a disfiguring "dirty-bathtub ring." But then the wind rose a notch, veered, began to blow diagonally across open lake. I looked out over sudden, sullen waves. The flat western shore promised little protection, but in its lee the going could only be easier. I swung out into the wind, across open water.

Now, I rowed hard. Soon, flat-out. But our progress pitifully slow. Halfway across the lake, a few yards to my left, battling the wind on a parallel course, a small white butterfly. This flimsy and fragile fellow traveler, buffeted by every gust, kept dipping and deflecting, swerving and correcting, bravely holding course—and making exactly as much headway as I did. Bound in curious linkage—twin slaves under the regent's thrall—we slogged on together over the wind-churned water. We must have been two-thirds of the way across when another white butterfly came creaming toward us. It flashed between its cousin and me at full sail, barreled on downwind, vanished. Moments later my co-voyager turned tail and followed.

Nowhere on the reservoir could I see—nor would I—any human co-travelers. But a highway skirted the western shore and along it beetled vehicles, presumably piloted by humans.

I reached the new lee shore, turned downlake. Indeed a thin strip of calmer water. But the wind up another notch. Progress still a crawl. Close inshore, the water was so shallow that my oars kept hitting bottom. Once or twice we grounded. But if I moved into deeper water the wind braked us almost to a standstill. I kept yo-yoing to and fro: sheltered but shallow; deep but windblown. Then I saw a way out.

Fontenelle Dam had been built twenty-five years earlier, but its reservoir filled for only a short spell each August and September before being drawn down; and for the past three years, during repairs to the dam, it had never filled. So when I looked down in the shallow shoreline water I could see pastureland virtually intact: occasional eroded gullies, cattle trails winding across green grass, even unimpaired cow chips. Submerged thistles stood erect and whole. One still bore purple blooms.

It was probably the cattle trails that flagged the way out for me. Anyway, I rowed close inshore, shipped oars, grabbed the bow line, stepped out into submerged pasture and began to walk, towing the raft behind me.

It worked. Faster progress. Less effort. Before long, as I slopped happily on through the shallow water, it occurred to me that in this mode of travel—leaning forward to take the strain of the bow line over one shoulder, dragging the raft in my wake—I was reenacting Humphrey Bogart's recurring boat scene from *The African Queen*. That was fine. Fun, in fact. I rather think I began to sing. But then I came to a series of eroded gullies too deep to wade. At each gully I had to pull the raft up level with me, position its bow out ahead, over the gully, shove as hard as I could and leap aboard—then leap off again the moment we reached the gully's far side, before the wind drove us back. During the third such operation it dawned on me that from the nearby highway, with the gullies invisible, my antics must look utterly crazy. One or two vehicles did seem to hesitate before speeding on. But when I resumed straightforward Bogie-ing across open pasture, I found myself relishing the role of regent's court jester. At one point, leaning lustily into my work, I shouted to a speeding red sedan, "Where's Kate?" The wretched pilot didn't even slow down. No movie buff, I guess.

For the next twenty-four hours the regent continued to rule—and I subserved.

The wind shifted again; the lake serpentined. I rowed out of Bogart country toward a new lee under the eastern shore. Two more hours, and wind and reservoir had again changed bearings. Back across open water. A quarter-gale raising white-crested, three-foot waves that rushed, one after the other, onto my port beam. The little raft lifting and sideslipping and corking along—crest and trough, crest and trough. Yet reassuringly stable.

Next morning, flat calm. I rowed hard toward the still-invisible dam. Then, the wind again. But this time the dam supervisor's north wind. It strengthened. I sailed downlake, beam-on and fast and grateful. Before long, a half-gale. I swung bow-on for safety, but the raft still acted like a spread sail.

By the time I reached the dam, soon after midday, the sea was running so high that two Bureau of Reclamation men working on a protective boom—conveniently so, because the supervisor knew I might be arriving—had had to stop work. But they moved beyond the call of duty and battled the whitecaps and managed to maneuver my raft onto a trailer attached to a pickup. We drove to the dam office, picked up the supplies I'd left there, relaunched the raft below the dam.

I camped that night just below the dam, sheltered from wind, beside the swirling river. It felt good to have King Current back on the throne, making quiet and familiar proclamations.

Late next afternoon I pulled in for a catch-up-with-chores stopover.

Because it had been simpler to store the outboard motor at Fontenelle Dam rather than at Green River, Wyoming, sixty miles downriver, I now had it stowed inboard. It would travel that way for a few days, strapped securely in the stern. But when we floated out onto Flaming Gorge Reservoir, just below Green River City, I would begin to use it—and state laws, all down the river, demanded that every motor-powered vessel, even an inflatable raft, display its license numbers. The prime chore at my stopover was stenciling those numbers on each side of the raft's bow.

The stenciling took longer than expected. So did fine-sorting stores picked up at the dam. Other backlog chores, too. But the extended stopover gave me a chance, when I took leg-stretching strolls, to absorb the schizoid nature of the local landscape. Softly whispering river flowing free between unsullied greenery; downstream, a majestic, curving sweep of sandstone bluff. But in the background, rashes of squat, determined buildings; a scattered pockmarkery of spindly, girdered metallic structures, silent but suggestive.

That cloven place set a stage. For the next fifty miles we oscillated, the river and I, between two worlds: a largely untamed prehuman setting; slashes of modern industrial life.

The river itself flowed fast and free, untrammeled, still playing its wild-life themes and variations. It sang new songs, too. New for this journey.

A beaver, as big as any I'd seen, paddled gently against the current, upperworks barely awash, casing me with care. A mile down, a small head surfaced briefly and performed enough little bobs and interrogations to put ottery ideas into my own head, but not enough to remove all shadow of doubt; then the animal dived—and not only revealed what was indeed a slim, lithe, otterlike body lacking a flat beaver tail but also raised new doubts by making me realize I had no idea what a waterborne mink looked like.

On the left bank, a big metal trailer and a white pickup and a Sears delivery van clustered around a log cabin. Soon, billboards warned that a natural gas pipeline ran under the river.

Around me, swallows slashed past, scything the air. Nighthawks—which are not hawks and not necessarily night flyers—patrolled the river, swooping low and annexing insects like outsize swallows with white "windows" in their wings.

The land bordering the river eased over into barren desert. Bankside, a big-wheeled pump thump-sucked river water into a tanker truck.

Along the quiet river, great blue herons still stood regular sentinel. Flocks of pelicans took off—and reminded me how, seen from the side, with necks arched forward like curving prows, they carried galleon overtones; yet seen from the rear, the airborne bodies' heavy, ponderous lines reverberated with unexpected echoes of World War II bombers.

In the middle distance, left, a couple of gaunt buildings rose massive and factorylike; beside them, big yellow machines grunted and roared. Then the country opened up for a spell, and power pylons came marching across the desert from another world, leapfrogged the river, tapered off into the other distance.

An unfamiliar flycatcher in a bankside willow sent me to the bird book—and a surprise answer: Eastern kingbird. Downstream, a big black bird identified itself by standing erect in shallow water and spreading its wings out to dry in characteristic ragged-old-cloth-on-washing-line fash-

ion—and triggered me into reciting to the open river my earliest scrap of
bird lore, gleaned in well-spent youth from a nonbird book:

> *Common cormorants, or shags,*
> *Lay all their eggs in paper bags.*
> *The reason, as you'll see no doubt,*
> *It is to keep the lightning out.*
> *But what these unobservant birds*
> *Have never noticed is that herds*
> *Of wandering bears may come with buns*
> *And steal the bags to hold the crumbs.*

Silence reenveloped the river. Far off to the right lurked twin structures
with an oil or mining stance; a huge bulldozer belched dust.

Sometimes, now, the river was still an overgrown trout stream—all runs
and tongues and pools. Then it would gather itself into a more or less solid,
300-foot-broad tide that swept me along without effort or hindrance. We
passed into and then out of a national wildlife refuge. Little seemed to
change.

The refuge was clearly for migratory birds, not mammals, and by now
I'd resigned myself to the idea that down here where industry ruled we
were out of the big-wildlife country. Beyond the moose, anyway. There'd
been none for some time now. And even earlier, all down the river, our
meetings had been strictly low-key. Not to be compared with what I remembered from Alaska. And it wasn't just a matter of size. The Green
River moose were wild animals all right, but repeated contact with humans
had blunted the edge of their wildness. They tended to be bovinely curious.
Curiously bovine. And that made a difference. Still, it seemed a pity I'd not
had at least one vivid encounter. Something close-up and dramatic, preferably featuring a big bull . . .

Ahead, a half-submerged rock demanded attention. I maneuvered us
around it. We swept on. Beyond our bulging blue raft limits, the water
swirled and glinted. The sun beat down.

We passed under a couple of big new bridges that provided momentary
and welcome shade but remained gaunt, ugly.

Big Sandy River—not very big, and muddy rather than sandy—joined
us. Together, we moved steadily south and seaward.

By mid-afternoon the sun was hammering down. I put on more sun-
screen, took off the life jacket. Cooler without it, and freer.

About five o'clock, ahead and to the left, more industrial noise. A subdued but steady hum. I stood on the dry box, precariously, and glimpsed,
just for a moment, through binoculars and a gap in the vegetation, an enormous gray factorylike building.

A browsing bull moose breaks the monotony of low riverbanks.
"The Green River moose were wild animals all right, but repeated
contact with humans had blunted the edge of their wildness."

We'd covered more than twenty miles now. Another hour, and it would
be a thoroughly good day. But first I'd pull in and stretch my legs and
chase the heat daze away, ready for the final lap. Just a brief pause.

Around a bend, river right, a branch creek tapered back into a willow
thicket. Below it, an open pebble bar: a perfect place for some quick calis-
thenics to wake me up. I pulled in beside the bar.

The raft grounded. I stood up, began to step out into the shallow water—
and with my left foot still in midair, froze.

My recollection of the precise order and causes of events at this point
becomes clouded. Perhaps I froze because I didn't want to disturb what I'd
seen. Or perhaps I was startled into immobility by the violent reaction of
what I saw. Anyway, I froze—or tried to—with one foot still in the raft and
the other poised.

What I saw, up the branch creek, at the edge of the willows, no more
than thirty or forty paces away, was an enormous bull moose. He may still
have been munching peacefully away at the willows when I saw him—in
which case I froze instinctively, to avoid scaring him. I rather think this is
what happened. But it may be that what froze me with my left foot still
midair-poised was that the moose saw me and panicked.

Whichever sequence of events occurred, the moose saw me. I think I
glimpsed the terror in his dilated eye. I know I saw his great spreading rack

flash in the sun. Then he'd pivoted left and plunged off through the creek's shallow water. The huge beast pounded away downriver along open bank and I was left with the poised foot at last down in shallow water—on slippery, weed-coated, pebbly bottom.

I set the foot as firmly as I could and tried to lift my right foot out of the raft. It would not budge. I strove to unjam the sandal; failed; became aware that the raft had spun with the current and begun to drift downstream; took my eye off the fleeing moose and concentrated on freeing the right foot; continued to fail; felt the left foot—pulled by its leg which was pulled by the other leg which was pulled by the moving raft—begin to slip; grabbed the raft and tried to hold it in place; failed at that, too; felt myself being spread-eagled; spread-eagled wider; felt the left foot slide out of control— and began to fall. I fell backwards, the sandal somehow wrenched free— and I found myself sitting chest deep in water.

I stood up. The moose was still pounding away at full throttle along the riverbank, heading for the next county, already too far away for me to hear if he was actually laughing. He vanished. I began to wish I'd had a companion with a movie camera. Played back in slow motion, the scene would have been hilarious.

I beached the raft, took stock. The only casualty seemed to be my fancy, fully automatic camera. Had I been wearing my life jacket it would have been tucked inside and would probably have stayed reasonably dry; but because it hung by its neck strap it had been comprehensively dunked, and now it dripped water, steadily and sadly. Without delay, I rewound the film into its cassette, opened the camera and wiped everything dry with toilet paper. But mist still clouded the viewfinder. When I replaced the battery, the film indicator registered "empty." Nothing else worked. I set the camera in the sun, back opened up, and sat down.

Prompt and prolonged sunbathing seemed the best and perhaps only chance for the camera, and that open pebble bar the best and perhaps only place. I checked maps, refigured Green River City plans, set up camp. Then I went fishing and caught a rainbow trout.

Before dinner I strolled back into the thicket beyond the place I'd surprised the moose. The willows grew tall, dense. Yet the moose, or his brethren, had tunneled big swaths through them. I stood surveying the thoroughfares. It wasn't easy to picture how you could, as a bull moose with an enormous spread of rack, get in among the willows, let alone tunnel out swathways.

I walked slowly back to camp.

Judging by the way he bolted, the moose had suffered as violent a surprise as I had. Until our paths crossed, he'd been quietly browsing the tag end of his day away. I'd meant to pause for only a few minutes, then push ahead for another hour. Not for the first time, chance had ganged up on the best laid schemes o' moose and man.

I began to cook the trout. Come to think of it, the same wind of chance had blown the sensitive chaos of its life terminally a-gley.

All night long, at my camp on the open pebble bar, a low but insistent *woo-woo-woo-woo* pulsed up and across the river, punctuated by an occasional labored thump that suggested machinery suffering indigestion. Peering into the darkness, I detected a faint glow, assumed that both glow and rumble came from the big gray factory I had glimpsed.

Next morning I was striking camp when, at 7:45, a hooter sounded. It sounded again at eight o'clock; and once more at 8:17.

I launched, began to move downriver. The noises grew louder. Soon, I could see the place clearly.

It was a sprawling complex of square gray buildings with tall gray smokestacks and girdered gray structures and fat gray overhead pipelines. Plumes of gray smoke spiraled up into the desert sky. As I moved closer, the factory's basic roar fermented into a tangled disharmony of inhuman thumps and grindings.

I'd pulled almost level before the place revealed its redeeming feature. On the edge of the complex, at its closest point to the river, stood a cluster of big conical-roofed tanks. All except one of these tanks were white. But the conical upperworks of the outermost and biggest tank bore a gigantic, whirling, red-and-white helical design, and the effect was gay and attractive, unbelievably and delectably out of place.

Now, the flats on which the factory stood were part of the ancient alluvial bed of Lake Gosiute, and I had read that at least part of that bed was "trona." Trona is impure sodium carbonate. And when I came close to the red-and-white-helical dome and saw that big pipelines fed it—and the other tanks, too—with what I assumed was the factory's finished product, my tentative assumption that the place processed soda got a boost: on the white lower portion of the gaily decorated dome I made out, through binoculars, the inscription, "Stauffer Chemicals."

I rowed on. Here, the river ran straight and dull. All around, the land stretched flat and dull. If you had to industrialize, it seemed a fitting place.

Soon, minor industrial structures, possible factory satellites, dotted the riverbank. Four powerhouses. A small boxlike building, probably a pumphouse. Two of the buildings had been painted green. A tree planted beside one of them softened the inevitable chain-link fencing. I rowed steadily on. Red helix, green walls, a tree: it was good to know that we seemed to be learning something about minimizing the impact of ugliness.

The wildlife seemed to have been left reasonably unhassled, too. A lone pronghorn bounded away along a riverside skyline. Swooping nighthawks skimmed insects from the river's sunlit surface. Trios of magpies did whatever magpies do. Several beavers loafed and puttered. And directly across from the boxlike pumphouse stood the first full-fledged beaver lodge I'd seen in a long time—so recently built, or at least improved, that unwilted vegetation still fringed the sticks that made up its walls. I stopped rowing and looked back up the shining river, past the green beaver structure to the gray, smoke-belching factory. Maybe we were even learning to live together.

In early afternoon the low alluvial banks ended. Bluffs began. Their convoluted, water-carved strata made stimulating new stage sets that screened off whatever was happening out in the flat gray valley. Although I didn't yet know it, they also signaled an intermission. An agricultural entr'acte.

Occasional washes breached the bluffs, and sometimes the washes cradled clusters of ranch buildings. Once or twice, a brave, relatively new structure; but mostly the buildings were weathered brown hulks sinking back into the sand.

I'd just passed one such abandoned ranch that stood close to the right bank when it occurred to me that it looked an interesting place. I checked watch and map. The ranch was the last the map showed above Green River, seven or eight miles ahead. I'd planned to camp on the town's outskirts, so plenty of time to visit the ranch. I looked back upriver. Almost a quarter of a mile below it now. In that fast, unbroken current, just about impossible to pull back up. Especially into the northerly breeze. I sighed, rowed on. In a raft, as in life, you travel on a one-way ticket.

It's not often in life that you get an immediate second chance.

Around the next bend I came to a wash, river left, that the map called Alkali Creek. The map showed no ranch, but at the mouth of the wash stood a cluster of weathered, dilapidated buildings. I pulled in and moored the raft on the alkali-encrusted shore.

A few yards inland, the remains of a fence paralleled the shoreline. I went through an old gate that still hung on its hinges and walked slowly down a dirt track that wound through the center of the ranch buildings. The track, though faintly whitened by alkaline deposits, was greened over with stunted vegetation.

There must have been a dozen structures. Some were adobe-walled, some entirely wood. One or two had collapsed into wigwamlike piles. Others leaned and yawned. A few stood stalwart, only slightly tattered. One, off to the left, seemed to be the main ranch house. It retained shape and dignity.

On my right, the detached white cab of a pickup truck, late forties or early fifties vintage, was heavily rust-pocked. Vegetation half-enveloped it to steering-wheel level. A rabbit erupted from beneath a nearby pile of vehicle parts, scuttered into greenery and safety.

I walked on down the track. A dilapidated sign warned against trespassing. The track curved and I saw, down at its end, where it T-ed into a worn-bare cross track, a strange vehicle. At first glance it looked like an old-time prairie schooner.

I moved closer. The prairie schooner began to reveal anachronistic hints.

The curved top turned out to be not stretched canvas but galvanized sheet metal. And the wheels had inflated rubber tires. I took a few more steps. Stacked beside the vehicle were several cardboard boxes with an up-to-date supermarket cast. Beyond them, stuck into a block of wood, an axe. Beside it, a coil of modern fence wire. And then there was a voice. I stopped dead. The voice didn't sound as if it were talking *to* anyone. More like someone talking to himself.

I think I moved back a few yards. I know I hesitated. On balance, I decided, innocence was probably the best approach. I walked forward to within hailing distance and called out, "Anyone at home?"

No reply. But the voice had stopped. I came alongside the schooner.

"Hi there! Anyone at home?"

Around the vehicle's far end, down from inside it, stepped a youngish, blue-jeaned, bare-headed, pleasant-faced Indian.

"Can you tell me," I said, feeling my way, "how far downriver it is to Green River City?"

The Indian shrugged. "Oh, 'bout ten miles."

He confirmed that we were at Alkali Creek. Gradually, question and laconic answer revealed more. The ranch had been lying unworked since 1968, or so his boss had told him. Yes, it sure looked older than that: they'd put a lot of work into it. Yes, the Indian was putting up fences for a guy who owned a big spread that included this ranch. Been working for him for a month. But on what this boss paid, he was starving. Going back home soon. New Mexico.

"Navajo country?"

"Yeah," said the Indian, and smiled.

I asked about the schooner.

The Indian grimaced. "Yeah, it's an old wagon with *this* put on top." He gestured with one hand and considerable contempt.

"D'you mind if I take a picture of it?"

"Sure. 'Long as you don't take me." He stepped back, off to the right, well clear.

I took my small backpacking camera out of a pocket and moved forward for a shot from beyond and to one side of the caravan. Its chassis was indeed a simple modern farm wagon. At its far end, above a stout triangular towing hitch, was a full-height door. It stood wide open but I couldn't see inside.

"You guys boating down the river?" asked the Indian.

I nodded. The man appeared utterly amiable, but there seemed no need to advertise my lack of companions.

"How far you come?"

"From the source."

"That's a long ways."

"Couple of hundred miles. Still fifteen hundred to go."

The Indian nodded, slowly. "How far you going?"

"To the sea."

The Indian emitted a grunt so subdued it might have been just "Hm."

By this time I'd moved back to a position flush with the caravan's door and was facing at an angle away from it, but as we talked I sensed, from the corner of one eye, a bulge in the door's line. The bulge materialized very slowly, like seeping oil, and it never became more than one sector of a broad-brimmed hat and a one-eyed sliver of a bronze face and perhaps the very beginnings of a suggestion of a body. The apparition held position just long enough to take a good look at me, then melted back indoors.

The first Indian was talking again. "Why you guys doing this river thing?"

Trying to explain, I had to come clean about my lack of companions. The Navajo did not reciprocate. A few minutes later we shook hands. I walked back up the curving track, turned off into the old adobe ranch house.

Doorways and window frames gaped empty. Inside, the usual dust-covered jumble: furniture skeletons; wall and ceiling fragments; plastic bottles and other post-pullout squatter detritus; several white-enamel kitchen appliances. Everything seemed to confirm the pickup shell's evidence: forties or fifties. Perhaps the owners had indeed lingered on, fighting alkali and economics, into the late sixties; but the real breathing and living must have taken place much earlier.

I walked back onto the track, turned right, went out through the gate toward raft and river and the present.

Halfway, I stopped, looked back. The weathered buildings clustered tight, still resisting, still determined in their fashion. The gate swung gently in the wind, creaking.

Half an hour later I was floating down the still-unspoiled bluffs-then-greenery river beneath a thin white cloud layer that diffused the light to photography perfection, when I saw, parked on the left bank in the shade of some cottonwoods, a pickup and small camper. I pulled into a back eddy, moored the raft, walked up toward the camper.

I was still a few paces away when I heard a man cough.

"Say, sorry to trouble you," I called out, "but could you possibly take some photographs for me? I'm rafting down and want some shots of myself out on the water. Can't very well take them myself."

From inside the trailer, a muffled grunt. Through a small window I vaguely made out a figure raising itself up from a bunk. A dog growled. A man's voice muttered something about being asleep.

"Oh, I'm sorry. Didn't think of that. Really sorry. Please forget it." I turned, walked back to the raft.

I stood beside it, trying to decide if I could mount a tripod on the stony

*A few miles above Green River City, Wyoming. For this
stretch of river, logistical constraints demanded that I stow
the small outboard motor aboard—though I did not use it.*

beach, row out into the big back eddy and take some of the self-portraits I'd been meaning to shoot for several days. Here, where the banks still ran green and unspoiled was as good a . . . Footsteps behind me.

"Sure I'll take some photos for you," said a voice. "Hell, I was still half-asleep when you asked. What kinda shots d'you want?"

The man was around forty, muscular, heavily tanned, stripped to the waist. Blue jeans. At their cuffs padded a brown female retriever, over-weight, distrustful.

We chatted. It was fun: the man had a herd-instinct deficiency. He was a miner. Worked underground in one of the four or five mines scattered around the area, and this was his day off. Always came out and camped like this. Just needed it. Yes, the Stauffer plant mined trona. Manufactured soda ash.

The miner seemed to understand photography, too. We discussed the best shots to take and I explained my doubts about whether the dunked au-tomatic camera was working.

For fifteen or twenty minutes, then, I kept maneuvering into favorable places and stances, and using the eddy to help bring me back. The man took shots with both cameras. The dog relaxed, turned friendly.

After the last shot I asked about campsites above Green River City. The man's advice was detailed, informed. He began to ask questions about my trip. I outlined aims, intents.

"All the way on your own?"

"Sure. That's how I like it."

I finished stowing the cameras away in the raft. We shook hands, ex-changed names.

"All the way on your own, eh?" said Bill Arnell. He glanced over at my raft, looked up along the wide and swirling river, down at his dog, then back at me. "Yeah, guess you're right, too." He grinned. "The more I see of people, the more I like my dog."

Half an hour later I pulled in on the left bank. The camp turned out to be an apt final curtain for the fifty miles we'd spent—the river and I—oscillating between the primitive and modern worlds.

Some way before I camped, Interstate 80 had swung in, parallel to the right bank. Traffic roared along it. Beyond and above ran the Union Pacific tracks. A freight train gnashed and rumbled by. Buildings began to crowd in.

Then, three or four miles above Green River City, the river curved away from highway and railroad. Now, tall trees on the right bank veiled them both. And the left bank became a pale brown bluff with an apron of greenery. Soon, a small sandy alcove prefaced a dry and sandy side channel that wound away into green willows.

I pulled toward the alcove. Just before I reached it I saw for the first time, a few hundred yards downstream, the bridge carrying the interstate across the river. Two trailer rigs loaded with enormous black pipes were lumbering over it, outlined against a distant escarpment.

I grounded at the alcove. Thirty paces up the dry side channel, a browsing deer froze for an instant into immobility. Then it sprang off in half-panic, kicking up spurts of wet sand, stopped abruptly, stood peering back at me through a gap in the willows.

I set up camp at the sandy alcove, behind a screen of bushes and silence, then wandered along the foot of the sandstone bluff.

It rose almost sheer. Close-up, I could see the individual layers, each a little different from its neighbor in color and texture and the way it was crumbling back into sand. Some layers, a fraction of an inch thick, might have taken only a few thousand years to accumulate. Other layers were several inches deep. One presented seven or eight feet of solid, undifferentiated face: no guessing how long that took to build. I wandered on. The cliff was seamed with fissures that river and weather had cut. Rocks that were blocks of severed sandstone hung poised, ready to come crashing down on my camp some time in the next few hundred millennia.

I walked back to camp, watched the day taper.

Afternoon eased into evening. I dined. Evening drifted toward dusk. I sat looking out across the quiet, swirling river.

Over on its far bank, out of sight behind the tall trees, traffic still roared fitfully. By common interstate standards the highway might seem underused. By Big Sky standards it seethed. Beyond it, occasional freight trains rumbled heavily by, silhouetted against the skyline in a way you rarely see trains.

In among the tall trees screening the highway grew flat green grass and several small colored flags on thin poles, and over the grass flitted shirt-sleeved men wearing white caps and white gloves. They drove white go-carts and kept stepping out of them with thin sticks and hitting little white balls in various directions, and every now and then they'd gesticulate wildly and shriek in ecstasy or agony.

I leaned back, recognizing how painfully easy it was—and strangely delectable—to belittle other people's pleasures and mores when you're positioned squarely outside their worlds. Easy to be snide, for example, about white-gloved men hacking away with thin sticks at small white balls when you're a detached rafter camped across the river from them—though you may in other modes be a dedicated, sweat-banded maniac hacking away with a nylon-netted racquet at slightly bigger yellow balls.

On my side of the river, now, the silence lay thick over alcove and willows and crumbling sandstone bluff. The sounds from the golf course didn't truly make it across the river. Nor did the sights, really. The reality of that world was blunted, almost dissolved, by the silvery, swirling ribbon that divided us, joined us.

Dusk deepened into darkness. The river flowed on. I could still hear it, still discern its restless lineaments. It flowed steadily on toward the sea, oblivious to the roaring traffic and the rumbling trains and the now-departed men in white gloves and the lone, detached traveler still tucked away in his camp on the quiet side, under his crumbling cliff.

It was almost one o'clock and I had finished doing all the things that had to be done in Green River—phoning John and Victoria Sexton and arranging for a replacement automatic camera to be shipped to Flaming Gorge Dam, picking up mail and stores, buying gas for the outboard motor—had finished all these things and was back under the bridges.

Back under the twin downtown bridges, beside my moored raft. Back under the bridges beside their ugly gray concrete piers, spray-painted so densely with graffiti from ground level to upper teenage-arm-reach that one blood-curdling, puerile or gross-out message often overran another and rendered them both mercifully unreadable; but this whole can of multicolored worms headlined, loud and clear, DUKE WAS HERE and BRIDGE GANG IS AWESOME. Back under the bridges, glad to be quiet again after the town-bustle. Back under the bridges, alone with the ghost of John Wesley Powell.

Powell's ghost has become an almost inevitable companion to any modern who runs the Green or Colorado, especially if he starts at Green River, Wyoming. And people seem unable to avoid drawing parallels. Before I started, several said, "Want to duplicate Powell's trip, eh?" But a root-deep fallacy undermines all such knee-jerk comparisons. Powell's journey can never be duplicated.

On May 24, 1869, the thirty-four-year-old Major Powell—who seven years earlier had lost his right arm at the battle of Shiloh—set off downriver from Green River with nine companions and four wooden boats. The boats had been specially built in Chicago and brought to Green River on the Union Pacific Railroad. The party took *"rations deemed sufficient to last ten months, for we expect, when winter comes on and the river is filled with ice, to lie over at some point until spring arrives."*

Powell, by now a "self-made" geology professor at Illinois Wesleyan College, had done much wild-country exploration in the Midwest and around the Colorado plateau, and his overriding aim in making the river journey was—if you discount personal ambition—scientific exploration. Wallace Stegner describes the purpose as "Only to discover. To find out. To observe, analyze, map, comprehend, *know*." Powell disclaimed any "adventure" element, but it's difficult to believe the physical challenge did not loom.

I don't mean merely that no human was known to have run the stretch of river they would attempt—which was thought to be "a three hundred mile canyon" but turned out to be a chain of canyons extending more than a thousand miles. They were entering what the maps of the day showed only as a blank, "as big as Texas." And myths about this void ran rampant. "Folklore and Indian reports both spoke of inaccessible and probably un-runnable canyons, rapids, falls, 'sucks' and cataracts." One rumor even maintained that the whole river ultimately vanished into a huge hole in the ground. In other words it was the unknown—the expedition's very raison d'être—that also lay at the core of their journey's physical challenge.

That is why Powell's original journey cannot be duplicated. Even his second trip, made two years after the first to gather further scientific infor-mation (which he eventually embodied in his account of the original jour-ney), was not really a repetition—because for sheer, raw, soul-plumbing, testicle-tingling scariness, the challenge that he and his crew faced when they floated away from Green River, Wyoming, in May of 1869 has gone. They dissolved it. After their pioneering success, the unknown was known. And it is the unknown, above all, that scares the living daylights out of us—and draws us like moths to its candle.

So when I stood beside my little raft under the twin bridges at Green River City I was bitingly aware that much more than a hundred and twenty years separated me from John Wesley Powell and his men. Much more than the wealth of river-running technique that had been honed and handed down to me by them and by those who followed. Much more than a changed, part-tamed river. Much more than a different set of aims. Much more than a different starting point (Green River, Wyoming, had for Pow-ell been the natural place to start, because of the railroad and because it lay on the fringe of the unknown he was determined to explore; for me, it was simply a supply point, 225 miles down the river I was determined to expe-rience as a whole). For although certain unknowns lay ahead of me—at once magnetic and scary—I knew they could not, by the wildest stretch of knee-jerk imagination, be compared with the unknowns Powell had faced.

So my journey could not be compared with his. Any attempt to do so would be empty, pretentious, mere puffery.

In spite of all this, I think I expected to experience, as I stood below the Green River bridges and prepared to cast off, at least a mild surge of Powellish feelings. I did not.

At a guess, the main reason for this deficiency lay less in an awareness of the empty comparison than in a personal attitude toward history—an attitude I recognize but can't confidently explain. It's not really that I'm insensitive to echoes from the past. On my day, I can hear them loud and clear, especially if the scale is small and it seems possible to picture vivid segments of little-known lives. But in general I have a block against the kind of history that has been told and retold a thousand times so that it has hardened into folklore and reaches us with its vitality congealed. My antipathy to such varnished lore is by no means absolute. I had read, more than once and with pleasure, Powell's account of his pioneering journey— a graphic telling that has helped keep the varnish thin. But the varnish is still there. To my eye, anyway. And when I finally cast off from beneath the Green River bridges I did so with an entire absence of true Powell-resonance. I also failed to detect ghostly echoes from any of the others who down the years had cast off from this place and followed Powell downriver. At that moment, I don't think I even remembered Buzz Holm-strom, one of the least known canyon runners but the one for whom I felt most empathy.

Weather and scene may also have contributed to the flatness of the moment.

A cloud pall now covered the sky, and even after I'd emerged from the bridges' gloom and graffiti the expanse of land and water that stretched out ahead lay bleak and sullen. Distant buttes that should have exuded drama sat gray and lifeless. Along the left bank crouched a gray corrugated-iron storage shed. And when I looked back just before the first bend, my final message from Green River, Wyoming, was the writing on a wall: DRIVE-IN LIQUORS.

Around that first bend, worse. The river now lacking riverness. Its water turned greenish—not the sort of green it had been above Fontenelle but a murky green. Plain dirty. Soon, on my left, a jumble of Union Pacific freight cars. Telegraph poles spiking the land. And garbage crudding the water: oil drums, tires, uprooted trees. A few raindrops fell, cold on bare arms and legs. They pockmarked the leaden river.

I rowed slowly on, still making reflex attempts to focus the ghost of John Wesley Powell. By design, his journal was not among the books now stored at my feet in the dry box, waiting to be read: from the start I'd intended that rather than trace his path page by page, relentlessly, distractingly, I'd hear only those echoes strong enough to have snagged firmly in my memory.

One echo that had snagged and remained lodged was that the Powell party had while readying their gear in Green River camped on an island. I'd forgotten to inquire in town, and now I began trying to identify it. The only possible candidate—a low, scruffy pebble bar currently populated by pigeons—hardly qualified. In Powell's time, if it existed at all, it could well have been underwater. Weather aside, it was difficult to know what might have met his party's eyes just after they cast off, that May morning in 1869. The Union Pacific freight yard perhaps—though in miniature and with less clutter, less rust. The other gray elements, probably not at all. And the first Powell place I had any chance of identifying was his first camp.

While reading his journal I'd checked the map and guessed at the site of that first camp. Although I thought I'd marked it on the map I now found I'd not done so. But I remembered his description of the place, even if less surely than I'd hoped: near a bluff, where the river swung left. I rowed on downriver, began to look for the bluff. The grayness still lay heavy. Occasional raindrops still fell.

By degrees, the river regained its riverness. Willows and other vegetation grew thicker, greener, healthier. Low bluffs gained stature. The cloud pall even began to lift and thin. And though beer cans, plastic bottles and Styrofoam still cluttered water and shoreline, they too were thinning out. On most rivers, urban detritus signals the beginning of the end: from this point on, you know, man will press in ever harder, dirtier. Here on the Green, it seemed to me, the trash signaled the end of the beginning.

Soon, a big flock of mergansers sitting on dry land. Upriver, mergansers had been one of the more common species of ducks, but I'd always seen them afloat. Now, sitting there with creamy breasts prominent, they had a quite different presence. They formed an almost solid phalanx, every bird more or less upright but all leaning at the same slight angle, like fey penguins. When they took off at last, they reminded me of a comic chorus from a well-choreographed Gilbert and Sullivan production.

I floated down toward a fisherman, patient on a promontory. As I passed I inquired about the Powell island.

"Sure, up above the bridge. The one with the big gray building."

"Hm, thanks. D'you happen to know where his first camp was?"

"Oh, he probably went down to . . ." The fisherman named a ranch. " 'Bout five river miles."

But by that time, as happened in such conversations, we were easing out of earshot.

Within two miles I came to the bluff I'd assumed was Powell's first campsite. I pulled in just below it. At river level, hardly enough room for ten men. But I climbed onto the bluff, as Powell had done. The cloud pall was dispersing now, and the wide downriver view from the top of the bluff, a hundred feet up, held life and energy. Powell, I remembered, had been impressed by the rock formations. Downriver, certainly, the geology shrieked at you. Powell could have caught only a glimpse of that country from Green River City, and it would all have been new to him. But it was essentially what I'd been seeing for a hundred miles. True, this variation on the Lake Gosiute alluvial theme was played with more brio than before. And it stood closer. Yet it failed to move me. I guess there's a limit to how long you can remain ecstatic about the dry bed of a 60-million-year-old lake.

By now, anyway, I was suffering profound doubts about whether this was indeed Powell's first campsite (doubts that would much later, when I rechecked his journal, harden into a certainty of error).

I scrambled back down to my raft, to the present, and cast off. On reflection, my failure to make a genuine Powell connection seemed salutary. From time to time in the miles and months ahead his ghost would no doubt

*The river and Lake Gosiute alluvial geology from bluff
above putative first Powell campsite. My raft is tethered
bankside, below.*

rematerialize. With luck, it would appear at proper moments, and in sharp focus. What I'd been doing, though, was ridiculous: striving to conjure the ghost up at will—my will—as a sort of obligation, a duty. I should not, indeed could not, ignore Powell's journey. But the one I must live was my own.

6

FLAMING GORGE

Mile 235 to Mile 320
August 10–14

Next morning, when I rowed on southward, the current soon began to slacken. Before long its last swirls ceased. Living river faded away into the dead water of Flaming Gorge Reservoir.

I pulled inshore, got out, clamped the outboard motor onto its transom, rowed a few strokes until the water was a couple of feet deep, then tilted the motor down into operating position. All I had to do now was start it.

But the morning sun beamed down and everything was beautiful and peaceful. We floated on the calm water like a painted raft upon a painted reservoir. I sat savoring the moment, reluctant to end it. Then a breeze ruffled the water. I looked down the reservoir. Hints of a headwind. Still reluctant, I started the motor—and changed the tenor of my travels.

For more than 200 miles the raft had been a delectable means of transportation. Softer than silence—because it whispered sweet nothings to the river. Responsive to each subtle hint my palms conveyed through its oars. Rich in the way it let me—sometimes even helped me—maintain contact with both land and water.

But the moment I started the outboard motor the raft became an impoverished power vessel. Engine noise blocked off all outside sound. A constant vibration, though damped by the long and flexible extension tiller, throbbed into my steering hand and pulsed through everything else. After only one filling of the tank, a thin but persistent residue of gas and oil coated both my palms.

The motor was about as benign a choice as I could have made: a little

3-horsepower unit, made by British Seagull, that had a reputation for simplicity, reliability and relative quietness. But only relative quietness. The problem lay in motors as an ilk.

Twenty years earlier I had, as a backpacker, promulgated the Law of Inverse Appreciation: *The less there is between you and the environment, the more you appreciate that environment.* Now, as soon as I started up my motor, I learned how aptly the law applied to waterborne travel—and that size wasn't the only barrier.

Size counted, though. In the course of the next three days, as I pounded down the 80-odd miles of Flaming Gorge Reservoir, huge powerboats roared by, carving tidal-wave wakes across the lake. (Flaming Gorge Reservoir is a national recreation area, so in official parlance the euphemism "lake" has Greshamed out "reservoir.") And it several times occurred to me that anyone transferring from one of these rampaging behemoths into my raft would perceive it, even in power-driven mode, as a quiet and simple vehicle—one that kept you in close touch with the natural world moving slowly past. As I pounded on southward I knew better.

But my outboard motor was not the only barrier to pleasure during those three motorized days on Flaming Gorge Reservoir.

Earlier, the living river had in its last miles kept branching into minor channels, and I had kept taking the narrowest and getting a kick out of it. I guess I enjoyed the throwbacks into youth: most of us are suckers for nostalgia. But the setting had been beautiful, too. Dramatic desert bluffs and buttes, red then gray. When their cliffs pressed close, the first canyon-country sensation of sinking deep into the earth. Along the shoreline, though, narrow sandy beaches, often cloaked with greenery. From a distance this vegetation looked exquisitely smooth, like a diffused dream meadow. Close up, it turned out to be not grass at all but dense stands of very small bushes, so young and tender that they seemed little more than sprouts—though they owed their smooth and strokable texture to massed, fluffy seed heads. All in all, a soft yet jagged country.

Once I'd moved well clear of the river, the shoreline softness vanished.

Flaming Gorge Reservoir, unlike Fontenelle, was not full: it had been drawn down twenty feet below its highest level. A "dirty-bathtub ring" therefore encircled and disfigured it.

At the start of those three days of pounding down the reservoir, the bathtub ring was only a thin and distant line along each shore. The first day, clouds soon drew a veil over the sky. A few spits of rain fell. The drab gray light softened the bathtub effect but left the shores lying flat and torpid. For hours on end, I hardly noticed them. I just putt-putt-pounded on into the headwind at full throttle, head down, brain benumbed. At full throttle because weather, setting and schedule seemed to demand it—and because the instruction book for the little Seagull warned that slow speeds during the first twenty hours of operation were harmful, and recommended "hard running."

Those three days on the reservoir generated only three episodes that, in retrospect, stood out.

Evening, that first day. The clouds had began to break up, and all at once, ahead of me to the south, seeming to block the foot of the lake—though I knew it did not—loomed the escarpment of the Uinta Mountains, blue and forbidding and inviting. Barely a hundred miles, now, to the Gates of Lodore, where the river began its improbable breach of the range. Barely a hundred miles to the first big rapids.

A little after six o'clock I pulled in to the eastern shore and camped. The place was simply an open beach, like miles of beach on either side, and I stopped there for mundane, practical reasons. Because it was time to stop. Because I'd covered close to thirty miles and could stop without guilt. Because the sandy beach seemed to defy the barren, lifeless bathtub ring imposed by the reservoir's drawdown. And because a gently curving shoreline promised some slight shelter from the south wind.

After dinner I sat watching the light seep away. Sat looking at the barren, curving shoreline—appreciating the way the sweep of the land had a rightness to it. Seeing, now, how the evening light slanted in low and lucid. There was a harmony, I saw, between the scene's many lines: water, weed bed, sand, scattered vegetation—and finally an open slope, more thickly greened but undeniably desert, that slanted up to the skyline. The long, gross, noisy day began to fade into the past. . . .

Something up on the skyline caught my eye. Or perhaps my ear. Blue-gray clouds hung heavy in the dying light, and against their somber backdrop I saw, in racing silhouette, a lone pronghorn. The antelope gave the impression of running well within itself, but it moved at astonishing speed, with lambent liquidity. Almost at once, it angled down off the skyline and dissolved into the murkiness of a shallow draw.

I raised my binoculars. Details of the draw leaped out. Dry gullies. Low, scattered bushes. Just below the skyline, a shallow natural cup. Grouped in this cup, I could now see, were not only my lost pronghorn but six others. And the troupe of seven was dancing. They seemed to be animated by the same odd, playful mood that sometimes strikes a band of horses and sends them at a gallop, manes flowing free, in wild, wanton, illogical patterns around a pasture; but the pronghorns danced with a grace and lightness beyond equine reach. There were moments when their dance seemed touched by logic: they would pause and, as far as I could discern in the shadowy gloaming, look down and recheck me; but soon they'd resume their reckless, feckless, pixilated ballet. Once, one member made a short straight-line run—just twenty or thirty yards, but all bounding near-levitation, downhill and away from its partners—then quietly rejoined them. As a finale, when the whole band had moved leftward and upward, still performing, one of them did a long, beautiful crazy-horse gallop along the skyline. Then the whole troupe had vanished.

I slept well.

Next morning, after pulling away from the beach, I shipped oars, sat looking back. The curving harmonies were still there. But the shallow draw in the slope behind the beach looked like any other desert draw: prosaic and unpixilated.

As I tilted the outboard down into operating position and reached for its starter cord, I thought of all the apparently prosaic campsites—backpacking and now rafting—that I'd chosen for mundane reasons but would remember for flecks of magic. Maybe I could formulate some profound law, dripping with overtones, about the incidence of such serendipities. I pulled the starter cord. The motor roared into life—and banished my profitless, invaluable daydreaming.

The second mildly notable episode occurred that same day.

A little after one o'clock the map reported that I was moving out of Wyoming—which had lived up to its reputation as an open and friendly place—and entering Utah—with its tighter, more money-conscious, development-minded, religion-oriented persuasions.

Soon, I pulled into a marina: acres of asphalt parking lot, line after line of moored pleasure craft—all the relaxed, pleasure-inducing enchantment of a concentration camp. The store, at which I bought a few groceries, levied a five-percent surcharge on the credit-card transaction. Down on the dock, where I wanted only a gallon of gas, because that was all I needed, the attendant—a mildly scruffy, rather guarded fellow—told me there was a ten-dollar minimum for credit-card purchases. When I explained that I was carrying very little cash, and why, the attendant suddenly warmed. "Oh, have it on the house," he said. "And I'll pray to Jesus to keep you safe."

The third and last notable episode began late next day.

By then the lake had narrowed. Often, cliffs plunged sheer to the waterline. And I had passed through the heart of the place John Wesley Powell christened Flaming Gorge. Had passed, rather, through the cadaver of the magnificent red canyon, whole and harmonious, that Powell had traversed.

*Flaming Gorge Reservoir. In Kingfisher Canyon, no
kingfishers; only the reservoir's lifeless bathtub ring.*

Its upper walls—all that remained—were still magnificent in their way. If
you looked at the scene without prejudice—that is, without imagination—
and could somehow ignore the bleached bathtub ring, it was still a beautiful place. But it was deranged.

The derangements included lacks and disharmonies that were subtle yet
profound. Among the more obvious deficiencies, wildlife: no beavers; no
great blue herons; in the canyon Powell had named Kingfisher Canyon, no
kingfishers. Among more obvious dissonances, the traffic that roared
through the narrows. Not only the rampaging behemoths—some with gar-
ishly futuristic lines and adornments that suggested they'd been designed
for selling rather than sailing—but droves of smaller, equally snazzy cabin
cruisers and speedboats. Square blue houseboats, too, chugging slowly
past—floating reminders of suburbia. And bobbing along the shoreline, a
wreath of discarded plastic and paper.

Perhaps it was the increase in boat traffic that made me check the calendar. Anyway, I suddenly realized that it was a Saturday morning—and that
if I pounded on down to Flaming Gorge Dam as planned I'd reach there on
Sunday morning. The dam supervisor had warned, when he kindly made
arrangements to move my raft around the dam, that he'd have men avail-

able only during weekday working hours. So there was no point in arriving before Monday morning.

About four o'clock that Saturday afternoon I camped at the mouth of a small creek in the farthest recesses of a narrow, curving fjord that before the flood had been a side canyon.

My hideout seemed to offer many things.

So far, in spite of striving to ignore the barren and lifeless bathtub ring, I'd failed to achieve any affection for the reservoir—and there were reasons for trying to like it, beyond plain enjoyment of what I was doing. One was a recognition that an "environmental" outlook might be unduly coloring my vision. Another was a sense of obligation toward the Bureau of Reclamation. Throughout the planning and then at Fontenelle, its people had been unfailingly helpful. And unfailingly pleasant. Yet to us environmentalists they tended to be "those bastards in the Bureau."

But now I had met the enemy, and I liked him. Personally, at least. And I felt I owed him an honest attempt to like the bodies of water his dams had created, and of which he was so proud. As a start I should learn more about this reservoir.

What I learned above all, though, in my hideout at the head of the curving fjord was more about the bathtub ring.

When I first saw the campsite, from a distance, it seemed to offer a pleasant little beach at the mouth of the feeder creek. No rock wall, only gently sloping land. I assumed that vegetation would have covered, or at least softened, the lifeless bathtub ring. But it turned out that the soil beside the feeder creek had been shallow, and the reservoir had stripped it bare, down to naked talus. The small sandy beach, though pleasing enough in itself, lay cradled in the barren zone, like a crib in a morgue.

Lacking any better alternative, I carried all my camp gear up almost a hundred yards to a small flat place at the foot of a juniper tree. There, although the barren zone still hung in a corner of my vision, the greenery cushioned me.

Sitting in camp, I enjoyed having the tinkle of the little creek's living water, below and to my left. But when I went down to fill the canteens I found that the creek, in spite of its swirls and vortices, was biologically dead. The running water had been killed by the still water—or, rather, by the way the still water rose and fell without natural rhythm. Now, the running water cascaded over bare rock or talus. No weeds. No life of any sort. Just inert silt. Mere dirt—because it met Lord Acton's criterion: *"There is no such thing as dirt, only something in the wrong place."*

Not until my second day at the hideout did it occur to me that all through the normally bird-rich evening and early morning I'd neither heard nor seen a bird. No small songbirds. No ravens. Not even a hawk. And apart from a few small tracks near camp, possibly mouse-made, the only signs of animal life were a few beer cans along the water's edge.

But as the lazy layover day ticked by, I began to see that life had in fact begun a patient reclamation job.

A chipmunk guided me.

He seemed to live in the greenery above the creek but he kept foraging down into almost bare talus at the edge of the barren zone. What attracted him were a few thistles scattered among the skimpy vegetation. He would bite off one of the thistle's purple flower heads, carry it to the top of a prominent rock and sit there—where he commanded a healthy view of his universe—holding the flower head upside down between his paws and nibbling away at its base. As he ate the seeds, the not-yet-fully-mature thistledown fell away. He nibbled on. The thistledown collected around him. Before long he was sitting there on what had been his bare lookout-dining-room floor, surrounded by a gleaming white carpet two or three times his size—and this carpet or apron glistened in the sunlight and framed him as with a halo. When he'd finished one thistle head he collected another, came back to his rock, started over. And when that course was gone he'd forage for yet another. Once, when he was off foraging, a house-cleaner breeze dusted away his white halo-apron.

In late afternoon I went for a walk up the little creek's canyon. At first I followed a trail, apparently worn by explorative boaters, that meandered up through sagebrush and junipers. Within a few strides it occurred to me that the little canyon was prime rattlesnake country. My left hand checked the rubber snakekit in my shorts pocket—and my mind clicked back three days.

I'd been camped beside the river, just above the head of the reservoir. After breakfast, when I was ready to cast off, I walked a few paces down the open beach, then turned up toward some underbrush in order to untie the bow line from a bush, several yards inland. As I did so it occurred to me that the underbrush looked like prime rattlesnake habitat, and that with the sun only just up it was prime rattler time. My left hand checked the snakekit I'd put in my shorts pocket near La Barge a week before, when I left the rattler-free high country. And just as I was about to step into the underbrush I saw at its edge, half-concealed among stones and vegetation, a snake. It was a small pale brown snake, little more than two feet long, but even before I checked its tail I'd recognized the flattened, triangular head. And in its mouth the rattler held a freshly killed breakfast. The mouse was

Rattlesnake breakfasts on mouse.

inert, no doubt already dead from the venom injection. But only its head had been drawn back into the snake's throat. Most of the little gray-and-white body lay out in the open, awaiting ingestion.

At first the snake showed no sign of alarm. Taking care to keep my shadow from falling on it, I retreated, walked softly to the raft, got my camera, came back. The snake still lay in the same place. I eased forward, camera ready. The pale brown body had mottled markings all right, but they were very faint, barely discernible. I moved in closer. Closer still. The rattle was complete and undamaged: six or seven rings plus the button. Closer yet. Only when the fully zoomed lens was three feet from the snake's head and I'd begun to take pictures did it respond. It began to withdraw, slowly, tentatively, into the underbrush. At first it did not seem alarmed, only suspicious. But when it was almost half-concealed by brush, with little more than its tail still visible, it raised its tiny rattle and shook it. I saw the shaking clearly—and heard nothing. Seconds later the snake had vanished into the undergrowth.

Now, walking up the canyon behind my fjord camp, left hand again checking the snakekit in my shorts pocket, I found myself thinking about more than the lack of audible warning from that shaking rattle, and its significance should I meet another rattler beside this trail.

That riverside camp three days earlier had been before the river once more sank into abeyance; before the onset of the barren bathtub zone. Next night, the pixilated pronghorns had performed outside the zone, in living desert. The marina had been asphalt jungle. And now I could look back and recognize the little rattlesnake and his mouse breakfast not only as a combination that had scared and then intrigued me but also as a proclamation that the land there beside the river had been alive and functioning. Had, until now, been the last live and functioning land I'd set foot on.

I walked on up the trail. The little canyon was not a remarkable place. Mostly sagebrush and junipers and boulders and stony brown soil. But the trail soon petered away from obvious human imprint and became more like a game trail. It crossed and recrossed the creek—now not only tinkling but greeneried, viable. I passed some deer droppings. Birds flickered tantalizingly behind junipers. One was probably a speckled towhee, but I couldn't be sure. Labels didn't matter, anyway.

After a while I came out into a desert flat—the closest approach to a meadow that such country offers. It was still nothing special. Just the same mix of sagebrush and junipers and boulders and dry, brown, stony soil. The creek was no longer visible. Yet the junipers seemed a slightly richer green. And when I went up another faint game trail I found a little garden of prickly pears and barrel cacti. That was about it. Except, perhaps, because of the way the flat tapered off into brush, a certain richness of edges. "The edges are where things happen," somebody has said. Seashores, riverbanks, forest edges, the fringes of society. . . . Yes, and now this desert flat, too—even though it was essentially just this more or less level place, rather more open than the rest of its little canyon. This apparently inconsequential place with its far end sloping and tapering up into the draw from which had washed, long ago, the eroded rock fragments that the ages had transformed into its present dry brown soil.

Yet there was more to the flat than its components. More than the brilliance of the low afternoon sun and dark shadows reaching out behind juniper trees. The place was undamaged, whole, wild, alive. And each element meshed with its neighbor.

When I'd explored as much as seemed necessary, I stood for a while at the edge of the flat, looking out over it. Then I turned and walked back down the canyon.

Back at camp, although the sun had now set, the bleakness of the barren zone had been mitigated. Or at least rendered less final. Its web of life had indeed been torn apart; but now I had not only the desert flat and its harmonies, back up the canyon, but also the chipmunk haloed against a white thistledown apron that glistened in brilliant sunlight. Life's bureau of reclamation was already at work.

I dined. Night fell, annulling the bathtub ring. Before drifting off to sleep I found myself wondering how long it would take for life to reclaim Flaming Gorge Reservoir after the dam went. How long would it take to grow new cottonwoods that would entice explorative beavers from up and down the restored river; to re-station great blue herons along new shallows; to put kingfishers back in Kingfisher Canyon? Four or five hundred years? A thousand? Not long, anyway, by life's clock.

In mid-morning, under a leaden sky that leaked occasional mild warnings, I reached Flaming Gorge Dam.

The Bureau of Reclamation people outdid themselves. As promised, they moved my raft, fully loaded, down to the foot of the dam. Then the supervisor and his office staff went out of their way to ease my administrative chores. There were plenty. Phoning, among others, John and Victoria Sexton, a whitewater equipment supplier and a man who helped clarify some of the uncertainties still clouding that final, Mexican leg of the journey. Packing the outboard motor, along with its transom and fuel can, in the wooden box I'd had made for it and which the Bureau people had brought down from Fontenelle Dam; then arranging to freight the motor to Hite, near the head of Powell Reservoir, 450 miles downriver. Above all, checking the supplies that had been sent ahead to the dam and stored there.

All this took time. It was late afternoon before I was ready to help the maintenance crew, down at the foot of the dam, off-load the raft from trailer into river. For some time, a light rain had been falling. And just as we began the off-loading, the sky sluices opened.

We took refuge in the cab of the truck that had towed the raft-bearing trailer, and sat chatting. Half an hour later the rain was still pounding on the truck cab's metal roof, still streaming down windshield and windows. Bill Russell, the crew chief, said it might last all night.

That would matter. Before I went on downriver I needed to lay my new stores out in the open to make item-by-item decisions about packing them tactically in the raft. Most of the stuff was packed in cardboard boxes, and it included a lightweight down sleeping bag, a replacement zoom camera and dehydrated food for several weeks. When the rain showed no sign of letting up, Bill Russell suggested I spend the night "in one of our guest houses."

Briefly, I struggled with knee-jerk reluctance. A break now might snap the journey's continuity. Pride probably came into it, too. But at last I said thank you, maybe it made sense.

"Good," said Russell. "Let's get her back inside."

My "Camp 34" therefore turned out to be in Dutch John, Utah, under a roof.

Dutch John is a Bureau of Reclamation "company" town, three miles from the dam. The guest house was a low, detached, suburban "home"— one in a line of them strung along a wide, curving suburban street. Inside, more of the same: loaded with convenience, devoid of soul.

Among the conveniences, of course, a tub. I soaked long and hot and luxuriously. When I'd heaved myself out at last and toweled off, I turned on the TV.

Soon, a newscast. The usual heartwarming stuff. After fourteen years, Christians and Muslims still killing each other in Beirut. Northern Ireland celebrating the twentieth anniversary of Protestants and Catholics killing each other in their current duel. After the news, a story on adolescent drug addicts. I remembered why I no longer owned a TV.

But when I turned off the set, went to my bedroom and switched on the bedside radio, Glen Gould was playing Bach, accompanied by his standard hum-along. In spite of everything, I decided, we were a remarkable species. At times you could even see us as worth it all.

7

BROWN'S HOLE

Next day, a little before noon, I cast off from the boat ramp below Flaming Gorge Dam and began to float down Red Canyon. Within minutes, it seemed, the lingering guest-house reality yielded to river reality.

The canyon was a beautiful place. Its red side walls tumbled steep and almost bare, then steep and pine-treed. The sun beamed down from a cloudless sky. And the river had taken on a new lease of life. It ran cold and clear, swirling and eddying like an overgrown but vigorous and still youthful mountain trout stream.

Which it was. From its silvery surface, big trout sipped small insects, natural and artificial—and on it floated flocks of fly fishermen. But nearly all fished from rafts or boats and moved steadily downriver at much the same speed I floated, so that at any one moment I was able to see few if any of them.

Much of that afternoon, I also fished. I caught just enough trout to keep me excited, not enough for the pleasure to pall. The fish were big and healthy and they fought fiercely and it should have been a perfect day.

Up to a point, it was. I enjoyed myself. But only on the surface. And from time to time, as I floated on down Red Canyon, a sense of unfulfillment clouded the cloudless afternoon sky.

A contributory reason may have been a sense of nostalgia. Nostalgia in its root sense, involving pain. I knew that the beauty of Red Canyon was a sweet but sad memorial to what had been lost a few miles upriver when the reservoir liquidated Flaming Gorge.

But the real and deeper reasons revolved around artificiality.

The beautiful canyon supported precious little wildlife. I saw no non-human mammals, few birds. One nighthawk did swoop low, filching insects from the trout's floating larder. And once, in bordering shallows, a dipper bobbed busily among wet stones.

It may have been the dipper that flicked my mind back twenty-four hours.

The little slate-gray bird might be undistinguished, commonplace; but it was three-dimensional, wild, unpredictable. Truly real.

In the Dutch John guest house, before the news, I'd caught the tail end of an African wildlife feature rich with magnificent photography. A short clip of a cheetah hunting at full speed was sheer poetry. But it had no part in the story. The commentary didn't even mention it. That's one of the problems with television: its intrinsic artificiality.

As always, I'd found the screen's images superficially attractive, mildly hypnotic. But something was wrong—beyond the way the script imposed an abrupt, urban, Marlboro-Man sheen. In the end, I've found, even the best TV wildlife features come up tainted. Have an inherent flaw. An unreality dimension beyond the missing third. Beyond the lack of scent, of potential danger. Perhaps it's the telescoping of time and a covert implication that the dramatic or poetic moments captured on-screen are the norm. Somehow, anyway, the essence is lost.

But as I floated down Red Canyon, comparing commonplace but real dipper with poetic but artificial cheetah, I knew that wildlife is only one, rather obvious, victim of television's artificiality. It's always the same, to some degree. The medium mauls the message.

Off to my right, a trout rose, close under the bank. A real trout. I cast my artificial fly. It landed in precisely the right place and floated down, tantalizing and deceitful as any television commercial. The trout rose like an unsuspecting couch potato—and was hooked, solid. Minutes later I brought it, played out and unresisting, alongside the raft. It was the best fish of the day—a sleek rainbow, all of three pounds. In compliance with local catch-and-release regulations, I eased the hook free, watched the fish swim slowly down into dark depths.

And that was part of the trouble.

If challenged to define the universe, I'd no longer call it a place created for humans to fish in; but the right combination—big trout that rise to dry fly in fast water in a beautiful place, for example—can still unlock my enthusiasm. And that afternoon below the dam, floating down the beautiful red canyon in brilliant sunshine, I almost recaptured the old enchantment. Yet even in the fishing, a sense of artificiality intruded.

I like to think I fish for pleasure, not food. Many a long day's fishing has left me empty-handed yet immensely satisfied. And I support catch-and-release regulations—which require you to return every fish to the water, immediately and unharmed. Support them in theory, anyway. (They're imposed because in the face of heavy fishing they are the best or only way to preserve a viable stock of big fish.) But in practice I've found fishing under such constraints an unsatisfying business. I don't much like admitting it, but I know that's how things are. I fish with tarnished joy, beneath a shroud of unreality.

The regulations in force below Flaming Gorge Dam are not, strictly speaking, blanket catch-and-release: you can keep two fish under 13 inches and one over 20 inches. But every fish I caught measured between 13½ and 19 inches. So did every other fish I saw caught. A professional guide in a passing boat smiled and said, "Yes, that's how things are down here." And I have to confess that in the end I grew tired of it. I guess we evolved as hunters and remain so at heart.

In camp that evening, nine miles below the dam, I had time to reflect on the abundance of big trout and lack of small ones. I assumed that trout existed in this stretch of river only because of the reservoir. And later I confirmed details. The fishery was an artifact—the result of intensive and expert management. Water released below the dam came from carefully calibrated depths in the reservoir—from specific temperature layers. The fish did not breed but were regularly replenished under meticulously calculated plans. Technically, it all verged on being a work of art. And on the surface, the results were fabulous. They'd have sent the boy or young man who fished under my name into transports of delight. But now, for reasons deeper than catch-and-release regulations, it failed to fulfill. The underlying problem, I saw, lay once again in disruption of harmonies. The artificial lowering of water temperature, for example, though bully for trout and human fishermen, must have played havoc with other lifeforms.

At this time—as we'll see when we float down into Grand Canyon—the whole question of water releases from Colorado River dams was under sharp public scrutiny. Among many issues: the effect of artificially cold water—along with unnatural flow patterns and sediment loads—on the future of four endangered species of indigenous fish. Among many concerned citizens: environmentalists and their sometime allies, trout fishermen. And even there in my first camp below Flaming Gorge Dam it seemed possible to hear a fisherman tackling an environmentalist: "I mean, hell man, who are you kidding? Squawfish? Razorback suckers? Bonytail chub? Sluggish brutes, all of 'em. Ugly, too. No damned use to anyone."

But the point, as always, is not the endangered species themselves. They're only acting as a miners'-canary early warning that danger threatens. Warnings, this time, not about hazardous explosive gas in a mine but about insidious disruption of our whole system.

Whether we join the exploding list of endangered species may depend on how soon we understand these warnings and how wisely we act. I guess you could make a case for the benefits of our extinction. But hardly for the tragedy that might follow if, on our way down, we tore things apart.

And now, please, time out while I adjust my surplice.

At that nightcamp below Flaming Gorge Dam I kept worrying away at my vague sense of unfulfillment, and before falling asleep I recognized it as an attenuated hangover from the break at Dutch John. A hangover from television reality—that primitive forerunner of virtual reality, threatening to mold virtual humans. At midday, when I cast off below the dam, it had seemed as if guest-house reality had within minutes yielded to river reality. That had been an illusion. Even now I wasn't fully back in touch with the river. The barrier might be only a thin, lingering screen, but it was enough to spoil our relationship. What I needed was something wild, something unquestionably real, free of artificiality.

Next day I came to Red Creek Rapid.

It was the tenth rapid shown in my river guide.

River guides are softcover books, printed on waterproof or water-resistant paper, that map a river's every twist and turn. They show mileages from some specific point, and just enough contours on both banks to help you identify your position. Photographs and quotes in the margins may add historical information. And there may be supplementary sections on geology, paleontology, anthropology. But the core is the ongoing map of the river. As you float down you keep turning pages, and the map-river flows on.

As a backpacker, I had long loathed trail guides. Loathed them strong and sour, from the pit of my gut. They tend to lead you by the nose, impose tunnel vision, predigest what should be fresh discoveries. To constrain, that is, the freedoms you are walking to find. But backpacking is not river-running. I guess I'd glimpsed differences between them—of nature, not merit—back in the planning stages, because I let experts coerce me into buying guides for the whitewater canyons. And now, after only one day's use, I was already halfway a believer.

My river guide could not limit a nonexistent choice of routes, and the information it gave was so sketchy and narrowly confined that it rarely threatened to damage discovery. It also did more than maps to help me select good campsites. Above all, though, it warned of imminent rapids.

Red Creek Rapid was, as I say, the tenth my guide had shown since the dam. The first nine had been little more than riffles: mildly good practice; just enough to whet my appetite—and cue latent fears.

The white slashes indicating Red Creek Rapid covered only a slightly longer stretch of river than had most of the others. There was no specific warning notation. But a margin photograph showed a wooden boat jammed beam-on against a rock, tilted almost vertical and half-filled with water. A more or less naked man perched on the gunwales was apparently struggling to free it. A caption read: *Current pins Todd-Page boat in Red Creek Rapid, 1926.* Powell's journal does not mention Red Creek; but I knew he'd lined or portaged many that he doesn't specify.

Two miles below my nightcamp, I floated down toward a bend. Beyond it I should be able to see Red Creek Rapid, and I tried to recall details of a conversation with Bill Russell, maintenance crew chief at the dam.

I'd not really expected any serious rapids before the Gates of Lodore, but to be on the safe side I'd asked Russell about them, and he'd said, "The only serious one is Red Creek. But it's given a lot of people trouble."

"How should I run it?"

Russell had offered what sounded like good, informed advice. But now I fumbled. The best I could come up with was that he'd said either "It looks as if you should go left, but you go right" or "It looks as if you should go right, but you go left." And that was hardly helpful.

I floated around the bend.

From above, the prospect looked uninviting. The main channel frothed white, close to the right bank. But the rapid was divided longitudinally into two distinct halves, and over on the left things looked more relaxed. I eased left. The wind, which had been gusting in different directions, now blew upriver and held us in the safety zone. I landed on the left bank, walked down, scouting.

The left run at first looked easy enough: rather shallow; no great power; little white water. But as I walked down beside it I saw that a maze of hidden boulders, barely submerged, posed a confused succession of problems that would come so fast, one after the other without break, that they'd leave no time for maneuvering.

From where I stood, the far run wasn't easy to assess. It cascaded white and wild, but there just might be a viable route, left of the main frothings. Halfway down, a boiling white turmoil looked like a "hole"—a pulsing water cavity downstream of a boulder, capable of flipping a boat or raft, even of holding it helpless. But this "hole" might be just a wave. I couldn't be sure. If I could maneuver the raft past its left edge, though, there should be time to pivot into ferrying position and avoid—either left or right—a boulder that thrust up from the foot of the run like a small haystack and looked remarkably like the one that had pinned the Todd-Page boat in 1926. Achieving the right line would largely depend on hitting the right point of entry.

I stood for a long time, there on the left bank, weighing pros and cons.

Red Creek would be by far the most challenging rapid I'd attempted alone. I'd made more difficult and dangerous runs during my thirteen-day initiation on the Idaho Salmon, two years before, but there'd always been experts ready to rescue me if things went sour. And now there wasn't much doubt about being alone. The day fishermen had all pulled ashore at a designated ramp. Since leaving nightcamp I'd seen no one.

I reassessed options. With a lightened load, I should be able to line the raft down the boulder-maze left run. Or I could portage. Portaging would be a sweat, but safe.

There was more to it than safety, though.

The far run was the challenge, because it scared me. If I let fear prevail here, this first time, I'd probably never overcome it. On the other hand, a successful run would give my confidence a vital boost.

In the end, there really wasn't much choice.

Much later I discovered that on October 9, 1937, at 2:30 in the afternoon—about an hour later in the day than I reached Red Creek Rapid—Buzz Holmstrom, also traveling alone, came to the same place. He, too, grappled with indecision. In his journal he called the rapid "a dirty son of a gun to put it mild," and hinted at thoughts much like mine.

Buzz Holmstrom and I shared more than just traveling alone. He was a mediocre swimmer, too. The year before, he'd run the Idaho Salmon. And there were things about his approach to river and journey, most of which I came to understand only slowly, that plucked empathetic chords in me.

But huge differences divided us. Buzz traveled not in a raft but in a 15-foot boat he'd built from a downed log of well-cured cedar he found near his hometown of Coquille, Oregon, where he worked as a filling-station attendant. It was a well-designed craft, stoutly constructed; but no wooden boat is as forgiving of fast-water errors as a good inflatable raft. And although Buzz had more river experience than I, he lacked the huge advantage of expertise honed and handed down by the river-running pioneers. Pioneers who, in my case, included him.

On the other hand, Buzz, at twenty-eight, had forty years less wear and tear on him. And he had, like Powell and with the same relief and elation, already run serious rapids now buried beneath Flaming Gorge Reservoir. Also like Powell, though, he'd launched at Green River, Wyoming, and so had had less time than I to forge confidence in boat or abilities.

One major difference between our situations at Red Creek Rapid is difficult to evaluate. It's one that always intrudes when you try to compare journeys made before and after the big dams were built. The day I reached Red Creek Rapid, the river was flowing at a little over 1100 cubic feet per second—slightly less than the flow when I left Fontenelle Dam. Buzz's description of the rapid suggests that much more water was pouring through—yet the way he reports running the minor rapids I'd run the day before suggests the opposite. Remember, though, that some rapids are easier in low flows, some at high. And rapids change over the years. Remember these uncertainties when you read what Buzz wrote in his journal:

I might have tried to run it if close to home and everything favorable, but here there is too much to lose by a smashing, so I portaged the boat over a beaver dam down a little side channel, then ran down to the foot light... I hated to break down and portage, as I have not done so before, but what I am trying to do is to see how far I can get rather than how many I can run.

Now, more than fifty years later, as soon as I'd made up my mind, I battened the raft down.

Loose articles went into the big dry boxes, cameras and binoculars into their padded watertight box, lashed at my side. I told myself it was worth doing the job properly not because I really thought I might flip or even get bounced seriously around—though it paid to be careful—but because it was valuable practice for what I'd absolutely have to do beyond the Gates of Lodore—now less than forty miles ahead—and then, intermittently, for almost a thousand miles, until I moved out of Grand Canyon.

Everything ready at last. I cast off and rowed out across the smooth, swift water, keeping well above the place it slid over and down into the rapid.

The wind was still gusting, still changeable. But I managed without real difficulty to position myself at the head of the main run, not far from the right bank. There, by pulling gently on the oars, I held us stationary, bow leading.

The view downstream was less clear than I'd expected. Partly because of the drop-off. Partly because the obstacles and clear runs I'd carefully catalogued from the bank were now more or less lined up and difficult to distinguish one from the other. And partly, I think, because my heart was pounding.

A long, hanging interlude of uncertainty. Then I let us drift down toward the most likely-looking entry point. Before committing myself, I'd take a closer look.

At that moment the wind swung around and gusted hard, directly down-river. I felt it nudge the raft toward the brink. Felt the current grip us. Tried to pull back. Failed. Saw that the best course—by now probably the only one open—was to trust my preliminary choice of entry point. I pushed hard with both oars, downriver, the way you must if you're to establish enough momentum to carry you over big waves.

Almost at once we were racing through a boiling white cauldron. Slight pressure on the oars—their blades kept just below the surface—held the raft straight and true. Then the hole was there—a huge, white, glistening mound-then-pit. It throbbed, pulsated. We careered past, closer than in-tended; sort of ran through its left edge. I held my breath. But all that hap-pened was a minor bump. And before I'd really asked myself, let alone decided, whether the hole had been hole or mere wave, we were beyond its pulsating grasp, without check and dead on course, hurtling on down to-ward the haystack boulder. The boulder's black shape was clear now, and I counter-pressured the oars so that we'd swing, stern right, into half-beam ferrying mode. The raft responded. I gave one or two quick strokes—and saw that we'd clear the boulder, right, with something to spare. I pivoted back bow-first. As we slid past the boulder, left gunwale three or four feet clear of its black, granular flank, I lifted my left oar from the water and slanted it back, out of the boulder's way. Then I had the oar back in place and the river's power had slackened and nothing loomed ahead except a few scattered boulders.

We moved clear of the last boulders. I took a deep breath. Now the oars seemed to keep the raft straight almost without my help.

Down beside my feet, something silvery caught my eye. A small can of chicken meat. I smiled. I'd opened it while scouting along the left bank, and before pulling out above the rapid had put the open, half-eaten can on the rubber-surfaced foot-thwart. It was still there, in more or less the same place. My little raft, in its first real whitewater test, had sat down like a sports car. But Red Creek Rapid had done much more than erase lingering doubts about the raft's stability. I'd run my first unchaperoned rapid. With luck, I no longer had to fear fear itself.

That evening I camped in a cottonwood grove near the head of Brown's Hole. Sitting in a little folding chair I'd picked up at Flaming Gorge Dam, leaning back at ease beside the heavily ribbed and extravagantly contorted trunk of one of the biggest cottonwoods and still riding a residual elation from the Red Creek run, I could look out over pale grassheads and the gleaming river to the long dark line of the Uinta escarpment. Clouds from an earlier thunderstorm were now disbanding, and my view out over the river, framed by the cottonwood's branches, constantly mutated. Sunlight and shadow cast brilliance, then blackness.

I sat for a long time and watched the light paint fluctuating scenes over desert and river. Watched silently wheeling nighthawks, busy at their insect-gathering.

Once, as the light failed, I walked down to the raft. There, the river world was even richer. Whispering water. Shifting shadows. Silently swooping shapes that might still have been birds but were probably bats.

Soon, a new storm thunder-and-lightninged its way toward me from the Uintas. But no rain fell. And by the time I slid down into my sleeping bag and lay staring up through the cottonwood branches, the stars were back.

Before long there floated across the river, as there always seemed to float when the need arose, a coyote chorus. I lay listening. The chorus faded away. I closed my eyes.

Out beyond my feet, the river still murmured. The restless river. The river that went on and on, forever. Now, I could hear its message, clear, unimpeded. The thin, lingering screen that had hung between us since the break at Dutch John was gone. Time had restored the old reality. We were back, the river and I.

Next morning I went on down into Brown's Hole.

Brown's Hole is a huge natural sink: a 35-mile-long, relatively flat-floored trough encircled by 3000-foot escarpments. Its formal name is Brown's Park, but the earlier and rougher label persists, especially in speech. And the moment I heard it, long before planning this raft trip, the name had burred irrationally onto my fancy, the way names sometimes do: Jessamy, say, or Skaneateles or Campi ya Moto. But when I floated down into Brown's Hole, out of fancy into fact, I found myself unattracted. Almost repelled.

I suspect this was largely a subjective reaction. Buzz Holmstrom called Brown's Park the "prettiest place I ever saw." But even objectively, the place is not what it used to be.

In the late 1800s it was rich grazing land that supported several ranches, run by pioneers with wildly independent turns of mind. The grass and the escarpments—which at each end of the trough pinch together into steep canyons that effectively seal the place off—also made it a perfect hideaway for cattle rustlers and general-purpose outlaws. Notably Butch Cassidy and his Wild Bunch. But the water table has long since fallen—possibly because its feeder streams dug deep channels into the soft white soil—and the rich grass has given way to desert.

The Wild Bunch may have had something to do with my negative reaction. Their story has been told and retold and retold. Its reality has vanished under varnish. So I guess I was ripe for disenchantment. A posed studio photo in my river guide showed the real Bunch—five business-suited, bowler-hatted men exhibiting no sign of gusto beyond a couple of jaunty hat angles—and, sure enough, I failed to detect in Butch Cassidy (real name, Robert LeRoy Parker) and the Sundance Kid (Harry Longabaugh) any resemblance at all to Paul Newman and Robert Redford. Letting personal prejudices about history alienate me from Brown's Hole would, of course, be ridiculous—though quintessentially human—and the problem may have lain elsewhere.

Weather seems a likely culprit.

The rain had begun back in Red Canyon, the afternoon before I emerged into Brown's Hole. Soon the world had turned black, the raindrops huge. A cold wind rose. Hail fell. I rowed on, battened down inside my rainjacket, hood pulled tight.

The wind solidified to a gusting upstream horror. Its edge sharpened. I felt glad of the life jacket's warmth. At the height of the hailstorms I covered bare knees and thin shorts with an impermeable yellow rainjacket that one of the dam crew had given me. The jacket was too sweat-generating to wear while rowing but it worked fine as a knee cover. The hail passed. The rain tapered off.

Then a new blackness slid across the sky. Thunder reverberated. Ahead, along an escarpment, lightning flickered. Once more, wind buffeted, rain lashed down.

That afternoon set the pattern for the next three days. All too often I had to travel battened down under the rainjacket's hood, cut off from the world. And this no doubt colored my perception of Brown's Hole.

Yet those days of floating down the final lap to the Gates of Lodore were anything but grim. At times, they glowed.

Just after sunrise at my first Brown's Hole camp I opened my eyes and saw the ribbed patterns on a campside cottonwood trunk. Patterns that the sun's first rays dug deep and shadowed, sharp and rough and leaping. In the rich and lazy interlude before I stirred, a rabbit and a magpie and an eastern kingbird visited. After breakfast I sat quietly for a spell, checking on the universe. Our sun levered slowly upward. Its light, slanting in across the river now, made the view less dramatic than it had been the night before, but softer, friendlier.

I sat there for a long time in the warm sunshine, wearing only shirt and hat and sandals. The journey had matured enough for laid-back relishing of such moments. No big-deal "Ah, what an adventure I'm having!" Just "Hm . . . Nice. Yes, this is how life is right now." At least, that's the way it mostly was.

But that morning under the cottonwood tree I suddenly said, out loud, "Oh, what a life!"

People labored all their lives to be able to buy a house with a view, and even those that succeeded could grow tired of their treasured vistas. But I woke every morning to fresh views, many of them magnificent, all of them free. And then, each morning, I floated off into the unknown. Not into the Unknown with a portentous, pretentious capital "U." Just toward a fresh new quota of life and river and landscape unknown to me. Unknown and inviting.

I got up from my chair, felt the sun warm on bare legs. It would be difficult, I decided, to dream up a better life.

After that, though, the weather deteriorated. Hour after hour, during those days of floating through Brown's Hole, rain fell. Often heavily. Even when it stopped, the wind still gusted. Overcast hung gray and low over the flat gray valley floor.

And the river had undergone a transformation. Had shed its broken, pool-and-run, trout-stream character. Had slowed, lost its clarity. The water wasn't exactly dirty; just murky. But now the dull and sluggish river was all gravel shallows and barren sandy flats. Wind ripples masked its surface messages concerning such issues, and if my attention wandered I was liable to ground on a hidden shoal.

In spite of its shoals the river had softened, almost without my noticing it, into a broad and shallow and uncomplicated waterway. It seemed content, now, to take its time. To hold itself in check, in preparation for what was to come. To move like a traveler easing through a placid interlude, through a lull before a storm.

We all experience such interludes—as individuals, communities, nations—but tend to recognize them only in retrospect. At the time, the days or months or years simply roll by. Beware of masked bandit! Such peaceful interludes are liable to lull us into forgetting—individually and collectively—that at the most innocent-looking and unexpected moment we may come to grief on a hidden shoal.

The river's transformation had failed to enrich the wildlife—though the season may have had something to do with it.

Near the start of Brown's Hole we floated for two miles through Swallow Canyon. Along its bluffs, sure enough, pale brown swallows' nests clustered in elongated condominiums, each tucked protectively and Frank

Lloyd Wrightly under a pale brown overhanging ledge. But the nests sat empty, silent. When Powell passed through and gave the canyon its name—he's responsible for most of the geographical names still in use, up and down the river—it was June 4, and he reported the place alive with flying adults, *"and young ones stretch their little heads on naked necks through the doorways of their* adobe *homes and clamor for food. They are a noisy people."*

Later I glimpsed on the right bank, wedged just for a moment into a gap in thick undergrowth, a furry brown face with ears. It vanished too quickly for me to know whether it had belonged to fox or coyote, but I was surprised to realize that, whichever it had been, and in spite of the many coyote choruses the river had provided, the face marked the first actual sighting of either. I don't think I saw another mammal.

The birdlife meager, too. Six Canada geese. A pair of mergansers. A single great blue heron. Then, near a nightcamp, under gray skies, in the bay of a reed-fringed, wind-whipped lake, a flotilla of pelicans riding at uneasy anchor, head-on into an approaching storm. My third day in Brown's Hole I floated past two turkey vultures, or buzzards—the first of the trip—sitting on a riverside fence, and one took off and made a gliding, dipping reconnaissance of the raft. I called out, "Sorry, chum, no food—still alive," and it swung away.

Soon afterward the river's banks played reverse variations on the artificiality theme. Played harmonies implying that we'd begun to understand; even, in a small way, to act.

That morning I'd crossed from Utah into Colorado. And into a national wildlife refuge. At least, so the river guide said. But a series of big modern water pumps along the banks suggested ranching rather than a refuge. Then, around noon, I came to a house on the left bank, close to the river, that the guide labeled "Refuge Headquarters."

I pulled in alongside a sheer section of bank, fifty paces from the house, tied the bow line to exposed tree roots, lunched and siestaed. I was still caffeine-fixing myself back into a fit state to walk up to the house and make inquiries, when a figure appeared on top of the bank.

In spite of a gusting wind, we talked.

No, he wasn't the refuge manager, just a refuge officer and maintenance worker . . . but he'd been here seven of the sixteen years the place had existed. Well, his house *used* to be the headquarters but was now the *sub*headquarters.

The refuge was only a thin strip. Varied from an eighth to three-quarters of a mile wide, on each bank. This stretch of river formed part of the Pacific Flyway, and one of his main jobs was flooding old oxbow lakes and re-creating the marshes that used to attract huge flocks of migrating birds before the dams went in.

"Ah, that's what the pumps are for?"

"Sure. And it works pretty well. The birds stop here regularly now. But we've found that to maintain the supply of food they want we have to let the marshes dry out occasionally."

I nodded. "You mean, you're trying to reproduce what happened naturally when the river used to flood and recede, regularly?"

"That's it. We tried burning, but it didn't work. Made the cattails grow even thicker, and they crowd out the bulrushes that we need . . .

"No, you're right—not too much wildlife around this time of year . . . Right again—this late in the season, this is about as far upriver as the turkey vultures come. Maybe the winters get too cold farther north. I used to be up at Seeskadee Refuge, in Wyoming, and by August we didn't have any there. But there's always a few around here."

The wind rose a notch. The refuge officer looked down and across the river at new and threatening cloudbanks. "Well, guess I'd better get back to painting my house before winter comes."

Afterward, floating on down, I checked my calendar: August 18. Hardly winter yet . . . but the snow at the source had left me still thinking of it as spring.

Two more miles, and I saw the Gates of Lodore. Remodeled.

The Uinta escarpment had for some time been hidden by a series of low hills along the right bank. Now, abruptly, the hills ended. And out beyond broad river and suddenly flat desert I saw—still five miles away, but appearing much closer—an illuminated, three-dimensional version of the black gash I'd glimpsed in earlier, more distant views.

The afternoon's storm threat had passed and sunlight now slanted down onto the escarpment's face, into the Gates. On either flank, foothills stretched smooth and almost luminous. The escarpment rose steep and dark. The canyon sliced into it: huge, savage, improbable. Plunging wall buttresses stood out sharp and shadowed. I stopped rowing, stared.

Then I made a connection; checked the river guide. It was there all right, just ahead on the left bank: a lone building labeled "Lodore School." Earlier, I'd halfway decided to land and inspect the place, and this new, urgently immediate image of the Gates cinched it. A school that endowed its students with such a vista, day after day, might offer a glimpse into real, unvarnished history.

The school, which my USGS map called "Community Center," came into view: an old frame building standing stalwart and stark on the crest of a low, barren spur. I landed, walked up onto the spur.

The simple school building stood foursquare in the Old West. With its rich brown weather-beaten clapboard sides and steep roof, unadorned except for a small red-brick chimney and a squared-off cupola, it would have made a resonant title-backdrop for many a lush modern genre movie.

Up close, though, that was all. Just backdrop. I did my best. But with its locked doors and small, dusty, curtained windows the old schoolhouse remained—for me, that day—a mere building, not history.

I walked the few yards that separated old schoolhouse from old cemetery. The fenced cemetery, framed in that sun-and-shadow setting of flat scrub desert with its backdrop of distant blue hills and billowing white clouds, would have made an equally eloquent movie shot. Its gravestones, some surprisingly modern, bore family names echoing Brown's Hole history I'd already heard, faintly, from the river guide: Carr Place and Wilson Place, both "Abandoned"; and Harry Hoy Bottom and J. S. Hoy Bottom, two flatlands along the river.

But the cemetery was not what I'd come ashore to see. I walked on beyond it to a big and very square but apparently natural block of red sandstone that looked wildly out of place on that barren sandy flat. On the shadowed side of the block, a bronze plaque sounded an unexpected note: *Fort Davy Crockett, built in this valley in 1837 by mountain men Thompson, Craig and Sinclair, was the winter rendezvous of traders, trappers and Indians until 1840, after which it fell into decay and was abandoned.*

Interesting, but still not what I'd come for. I moved around the sandstone block to its sunlit side.

The red sandstone block was five feet high, flecked with lichen, almost free of cracks or roughness. I stood beside it, trying to shrink back into boyhood. If you were still too small to reach up and get a grip on its sharply squared lip, the block would present a fearsome challenge. Once you grew tall enough, though, it would demand only brute arm strength; then you could stand on top in triumph and gloat down onto the lesser fry still stranded, earthbound, below. But the ghost of that block looming huge and red and unclimbable would surely lurk in some corner of your mind for the rest of your days. If you came back, years later, the challenge it posed might look puny, almost contemptible. But the ghost would still lurk.

I turned and walked a few yards beyond the main building to some hitching posts, those older and gentler parking places. Most Brown's Hole children, I imagined, rode horses to and from school, and the view I saw was the view they saw when they parked their horses.

Below, the river swirled blue and eternal. Beyond it, the Gates of Lodore. For the first time in days the sky above the Gates was almost clear—just a few remnant flecks of white cloud—and sunshine still angle-lit the buttresses of the canyon's far wall into sharp-edged brilliance. But I'd moved downriver since that surprise sighting from the raft, and stood higher, and so could look a little deeper into the canyon. Not far, but far enough.

I rested my arms on the rough hitching post crossbar. It may once have been worn smooth by the friction of many halter ropes, but the wood had now roughed it through many summers of dry wind and desert sun, many winters of gale and snow.

A lot would depend, of course, on the schoolteacher. If he or she—almost certainly she—could reach and teach out beyond the three R's, then perhaps the boys and girls of Brown's Hole were indeed exposed to facts and fancies about the dark and ever-present chasm that hung there beyond the river, day after day, mood after mood. If so, a few of them might have carried away, when they left school, at least a blurred and shadowy understanding of some of its meanings. But it seemed to me that even if their teachers did not grasp meanings beyond the surfaces, or failed to convey them, that huge gash in the mountains would, willy-nilly, have lurked in the kids' memories long after the milestone day they left school for the last time and moved on to face the wider world. And if the memory lurked it would have lasted forever . . .

I ran a hand over the surface of the rough hitching post crossbar.

For me, as an adult, "school" had always meant the third of the three I'd attended—a cluster of dignified stone buildings on the edge of Exmoor, in north Devon. It was a boarding school, recognized as "tough." That was why my overadoring but acutely aware mother had sent me there.

At first, as a twelve-year-old, largely home-spoiled brat, I'd loathed the place. The grim gray buildings. The rain. The bullying. The discipline. Everything.

The academic standards were, I think, anemic; but looking back, I know we were taught things more lasting and valuable than academic knowledge. The value of discipline, for example, the satisfaction of overcoming challenges. And although the school offered no Gates of Lodore, memories of that place and time now swirl rich and warm around the moorlands of my mind. The rough gray stonework of the buildings. The monkey-puzzle trees at the foot of the east drive, tall and dark, intricate and enigmatic. Long walks through rolling farmland. Small streams tumbling down green valleys, or "bottoms." Playing rugby with benumbed hands in cold, driving rain. The big oak tree, ancient and reassuring, under which stood the heavy roller that rolled the cricket pitch. The simple granite war memorial with its message that now has a parochial and outdated ring—the odor of varnished history, too—but at that time, just before World War II, tolled solemn and resonant: LIVE THOU FOR ENGLAND, WE FOR ENGLAND DIED.

When, after five years of growing, the time came for me to leave the school, to move on and face the challenges of a wider world, I knew that I loved the place. During the final days I even said something about "the best days of my life." That was hardly standard talk for reserved British schoolboys furnished with stiff upper lips, but . . .

A turkey vulture, planing past, made the sun blink. Afterward, the hitching post was rough again under my hand. And beyond the flowing blue river loomed that dark gash in the Uinta escarpment, waiting for me to move on and discover what lay beyond.

An hour later, floating downriver, I came level with the old, abandoned Wilson Place. Not far inland ran a line of rolling white hills with bare, rounded crests. Such hills had been catching my eye for three days now, and I'd kept telling myself I should take a sidetrip and stand on them and get at least some feel for Brown's Hole. But the weather had bonded with my procrastination. Now, three miles above the Gates, I had one final chance. I needed a good walk, anyway. And it was time to camp.

Ahead, over the Uintas, heavy clouds had piled up again, gray going on black. Others, just as somber, hung along the escarpment on the far side of Brown's Hole, beyond the rolling white hills that were my target.

I pulled in to the left bank, tied the raft securely, shoved a few candies and a baby bottle of water into my shorts pocket and, without even unloading any stores, set off inland. Almost an hour and a half of daylight left. Just enough. With luck it wouldn't rain before the light failed.

Forty-five minutes, and I stood on a stark white hilltop, looking out over Brown's Hole.

The clouds had now massed into angry armies. They hung poised along the crest of the escarpment. An almost unnatural calm lay heavy. Lightning flickered. All I could see on the floor of the dark and dismal trough, really, were cottonwood groves fringing the river and broad, open flats. Bleak, treeless flats.

For four minutes—all I could spare if I was to be back at the raft before dark—I scanned this dreary landscape. Then I turned, began to retrace my steps.

Forty minutes later, and as I hurried the final few yards in the last dregs of daylight and glimpsed the raft outlined against a slight paleness that I knew was the river, I found myself in a state bordering on elation. I unloaded the gear, started to set up camp. It had been good to see Brown's Hole in panorama at last, even under that ominous gray pall. But what had lifted my spirits was the walking.

The sidetrip's value lay in the granular gifts of foot travel. Route-finding through marsh and wash and featureless foothills. Making sure, as I went, that I could find my way back. Bulling through bulrushes and feeling the rough and secretive textures of their world. Pausing in a sandy wash to eyeball the roots of a coarse grass or reed reaching out across the surface of the sand, single root by single root, for twenty, thirty, fifty yards in an act of recolonization so eloquent you could almost see it taking place. Pausing again, just a moment, to delight in the ghostly beauty of a grove of dead trees standing stark and skeleton and grotesque—eerily abstract in that heavy, unnatural calm—against the flat grayness of a low, bulging, motionless thundercloud. These were the things the hurried walk had given me. And being in close touch with this changing tapestry of commonplace natural wonders had reminded me what I'd been missing. Rafting was wonderful, no doubt about it. But walking, my old love, could still seduce. I began to roll out my bed in the only place that offered shelter—between a clump of salt cedars and a fallen tree trunk. Somehow, I must find time for more sidetrips.

A tearing wind sundered the unnatural calm. Within minutes it had whipped the salt cedars into a frenzy. A stylized sort of frenzy. Each supple component of each bush flailed away in unison with its fellows—like a Greek chorus gone berserk or a troupe of latinized banshees exorcising evil spirits in a wild tarantella. But the new bedlam absorbed their tormented cries, swept them away unheard. Out on the maelstrom river, foam madcapped.

Then the rain began. Just in time, I spread my big blue tarp over everything and anchored it with half-full dry bags jammed under the slope of the fallen log and with oars and anything else I could find. Crawled in under it.

The rain continued to lash down. I cooked dinner in my blue tarp cavern. Outside, all hell was letting loose. The rain still lashed, and lightning illuminated the outline of my one small cavern window. Thunder thundered, close. Yet I found I was still enjoying myself: no longer elated, but quietly content. Before long, replete with shrimp Alfredo and bourbon and candies, I fell asleep. Sometime during the night I woke to find the world once more tranquil. I peeked outside. Stars glittered. I pulled the tarp back out of the way.

But soon after dawn the storm circled back. I re-created my cavern. This time the rain had a steady and ominous rhythm, as if it might go on all day. Caverned happily under my tarp, I brewed tea, ate breakfast. After breakfast I lay thinking of a good friend who would shake his head at my predicament. "Crouching there under a tarpaulin," he'd say, and launch mock-serious barbs about masochism. Like other incognoscenti, he failed to understand the quiet satisfaction of being comfortable under such conditions without real effort, just as a part of normal competence. He didn't know about the other rewards, either. The rhythm of the rain. The way the salt cedars only rustled now, like a troupe of exhausted dancers stirring in deep sleep. Or the aftertaste. For when the rain stopped and I went outside, there was the river, still flowing by, still just rollin' along. And the rain-washed air heavy, fragrant.

By mid-morning the sun shone. I loaded up and floated on. Floated past the mouth of Vermilion Creek—dry or close to dry, but with bright red banks trumpeting the origin of its name. Crossed from Brown's Park National Wildlife Refuge into Dinosaur National Monument. Pulled in at Lodore Ranger Station boat ramp.

At the ranger station I picked up some stores I'd mailed ahead, a permit to run Lodore Canyon and some advice about its rapids. Then I camped on the fringe of the official campground.

The Gates of Lodore now stood less than a mile downriver. Yet from camp they looked less impressive than they had from the school. A spur angling out between us concealed both the river's point of entry and the lower halves of the canyon walls. In flat evening light, the visible parts of their buttresses no longer stood out sunlight-and-shadow stark. Gray clouds had moved in again, and the place had a newly gloomy, almost morose aspect.

Later, rereading John Wesley Powell's journal, I found that when camped in about the same place he wrote that at noon *"the canyon opens, like a beautiful portal, to a region of glory"*; but by evening it had become *"a dark portal to a region of gloom—the gateway through which we are to enter on our voyage of exploration tomorrow. What shall we find?"*

It was Powell, as usual, who gave the place its name. Actually, he used the singular, "Gate," and some people still do.

The name "Canyon of Lodore" was suggested by one of Powell's men—Andrew Hall, a nineteen-year-old Scot—after *The Cataract of Lodore*, by the English poet laureate Robert Southey. Southey wrote the poem for his children, and it reads like it—though there's a certain charm and aptness in the way the heavy rhymes sometimes cascade.

Dusk deepened. The Gates blurred toward blackness. I leaned back in my folding chair.

Poised at last on the brink of my first serious whitewater challenge, I found myself remembering a river-runner I'd consulted soon after the thirteen-day initiation on the Idaho Salmon had boosted my confidence. The man turned out to have undeniable whitewater expertise but a morose temperament. His prime and almost sole contribution was a repeated, "I really think you'll be operating beyond your competence."

Around that time, some preparatory reading at first amplified my misgivings—then allayed them. The Colorado, I found, had claimed many lives. But most losses came in the early days, before viable whitewater equipment and techniques had evolved. All the pioneers started very "green."

Powell, though he'd traveled many river-miles in small boats, had never faced real white water and had presumably based the designs of his specially made boats on intuition and guesswork. He also ran rapids bow-first, as in conventional rowing, with the oarsmen unable to see what lay ahead: they rowed at full speed, to give the rudderman some control with his big sweep oar. The forward-facing rudderman acted as coxswain: he tried to glimpse what lay ahead, would shout "Right!" or "Left!" and the oarsmen would try to respond. Powell himself eventually improved his view ahead by fitting a wooden chair on his boat's upper deck. It helped, but it made his boat top-heavy. From the start, anyway, boats kept slamming into rocks, being swamped, overturned. One was lost in Lodore Canyon, in the rapid Powell called "Disaster Falls." After that, he lined or portaged around many of the major rapids.

Some later pioneers started with even less boating experience. Ellsworth Kolb, in his book on the 1911 run with his brother Emery through the main canyons, wrote that when they set out Emery could row fairly well but *"had never gone over any large rapids."* Ellsworth himself *"had done very little rowing . . . so little that I had difficulty in getting both oars in the water at the same time."*

By comparison, I felt in good shape. Desultory rowing, all through my life. The Idaho initiation. Now, almost 350 river-miles, including Red Creek Rapid, safely under my life jacket.

Today, of course, we're spoon-fed. Any Tom, Dick or Colin can, for unexorbitant sums of money, buy refined specialized equipment and can learn at least the rudiments of proven techniques from professionals. As in most fields of human endeavor, we are, compared with the pioneers, coddled.

I stirred in the chair, newly aware that my feet were cold. Downriver, the Gates had dissolved into the night. I stood up, stamped.

Then there was that other gulf separating us from the pioneers. Mostly it seemed profound, occasionally a mere matter of degree. I stood peering into the darkness. To some extent, each of us faces the unknown. The unknown that, for all its magnetism, scares the living daylights out of us.

I cleaned my teeth, went to bed, lay listening to the soothing, incessant, ever-changing murmur of the river I had by now grown used to sleeping with.

8

THE GATES OF LODORE

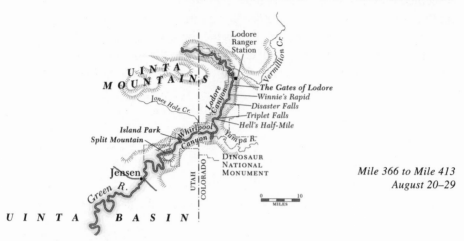

Mile 366 to Mile 413
August 20–29

Next morning I woke to find the river transmuted. Now, Powell would have recognized it.

The water had risen little if at all, but it ran red-brown and opaque, like a thick blood-and-chocolate soup. Patches of foam mottled its surface. I assumed, and later confirmed, that the heavy rain had sent flash floods roaring down Red Creek or Vermilion Creek or both, scouring up their rufous sediments.

Even from camp, the new river had a different persona: less open, slightly sullen. And when I launched the raft and we floated down toward the Gates in bright morning sunshine, nothing changed.

We came around the spur that from camp had half-hidden the Gates. Back upriver, I'd understood why someone had called them "a great stone mouth drinking a river." Close up, they still drank the river, but now the mouth had become undeniable gates: two red slabs of cliff that could have been monstrous hinged doors held ajar by the river's current yet always ready, if the current faltered, to swing back, snap shut. I don't know if it was this hollow threat or the contrast of black, in-shadow Gates against sunlit canyon walls beyond, but even on such a shining morning the place seemed somber, going on sinister.

I eased the blue raft down the red river. Its surface swirled and eddied. Off to our left, a man and three kids sat silent on a rock, watching us go.

We passed through the Gates. The rock walls closed in, sealing us off from the flatlands, from civilization.

We floated on down. The canyon stretched ahead now, quiet, untouched, beautiful. The sun floodlit broad slabs of red rock. And the rock no longer intimidated. Along its base ran a thin, irregular line of pale sandbars and bright green vegetation. At last, true canyon country.

Upriver, nothing had quite qualified. Flaming Gorge: mutilated. Red Canyon: whole and beautiful, but with always-sloping walls. And some element of slab-sided sheerness—though it can be intermittent, even illusory—must be there for a place to qualify as part of the red "canyonlands" of the American Southwest.

The river narrowed. The rock pressed in tighter, unyielding. We slid through a riffle—and the river's new persona made a difference. Small swirls and eddies of a kind that for many clear-water miles had been mere pleasantries that I hardly noticed now roiled red and opaque and vaguely ominous.

We ran two more riffles. I began to get used to the turbid redness; began to relax, to enjoy myself.

The day before, I'd asked the ranger at Lodore, "Will anyone else be running the canyon tomorrow? These are my first big rapids, and . . . well, I might be glad of a . . . a sort of chaperon. 'Careful Colin' they call me."

"Yeah, there's a Hatch party due to go down. Good commercial outfit. All their boatmen are first-class. Let's see . . . probably leave here around noon. But you say you ran Red Creek Rapid? River right? Then you shouldn't have any trouble.

"Still, when you get down to Disaster and scout it, if you don't feel too sure about running it alone, just wait for the Hatch party. I'm sure they'll be happy to have you go through with them. . . .

"Oh no, nothing before Disaster that you won't be able to handle on your own. Winnie's is the only real rapid—and it's just a matter of keeping right of one big rock. Don't go left, that's all. Some guys have tried, but I never heard of anyone who made it."

A photo in my river guide echoed his warning: a raft trying to pass the rock left had slammed into it and was tipping at a dangerous angle. But no need to worry about Winnie's Rapid yet. "It's just below Wade and Curtis Campground," the assistant ranger had said. "And you'll see that on the right bank."

We eased on down. Two big midriver boulders; the current picking up speed. We moved into another riffle. Ahead, around a bend, the sound of broken water; but still no sign of a campground. I pushed on, bow-first. The opaque water seemed more difficult to read, but adjusting to the change was fun. Confidence surging back, strong.

We came around the bend. Ahead, beyond a stretch of sunlit river, a block of shadow reached out from bank to bank. My eyes took a moment to adjust to this change; to register that we were in more than a riffle. For the water continued to accelerate; and it swung right, then funneled into a narrow gut and vanished over a line of broken water. No . . . over two lines. Through two narrow gaps—one on each side of a big, dark rock. I think I'd pivoted into ferrying position and begun to pull toward the right bank before I fully comprehended that I must have failed to notice Wade and Curtis Campground.

By then it was too late to stop and scout, even to pause and reassess: the current was sweeping us irresistibly down toward the big, dark rock. The ranger's warning echoed in my mind: "Don't go left, that's all." The river guide photo flashed across my vision.

For the next few seconds events moved so fast that I'm not sure of their sequence, but I think what happened was this: I pulled on both oars, hard. The almost-broadside raft responded. We slid toward the right bank. The current raced faster. The rock loomed closer. Much closer. We continued to slide right. The gap to the right of the rock still looked very narrow. We were close to the right bank, but I still wasn't sure we'd miss the big rock. Then there was a small boulder, not far from the right bank, not far from our stern. I stopped pulling. Then we were past the small boulder and I was pulling again, briefly, because I was still not sure about the big rock. Yet at the same time, I was trying to pivot the raft so that we'd take the broken water bow-first. And then we were plunging down into the broken water and the big rock was safely on our left, with a foot or two to spare. And then, although we weren't yet running quite bow-first—were still angled slightly, because there hadn't been time to complete the straightening up—we were bouncing through the gap, clean. Almost before I knew it was over, we were floating in a back eddy, safe and sound and miraculously motionless.

I rested on the oars. Funny, it didn't look much now. Not from down here. It would have been very simple, in fact, if I'd been ready. Or even if the shadow hadn't obscured things for those few vital seconds. But given the unforeseen hurdles I could hardly have asked for more. I pulled back into the current, floated on down.

Three more miles. Half a dozen unnamed riffles—some that flirted with being rapids, none that quite made it. No scouting; no problems. I began to read the opaque water better. Noonday sun filled the canyon, extinguished the shadows, the last vestige of intimidation. And around one o'clock we reached Upper Disaster Falls.

I landed, river right, and scouted.

At first glance, mild relief. An obvious route down the first drop:

through a narrow, well-defined midstream chute. If it was as straightforward and unimpeded as it looked, probably no problem. But if that torrent thick-souping through the chute concealed any obstacles . . .

Before long I'd figured out an alternate route.

If you ferried left down the smooth tongue above the rapid and established momentum toward the far bank, a few fierce strokes at the proper moment should take you beyond the boulder that formed the left flank of the chute and into a small, relatively slack patch of water. From there, an apparently easy route bypassed the main drop. Below, a short stretch of water without major obstacles would give you time to set up for the rapid's second part.

I walked a few yards downstream and scouted that second and principal part of Upper Disaster.

Its main channel ran for perhaps three hundred yards, right of No Name Island, in an almost straight line. But it ran broken and confused. I formulated a tentative agenda: enter right of center; try to ease left until winging along close to the island; then, just beyond a big angular boulder, move back center for a clear final run to the tail. But I knew it was a very tentative plan. A mere expression of intent. I'd have to feel my way down, making moment-to-moment decisions, obstacle to obstacle.

Lower Disaster Falls still lay out of sight, around a bend. Walking down to scout it promised rough going. And marginal gains. I might miss the Hatch party, too. I turned and began walking back to the raft.

On balance, still mild relief. The whole thing looked very runnable. In spite of its name, unhorrific.

"Disaster" was another of Powell's labels. An understandable one. In Disaster he lost one of his four boats, the *No Name*. Its crew survived. Below the rapid Powell found the remains of a boat that General William Ashley, the beaver trader who once caroused at Fort Bonneville, had wrecked there more than forty years earlier, on what was probably the first passage of the canyon by white men. In that disaster, Ashley apparently lost some of his crew.

Back at my raft, just above the first chute, I ate lunch.

Yes, still a mild sense of relief. But I'd wait for the Hatch party. Careful Colin.

It was difficult, now, to assess Powell's judgment of the place. Difficult even beyond the way the pioneers had faced a gaping unknown with primitive equipment and inadequate techniques. Difficult to assess because of the way people did things before we began to watch our modern p's and q's—our compulsive photography and obsessive quantifying.

My river was running, that day, at about 1400 cubic feet per second. The flow when Powell passed through Lodore is shrouded in uncertainty. One expert I consulted wrote that by mid-June—the season Powell entered Lodore Canyon on both his expeditions—the peak runoff was often, in those pre-dam days, past; but that some years the river could "be really flooding then." He went on: "[Powell] did mention running into sandbars and gravel bars on his first expedition, which would indicate the water wasn't overly high. . . . In looking at the Beaman photographs from the second expedition, there are mudbars and rocks exposed that I would not expect to see at higher levels. I would have to guess that the water levels were less than 3000 cfs. Don't mention my name if you publish that figure. Every river-runner in the West has his own theories on every aspect of the Powell expedition."

After lunch I found a comfortable nook that commanded a clear upriver view, settled down to wait, began reading a book called *River Rescue*—co-authored by Les Bechdel, who a year earlier had given me a day's one-on-one instruction in solo lining. Here at the head of my first prolonged stretch of white water seemed an elegantly appropriate time for a refresher course.

I'd read only enough to know that the book promised to be mercifully less dull than I'd feared, when the sound of voices drifted downriver. I looked up. One medium-size gray raft; four guys. The raft floated down, came within hailing range. Along one side tube ran a weathered inscription, not yet decipherable.

"Are you the Hatch party?" I called.

The young man at the oars turned, smiled. "Yeah, that's right."

"How many boats?"

"Just this one."

I explained about wanting to go down with a pro, if possible.

The boatman pulled into an eddy. Sure, he'd be happy. As soon as I was ready. He seemed dovetailed into his niche: quietly competent, relaxed, a mixer.

I asked about the chute.

"No problem. Good, slippery rocks. Even if you're a touch off line, you slide through."

"And below?"

"Oh, you just read your way down."

A few minutes later we ran the chute, the Hatch raft first. I aligned my bow dead center on the taper of smooth water that, from above, was all you could see of the chute, then let us ease forward. The flow did the rest. One moment we were running smooth and level, then the bow dipped and we surged down and forward—and almost before I'd registered that we were holding straight and true we were back level and moving on down the mildly white water below.

By now the Hatch raft was too far ahead for me to discern its route, so I followed my tentative agenda: enter right of center, react to each obstacle as it presented itself, ease left when I could. It turned out to be not at all a scary business, just intensely absorbing. At one point I became vaguely aware of winging it, on schedule, close to No Name Island. Then, unexpectedly soon but exactly as planned, I was making the final run down the tail of the rapid.

The Hatch raft had pulled off in an eddy.

The boatman was grinning. "You see, I told you no problem." Lower Disaster would be much the same, he said. "Just keep clear of the place, river right, where the current undercuts a cliff."

I nodded. The first few pages of *River Rescue* had warned about such places: undertow could suck you under and pin you there, helpless, until you drowned.

We moved on down. I steered well clear of the cliff, read my way safely through. The day's only bad moment came in fast but easy water just below the rapid.

I was ferrying down almost broadside, looking ahead for obstacles and holding position with gentle oar movements, when to my surprise the downstream oar hit bottom: the murky water had concealed the shallowness of the place. The current, carrying the raft on down, jammed the oar blade tight. Before I realized what was happening, the oar had flipped out of its oarlock, out of my grasp. I watched it pinwheel free, splash down just ahead of the raft—and vanish. I leaned overboard, plunged one hand into the swirling soup at the spot I'd last seen the oar—and there it was, nestling round and firm in my grip. Within seconds I had it back in the oarlock.

A mile downriver the Hatch raft beached at a campsite, river right. I pulled alongside. The boatman introduced his three clients—young fellows from back East—and himself—Brian Rasmussen, from Arizona. I thanked him for running convoy, and a little hesitantly said I hoped he'd understand if I went on down a little way and camped alone.

"No problem," said Rasmussen. "I'd do the same myself. And if you'd like to run with us again tomorrow, that's fine. I'll be happy to show you the bad places."

We sat on a rock and chatted.

"Just three more real rapids in Lodore," said Rasmussen. "With the water at this level, Hell's Half Mile is the only one could be a problem. The first move, anyway. I'll probably scout it."

He agreed about the difficulties of reading the opaque water. Even churning stuff that was normally white now looked brown, so you didn't have the color contrast to help you judge what it hid. The best way, he'd found, was to read the texture of the calm water beyond an obstacle.

I asked whether the alternate route I'd scouted, up at the first chute, would have worked.

"Sure. In fact, I went that way once." He smiled. "I was talking to my party and forgot exactly where I was. Just reading the water. And I did exactly what you said—ferried left into that slacker place. Went fine. It was only after I'd passed it that I thought, 'My God, that was Upper Disaster!' "

I told him about losing the oar. "Felt a bloody fool," I said.

"Oh, don't worry, it's easy enough to do, particularly in water this dirty. Just try to keep your downstream oar close to the surface. Always. You'll find that after a while it becomes automatic."

I rowed on down for half a mile before camping.

Next morning the Hatch party caught up with me at just the right moment, before I'd reached anything big. We ran Triplet Falls without scout-

Lodore Canyon. Rowing down a flatwater reach.

ing, without problems, then came to Hell's Half Mile—another of Powell's vivid and daunting labels.

Brian Rasmussen pulled in left and walked a few yards down the bank. I joined him. Responsible professional boatmen routinely scout certain rapids, no matter how often they've run them.

As we stood together on the bank above Hell's Half Mile, Rasmussen said that every time he saw the chute and churning torrent that prefaced the long rapid it looked different. At this water level, different-sized rafts would have to run it rather differently. Because his was bigger than mine, and more heavily laden, he'd have to run bow-first more or less down the center of the entry chute, then turn and trust he could pull left quickly enough to avoid a massive boulder that jutted up just below, high and dry, almost dead center in the main current. But he'd now seen enough of my raft to feel sure I could go down the extreme left edge of the entry chute and glide over a barely submerged boulder there—and then, if I turned quickly enough and pulled left, I should have no difficulty in passing well left of the dangerous boulder. I must go over the center of the small boulder, though, turn the moment I was past, then pull like hell. The rest of Half Mile was more or less like Disaster: you just felt your way down, obstacle by obstacle.

We stood there for some time, evaluating every swirl, discussing moves. My adrenaline, I couldn't help noticing, flowed about as fast as the chute.

Rasmussen went first. As soon as he dropped down the chute he was out of sight. I waited until he'd had time to clear the big boulder, then eased down bow-first, pulling strongly enough to hold back so that I moved more slowly than the water. That way, I had more control over the raft and more time to pick up my marker—the hump of water that poured over the small boulder, left of the chute.

By this time the adrenaline had subsided. My attention focused, tight and tunneled, on the technical problem. No room, now, for fear.

I came down toward the marker slowly, under control, exactly on line. The current accelerated. I went with the flow—eyes riveted, now, on the swirling brown hump that was my marker-boulder.

And then, a few feet above the hump, when I was already committed, with no hope of pulling back or even holding in place, I saw, ahead and below, the Hatch raft. It was tilted up, broadside on, wedged against the massive mid-current boulder. Figures moved feverishly, trying to push it free.

Almost at once, I had to look back at my marker. We went over it dead center, without touching and without deflection. I counter-pulled on the oars, felt the raft begin to pivot, stern left. At that moment I snatched a glance ahead: the Hatch raft had come free and was moving on down the rapid.

My stern came fully around. I pulled on both oars, hard and in unison. With almost surprising ease we moved left, clear of the line that would have taken us down onto the big boulder. Then we were shooting past it.

I narrowed the ferrying angle, began to maneuver. Obstacle succeeded obstacle. The spray-drenched top of a black boulder. A staccato brown turmoil that meant a barely submerged boulder. A swirl that might have meant almost anything but plainly spelled "Stay Clear!" Then the same obstacles all over again, but shuffled, mutated. They demanded total attention, instant response.

A different kind of adrenaline now flowed. But adrenaline may be the wrong word. What I mean is the kind of kick you get from sheer elation. Or from elation boosted by relief. For even as I read my way down, obstacle to obstacle, I knew I'd made that first crucial move like a pro. Knew that if I could make every difficult move under such control, I'd be all right. I'm not sure I remembered just then that my route had been chosen and explained by a pro.

Below the last white water the Hatch raft swung off into an eddy. I pulled alongside.

Brian Rasmussen said that during that first move he'd "lost" an oar as he tried to pivot at the foot of the chute. Hadn't lost it overboard, but had had it "catch a crab" and jump out of its oarlock. And he couldn't get it back in place before he hit the big boulder. They'd only been tilted up against it for a moment and were never in real danger. He grinned. "Still, it wasn't exactly what I had in mind."

With a deadline to meet, he had to push on. But I was in no hurry now. And for various reasons I wanted to pull ashore right there, and camp.

Before we separated I thanked Rasmussen for his support. When I went on down, I said, I might try to latch onto another party—and I only hoped I'd be as lucky in my choice as I'd been with him.

"Oh, you'll be OK on your own," he said. "There's nothing much left in Lodore." And through the rest of Dinosaur—in Whirlpool and Split Mountain Canyons—all rapids but one were straightforward. You just ran hard down the middle. On the long run through Desolation Canyon there'd be only half a dozen rapids, and though some were interesting they were all straightforward, too. Later, Cataract Canyon might test me a bit. And then there was Grand Canyon.

"You'll be OK, though," he said as we shook hands. "I envy you."

After they'd gone I pulled ashore, river right, onto a narrow bench at the foot of a cliff. A big box elder overhung the bench. I walked a few paces back into its shade. Yes, a good campsite. (To reduce bankside impact, the Park Service normally allows river-runners to camp in Lodore Canyon only at designated sites. But I'd managed to get a dispensation: the essence of my trip, I'd said, lay in the assurance of solitude when I needed it and the freedom to stop at felicitous moments.)

I sat down at the foot of the box elder.

Fifty river-miles and I'd be out of Dinosaur National Monument, calling in at Jensen post office to pick up mail and supplies. But I didn't need or even want to arrive there for a week. So no hurry at all. Just as well, the way I was feeling. I leaned back against the tree trunk, dozed off.

It was mid-afternoon before I finished setting up camp; and evening before I registered that in a little over twenty-four hours I'd surmounted the first of the whitewater challenges—the one that had been hanging there from the start—in the course of perhaps the most pleasant and leisurely, real-vacation interval of the journey.

Next morning, sitting in camp and watching the river swirl slow and red-brown beyond a fringe of salt cedars, it occurred to me that I shouldn't have been surprised at the way this first major challenge had dissolved so quickly.

The highlights of any journey—the big deals we look forward to or back on—tend to be brief. Whether the journey is the passage of a river, the life of an individual or the history of a civilization, it will have such pivotal points. The bleak fifteen-minute exchange that you both know writes "finis" to an affair or marriage. The two-minute infantry charge that turns the tide of a two-day battle that decides a four-year war that undermines a thousand-year civilization.

There are also less dramatic pivot points, of course, slower yet cumulative. But we tend to overlook them. We visualize highlight challenges looming ahead; we remember the bleak confrontations, wars, infantry charges. Our more vivid wilderness trips, too. And within them, the craggy snowcapped peaks, raging rapids. In prospect or retrospect, that's the way we tend to see our cookies crumbling.

Such a slant has its truth. But when we have time to stand back and examine a journey as a whole—any journey, any life—a counter-truth comes yin-yanging out. Those elements that over the long haul make life worth living tend to flourish during our quiet seasons. Not in the quarrel that severs a romantic coupling but in the sharing that forged it. Not in the war we fight to protect our way of life but during the peace that permits us to practice it. Not in the rapid that sends adrenaline racing but during the languid interlude that gives you time to sit and stare. Not in the highlights but during the glowlights.

At my box elder camp below Hell's Half Mile I had plenty of time to sit and stare. Time to let myself become aware, slowly and somewhat vaguely, of double-wing seed pods hanging like butterflies among broad leaves, and of the way the pale pods and green leaves stood out, luminous yet subtle, against red-cliff background. Aware of a hummingbird in a downstream hurry that whisked by and barely missed me, then braked to a vertical halt beside a cluster of delicate purple mesquite flowers that overhung the slow-swirling, red-brown river. I sat on, dozing intermittently but aware of such things in a diffused sort of way, not so much as separate elements but as color and light and shade blending into a harmonious whole.

Not until my third and last morning at Box Elder Camp did I walk over to the cliff that rose sheer and red behind the tree's green canopy. I stood looking at the rock, trying to look into it—trying to see beyond the slanting sunlight that italicized its smooth yet textured surface. Stood there worrying away, as happens from time to time, at the problems most rocks pose.

The cliff was Precambrian quartzitic sandstone—and therefore among the oldest we know. I found myself remembering the Precambrian rocks of Grand Canyon's Inner Gorge; remembering how old age had come to them, as it comes in the end to all of us who live long enough. The Inner Gorge rocks were gray or black, their wrinkled faces twisted and distorted by the terrible weight of the years. But this bright red Lodore Canyon rock looked youthful: smooth, open-faced, untrammeled.

I brushed fingertips across its gritty surface.

Yes, as undifferentiated, as free of layering, as Grand Canyon's limestone Redwall. It had probably—though I'm no geologist—been laid down in the tranquil waters of a lake or sea. That process was something I could visualize. Its constituent elements, anyway. This was the easy part. First, rain and wind eroding ancient mountains. The resulting particles being carried down and borne along as sediment in ancient rivers—much as the recent rain in Brown's Hole had scoured from Red and Vermilion Creeks the rufous sediments now coloring the river behind me. Then the emergence of those ancient rivers into a lake or sea. There, in still water, they decanted the sediment—much as the Green River decants sediment in today's Green River Lakes or in our temporary dam-reservoirs—and each particle sank slowly to the floor of the lake or sea. This simple process went on and on and on without serious interruption, grain by added grain of sand, day after day, year after year, century after century, millennium after millennium, until the sand had built a solid bed, hundreds of feet deep. Picturing that process was not, up to a point, very difficult.

The problem lay, as always, in what happened next.

The events themselves raised only minor difficulties—though mysteries still lurk. What happened on the floor of that ancient lake or sea was that— by a process probably involving heat and the immense pressure of later overlays—the entire sandy deposit was transmuted into rock. How long that process took remains unknown. What *is* known is that it happened at least a billion years ago.

This was the difficult part: comprehending those figures with more than my intellect. This was what had kept me worrying away, intermittently, for years.

It's the same for most of us, I think. Encased in our ephemeral human-lifetime envelopes, we cannot read the long-range messages of geologic language; cannot grasp the round reality of "a million," let alone "a billion," years. Faced by time's barrier, unable to find chinks in its armor, we stand screened off, fearful.

Once, after being immersed for long enough in rock and solitude, I'd seemed to penetrate the barrier. That revelation faded, as I knew it would. Echoes still lingered; but the best I could now do, from time to time, was to slide for a brief spell through some slanting fissure in the barrier and grasp an oblique intuition of time's mystery. That was all most of us could hope for. And now, brushing fingertips again across the face of the sandstone cliff, trying to grasp the immense spans of Precambrian time, I came up . . . well, if not quite empty-handed then with only a few grains of sand that trickled away between my unqualified fingers.

I stepped back, ran my eye up the towering red cliff, over and across its temporary faces and fissures. The shadows that slanting sunlight drew along these fissures were the shadows of this day, this hour, this minute. No enlightenment there. None at all.

I turned, walked a few paces toward the river.

Beyond the slow-swirling, red-brown, sediment-bearing water, massive red cliffs matched my campside cliff. Still seeking, I ran my eye along these temporary rock walls, sculpted from the solid block of ancient sandstone in only the recent, few-million-year history of the current river.

I took a few more steps, to the water's edge.

The cliffs beyond the river sometimes soared sheer, sometimes sloped talus-steep and buttressed. Downstream I could see—brilliant green in slanting sunlight—a few conifers that for a century or two had snatched footholds among the buttresses. Upstream, the sunbeams slanted toward me. They built a screen of light that blocked off the cliff, left its face in impenetrable black shadow. My eyes strove to penetrate this screen—became distracted by a cloud of small white specks.

Almost reluctantly, I refocused on the specks.

"Cloud" wasn't really the word. Not in the sense of the clouds that drift across our daytime skies. These specks formed no translucent mass. Floodlit by slanting sunbeams against the black rock-wall backdrop, they floated widespread and uneven, with denser clusters here and there. Like clouds of stars. Yes, that was it—like galaxies that hang motionless in nighttime skies, yet seem to float and swirl. Like the one galaxy our naked human eyes can discern as a star-spangled cloud—our own Milky Way.

But these shining specks above the river drifted and lifted and fell in a slow and graceful dance. Some dancers floated passively. Others performed little personal jigs. Like insects.

I lifted my binoculars.

Yes, insects. Tiny, fragile, gossamer-winged insects. The insects I knew I should now call "mayflies," but which I tended to think of as "Ephemeridae." For this is the label commonly given by British fly fishermen to the group of insects that Americans call mayflies, and the accident of my birth and upbringing made it the name that still floated most naturally into my mind. That morning beside the sunlit river, it also seemed an exquisitely apt name.

Ephemeridae—the old name for the order now called Ephemeroptera—celebrates the most conspicuous feature of the insects' existence. "Ephemeral," meaning short-lived, derives from the Greek *ephemera*—literally, "for a day"—and in their adult, air-living forms, Ephemeridae indeed live for only one day, or perhaps two.

That morning beside the river, watching the tiny white specks dance their dance, transfixed by slanting sunbeams against black rock-wall backdrop, I found myself immediately and intensely aware of the fragile insects' one-day life spans and the billion-year history of the Precambrian rock that formed their backdrop. The gulf between the two modes of existence seemed moving and poignant as well as difficult to grasp.

It made little difference, really, that I was seeing only the surface of things. This one-day airborne existence might be the sole segment of the insects' life readily visible to our unaided human eyes, but I knew the adult Ephemeridae were a culmination.

For a year, or in some cases two years, the insect lives underwater in an immature form both fishermen and entomologists call "a nymph." That stupendously inappropriate label identifies a lifeform almost infinitely distant from a beautiful damsel. A nymph is to the average human eye a homely creature, ugly as sin, going on repulsive—a wriggly little armor-plated being that devotes its life to grubbing about for algae or detritus, underwater or even underground, mostly at night. It has no sex life, presumably no sexual urge.

Then, when conditions are right, the nymph rises for the first time to the water's surface. Its armored envelope splits open. From it emerges a delicate, soft-bodied creature that unfolds translucent gossamer wings and—as soon as the wings dry—flies up and away. This new and aery being has only vestigial mouthparts. It cannot eat. Its sole "purpose" for the remaining one or two days of life: mate, reproduce.

The transformed creature wastes no time in going about its business. If you live only a day or two as an adult, you've got to get things moving.

Males and females fly ashore, alight on vegetation and do what no insects except mayflies do: they molt again after they've grown working wings. Their revised, pared-down versions are even more delicate creations—fragile, transparent, almost insubstantial. Not unlike some very old humans. But these organisms are vital. Ready and eager to create a new generation.

The males, as in many species, get the ball rolling. They congregate above the river in vast singles-club clouds. These were the clouds I now saw floating above the Green River, luminous in slanting sunbeams against their black-rock background.

Before long—or so I'd read—females begin to join the club. As each arrives, a male seizes her. They fly coupled, and copulate. The spent male then flutters away, soon dies. Within minutes—or at most within hours—the female lays her eggs, normally by dipping down, touching the water's surface with the end of her body, rising briefly, and repeating the performance until all eggs are deposited. Then she also dies.

What I did not know, standing there beside the river below Hell's Half Mile, was how to recognize the mating act. I sat down, studied the galactic mayfly cloud.

A stately sundance.

Part of its flow was due to a fickle upstream breeze. Like all of us, mayflies lived at the mercy of the winds of chance. Up to a point, anyway. But through binoculars I began to recognize choreographic patterns.

Mostly, the dancers danced alone. Occasionally, though, by accident or design, two of them would for a moment move close together. Surely no time for copulation. More like a brief attraction, then repulsion—as if instinct said, "Ah-hah, this is it!" and then, almost instantly, "Oh no, this isn't right," or maybe just "No, not yet."

I watched intently. Time passed. More patterns. A dancer would hover briefly, then move forward horizontally, then climb vertically with the two delicately tapering appendages that protruded from its tail—called "whisks" by fishermen and "caudal filaments" by entomologists—hanging downward. From the peak of each climb, the mayfly would slowly descend, wings extended, whisks held out level as if to assist the aerodynamic balancing act. Backlit by sunbeams, diaphanous body and extended whisks stood out in startling relief against the shadowed rock wall. And in each such interval of slow descent the dancer attained a peak of grace and beauty. Once, my binoculars isolated a descending insect that trailed a single long tendril—far longer than a whisk, more like a strand of gossamer spider's web. Then that performer glided out of the spotlight, back into anonymity.

Eventually I became aware that the galactic cloud had thinned. Lower binoculars, glance at watch. More than an hour since I'd become conscious of the performance.

I flexed stiff neck muscles. It remained unclear whether I'd seen a mayfly mating dance. But I had seen the dance. The dance of life. The dance we all dance. I had seen it before, in quite different places, at similar moments. But here I'd been more aware of its backdrop. And as I stood up I felt again the heartbreak significance, and yet the soaring hope, of those millions of ephemeral entities dancing their brief dance in sunlit beauty against a background of billion-year-old rock.

I turned, began to walk the few paces to my green box-elder canopy.

At a deeper level, you couldn't really call either dance or dancer ephemeral. Mayflies were astoundingly enduring creatures. Persistent in a sense presently beyond our grasp. They belong to the most ancient clan of winged insects. Fossils not very different in form occur in Cretaceous rocks, so those mayfly ancestors lived ninety million years ago. Ancestors that bear any close resemblance to us date back, at most, four million years.

I stopped, turned, looked once more across the river at the rock wall, black behind its slanting sunbeam screen. A few tiny insects still danced their brief dance. But against the time scale of the background rock, was there really much difference between twenty-four hours and three score years and ten? Was there any difference at all?

The remaining thirty-three miles of river within Dinosaur National Monument fulfilled Brian Rasmussen's promise. Few rapids, all straightforward, unchallenging. The country varied and beautiful.

At least, that's the way I remember it. But for reasons I guess I've been reluctant to admit, most events in the days below Hell's Half Mile seemed to take place behind a thin veil.

By now you've probably had a bellyful of my recurring ailments. I sympathize—and hope you'll reciprocate. The fact is that, from its conception, this journey had—as tends to happen in certain phases of nearly all our journeys—been colored by brushes with ill health. At such times, the malaise fills your horizons. And the reason I'd pulled ashore immediately below Hell's Half Mile was that I'd felt the beginnings of what—doctors notwithstanding—seemed to be yet another flu relapse. And it lingered.

Now, I don't want to overstate. By that third day at Box Elder Camp the mild relapse seemed over. But next morning, after floating on down, I took a stroll—"just to stretch my legs"—that somehow became an hour-long sidetrip up a steep canyon; and, briefly, it re-clobbered me. I think I imagined, afterward, that business went on much as usual. Only occasionally did I feel ill or acutely weak. Most of the time I traveled with a sense of quiet contentment. But in retrospect I could see that for five days beyond Box Elder Camp—until the evening of my last camp in Dinosaur—I operated in a slight daze.

The outside world kept penetrating my daze-screen, of course: a few incidents; an ongoing flow of impressions.

Always, inevitably, the river. Once we'd passed through the Gates of Lodore it had gained new life. Rapids aside, it still swirled and eddied past scattered boulders—once more a dashing young trout stream. Yet still the same river. Every time I struck camp and floated on down, there she was again, murmuring, waiting for me.

Slowly, the red-brown sediment thinned. For many miles below the Gates the water had been opaque to its outermost edges, but in the shallowest shallows I could now make out the shapes of submerged pebbles.

The Yampa River joined the Green. We moved from the Canyon of Lodore into Whirlpool Canyon. But I registered few details beyond the constant, ever-changing patterns. Glorious red-slab rock walls, sheer and angular, yet curving. Or gentler tree-clad slopes rimmed, far above, with conifer-forest hints. Capping it all, a strip of blue sky with fleecy white clouds drifting or scudding by. And back down along my river, twin tapering borders: pale sandbars; smooth emerald-green swaths of salt cedar, box elder.

Still no hurry. The first four days, barely twenty-five river-miles. Meandering down through daze and varied landscape, I had time to pause and rest and doze and read.

The river guide disclosed that we'd left Colorado, were back in Utah. Then that we'd moved below the 5000-foot mark. In less than 400 miles we'd lost half the elevation we'd lose in all our 1700-mile journey.

Time for books, too. I finished *River Rescue*—which had lived up to its promise—went back to *Sensitive Chaos*, the book on the nature of water. After an encouraging start it had squished over from new-angle vision to a

muddy mix of medieval "science" and old-fangled religion. Nuggets floating in drivel. An infuriating book. But its basic thesis still cast light, general and river-specific: water is not only the lifeblood of this planet but a
matrix builder for its lifeforms.

As the days passed, my daze-screen, like the sediment, began to thin.

Once, I even fly-fished up Jones Hole Creek. Trout for dinner, breakfast.

Once, a rock-wall indentation caught my eye, crystallized into unique-
ness. Indirect sunlight illuminated the place with a soft, subdued glow. I
backwatered, held.

Two rock faces angled into a clean-cut V. Walls annotated in vertical
staves by parallel water-weatherings. At their foot, erect on smooth silver
sand, a stone plinth. Perched on its summit like an exhibit, a lump of
rock—once an extension of the gray-brown, clean-cut plinth but now
weathered into complex, curving, pale pink surfaces. And each element
meshing, in perfect balance. The place had an ancient, druidic holiness. I
lingered for worship at Pan's Alcove.

Whirlpool Canyon ended. A brief interlude of relatively open flat-
desert: Island Park. Then, Split Mountain.

The curving, contorted strata of the dramatic gateway to Split Mountain
Canyon and the six-mile canyon itself both spoke, eloquently, of more
rock events than you could throw a geology book at—and I knew that John
Wesley Powell had helped write the book.

Pan's Alcove.

Powell, wondering why the hell a river should slice lengthwise through the heart of an isolated mountain rather than slide around its flanks, figured things out from scratch and reached much the same conclusion as today's savants. Their answer, simplified, is that the river established its meandering course in softer material that once overlay the present mountain—then met the emerging mountain massif and simply continued to cut down along the sinuous line already etched in response to earlier conditions. It happens all the time. Living entities, faced with changed circumstances, cling to old courses. Ants, for example. And penguins, dogs, people who play radios as they raft down quiet rivers. Also politicians, voters, writers.

In Split Mountain Canyon the Green drops at a rate of twenty vertical feet per mile—as fast as it does anywhere. There are four named rapids. I ran all without scouting and without problems. By the time I neared the canyon's end, my daze had about gone. Perhaps that's why I began to notice more wildlife.

All through Dinosaur, animals had seemed scarce. Not absent, by any means. But those that had caught my blurred attention and burred onto memory were a motley collection, not always very wild.

Once, river right, a bighorn ewe and lamb grazed among waterside stones, brown bodies rough against soft greenery. They ignored me. I rowed slowly to within twenty paces and saw that around the ewe's neck hung a big plastic tag inscribed "#53."

Whirlpool Canyon debouches into Island Park.

At a nightcamp, a shape that in moonlight had been a crouching bighorn, curiously immobile, next morning became a very ordinary rock outcrop.

A lone ladybug landed on the metal handle of my cooking pot, rejected that landscape, spread its wings, flew two inches, landed on the back of my hand, explored, still failed to find satisfaction, took off for fresh fields.

My plastic washbasin, left overnight with an inch of water in it, had by morning become a morgue. The victim of my chance intrusion: a poor wee stiffened mousie.

Four young mergansers and their mother patrolled an eddy, red-brown heads and gray backs burnished by sunlight, red-brown wakes glistening. They plunged heads underwater in unison, became five gray stones.

In water that had fined down to a pale, translucent brown, a carp eased languidly away from the bank and swam in a gentle curve to midriver, ready for the day's business.

Early one morning, floating down thirty yards from the left bank with the sun directly behind me, I found myself looking at a very large rabbit, inches from the water's edge, nibbling green salad. He looked directly at me, twitched ears, resumed breakfast.

A grayish jaylike bird captured some morsel on the wing, swooped down, stabbed at open sand. It looked improbably familiar. Up binoculars. Yes, a Clark's nutcracker—no doubt wing-loosing it down from the conifers that fringed the canyon's rim. At their 8000-foot elevation, the conifers were a mountain forest.

In Whirlpool Canyon, two good-companion species had made comebacks. A great blue heron standing morning sentinel reminded me that it was the first I'd seen, or at least registered, in many miles. A sleek gray shape slipping into the water at dusk did ditto; but then the beavers put on three successive nightcamp performances. And at the final show, moved stage center.

It was late afternoon when I pulled ashore. Around the next bend the river would emerge from Split Mountain—last outlier of the Uintas—into the flat Uinta Basin. And my campsite on a narrow, sandy, left-bank beach promised a fitting Dinosaur finale.

Out across the river, a hundred yards away, rose a sheer red cliff. The broad river, now fined down to translucent green, flowed fast but smooth. Behind my camp, pale pink limestone mounted to the horizon in mighty tiers.

Shadow had already fallen across the little beach, but the air was still hot, beyond need for clothes. I set up camp, then sat in my folding chair, suitably clad, and began writing letters for mailing at Jensen, eighteen miles ahead.

I kept looking up, though—looking out beyond the bulging blue lines of the raft, tethered eight or nine paces from my feet, trying to accept that this broad river must still contain a few molecules of water from "my source." I was still grappling with that profound problem when I saw a wide, engraved V curving across the smooth surface. Its path, directly away from me, suggested that it had probably originated somewhere near my raft.

The dark blob that was inscribing the V came close to the far bank, turned upriver. In profile it became, as I knew it would, a familiar brown flat-topped head equipped with a black button of a nose, a shining black eye and stubby yet prominent ears. The head coasted into shallows, kept moving upstream. Sometimes, now, the animal still swam; sometimes it walked; and when it walked its body lifted almost clear of the water. It was very big. Perhaps the biggest I'd seen.

It turned inland, up onto the sloping bank, then stopped, half out of the water, alongside something I'd not noticed until that moment: a much smaller beaver. The two dark schmoo figures sat close together, lazily eating waterside greenery. But "sat" is never quite the right word for what beavers do: a shape as amorphous as a schmoo barely has a butt. And this relaxed shapelessness contributes, I think, to the serenity that pervades almost any out-of-water beaver scene.

The serene aura is apt. In one sense, beavers deserve their knee-jerk label "eager." When occasion demands, they're indeed hard workers—though they work in a slow, deliberate, unstoppable, see-it-through-to-the-bitter-end-no-matter-how-long-it-takes sort of mode. But they are also, as one expert has said, "masters of the fine art of rest." And they eat with consummate restfulness.

Watching the two beavers eat side by side on the far side of the river I sensed—though I wasn't sure just why—a strong bond between them. An almost palpable affection. They were, I felt confident, either Momma and Child or Papa and Young Bride. Tentatively, I settled for Momma and Child. As sometimes happens, I reverted to Swahili and labeled them Mama and Toto.

Before long, Mama slid back into the water and swam toward me. Directly toward me. And kept coming, clear across the river. Just short of the raft, she swung briefly downstream, then turned and swam back upalongside it. She moved clear; paused to investigate me. She was so close now that I could see the way the wet brown fur on her face seemed to be streaked with black—though I knew it was probably just that the pale topcoat lay back in strands and the dark underfur showed through. For a long moment, Mama floated there, staring at me. Then she turned and swam slowly upstream—and I knew I'd passed her test. Had, provisionally, been judged harmless. Something that could safely be ignored.

I looked across the river at Toto. It was still schmooing peacefully. When I brought my eyes back, Mama had disappeared. But I could see a line of small bubbles that I knew must indicate her route (though whether the bubbles came from her mouth or from air trapped in her fur, I didn't know). The bubbles led to a rock spur that marked the end of my little beach. There, they vanished.

I looked back over the river. Now Toto was swimming across. Languidly, he duplicated Mama's inspection of raft and me, then swam up to the rock spur, waddled ashore and schmoo-sat under the spur's overhang, less than twenty paces away. Mama resurfaced, joined him.

Out in midriver, another full-sized beaver appeared, apparently from nowhere. It swam to a point just off the rock spur, paused, then came on down, passed close to the raft, swung out toward the far bank. The light was poor now, but through binoculars I watched its dark head cut V-ripples across the smooth water. Across and downstream. At the tail of the smooth pool, near the point it poured over into a diagonal line of white water, the beaver turned directly downstream, accelerated. Where the water began to slope away, it submerged. It had the determined look of being on its way somewhere. I christened it Papa.

Back at the rock spur, Mama slid down into the water. Before long she reappeared, towing a leafy cottonwood branch. I could not see her broad tail, but I knew she'd be holding it to one side, offsetting the drag of the branch which otherwise would have sent her swimming in circles. A swimming beaver uses its tail little if at all for propulsion, but extensively as diving plane and rudder. On land, the tail provides a firm base for such upright-body operations as tree-cutting and carrying construction materials held between forepaws and chest.

I could not see Mama's feet, either, but I knew the front paws would be tucked in under her chest like little fists: she wouldn't use them for swimming, only to fend off obstacles. A beaver's paws are remarkable instruments. They've evolved quite differently, fore and aft. The five-fingered forepaws are almost as flexible and dexterous as ours, yet the nails at their tips are stout and strong enough to dig not only bank dens but long canals through solid earth—neatly engineered canals that can be as much as three feet deep and 750 feet long. The massive hind feet, webbed like a duck's, provide almost all the power for swimming. They can propel the animal along at five miles an hour. In emergency bursts, even faster.

The hind feet also furnish their owner with an unlikely yet vital subsidiary tool.

Mama dragged her cottonwood branch to the rock overhang, came ashore, gave the branch to Toto. By now the light under the spur's overhang was very poor, but through binoculars I could see Toto chewing away at the branch. His self-sharpening teeth—self-sharpening because the softer material on the inside eroded faster than the tough outer layer—made short work of the soft wood.

Mama sat facing me, on the exposed river side of Toto. Her body was partly in the river, mostly out. Through binoculars she looked huge and bulbous, like a manatee wallowing to its Plimsoll line. Or a minor gorilla taking a bath. At first she just sat, doing nothing. But after a while, as far as I could see in the growing gloom, her body began to undulate with a gentle pulsing movement.

I set aside my barely started first letter and dedicated the evening to beaver-watching.

Most of the action—though that is far too energetic a word for what went on—took place under the overhanging rock spur. But occasionally Mama, and even Toto, would slide into the river for short swims. Mama tended to begin them with a reinvestigation of the raft and its beached hanger-on. And always she swam slowly, at ease. Not once, all evening, did I hear a ker-*ploosh*. (That tail-beating action is correctly thought of as primarily a warning to fellow beavers that danger lurks; but many beaver meetings, all down the river, had by now led me to the conclusion, later confirmed, that it can also be a message to intruders: "Get out of my territory, you bastard!")

Before long, most of the river and shore had dimmed to a deep, shadowy gray. But once, as Mama returned from a languid cruise, she passed through a sliver of the river's surface that was still floodlit shining pink by reflection from the last sunlight hitting high on a red cliff, and for a long moment her small black head with its protruding ears stood out sharp and clear, like a submarine gliding into a western harbor at sunset. Then she moved back into shadow. Soon, she schmooed up into the spur's overhang—and I had to let my eyes adjust before I could be sure, even through binoculars, that Toto was indeed still there.

For the rest of the evening both beavers sat in the spur's overhang, acting as if I did not exist, barely twenty paces away. I had made no attempt to hide my presence. The camp gear stood stark on the open beach, and I sat naked in my chair. At first I avoided unnecessary movements. And when I moved I did so slowly. But as time passed and the light faded I exercised less care. In due course I cooked and began to eat dinner.

Draping a bright red towel across my knees as tablecloth disturbed the beavers no more than had the roar of the cooking stove or the scrape of metal spoon on metal pot. As the light seeped away, they went quietly on with their business in the overhang that I now believed must be the forecourt to their den. Each of them had vanished occasionally into the water without seeming about to swim anywhere, and had later reappeared, just as quietly. The den itself, I assumed, must be down below the spur, in a natural cavity half-filled with water.

As I ate dinner, Toto continued to eat his. Or, rather, to eat his breakfast. Although beavers often wander abroad in daylight, the night is their time.

Sometimes Mama seemed to be chewing the cud, like a cow, but this did not seem to account for the slight pulsing movement of her body I'd noticed earlier and that had continued intermittently. At last, when she moved into a position that allowed me to see her rear leg—though only dimly—I understood what she was doing.

The unlikely yet vital subsidiary tools in a beaver's hind feet are splits in each next-to-inner claw. Each split claw acts as a fine-tooth comb with which the animal constantly preens its coat while applying oil from special glands. It was this grooming, I finally realized, that caused the gentle pulsing movement in Mama's body.

At least, I assumed she was grooming herself. But by the time I'd finished dinner—the last of it stonish cold, because I'd been preoccupied with the pageant being acted out in the overhang's proscenium—the light had almost gone. Near the end, before night dropped its final curtain, I thought I could see Toto cuddling up to Mama, breast feeding. But by now the dark shapes had become indistinct to the brink of invisibility. Even through binoculars they were no longer manatees, let alone minor gorillas. Not even schmoos. Just blobs that kept merging with their dark backdrop.

I bid the cast a whispered and grateful "Good night" and went to bed.

In the morning, before the sun rose, the beavers were still at it, rounding out their night's business. Papa returned from what I chose to assume was a nightlong foray below the rapid. Mama and Toto appeared briefly in the overhang. Then sunlight, angling through a gap in the far canyon wall, floodlit my little beach. It banished the last hint of mystery from the overhang-stage and left in its place a very ordinary, common-or-canyon pink rock spur, no different from a thousand I'd passed. The sun banished the beavers, too. Their daily nighttime dance was over.

By the time I'd packed up and was ready to leave Beaver Camp, the sun had kindled the mayflies' morning hatch. For a moment I stood beside my raft and watched the inaugural stages of this daytime, once-in-a-lifetime pageant. Stood and watched the swelling throng of tiny, diaphanous insects—insubstantial against the far cliff's ancient rock—begin their ephemeral dance. Then I stepped aboard, resumed my own.

Around the first bend, the river emerged from Split Mountain Canyon and flowed out into the Uinta Basin. Emerged from the sanctuary that is Dinosaur National Monument and flowed out into "the real world."

Most of our systems go through such emergences. Life on earth can be seen as doing so when those first scorpionlike creatures emerged from the sea and crawled up onto a beach and liked what they breathed—and thereby found, though they did not know it, a wide new world that they and their descendants would colonize. Farther down life's journey, the mammals can be seen as doing much the same when their small, insignificant, newfangled, warm-blooded offshoot of the establishment reptilian stock found itself unexpected heir to the world the dinosaurs had abruptly left vacant. Farther down these mammals' efflorescent line, the cultural evolution of *Homo sapiens* (Western bunch) can be seen as emerging from its limited confines when, liberated by new advances in travel and communication, the increasingly complex post-Neolithic civilizations beside the Tigris, Euphrates and Nile flowed outward into Asia, Africa and Europe. You could also, if you chose, see the system known as the United States echoing the process when, after the Louisiana Purchase in 1803 and the following year's Lewis and Clark expedition, its population began to flood westward across the New World.

Not all such emergences lead to high success, of course.

In our individual lives, a pivotal emergence normally takes place when we leave school and move on out into the wider world.

For children who went to old-style country schools—the Brown's Hole kids, say, who went to Lodore School—the process was not, at a guess, a true emergence. As long as the local grass grew green, most of them just stayed on their parents' ranches and worked—full-time now, without the long rides to and from school—and in due course took over from their parents. But in the modern, urbanized, more fragmented world, leaving school—grade or high school or college—for most of us means moving out at last into the unknown, out into what is often called "the real world," into that dreaded, longed-for first job.

It's a serious moment, that move. Or at least a solemn one. We stride out into the unknown, half-baked, seeking to pry open—though we hardly put it that way—the dark secrets of how the cosmic cookie crumbles. The trouble is that we've almost always got the cookie wrong. We tend to see the things around us—the physical things, the people and their positions, the mores and much more—as solid and lasting in that world.

At the time, of course, we understand little if anything about such things. At least, I had certainly not done so when, a few days out of school and still seven months shy of my eighteenth birthday, I went up to London to become a clerk in a suburban outpost of the British Admiralty. Although I didn't know it then, the new world I discovered there would within two months be rocked by forces and events destined to dam and divert the flow of much broader currents than those carrying my own little life along.

Below the first bend, on the fringe of the Uinta Basin, I pulled in at a boat ramp, dropped my park service permit in the proper campground box, so that the rangers would know I'd passed safely through, and was walking back to the raft when I met a husband and wife, vacationing in their RV.

They looked entirely human. "Has World War III begun?" I asked. "Or anything like that?"

They both smiled. "No," said the wife. "But World War II is over."

"Uh-huh. Anything else of note?"

"Well, Pete Rose has been banned from baseball for life."

I relaunched, floated on down, crossed Dinosaur's guardian boundary. River left, a pump mounted in a huge rusty scaffolding thumped away. Soon, a gravel operation scarred the plain.

9

UINTA BASIN

Mile 413 to Mile 531
August 29–September 8

For a hundred miles the river meandered across the Uinta Basin, and my journey and thoughts conformed.

Even before we moved clear of the Uinta Mountains' last fingers, the river slowed and broadened. Soon the water rose a few inches and remuddied. That complicated the prime navigation problem: finding routes around sandbars. And no matter how much we meandered, the winds that blustered across the Basin always seemed to hit head-on. Day after day I did a lot of hard rowing.

For fifty miles the landscape lay schizoid. Now, barren desert—especially bordered by river greenery—normally bewitches me; but although the Basin looked like a back-of-beyond place where nothing happened, I found I was rarely out of sight or sound of machinery. Gravel operations. Oil rigs—grasshopper and grosser. Industrial apparatuses of uncertain purpose but wide impact. Yet in spite of man's heavy signatures I saw few people. Winds or no, the Basin was a doldrum.

Day after day, the sun beat down. It flattened the desert into glaring ugliness, beat back up from wind-pewtered water, addled my brain. The river became beautiful only at nightcamps, in the cool and calm of sunset and sunrise. And only at the nightcamps did my thoughts flow. Even then they tended to follow tortuous courses.

A day after picking up stores and mail at Jensen, I paused for thirty-six hours at a left-bank camp to reorganize gear.

A group of cottonwoods furnished shade and greenery and also screened an oil operation on the far bank: at the head of the flat land within a big horseshoe bend huddled a scattering of metal buildings and junked vehicles laced with garbage. The wind had transported a garbage delegation of empty oil cans onto my shore.

The second evening at this camp it occurred to me in mid-dinner that the date was September 1. I put down the spoon, turned my right hand palm up and for the first time in years looked at a point near its center. It was still there: a small black mark embedded in what palmists call the line of life. A small black mark now exactly fifty years old.

On September 1, 1939, Hitler invaded Poland—and I, still a clerk at my suburban outpost of the Admiralty, was chosen to accompany my immediate boss on an emergency trip to headquarters in Whitehall. I can no longer recall the specific purpose of our trip, but I remember the sense of bustle and controlled consternation we found at headquarters, where everyone seemed—or so memory tells me—to be stacking files for safe storage against the bombings that the inevitable war would surely bring. And at some time during the hour or two we spent at the beehive Admiralty I jammed the point of a pencil into the palm of my right hand. The tip of the lead broke off. I pulled it out easily enough, but when the blood ceased to flow a black mark remained, precisely damming my line of life.

I picked up the spoon again, went back to eating dinner.

Little else about that momentous Friday still hung in memory. But next afternoon I was due to play in a cricket match, and because war had not yet been declared—our world was on hold, in a state of suspension—I went to the cricket ground. Three or four other optimists straggled in, but we never approached the quorum of twenty-two. By that time it had become fairly clear that England would declare war the following day, and after an hour or so we dispersed and, like everyone else, went on waiting.

I put down the spoon again, looked once more at the black mark on my line of life. It was a long time since I'd thought of those days when World War II began. Most of the memories had faded, but a few remained as clear and undeniable as the black mark—as clear as the hindsight understanding that those days had unleashed forces destined to dam and divert the flow of my life. Not to mention a couple of billion other lives.

Out beyond the river, the sun was setting on the junkyard of vehicles scattered around the oil outfit's headquarters. I picked up the spoon, resumed dinner.

By noon next day I'd rowed eight river-miles and was back within a mile of my campsite, across the neck of the big horseshoe bend. At the neck—at a place the map suggested was approachable only from the oil operation headquarters—I found myself floating down in the midday sun toward a pale gash in the right bank. From this scar rose dust and a mechanical roar. At the dust's point of origin, one or two figures flickered. Beyond them, a big yellow machine stabbed at the earth. I floated closer. Two fat white plastic pipes snaked down to the river. From them, muck poured.

I pulled in just above the pipes, hesitated, made fast. There were a couple of genuine questions I'd been wanting to ask someone, and they should mask my curiosity.

I walked up beside the fat white pipes, into the devastation. Two men were leaning over the machine that generated most of the roar and dust. They wore shirts and slacks and baseball caps. I walked toward them. The sun beat down. A radio blared from a parked pickup, but once I was past it the roaring machine drowned the music.

The two men didn't see me until I came close. When they turned, there was a furtive, vaguely guilty look in their eyes. And they hardly welcomed me with open arms. I asked my first cover question; bellowed it out over the machine's roar.

One of the men responded, curtly. Information had to be squeezed out drop by drop, question by question. "No, no poison oak around here. . . . No, no poison ivy. . . . No, them Russian olive trees don't do that, neither. . . . Midges, it'll be . . . Goddam little bugs you can't hardly see. Happened to me once. Face swelled up, jest like yorn." The man turned back to his machine.

For a minute or two we stood there, silent in the sunlit din. Then I asked, "Is this a gravel operation?"

The man glanced at his companion. "Yeah, guess you could call it that." He sniggered, turned back to his machine.

The machine stood in the middle of a shallow hollow gouged into the plain. The hollow was all bare-gravel trenches and ridges. A raped, sodomized landscape. The big yellow front loader prowled around it, scooping loads of gravel and delivering them to the machine. The machine agitated each new load and sluiced it with river water sucked up by the pumps. It shook onto a protruding tray the riches it had winnowed from gross gravel and disgorged the waste into a growing pile. The two men bent tautly over the tray. It occurred to me that they probably had no mining permit. That would account for their guilt and furtiveness.

The nearest man straightened his back, turned and stared at me. I asked my second question. Yes, the Indian village of Ouray was maybe thirty miles down. . . . Stood a hundred yards back from the river . . . How big? Oh, about two houses.

I lingered, just standing there, surveying the scene. The place was clearly no one-day operation. Quite apart from the size of the gouged-out gravel pit, electric power poles ran down into it. "Are you from the oil operation up there?" I asked.

The man hesitated just a split second. "No." He almost spat the word. A child might have believed him.

For the first time, I remembered it was the Saturday of Labor Day weekend, when nobody labors. So the shirts and slacks and baseball caps instead of work clothes and hard hats probably meant that this was the men's idea of a vacation.

I turned and walked back to my little blue raft, cast off, floated on down the sunlit river. I did not look back at the placer miners making war on the earth to satisfy their gold lust.

Late next day I camped in a national wildlife refuge. The refuge embraced only a narrow strip along the river and I could still hear, off to the east, the low rumble of what sounded like very heavy machinery. Hours of steady rowing, mostly into a headwind, under a pitiless sun, had tired me, and once I'd set up camp I sat for a long time in my little chair, sipping bourbon. I was staring out over the river, watching the evening shadows lengthen, thinking idly that it was good to have it always there, flowing past, when I remembered that the date was now September 3.

Long before 1939, September 3 had been a day of note in the history of my native land. "Cromwell's day," it has been called—because on that date, in different years back in the mid-seventeenth century, Oliver Cromwell won two of his major Civil War victories, overcame a crisis with a recalcitrant parliament and, eventually, died. Early on September 3, 1939—a Sunday, like this one beside the Green River—BBC Radio announced that at eleven o'clock Prime Minister Neville Chamberlain would speak to the country. Clearly, he would be declaring war. With a sagacity that now surprises me, I decided that there was nothing I could do about the event and that I should therefore carry out my original plans for the day. I duly bicycled twenty miles west and went fishing in a huge, flooded gravel pit. But I knew that the inevitable had indeed taken place when, a few minutes after eleven o'clock, air raid sirens wailed, all around me. World War II had begun.

Out on the river, a beaver ker-*plooshed*. I took another sip of bourbon, began to reflect on the war that had consumed six years of my life. What I found myself remembering, to my surprise, was Tony.

In 1940, Tony Gale and I had known each other briefly as marine recruits in neighboring squads. Three years later we'd found ourselves, now twenty-one-year-old lieutenants, in the same commando unit. Once again we became, if not close friends, then colleagues on very cordial terms. Tony was a tall, gangly, fair-haired guy who enjoyed life—a good soldier but really a man of peace, not war. Now I remembered his mentioning to me, just before D-Day, a week he'd spent in London with his girlfriend: although he avoided details, the sheer joy of the interlude shone through. But the conversation with Tony that I remembered most vividly—well, fragments of a conversation—took place in Normandy, the morning after D-Day.

A unit "O group"—an assembly of troop commanders and others at which the commanding officer gives orders for an impending operation—was taking place in a shallow, scooped-out hollow on the slope beyond the canal and river we'd crossed the day before. Tony and I were not part of the inner group but by chance found ourselves lying side by side nearby, waiting for our own orders. German mortar shells kept landing uncomfortably close and often. Dust from their explosions blurred the summer sunshine. Each shell reloaded the air with suppressed tension.

Between explosions, Tony and I exchanged occasional thoughts. The central "O group" included a major from another commando in our brigade whose troop had been attached to us for the coming attack on an enemy-held village and gun battery. The major, whom I knew only by sight, was tall, statuesquely handsome, deadly serious—an almost heroic-looking sort of man who you felt sure would make his mark on the world. At one point, Tony nodded toward him.

"My God!" he said. "Just look at John Pooley! We were at school together, you know. He was a bit ahead of me but . . . I didn't realize until now how much he's aged."

Soon afterward, we moved off in the sunlight for the attack on the village, down near the mouth of the river we had crossed. By sunset that day, John Pooley was dead. So was Tony Gale. And now, forty-five years and five thousand miles away, here was I, alive and remembering, on the banks of another river, waiting for the sun to set.

Shadows reached out across the river, touched the far bank.

Nowadays, the war no longer made much sense. Not war in general, that is—war as a way of life. Certainly not the memories that lingered sharpest. The almost incessant, all-pervading tiredness, for example: a popular saying in our unit had been, "Roll on, death, let's get some fucking sleep." Sprawled bodies with bloated, purple-black faces. Or what had once been faces. Bits of bodies just lying around—a leg, an arm, a hand—still starkly white but stripped of all identification, so that you didn't know whether they were bits of our guys or theirs. Not that you thought too much about that. You couldn't. When you're young and fighting a war you more or less have to deny the potential imminence of death. Otherwise, you can't operate. But if you live, and half a century later move into prime dying time, you discover a different set of rules: you'd damned well better have come to grips with the imminent reality or, in a different but almost as compelling sense, you once again can't really operate. Not, that is, in a full, rounded, productive way.

Across the river, the shadows had captured the shoreline. Sunlight's only surviving citadel was a thin pink line, high on a distant rock escarpment.

Even if you stood far back, now, and looked at the whole bloody war, it didn't make much sense. The country that Tony Gale and John Pooley and I had been fighting for—the only major power to fight (along with its Commonwealth partners) through the entire six-year affair—entered the war as hub of an empire so powerful that a quarter of the world map was painted its color; now it was a third-rate power, and sinking. My adopted country, joining the party late again, had done rather better, so far. But the craw-sticking irony was that the countries we'd together defeated—the countries our victor-written history still labeled the aggressors—now ruled wide sectors of the economic roost, and were gaining.

Somewhere out on the darkening river, a beaver slapped its tail. I poured myself another bourbon.

In the course of the next three days I passed out of the wildlife refuge, through an Indian reservation and into Bureau of Land Management territory. Nothing changed. Out beyond both banks, the landscape still stretched flat and deadly. And the furnace kept building. Some days, by the time I launched, around eight o'clock, the sun already beat hot on my bare skin. Once, around noon, a flock of domestic sheep, clustered in the shade of riverside bushes, seemed to peer out with pity, as if expecting to see a mad dog accompanying this Anglo-raftsman who persisted in going out in the midday, out in the midday, out in the midday sun. Taking an occasional swim as I floated down helped cool me off—though I found that unless the water was shallow and I could push up off the bottom, it was surprisingly difficult, wearing a life jacket, to clamber back over the raft's smooth, bulging gunwales. So instead of going for swims I took to dipping my shirt in the river, putting it on while soaking wet and letting it dry as I rowed. It worked well. Even so, the heat had by mid-afternoon often hammered my brain into a semi-catatonic state.

Eventually, the rest of my body began to complain. One day, significant time passed before I succeeded in dismissing mild chest pains as due to a mix of indigestion and unusually long hours spent rowing. The mosquitoes didn't help, either. Nor did the wind, which still seemed to blow almost constantly upriver. And the wind, paradoxically, deepened the doldrum effect.

But all through those dreary ten days I spent crossing the Uinta Basin, wildlife generated welcome little puffs of fresh air—and one brief pleasure-gale.

Most appearances were established acts. A mule deer buck sauntered across shallows. Beavers patrolled and people-watched and tail-slapped. Great blue herons stood regular, severe, solo sentry duty. But once an ill-disciplined squad of them, mustered a dozen strong on a sandbar, took flight before the blue-raft intruder closed to within authentic camera range. A fat carp, lying on its side in a shallow sandbar inlet, about to die as the river fell, exhibited no obvious sign of gratitude when I nudged it back into deep-water safety. A killdeer stood solitary and stoic and silent as I floated by, ten feet away; listened indulgently to my "Killdeer! Killdeer! Killdeer!" salutation; then stalked inland—leaving no doubt that my performance had fallen pathetically short of professionalism.

But not all acts were encores. A sage grouse erupted from bankside sagebrush and fluster-flapped off, overland and low, looking surprisingly bulky, anything but sage. A very large rabbit came up out of a crouch, revealed unfittingly long ears, hared away. I landed to scout a campsite and a porcupine wambled from center stage into shadowy wings.

And then, one hot and windy afternoon, an open sandbar presented an unexpected matinee.

Not until the star and sole performer focused in my binoculars did I identify it: the first of the trip—and the first I'd ever seen. I think I'd always been vaguely puzzled by the temperament of Badger in *The Wind in the Willows*: he was supposed to be at once sagacious and rather remote yet profoundly amiable. Now the medium-sized, low-slung animal defined in my binoculars as it trotted up the sandbar exuded each of these characteristics—and melded them.

There was sagacity in the slightly upturned nose and air of confidence; remoteness, somehow, in the general shagginess of his coat and in the way he seemed oblivious of or uncaring about the big blue raft passing barely thirty yards away; and amiability in his walk—in the way he flipped up the tip of each forepaw just before he put it down and then, when each stride was over, lifted it far back under his body before bringing it forward again. But the amiability ruled. He looked a most friendly beast. I doubt if he was, but he looked it.

To my surprise, there was something doggy about him—not just in the way his paws flipped but also in his straight-ahead, going-for-it attitude.

His coloring was not what I'd expected, either. I think I'd pictured badgers as having heavy black and white markings over the entire body. A sort of zebroid skunk effect. This animal's shaggy coat kept ruffling in the wind, so it was difficult to be sure, but it seemed to be an overall muddy gray. The long, pointed head had markings all right—vaguely like the piebald face of an acorn woodpecker, much faded by time and sun. Almost before I'd registered even these superficial impressions, the badger's straight-line, get-out-of-my-way path had carried him into thick undergrowth. I waited. He did not reappear. I rowed on downstream, semi-decatatonicized.

One of the rare people-meetings cheered me, too. A man, car-camping with his family in the shade of a riverside tree, called out as I passed, "Hi, Captain! What have you done with your girl?"

"Oh, left her at home."

"How far you going?"

"Just down to the ocean."

"That's not far."

"Another four months."

A pause. Then, "You're serious, eh?"

"Sure."

"Where'd you start?"

"The source. 'Bout two months ago."

"Hm, sounds like fun."

"It is."

On my eighth doldrum day in the Uinta Basin, as I passed the journey's 500-mile mark, scattered buttes and then low bluffs along the river began to leaven the landscape. The river quickened. We moved into the fringes of the Tavaputs Plateau; the bluffs grew taller. Clouds gathered ahead, over the Plateau. Soon, for the first time since back in the Canyon of Lodore, it was raining. Not heavily, but enough to disband the mosquito swarms and drop the temperature and restore my brain to modest working order and inject hints of promise into the proceedings. Before long my mind was replaying the dreary crossing of the Basin and commenting that even occasional distant white stratified buttes had failed to remind me that an extension of Lake Gosiute once covered this flatland. The loss of a profound geology lesson left me singularly unmoved.

The bluffs continued to grow taller. Rose yet higher. The river gained speed and character. And on the tenth morning I pulled in at the Bureau of Land Management Sand Wash Ranger Station, entry control point for Desolation and Gray Canyons.

The Uinta Basin's hundred-mile doldrums were past. A hundred miles ahead—beyond Desolation and Gray Canyons—lay the town of Green

River, Utah. Looking ahead, I found myself relishing, just for a moment, the prospect of holing up in a motel for a couple of days—of soaking in a bath, sipping beer, until I developed wrinkles; then gorging on fresh food served at a table, with cold wine.

On the beach at Sand Wash, two men were loading gear into a small inflatable raft. We chatted briefly. They were putting in that afternoon and would take out ten days and a hundred miles later, at the foot of Gray Canyon.

I walked on up to the ranger station.

Back at Jensen I'd phoned the BLM Recreation Planner at Price. "Oh, if you've come this far," he said, "then you shouldn't have trouble with any of the rapids in Desolation or Gray—though with the water this low a couple of 'em may be interesting. But beyond the canyons, eight or nine miles above Green River, there's a diversion dam." The dam had caused at least one drowning in recent years. Normally, he said, the problem was that the white water along its entire foot curled back in an unbroken pattern known as a "double-reversal hydraulic," and that was dangerous because if you got caught in it you couldn't get out. "But with the river this low I don't think that'll be a problem. What worries me is whether there'll be enough water for you to go over the dam at all."

The volunteer ranger at Sand Wash had never been down as far as the diversion dam, and had no up-to-date information about it. She'd taken this unpaid job, she said, because it gave her a chance to concentrate with little interruption on her freelance graphics work. She liked the remote country, too, and the river. "Oh, I'm sure you'll enjoy it through the canyons," she said. "And you should have the river to yourself—except for the two guys you met on the beach just now. At a guess, you'll keep meeting them all the way down. They both seem real nice guys, though. And there's nobody else immediately ahead or behind you. . . . No, after Lodore, you shouldn't have too much trouble with our rapids. But I think you'll find the whole river interesting."

10

DESOLATION

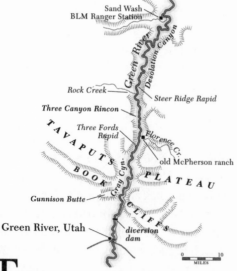

Sand Wash
BLM Ranger Station
Green River
Desolation Canyon
Rock Creek
Steer Ridge Rapid
Three Canyon Rincon
Three Fords Rapid
T A V A P U T S
Florence Cr.
old McPherson ranch
B O O K
Gray Cyn.
P L A T E A U
Gunnison Butte
C L I F F S
Green River, Utah
diversion dam
0 10
MILES

Mile 531 to Mile 618
September 8–17

T he Sand Wash ranger turned out to be right on all counts.

But almost every process—journey or job, marriage or life—has segments in which the ongoing events that seem to form its motif prove to be only a stage setting. The essence, you come to see—perhaps at the time, perhaps only much later—lay in sideshows.

Desolation and Gray Canyons unreeled as promised: interesting, beautiful and varied. Only two rapids posed challenges. Except for the rafters I'd met on the beach at Sand Wash, I had the river to myself. And the diversion-dam question mark hung there, intriguingly, until the very end. But the things that really made my ten days through Desolation and Gray lay elsewhere. In the river's songs and cameos. In rare meetings with the two rafters. And in two sidetrips.

Below Sand Wash, the canyon walls continued to gain stature. Soon their rims towered a thousand feet above the river—providing both practical and aesthetic solace.

The cliffs projected pyramids of shade across the winding river, and the air within each shadowed pyramid was always comparatively and deliciously cool. Temperature gradients between shade and sunlight even created pleasing local breezes.

At first the cliffs swung gray and smooth in sweeping curves. But their grayness varied. And buttresses in regular series counterpointed their smoothness. Then the cliffs became red and less friable rock walls—sometimes rising almost sheer, sometimes slanting back in eroded, beautifully stratified benches. The light changed minute by minute, hour by hour, thrumming on the rock walls' theme, constantly transfiguring it. Grandeur. Mercurial shifts of mood. Slowly, they smoothed away the corrugations that the Uinta Basin had inflicted on my spirit.

Before long my mind was alert enough to absorb a river-guide explanation of why the canyon's walls kept changing.

Fifty million years earlier, Lake Uinta—a sometime outlier segment of Lake Gosiute—had fluctuated wildly. The lake was very shallow—"probably never more than 100 feet deep"—and its shoreline often moved many miles. When feeder streams from surrounding highlands rose in flood they dumped coarse red sand and silt in tongues that might reach far out across the lake bed, and when the floods subsided the now-deeper lake overlaid these tongues with the fine gray mud—formed from organic materials and clay—that it was always and steadily depositing. After the lake had finally dried up, the southern part of its bed was uplifted, and tilted slightly, to form the present Tavaputs Plateau. Desolation and Gray Canyons cut through the interleaved tongues of gray "mudstone" and red sand and silt. Hence the changes in their walls. (These Tertiary period sedimentary rocks, less than fifty million years old, are the youngest the Colorado or its tributaries expose in any major canyon.)

During my early days in Desolation, the river itself also helped me recover from the Uinta Basin war.

At first its character remained much as in the Basin: swirls and sandbars. Then the rapids began. Soon, the river once more became a necklace of pools and runs—a trout river, lacking only trout. And by now it had fined down again, to palest brown. Every morning, no matter how pleasant my nightcamp, it was good to get back onto the wide, inviting waterway.

The third day below Sand Wash, I reached Steer Ridge Rapid—the first of two I'd been advised to scout. I scouted. Entry was the problem: a milder mirror image of the first move back in Hell's Half Mile but offering two choices. I consulted my fears and ambitions, chose the more elegant route, executed it to perfection. And afterward, filled with now-familiar elation, I found that something had changed.

Until then I'd tended to see rapids as mere obstacles—challenges to be overcome if I was to complete my journey. But they'd become fun. In a sense, of course, that was the way I'd regarded them all along. But the fun had begun to elbow out, in a contortionistic masterstroke, my stiff upper lip. And it was probably about this time that there crept into my mind the idea of trying to run all remaining rapids instead of avoiding the most difficult, as I'd planned, by lining or portaging.

This change of attitude reflected, I suppose, a new confidence in my rafting ability. But within ten miles the river issued a gentle warning against overconfidence.

Trail Canyon Rapid turned out to be a long, undemanding rock garden. The first half, dodging boulders left and right, was fun. Then the entire flow massed into a solid tongue and slid right-handed over a ledge. By the time the current flared out again into another rock garden it had swung almost ninety degrees right, and without warning I found myself looking directly into the late-afternoon sun—into a blinding, fractured sheet of light that reflected off the swirling river. "Goddam!" I said out loud. "Can't see a bloody thing!" The words were still floating across the river when I felt a jolt. We were stuck, firm.

At first the apparent facts made no sense. On either side of the raft, the river swirled past, seemingly deep and unimpeded. I unshipped an oar and prodded vertically into the racing current. Yes, deep. And deplorably strong. Slowly it dawned on me that we were impaled on a rock pinnacle. With the oar, I pushed and pulled. We rocked and rolled but did not budge. More oar probing finally revealed, though, that neighboring pinnacles rose up from the depths. And eventually I was able to step-stretch unsteadily onto one of them, rope in hand, transfer to a third pinnacle, downstream, jiggle the lightened raft free and, just in time, jump back aboard. For a few more yards I could still see only the blinding, fractured sheet of reflected light. By sheer luck, we hit nothing else. Then we'd floated down into shadow and I could once more read the water.

The pinnacle had not damaged the raft, only my pride. But I knew I'd been lucky. And as I floated on down I understood in a new and healthy way that a single split-second change of conditions could transform a cakewalk into a catastrophe.

All through that week in Desolation, the river was there, singing me many songs, from solace to warnings. But as I've said, the sideshows were the thing.

Some sideshows were staged as fleeting scenes glimpsed as I floated by, others at nightcamps or on brief trips ashore.

Several raft-borne glimpses of the passing show featured oddities. The first day below Sand Wash, successive side canyons presented troupes of "hoodoos." A hoodoo is a geological mushroom by Disney. Rain erosion of very soft alluvial soil has been thwarted by a hard, disklike boulder that once lay on the surface; rain has washed away all surrounding soil but has been unable to penetrate directly below the boulder and has left it as a caprock on a long, spindly, alluvial stalk. Some of the side-canyon hoodoos looked at least thirty feet tall. Some caprocks were cocked at rakish angles, and I think I half-expected the hoodoos to break into a dance: the *trepak* from *Nutcracker*, say, as mushroom-pranced in *Fantasia*.

Some sideshows were quiet natural cameos. Just below the hoodoos, a single sunflower plant grew stalwart on a riverside mud terrace. Its backdrop, sharply tiered: the vertical stalks of pampaslike grasses etched subtle green against brown mud wall; then their seedheads waving straw-pale against horizontal red rock strata. And each element—sunflower, mud, grass, rock—innocently coordinated with delicate, Japanese artistry.

One passing sideshow, routine in itself, carried invisible freight. High on the canyon walls, a cliff. At its foot, a long talus slope. Snaking down the rough pink surface of this talus, several smoother and paler pink lines. Below, on a desert flat bordering the river, the boulders that had broken off the cliff and come crashing down the talus in clouds of dust as they gouged those pale, snaky lines. Now the boulders lay inert and powerless.

I'd been passing similar scenes for weeks. But the day before I'd begun to rebrowse, with renewed pleasure, through Barry Lopez's *Desert Notes*. I still wasn't sure I always understood exactly what Lopez was getting at, and sometimes I almost hoped he didn't quite know, either. But sometimes we both knew exactly what he meant:

> Coyote climbed to a mountaintop to ask Akasitah to change things in the world, so that the Shisa no longer ruled. Coyote had seen a party of Shisa come loping over the desert and find a gully full of rattlesnakes, and he remembered how they *"yelled and beat the snakes to death with sticks. Long after the snakes were dead they beat the snakes and threw them away, kicked them under the bushes."* Coyote also remembered *"the time the Shisa had cracked open the sacred mountain with a great machine and taken the blue heart of the mountain away in chains."* Up on the mountaintop, Coyote knew when he was in the presence of Akasitah: he *"could feel the warm spot in the wind."* He began talking. *"Below,"* he said, *"it is chaos because of the Shisa. . . . Soon there will be nothing left. The Shisa will take even the desert."* On the mountaintop, there was a space in the wind, and Coyote heard words: *"The Shisa are like a great boulder that has broken away from the side of a mountain. The boulder makes a great noise as it comes down the side of the mountain. It tears away great chunks of earth and rock . . . throwing up a cloud of dust against the sun and you are afraid for your life. . . . But soon the Shisa will hit the earth at the bottom of the mountain and roll out into the desert leaving a little trail in the dust. The boulder will come to a stop. You can sleep on it at night. Do not worry. Go."*

Two shore-stops to inspect artifacts focused a pair of former acts from the passing river show; and one ongoing act.

In the river guide, a photo caption read: *"Iron-prowed skiff left under ledge just upriver from Gold Hole."* It was there right enough, tucked in under its rock ledge, high above the present river level. But an air of sadness hung over the place. The soft gray earth around the skiff had been worn smooth by the feet of all of us whose curiosity had been piqued by the river guide. And the skiff itself was a flimsy and unstable-looking affair, difficult to take seriously as a whitewater boat. The sturdy iron prow—a casting borrowed from something else—was secured with a stout bolt; but the planks forming the hull were thin and cheap-looking, and the thwart seat—now missing but visible in the guide photo—had rested on two pieces of wood held in place by nails driven in from the outside and left with their heads turned over. Yet the stern was solidly made. The overall result looked in some ways like a kids' boat, and in some ways did not. Its design had apparently been based on the assumption that you'd run the river bow-first, and that if you hit anything you'd hit it head-on with the iron prow. But except for a small metal patch on one side, suggesting repaired damage, the boat showed no signs of battering. In the absence of facts (I never did manage to ferret out any information about the little craft—even its age) I assumed its owners had run only a short stretch of river, found their vessel wanting, pulled it up onto the ledge at high water and abandoned it.

Next day I went ashore to inspect an artifact that could be dated in only a round-number sense. I'd landed and was about to walk inland to look for some "petroglyphs" marked in the river guide when the two rafters I'd met at Sand Wash pulled in alongside.

We had several times floated past each other's campsites but had exchanged only a few words. This time, we talked. Mike George and Pom Collins had met fifteen years earlier, at college, and become great friends. Then involvement with families and vocations had prevented them from getting together and doing the kinds of things they used to. For three years they'd not even seen each other. Now, in what I guessed to be their late-thirties, they had with great determination managed to mount this "George-Collins Expedition"—and were having a ball.

Mike George, a stalwart fellow with a shock of dark hair and a beard already flecked with gray, was a ship's captain; he lived in Austin, Texas, and operated out of Houston, ferrying supplies to and from oil platforms in the Gulf of Mexico. Pomeroy Collins, more slightly built, was a physician: he'd done volunteer stints in Guatemala and in Cambodian refugee camps but currently found great satisfaction working as a general practitioner in a migrant workers' clinic in Portland, Oregon.

Pom had done a little rafting and was the expedition's official captain. I asked Mike how he felt, as a seagoing captain, about approaching white water in a near-broadside "ferrying" stance.

He laughed. "At first it scared the hell out of me. But . . . well, we haven't come to grief yet, and I guess I'm getting used to it."

We located the petroglyphs, dutifully photographed them. They were, as always, intriguing: spindly drawings of animals and men and assorted unknown objects scratched into a section of smooth red cliff face that stood in the open, easily visible, but was slightly overhung and reasonably protected from weather. Now, perhaps a thousand years after they'd been inscribed, the lines still stood out, pale pink on red rock. In at least one way, this exhibit echoed the graffiti I'd found under the twin river bridges at Green River, Wyoming: in its main section the figures and devices crowded more closely than most I'd seen, as if successive canyon gangs had by macho habit kept coming back to this chosen rendezvous and answered a deep need to leave their imprints, even when space had run out. The drawings jostled, even overlapped. Bighorn sheep with back-curving horns. Square-bodied men, related to playing-card royalty, their cavernous abdomens embellished with dots or squiggles or possible intimations of anatomy. Thin men with horns and dervish-dancing arms and legs. Squiggles that might have been snakes. Sunbursts with star centers, helix centers. Strings of beads that probably did not represent DNA. Patterns that defied modern guesswork.

In this crowded main exhibit each lithograph was drawn primitively, yet with vigor. But off on their own, high and left and different, a dozen small men, one behind the other in orderly line, marched off to nowhere. Though mere sketched suggestions, they were drawn so deftly and naturalistically that each individual seemed to be at a different stage of walking, and each had his own character. If the weathering had not proven—or close to it, for my uneducated eye—that these subtle figures were as old as the primitive drawings below, I might have thought they'd been scratched there yesterday, by James Thurber.

"Yeah," said Pom. "And that's about the place he'd go put 'em."

Nightcamps often opened sideshow windows.

My third night in Desolation, I camped beside a huge boulder with the whole surface of one flat side-face, overhanging the river, covered with what looked like the seashore relics of a long-ago limpet colony—or perhaps the outlines of ancient cliff dwellings built by miniature swallows: a slightly raised network of white ovals, compressed together like a football crowd, sometimes even overlapping, with here and there remnants of the

*Petroglyphs, Desolation Canyon. (*Not *those shared with the "George-Collins Expedition.")*

paper-thin walls of tiny domes. Admitting the unlikelihood of sea limpets and pigmy swallows, but not knowing what kind of insects might have built the little white structures, I christened the place "Pupae Camp."

Then there was Moonwater.

When I pulled in at the long, open beach below Moonwater Rapid, I was feeling pleasantly weary. The sun had already left the beach, and as I stepped ashore I happened to note that it was 7:20—later than I normally camped. By now I'd honed my camping technique to the point I'd long ago reached in backpacking: things happened more or less automatically and, unless I wanted to putter, fast. That evening I made no conscious attempt to hurry. But I happened to glance at my watch again at 8:08. And I noted that by that time I had decided on a campsite, double-tethered the raft in routine fashion to two big boulders that protruded from the beach, carried everything across the thirty or forty paces of beach, set up camp, filled two buckets from the river, washed, dressed for dinner—light balaclava, down jacket, polypro pants—and was eating my rehydrated rendering of Chef Alfredo's famous shrimp dish and washing it down with bourbon. I don't know whether it was the pleasant weariness or the unexpected awareness of camping competence or the taste of my favorite dinner or just the bourbon or, more likely, a meld of all these things, but suddenly, sitting there in my folding chair, I became aware of the music of Moonwater Rapid and, beyond it, of a pinnacled rock palisade. On its highest upthrusting cliffs the day still lingered, residual red. But from behind its rim there now came floating up, silver and majestic, the almost-full moon.

I stood up, walked out onto the beach. Upriver, the moon danced on Moonwater Rapid. Downstream, out in a broad riffle, it illuminated huge angular boulders; painted stark shadows behind them. A little way down the beach, I could even make out footsteps in the sand—footsteps I'd vaguely noticed as I landed.

I went back to camp, sat down. The footsteps, I seemed to remember, had looked recent. And there'd been a lot of them. A party had apparently camped here within the last day or two. I looked up at the moon's dented disc, now clear of the palisade. It was difficult to believe that anyone camping here could fail to be moved; could fail, after a while, to feel a sense of unity with the river, with everything. It occurred to me that church parties might be wise to avoid traveling into such places. Some of their more probing members might run into problems. As the days passed, and the nights, they might be forced to connect. Forster connect, only connect. And afterward they might find it difficult to believe in a god whose central concern was man. In a god reputed to have gone so far as to make man in his own image.

The moon swung slowly away from the black, upthrust palisade.

Of course, we all spoke in metaphors. When we expounded the realities we fancied we knew, we used the metaphors we currently found most valid. And their usefulness would pass. The idea behind "connect, only connect"—and its semi-scientific equivalent in general systems theory—might to me sound like solid, unadorned fact; but later generations would most likely regard it, in its turn, as cumbersome and outdated metaphor.

I went to bed, lay looking up at the moon. All we could do, perhaps, was hope we could keep moving on to new metaphors, honed truer by time and trial. As sleep began to enfold me I found myself wondering, fuzzily, what metaphors had sounded true to the people who had recently camped on this beach.

Next morning, loading the raft, I happened to glance down the beach and see what looked like words inscribed in the sand near the footprints of the party that had preceded me. I walked across the open sand, stood looking down at the message they had left. The low morning sunlight etched it razor-sharp: "Fuck me running."

During the week in Desolation Canyon I at last found time for a couple of extended sidetrips.

Late one evening I came to a feature I'd long been planning to walk around.

In canyon country, a *rincon* (a Spanish word meaning "corner" or "nook") is an abandoned river meander—a dry oxbow lake. The river has cut an extreme horseshoe bend deep into the rock, then broken through the gooseneck, bypassed the horseshoe and left it hanging high and dry. As the river deepens its channel, so the height of the rincon's floor above the river increases. On a topo map, a canyonland rincon shows up as a startling reverse doughnut—the quirky sort of feature that's irresistible to any map junkie; and when I saw Three Canyon rincon on the map, long before beginning my journey, I'd made no attempt to resist.

As for why anyone should feel compelled to circumnavigate a rincon . . . well, perhaps the urge is linked in some way to a need for completeness—the sort of need that can drive a man to walk from one end of California to the other, or from one end of Grand Canyon to the other, or to follow the entire course of a river, source to sea.

By the time I reached Three Canyon rincon it was too late to start walking around the huge red reverse-doughnut trench, so I camped at its foot— at the point the river had, centuries earlier, cut through the gooseneck.

My dinner menu included five fresh brown trout, caught earlier that day in Rock Creek. Fried on one side and then turned over, and the cooked sides eaten direct from the pan, smallest fish first—with the procedure repeated when the other sides were cooked—they made a meal Chef Alfredo would have envied. After dinner I walked up the slope behind camp in bright moonlight, partly to ditch the fish bones well clear of river and camp so that scavengers wouldn't bother me during the night, and partly for another look at the rincon entrances.

When I'd hurry-scouted them just before dark, under lowering clouds, the place had been impressive: pale green sage-covered floors, dark green junipers dotting the gentle red flanking slopes, red-and-white-strata cliffs that soon thrust up from the slopes for close to a thousand feet. But now the skies had cleared, and by moonlight the place had a different feel. The flanking walls and the towering butte that the trench encircled—the butte that was the "hole" in the reverse doughnut—seemed, in blue-tinged monochrome, rather less majestic; but now they stood shrouded in mystery. The two huge entrances to the rincon tunneled back into the silvery night like trenches dug by immense ancient gods, no less powerful for being totally fictitious.

Next morning I slept late. By the time I began to walk up into the right-hand trench it was bathed in bright morning sunlight. But the start proved disappointing. A stand of burnt junipers. Then broken terrain, rougher and more steeply sloping than it looked from a distance. A few deer tracks. Nothing more.

Half an hour's steady walking brought me to the rincon's apex, and I found myself looking out over a flat, enclosed meadow dotted with big boulders. The dry grass glowed pale in the morning sunlight. I was sweating after the uphill walk and was glad to move into the huge dark shadow cast by the central butte; but it was cold in there, and I was glad when the shadow ended and I moved out once more into sunlight.

A few strides, and I stopped. Ahead, the return trench sloped gently and evenly back down toward the river. It, too, was all pale and glowing grass. But halfway, a juniper-clad spur thrust out into it from the right, dark and incisive. Over beyond the river, a jumble of cliffs and buttes and pinnacles flared red in sunlight or lurked hazy blue in lingering shadow. I turned and looked back. The boulder-strewn meadow still stretched straw-pale and glowing, quiet. Small shadows reaching out beyond its boulders echoed, in miniature, the huge shadow of the butte. For a moment I stood looking. Then I turned and walked on down, elated.

It was difficult to pinpoint a reason for my elation, but as I walked, it grew. The sun beat warmly down. A trail began, winding across the grass, labeled with hoofprints and horse dung. The trail meandered and sometimes petered out: made, I surmised, by grazing, not man-ridden, animals. I was wondering whether the trailmakers were wild or domestic horses when up from the grass, almost at my feet, flurried a sage grouse. I stopped, heart pounding for a moment, then walked on.

And all at once it was morning bird time. A small brown hawk scrutinized me from a sage bush, suspicious but unafraid. More sage grouse erupted from the grass. A large bird, almost certainly an immature golden eagle, cruised by. Yet more sage grouse erupted: within five minutes I'd seen more than during the whole trip. Once, I heard a Clark's nutcracker. And not only bird time. At my feet, suddenly, there was a single purple sunburst of a flower, lone and determined in that expanse of pale dry grass—so determined that its stalk embraced all three stages of flowering: at the top, as-yet-unfurled petals; on the flanks, opened flowers, some already easing over into pre-seedpod spikes; and at the base of the sunburst, big, pendulous, fully formed leguminous green pods.

I came level with the spur that jutted out into the pale grass. Now I could look directly up the trough of Three Canyon, feeding in from the right. It looked almost as big as the rincon trough, and as I walked on I studied the rockscape's curves and cliffs. To my nontechnical eye, they seemed to say that either watercourse could have cut them.

An hour and forty minutes after leaving camp, I was back. Nothing much had happened, really. Just a few birds and some pale grassland, a single flower, a couple of small unanswered questions and a lot of morning sunlight. But they had been more than enough.

(Much later I got answers to my two small questions.

According to the BLM area manager, there are no wild horses in Desolation Canyon but domestic horses do graze there. And "although there has been no definitive work that would settle the issue" of whether the Green River or the Three Canyon watershed carved the rincon—"likely the most peculiar geologic feature in the canyon"—two geologists and a hydrologist agree that it was probably the main river.)

Next day I spent an hour wandering around the old MacPherson Ranch, near the mouth of Florence Creek.

Even before I saw buildings I felt the presence of the place. Sensed harmonies.

It was mid-morning, and out beyond the shining blue bulge of my raft the river swirled and gleamed and danced. Along the left bank, sunlight angled luminous green through trees but left the pointed red buttes behind them in deep, contrasting shadow.

I landed on a sandy beach, pulled the raft's bow up onto it, and then, even before making it fast, walked a few paces to take a photograph from beneath the trees. But I could frame no satisfactory picture with my little wide-angle camera—and the night before I'd knocked my replacement zoom camera into dry sand and it had jammed. I went back to the raft, collected a couple of canteens to fill from the drinking water I was told still flowed at the ranch, then went up over the bank.

The first of the old ranch buildings stood close to the river, on a wide desert bench. At the inland edge of the bench clustered some modern, off-white motellike structures. I walked toward the old homestead.

The MacPherson family, I'd read, had settled the place in 1883 and worked it until 1939, when the Uintah and Ouray Indian Reservation was extended to include it. The Ute tribe leased the ranch back to the MacPhersons until 1941. Then the tenants left. I'd heard that the tribe now worked the ranch, but a vague question mark seemed to hang over that report.

I wandered around the old homestead. It showed no sign of being "worked." Three or four stone residences, walls intact but roofs all gone. A scattering of wooden farm structures, serenely disintegrating: a corral, barns, sheds. A rusty corrugated-iron shower, its galvanized overhead tank still gray and whole. An outhouse leaning drunkenly under the pressure of a fallen tree. Yet the place still had a warm, natural, welcoming air.

The main ranch buildings had been built with local red stone. Lovingly built. Had been hand-carved, block by block, from slabs of the red rock that formed the surrounding cliffs and buttes. Most blocks had standard right-angled shapes. But irregular slabs mingled in offbeat groups among their orthodox neighbors—yet meshed almost seamlessly with them, leavening the walls. They injected life and surprise but left the walls' sturdiness unimpaired, the way ethnic or social neighborhoods can leaven and strengthen a modern city.

There was no doubt about the walls' sturdiness. The unroofed shells stood foursquare, unbent and unbowed. And the buildings still melded with their desert bench.

Place and setting had harmony of function, harmony of form. Loosely scattered structures echoed scattered trees and rocks. And the stone walls' color and texture—mostly red and smooth, but leavened with rough gray streaks—stood in clear and present harmony with the rough-smooth, red-gray, cliff-butte background. And the roofless shells still spoke.

I wandered happily around the homestead. The log-walled outbuildings spoke, too. With standard log-cabin eloquence. But it wasn't until I stepped inside a small log-walled shed that had been the tack room, and saw four leather horse halters hanging from long, rounded wooden pegs that something in my mind clicked.

The halters had weathered. Had weathered dark and stiff. One had burst open to disclose pale straw padding. Yet somehow they looked as if they'd been casually slung there the day before, ready for use tomorrow. And all at once, certain dates sprang to life.

The river guide's collection of snapshots from the old MacPherson family album had failed to give me a handle on the reality of their time. One comment from the original Jim MacPherson about his occasional befriending of Butch Cassidy's Wild Bunch "when they needed grub or fresh horses" had certainly made him sound very human: "The outlaws were generally a lot nicer folks than the posse chasing 'em." But the Wild Bunch were now history. Dead history.

In the guide, a picture of a dead man bore the caption: *"Posse killed Wild Bunch compadre Joe Walker in his bedroll Friday the 13th May 1898, in high country behind Florence Creek."* This footnote on rough justice up among those red cliffs and buttes behind the MacPherson Ranch had until that moment also remained ancient history for me, as dead as Joe Walker. But as I stood in the old log-walled tack room, looking at its four weathered horse halters, something clicked: "Friday the 13th May 1898" had been my mother's second birthday.

That should not have made a difference, I suppose, but it did. When I came out of the tack room and began to walk up toward the cluster of modern motellike buildings at the far side of the bench, I found that the old ranch had moved partway into the present. Roughly speaking, its life had run in tandem with my mother's life; even with the early part of mine. My mother had lived only two years longer than the MacPherson Ranch: she died, age forty-seven, during World War II, when I was soldiering.

I walked slowly on across the dusty desert bench.

My mother was still with me, though. Her reality had faded a little, the way all realities do, though we may not like to admit it. But I still remembered her essence, vividly. And gratefully. Remembered many things she'd given me. Above all, she had given me, though I didn't recognize it until long after she was dead, the greatest gift a mother can bestow: the knowledge that, no matter what happened, I was loved. This knowledge lay deep, down where it mattered—a knowledge so safe and sure and natural that until long afterward it never occurred to me that things could be otherwise.

I came to the cluster of modern structures.

They were long and low and ugly. Two main buildings with the neat, soulless lines of motel-row suburbia. Pale walls and dark roofs. Jutting up from the roofs, square gray air-conditioner intakes. These upperworks all new and raw; yet the buildings' steps old and weathered, as if built many years before. A few windows with glass, but most of them just boarded up. One doorway boarded, too. It, and one boarded window, smashed open. Splintered.

The soil surrounding the buildings had been scraped bare. Nearby, a very new rubber-wheeled bulldozer. Scattered around, old bulldozer parts. Laid on the earth's surface, an angular snake of metal water pipe with water gushing from its end. Assorted modern litter. The dried-out tail of some animal, probably a skunk. The rusting pale green shell of a junked sedan, circa 1970, without wheels or hood. Over everything, silence lying thick.

I walked around the buildings. Two or three times I called, "Anyone at home?" No response.

Forty feet beyond the main buildings stood the shell of one of the old stone MacPherson structures, red and stalwart. Its roof had been removed, cleanly, to the last beam. I realized that all the other MacPherson roofs, too, were not merely missing; they'd been cannibalized.

I walked back around one side of the new buildings. There, in the sunlit silence, stood an old steel-wheeled MacPherson wagon, wooden bodywork warped and weathered but still elegant. On it lay an unweathered wooden sign bearing a single crudely lettered word in yellow paint: WELCOME.

I filled my canteens at the gushing water pipe, began to walk slowly back down toward the river.

The ancestors of today's Native Americans seem to have lived in harmony with their land. Their cliff dwellings were stone structures built, like the MacPhersons', from local stone. They therefore melded with the earth. But many of today's Native Americans have lost their own heritage—and succumbed to a sad Gresham's Law of cultural currency: in any transfer of mores, bad customs tend to drive out good. Modern Indians—like other peoples, elsewhere—had embraced our ugly motels, casually junked cars, litter; but they had failed to absorb some of our efficiencies. Our efficiencies that lubricate everyday life, allow it to go on, even enrich it. The habit of completing what you've started, for example, and of maintaining what you've built. For centuries, we of the "West" led the world in such mundane matters—until the Japanese yesterday began to outdo us at our own game. It was these mundane efficiencies—in tandem with "higher" attributes—that had enabled us, during those recent centuries, to sprawl as conquerors across the globe. Perhaps mundane, routine efficiency counted for more than we might like to think. . . .

I skirted the old MacPherson buildings, felt again the genuine sense of welcome, hints of the slow days and loving labor that went into creating such a place. Then I was skirting the end of a long, narrow rectangle of land, close beside the river, that had been bulldozed bare but was beginning to sprout knee-high vegetation. It was, I concluded, an airstrip. Beside it, on new-looking concrete supports, a few planks of unseasoned wood, recently a tabletop, were already warped and twisted, useless and ugly.

I reached the riverbank, went down to the raft—and found that when I'd pulled it ashore and walked those few paces to take a photograph, I'd forgotten to come back and secure it with even one mooring line.

I leaned one hand on the bulging blue bow. I'd been away an hour. A chance increase in the flow from Flaming Gorge Dam, far upriver, or a flash flood down any tributary, and I might have found an empty beach. As I slid the raft back into the river I vowed that my first potentially serious inefficiency of the journey would act as a hubris-deflating alert.*

.   .   .

* Much later, I got answers to some of my questions about the ranch.

BLM confirmed that the motel buildings had indeed been intended as "a dude ranch/hunting lodge" for tourists flown in to the airstrip. But the buildings, constructed in the 1970s, had been closed 95 percent of the time. Occasionally they'd been used for tribal meetings. That was all.

The comments I've made about the place will raise ire, of course. In these days of hypersensitive political correctitude, when we're exhorted, oh so straightly, to revise toward such sports labels as the Alternatively Pigmented Washingtonians, I shall be accused of racism. But I'm not talking about race, you know, only about time. And maybe the anatomy of decline. Besides, would you—or any Native Americans—picket alongside a Cambrian-American like me at Boston Garden to protest the label "Celtics"? I mean, how Keltic was Larry Bird or, for crying out loud, Bill Russell?

Three miles below MacPherson Ranch I came to Three Fords Rapid, the last in Desolation that I'd been advised to scout.

From a rock ledge twenty feet above, I looked down onto the head of the rapid. Onto the crux of the problem. Below me, the entire river's flow funneled through a chute barely thirty feet wide, and a submerged rock split the flow into two narrow tongues. Each tongue dropped into a white cascade, and each cascade steered you into immediate big-boulder problems. Below that the rapid tumbled on for a hundred yards or more—all boulders and white water but without convincing threat—until it petered out at a bend.

For a long time I stood on the rock ledge, mulling the entry problem. My final choice, after much internal debate: go left, young man. A few minutes later I was bringing us down toward the chute, holding against the current, aiming to split the left tongue dead center.

Very slowly, we eased toward its lip. The drop-off hid the cascade and boulders, down below. I made a couple of minor adjustments. Dead on line. I pushed hard, both oars.

The white cascade and two big black boulders came up into view; then

Three Fords Rapid. "Below me, the entire river's flow
funneled through a chute barely thirty feet wide, and a
submerged rock split the flow into two narrow tongues."

the bulging blue bow had dipped and the raft was careering downhill. We hit the cascade, bounced. The bow reared. Spray flew. But we held line as if on a rail.

Then we were in water that no longer frothed white but only swirled, and I was pulling with my left arm, pushing with the right. We pivoted ninety degrees, neatly as a dodgem car. A couple of quick pulls, and we were sliding past the black boulders, past the crux. I angled into ferrying position and maneuvered on down among less menacing obstacles.

At the foot of the rapid I leaned on the oars. From here it looked rather tame, the way most long rapids do from below. The curving riverbank hid the chute and cascade at its head but I could still feel the way we'd ridden them. Just bang, bang, bounce, sail on. Until that moment I'd still felt unsure of the raft's stability in big white water. But that tongue-and-cascade entry, though no doubt small by Cataract and Grand Canyon standards, was as big as any we'd taken. So it had been a test. Another landmark moment. Another rivermark.

I spun us around, headed on downriver. There was something beyond satisfaction, though. Unlike the runs back in Lodore, with Brian Rasmussen as adviser and safety net, this had been a strictly solo affair. So I exulted, too.

Three Fords Rapid marks the transition from Desolation to Gray Canyon, and there at the foot of the rapid I could see the geology of change. The towering walls of Desolation modulated within a few yards to lower and softer escarpments; from talus dotted with pine and juniper to gentler slopes no longer red but pale gray.

Gray Canyon is a trench the river has cut into deposits laid down twenty million years earlier than those of Desolation, and because these deposits erode more easily, the feel of the land changes. Its slopes are gentler, more rounded. They support smaller, skimpier plants. And as often happens in desert lands, you cannot see such plants from a distance. So the slopes looked bare.

For the two days I floated through Gray Canyon this pattern persisted, with variations. After a few miles the escarpments became taller, steeper, more staccato. The rock eased over from gray to pale yellow, even white; then to somber brown. But always, from a distance, the slopes looked bare.

Through this new country flowed the old river, playing familiar themes: whisper, chatter, clamor—then silence; glinting swirl, rumpled riffle, tumbling cataract—then gliding mirror. The river staged its customary wildlife cameos, too—featuring old players and new.

A great blue heron flapped away at my approach, suffered the intrusion, high and impatient, on a cliff-face rock ledge. A lone osprey waited me out on a snag in huffy, white-shirtfront dignity. Two quail-like birds scuttled into dense brush before I could confirm they were chukar. Two blue damselflies copulated on the raft's blue-and-white safety rope. As I pulled in toward a campsite, a doe and fawn, diaphanous in low-sun backlighting, held their ground until I was within a few yards, then ghost-melted away.

But my most startling—and echoic—wildlife meeting, all through Desolation and Gray, was one that never occurred.

Dark clouds had massed above the canyon walls, and as I drifted downriver in a postlunch stupor, wondering whether to take my siesta aboard, thunder began reverberating, rock wall to rock wall. Up on the rims, lightning struck. The clouds grew darker, more threatening. I could almost feel the rain hanging in wait.

The thunder moved closer. A clap exploded directly overhead. Downriver, deep in the gorge and not far away, lightning pierced the gloom. This time, I conducted no debate about whether sitting in an open, steel-framed vessel, the tallest object in a wide river, did or did not make me, even before rain started streaming off my bare legs, an impeccable lightning conductor: I pulled ashore, river left, grabbed a warm jacket and pants and waterproof dittos, jumped out onto the muddy bank, bow rope in hand. But even before I could take a few paces and tie the rope to a big bush, I stopped. Stood stock-still. There at my feet, deeply imprinted in the soft mud, sharp and compelling, were the tracks of a large animal.

The spoor were massive, distinctive: alternately triangular then stubby, with impressive claw marks. I'm a miserable tracker, but I knew at once what kind of animal had ambled down to the water's edge, apparently drunk its fill, then ambled away. I'd read in the river guide a report of ancient Indian dance rites, out in the Uinta Basin, performed "when bears wake from winter naps." The guide even showed pictures of bear tracks. I'd assumed, though, that both dance rites and bears were echoes from the past. But now, staring down at the tracks in the mud, I knew a bear had been here very recently indeed. I think I even looked, a little apprehensively, upstream and down.

Huge, cold raindrops hit my bare arms. The first of them began the slow, inevitable process of blurring the sharp outlines of the spoor at my feet. I moved on up the bank, ducked under the foliage of the big bush, tied the rope to its sturdy base, sat down and put on both the warm and the waterproof clothing. Outside the bush, the rain was now lashing down. I curled up, set confident course for sleep.

But something odd about the bear tracks kept gnawing at my mind. They had been totally unexpected; still seemed almost bizarrely out of place in that stark desert canyon. Yet there was something familiar about them. Something that echoed around my mind. And all at once, lying there warm and dry while the rain lashed down outside, I placed the echo.

After World War II, my first wife and I—married a year earlier—emigrated to Kenya. Another year, and we were co-managing an up-country hotel. Now, running a hotel—a job I'd failed to recognize as strictly not my line—keeps you tied firmly down. Almost never could both my wife and I be away at the same time. But each of us, separately, could now and again break free. At twenty-six I still half-believed the universe was a place created for young men to fish in, and one day I went with a fisherman friend named Leo on a long-planned trip down the banks of a highlands river. We started at an elevation of about 6000 feet, where the water still ran cool. Europeans had long before planted trout in the river, and we'd read that the trout could breed if the water temperature did not rise above 59 degrees Fahrenheit—and that the farther downstream you went, the bigger the trout grew. We therefore went, armed with a thermometer, in search of 59 degrees and the biggest damned trout in Africa.

We found no such fish. At the magic point, in fact, we found no trout at all. But just after we'd began to retrace our steps through the dry bush that bordered the river we stumbled on the carcass of a native cow. The animal's belly had been ripped open and a large portion of its flank gnawed away. Beside the half-eaten flank, the dusty soil was still wet from the spilled blood. Leo and I were standing together beside the carcass when we both saw, at the same moment, deeply imprinted in the soft, blood-soaked soil, clear and fresh and sobering, the print of a very large lion paw. The single spoor was so sharp and eloquent that we both swiveled our heads to scan the encircling bush. We could see nothing. Until then the bush had looked rather sparse, but now it seemed to offer a hundred hiding places for a disturbed and edgy lion. Warily, we resumed our homeward trek.

I had always remembered that one-day riverside safari. Above all, the moment when Leo and I stood together beside the gnawed cow carcass. And that single massive paw print in the blood-soaked soil had hung vivid in my mind, slightly blurred by the erosion of time but still riddled with hidden, unresolved meaning. When I ran into Leo again twenty years later he was a White Hunter.

Since Sand Wash, people had been rare.

Four days into Desolation, a raft-and-kayak party of four had hurried past. Otherwise, except for a few more brief meetings with Mike and Pom—when we exchanged only pleasantries but somehow seemed to establish temporary co-ownership of the river—I'd met no one. But late in the afternoon of my second day in Gray Canyon I looked up to see, tucked in among trees on the left bank, a vehicle and a tent. I checked the river guide. Indeed, a road. The end of a dirt road that wound up the canyon from the flatlands, now only eight miles downriver. I floated on, trying to subdue a surge of resentment. I knew it was ridiculous, but resentment always welled up, strong and acrid, when some innocent "intruded" into country that I had, often without realizing it, come to think of as "mine."

A couple of miles below the van-and-tent camp I heard the hum of a motor. It sounded too steady and striving to come from a land vehicle. I looked downriver: a motorboat, slicing up toward me. It came close, slowed. A small, outboard-driven dinghy. Three men. The one at the helm idled the motor, coasted up alongside within speaking range.

He wore gloves. "Seen any birds?" he asked.

I hesitated. Birders or hunters? A certain hawkishness beneath the peaked caps offered a hint.

"Not down here," I said. "But a ways back there was this white heron. Or maybe a cattle egret, I don't know."

The helmsman, sure enough, wasn't interested. "You been down this river before?"

"No."

"Usually see a lot of chukar partridge up here. But not this year."

I held my tongue. The man gunned his motor. The boat roared upstream. It left the air tainted.

I floated on. I could almost never see the dirt road—just a track, really—that the map showed as still snaking along the left bank. But it was always there, now.

Next day, in mid-morning, the canyon walls fell back and the river emerged into flatlands. We had come through a gap in the Book Cliffs—a spectacular escarpment, 250 miles long, that forms the southern and western flanks of the Tavaputs Plateau's uplifted bulk. Opposite Gunnison Butte—an eroded-away fragment of the Book Cliffs standing out on its own—I went ashore to say goodbye to Mike George and Pom Collins.

They were carrying their empty raft up to the top of the takeout ramp. They dumped it, came back down to their pile of unloaded gear.

Pom picked up a square cardboard box. "Say, how'd you like some bad wine? It wouldn't win any medals, but on the river it sure tasted good with dinner."

The George-Collins Expedition had more than lived up to their expectations. So had the river. Their only sadness lay in having to leave it. We exchanged addresses, chatted, compared notes on running rapids and on "owning" the river.

When I confessed to my resentment at seeing the van and tent in among the trees, Mike grinned. "I know what you mean," he said. "When I saw them my first reaction was 'How dare they? On *our* river?' "

Before I left, the local river guide who was to drive them to the airport arrived. I asked him about the diversion dam, now only a few miles downriver.

"Oh, shouldn't be a problem. The only question is whether there's enough water for you to go over. Haven't seen the river this low in twenty-five years. But if you do run it, make sure you pull right the moment you hit the bottom. There's a lot of bad stuff down below."

A couple of hours later I knew I was approaching the dam.

The river, which had already slowed to a dull flatlands waterway, widened into a minor lake. At its far end the water cut off straight and unnatural, beautiful yet ominous. And from this line emanated a steady sound that hung poised somewhere between a grumble and a whisper.

The wind had lulled, and the water in front of me stretched so placid that the dark line of bankside trees and the broken white clouds above them were mirrored in almost perfect replica. I rowed slowly forward, trying to encompass both beauty and challenge in a single embrace. And then, ahead, floating down from nowhere—catching my eye only in the last foot or two of its descent—there was a small pink balloon. It settled, very gently, on the mirrorlike water. The apparition was so unexpected and its touchdown so exquisitely soft that I stopped rowing.

The little balloon rode motionless, barely touching the water, directly between me and the center of the unnatural straight line that marked the end of the lake. Almost at once, I decided—not knowing quite why, and acknowledging the ridiculousness of all such things—that it could be nothing but a good omen.

Slowly, I rowed toward the balloon. It waited. I reached out, lifted it inboard. An ordinary pink child's balloon.

With it lying at my feet, I rowed even more slowly than before toward the unnatural line that marked the top of the diversion dam. Off to my left I could see a big wooden waterwheel, motionless; to the right, a brick wall and a square building.

Ahead, the lip suddenly close. White water began to appear, below and center. It growled now, rather than whispered.

We eased, bow-first, toward the lip. The lake began to gather itself into motion. The moving water was smooth, powerful.

At first I hung back, several feet from the brink, pulling gently on both oars to hold position. Then, gaining confidence, I eased us forward until our bow overhung the lip and I could look down along the surface of a sheet of glassy, racing water. It angled at about forty-five degrees, apparently clinging to the face of the dam. At the dam's base, perhaps ten vertical feet below, the sheet shattered into white turbulence. Beyond it, an ugly mass of protruding rocks. But the current flowed right, almost parallel to the dam, clear to the right bank. As far as I could see, the turbulence at the base of the dam was too small to pose a double-reversal-hydraulic threat.

I backed up a few feet to a point at which occasional oar pulls were enough to hold us in place. There, I sat and debated. That is, havered. First, the lip problem. I'd located what looked like the deepest flow of water over it; but how deep was it? If the raft grounded as we went over we'd probably swing broadside and might then break free, hurtle on down and flip as we hit the white turbulence. Second, the grounding-on-the-way-down problem. The results, though perhaps less dire, would be similar. But the only alternative to taking a chance on the water's depth seemed to be portaging. That would be a royal physical pain. Besides, the prospect now stuck in my craw.

As I sat there a few feet above the lip, pulling gently on the oars, havering away, my eye lit on the pink balloon bobbing about at my feet. I picked it up and—uncertain whether I was seeking information or dealing in omens or just procrastinating or simply having fun—dropped it overboard. Watching how it went over the dam might teach me something, I told myself: maybe I could see what ideas the balloon had on the subject. But the balloon did not move forward with the accelerating water. Instead it was caught by a breeze—a breeze so gentle that I could neither feel it nor see its effect on the water. But the balloon knew. The moment it touched the water it wafted off to the left. It gained speed, angling away from the dam. Helplessly, I watched it go. If anything, I decided, that had to be a bad omen: maybe the balloon had enough sense not to want to run the dam.

Eventually, though, I made up my own mind. I battened down—camera, binoculars, tape recorder, everything—moved us forward, aligned on the deepest water pouring over the lip, inhaled like a pitcher with the bases loaded, then pushed with both oars. The bow dropped. I looked directly down the sheet of racing water at the whiteness below.

Now, no turning back.

We went over the lip without touching. For a long, attenuated moment we were hurtling down the face of the dam, straight as a die. Just once, for a split second, the raft floor was grazing something. Then, still dead on course, the bow hit the white turbulence. We flounced over it without fuss. It was almost an anticlimax. Ahead, the dark rocks loomed. Quickly, I pivoted. Then I was pulling madly and we were careering along with the white water toward the right bank. A few strokes, and I knew we had it made.

By the time I reached the fringes of Green River, Utah, dusk was folding in over a calm and silvery evening.

It was a Saturday. If I went on into town I might fail to find a room in either of the two riverside motels. And I'd have to leave the raft moored beside the river, unguarded, all night. Besides, although the flossy urban delectables still beckoned—hot tub, beer, food served at a table and all the rest—their lure had dimmed. At that moment I felt in need of a decompression pause on the fringe, suspended between two worlds.

Once I'd camped, river right, trees hid a big road bridge, half a mile downstream, that I'd seen from out on the river. In the last of the light, while I cooked dinner, a patrolling beaver kept investigating me. When he drifted within conversation range, I said, "Hullo, beaver." He moved a few feet farther out into the current, then tail-slapped, decorously. A barely visible circle of ripples widened across the pale, silvery river. Night fell. Silence settled.

After dinner, I sat in the darkness, looking out over the blackness, still sipping a cup of Cabernet Sauvignon from Mike and Pom's plastic-pouched box. Yes, probably bad wine; but medals or no, in that place and at that time it indeed tasted good. In front of me, out in the blackness, the beaver intermittently slap-drummed aside the river silence. Off to my right, a scattering of lights flagged civilization. Closer, somewhere behind me, off in the urban darkness, a dance was going on, but all I could hear of the band was the bass line. Pom, pom, pom, pompompom—on and on, without variation. At ten o'clock, when I went to bed, the bass line was still booming away and the beaver was still intermittently tail-drumming.

Next morning the beaver was back, patrolling the resilvered river, re-investigating. But the human dance was long over. By now, probably, only hangovers lingered. I rowed down to the bridge, moored on the left bank just below a new and still uncompleted building, walked up to the first motel.

11

TIME OUT

Green River, Utah

Green River

Crystal
Geyser

Labyrinth

Canyon

0   10
MILES

Mile 618 to Mile 633
September 17–21

Four days passed before I returned to the river.

The first two days I holed up in a motel and reveled in the flossy delectables. I soaked in a tub, sipping beer, until wrinkling set in, and it was almost as good as I'd hoped. In the motel restaurant I ate food served at a table, and the food was awful and the wine worse than the wine in Mike and Pom's plastic-keg gift. I switched to cooking in my room.

Encaved there, back among walls and fingertip electricity, culture-shocked out of my gourd, I switched on the TV. Civilization just kept rolling along. Beirut still bled. The Tienanmen Square massacre still reverberated. Catholics and Jews were on warpaths over a convent at Auschwitz. But a thirty-three-year-old outdoorsman, paralyzed four years earlier in a motorcycle accident, petitioning for the right to turn off the ventilator that kept him alive—because he had "nothing left to enjoy"—had won. And I watched Joe Montana engineer one of his routine miracles for a last-minute Forty-Niner win. In other words, the old human story: as individuals, so much greatness and glory, so much to love; in bulk, so gross, so much to deplore.

Meanwhile, outside, a storm raged. Through a window I watched the rain lash down and felt no urge to leave my cave. But gradually I emerged from the maladjustment daze and began to grapple with administrative chores: paperwork; re-sorting my river gear now strewn around the room; much phoning.

Several real things happened, though, in Green River, Utah.

The second day, the Canyonlands National Park river ranger came to check, as regulations demanded, the adequacy of my equipment. Dave Stimson turned out to be a human first, a bureaucrat second. We inspected the raft, stored at the nearby Holiday River Expeditions headquarters, walked back to the motel to look at my still-strewn gear, then sat and talked about the river.

Dave confirmed that the next leg of my journey would at first echo the pattern established by Uinta Basin–Desolation–Gray. A couple of days across flatlands; a long and beautiful stretch, free of rapids, through Labyrinth and Stillwater Canyons. Then the confluence with the Colorado, and Cataract Canyon. Finally, Lake Powell.

With the water so low, Cataract's rapids would pose a stiff technical challenge but shouldn't be too horrifying—except at the end. "The last rapid's Lower Big Drop," said Dave. He smiled. "That'll be your first Holy Shit rapid. When you see it, you'll say, 'Holy Shit, am I going through *that*?' "

The third day the sun shone and I made my first contact with the river since trailering the raft up to Holiday's headquarters. A building across the road from the motel—the uncompleted structure I'd seen from the river—turned out to be a John Wesley Powell History Museum. I walked over. As I came up beside the still-empty shell I saw that the rain had turned the river deep red-brown—and there surged up in me a longing to be once more floating down it.

I stood at one corner of the museum, thinking that it promised to be an attractive place, half my mind watching the river. The museum's sidewall blocked my upstream view and the river flowed, as it were, out of the masonry. Without warning there materialized from this masonry, in midriver, a raft. It was a gray raft, a size bigger than mine, carrying a young man and woman. I felt a mild puff of surprise. Most raft parties took out opposite Gunnison Butte, as Mike and Pom had done; and this young couple didn't look like locals on a day trip—though something about the raft or their relaxed and competent air suggested they felt at home on the river. As I stood there, wondering, the woman looked up, directly at me. I waved. She waved back. Then the raft vanished under the big road bridge.

The fourth day I checked out of the motel. But reloading the raft at Holiday Expedition headquarters took longer than expected. The helpful people there not only invited me to stay overnight but ran film clips from Buzz Holmstrom's second river journey, in 1938, when he traveled solo in the same boat, accompanied by a movie-cameraman in a raft. The film revealed a compact, no-nonsense man who handled his boat with competence—and understood the river. In the journal of his solo 1937 trip, just before making the final symbolic gesture of bumping his bow into the huge, hated wall of recently completed Hoover Dam, he wrote:

> *Some people have said I conquered the Colorado. I don't say so. It has never been conquered and never will, I think. Anyone whom it allows to go thro its canyons and see its wonders should feel thankful and privileged. . . .*
>
> *The river probably thought, "He is such a lonesome, ignorant, unimportant and insignificant pitiful little creature, with such a short time to live, that I will let him go this time and try to teach him something." . . . It has been less kind to many prouder people than I.*

There was more, too. River historians tend to dismiss Holmstrom—the only other person to have run long whitewater reaches solo—as inconsequential. I began to see I'd been right to be intrigued by him.

Next morning the professional Holiday boatman who had trailered my raft up from the river—Karen Nelson, a statuesque blonde with a mind and niche of her own—trailered it back again. As we drove down to the launching ramp below the bridge we discussed the flatlands immediately ahead. "Oh, for the first two days," said Karen, "just keep your eyes closed."

A few minutes before nine o'clock on that fifth morning, under a sky laundered brilliant blue, I cast off from the ramp, waved to Karen, pulled out into the river.

It was good to be back. Good to be back in the billowing blue raft, enveloped by sunlight and space and silence; back where everything fitted, connected. The river was turbid and brown now, underneath, but its surface gleamed. We floated on down, blue and billowy, brown yet gleaming, quiet, connected. And I, at the center, tanned and lean, refreshed, eager.

Any long journey benefits from a break of the kind I'd taken in Green River, Utah.

First, your body needs a rest. When Karen came down to trailer my raft up from the river she'd pointed at my river-runner's sandals and smiled and said, "Ah yes, I can see you've been on the river a long time. Look at the way your skin's cracked. Especially around the heels. For us, it's an occupational hazard. Alkaline river water. We find the best stuff to put on is Bag Balm. Meant for cow's udders, but works great."

Your body needs respite from the sun, too. And from toil.

Above all, though, your mind needs time out. It probably doesn't matter much just what it does during the limbo-time so long as it gets a change. A total change. Then, when you come back to the journey, you find you're rejuvenated, impatient to discover what lies ahead.

You pay a tariff, of course, for such rejuvenation. All wilderness travelers know about the kind of maladjustment I'd suffered in the motel room—a maladjustment that you have to work through every time you return to the flasheries of civilization. Most people have heard of the "culture shock" (as distinct from jet lag) that you're liable to suffer if you transfer abruptly from, say, New York to Beijing, let alone rural China. Well, a switch from wilderness to the fleshpots is far more disruptive: a leap from an absence of culture into a streamlined one. But what most people fail to realize is that the reverse switch creates a mirror havoc. After a pause among the realities of civilization you need time to readjust to wilderness realities.

(Dedicated urbanites "know" beyond shadow of doubt—because doubt never raises its disturbing head—that civilization is the real world: you only "escape" to wilderness. When you're out and away and immersed, you "know" the obverse: the wilderness world is real, the human world a superimposed facade. But when you're suspended between the two realities you may hang in transient uncertainty. The controversy is, of course, spurious. Neither view can stand alone. Both worlds are real. But the wilderness world is certainly older and will almost certainly last longer. Besides, the second view seems far healthier for a human to embrace.)

Anyway, that first day below Green River, Utah, as I floated downriver—sun beating on skin, hot but welcome—I felt, though deliciously rejuvenated, screened off from the roundest realities of the river world by an invisible curtain. I knew I'd need time to readapt. The question was how much time.

I floated on. Even in my suspended state, I had trouble going along with Karen's "just keep your eyes closed" fiat.

The map indeed showed flatlands on each flank. But they were rarely visible. The river flowed between low bluffs—sometimes pale brown, sometimes charcoal gray—and they cut off all vistas. But the bluffs themselves, though unimposing by Green River standards, ran charming permutations on brownness and texture. If this leg of my journey did in fact turn out to echo the previous one, then perhaps all echoes would be raised an octave. Once, looking downstream at a tapering line of bluffs, I said aloud to present scenery and absent Karen, "Oh, but you should have seen the Uinta Basin!"

Still, it was clear enough why she'd warned me. Compared with some riverscapes I'd passed through—and no doubt with those ahead—the intermittent brown bluffs were humdrum. In twenty or thirty miles, only one "feature" disputed the monotony.

Four miles downriver I came to "Crystal Geyser"—proclaimed by a swath of riverside rock stained garish red-brown. The river guide said the geyser was no natural phenomenon but "an unplugged well unsuccessfully drilled for oil in 1936. Gases seeping into the well bore cause the 'geyser' to erupt periodically." I did not stop.

This sub-spectacle aside, the bluffs screened off the broader scene—so long as I stayed on the river.

But late on the first day, fifteen miles below Green River—just after we'd crossed the 4000-foot elevation mark—I pulled in at a narrow rock ledge on the right bank. And when I'd set up camp I climbed the bluff behind the ledge.

At its lip I moved out into a different world. It was a world that people unsensitized to desert tend to find about as attractive as a bomb-cratered parking lot. Understandably so. The landscape now spread out before me for a mile or more in every direction—away from the river and also back across it—indeed resembled rubble. Rubble that had been gouged into basins and gullies. Rubble that had mostly been pounded into small fragments. But rubble that was punctuated, here and there, by slabs of what could have been the scattered masonry from some razed but once monumental edifice. The color of this rubble, in spite of the setting sun's warm glow, was a pale, almost uniform, uninspiring gray-brown. And yet . . . It wasn't only that the last of the sun's rays cast mysterious shadows into the basins and gullies; not only that they etched elegant black wedges among the tilted slabs and rougher rock piles; not only that behind mesas and hillocks and escarpments they projected long and lengthening parallelograms and pyramids and broad, enshrouding night-blankets. Even without these pungent eventide embellishments, the dead-looking plateau lilted with life.

Once you know what to look for, this kind of desert always does. If you doubt it, you need only glance down at your feet. Around them, you discover, the blank, uncaring landscape simmers with intricate stony detail and supports stubborn clumps of low-growing greenery. When you let your eye lift again you find you can once more see only bare rock. But your brain, behind the eye, now knows that the rock is anything but bare, anything but dead.

Perhaps I've suggested that you cannot feel the pull of such landscapes unless you've been pre-sensitized. But the first time I walked out into such country (and walking is the key—if you drive, the car imprisons you behind an invisible wall) I found that after the initial shock I had fallen in love. In part, I think, it was the sheer starkness: the landscape's clear and total lack of concern for anything so recent and flippant as humanity. That, and its abstract beauty. For some reason I was lucky enough to be able to accept these things at my first real exposure to desert (thirty years earlier, a thousand miles downstream). But many people need time to adjust.

Some never do. Once you accept it, though, such desert always soothes your soul.

That evening I climbed the bluff behind my camp, I wandered for less than an hour through its glorious, rubbled nothingness. And I did nothing except stroll. Nothing you could call thinking. But when I came back to the lip of the sloping bluff and looked down at the little blue raft and my simple camp on the gray rock ledge far below, all now deep in shadow, I knew that already I'd begun to recross the barrier between man-world and river-world. And once you begin that passage, things move.

I scrambled down the bluff, dined. Afterward I sat looking past the tethered raft, out across the silent, still gleaming river. Beyond a strip of greenery along its far bank stood a line of low cliffs. I had registered with a corner of my mind the cliffs' slow evening mutation: from mundane grayish-white, through a pink that never quite achieved alpenglow, to a soft and restful gray. But now, as I sat watching, the cliffs rekindled. Began to burn with an almost incandescent brilliance. For a suspended interlude they stood out in startling contrast above the strip of riverside greenery. Then the whole scene faded. The cliffs subsided into no color at all. The greenery turned black. The raft was now black, too. But the whispering river still gleamed, very faintly, in the last lingerings of day.

I slid into my sleeping bag. At that moment the things that loom so large in the outside world—the loves and unloves, the friendships and quarrels, the successes and failures—seemed very small, very distant, almost petty.

I was back.

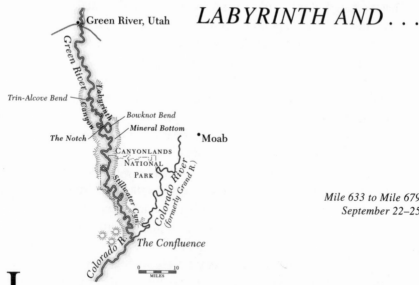

12

LABYRINTH AND . . .

Green River, Utah

Green River

Labyrinth Canyon

Trin-Alcove Bend

Bowknot Bend

Mineral Bottom

The Notch

•Moab

CANYONLANDS NATIONAL PARK

Stillwater Cyn.

Colorado River (formerly Grand R.)

Colorado R.

The Confluence

Colorado R.

0   10
MILES

Mile 633 to Mile 679
September 22–25

Late next afternoon the crumbly brown riverside bluffs gave way to solid red sandstone, low at first but quickly gaining stature. Soon, rock walls enfolded us. We floated on through the opening notes of Labyrinth Canyon, prelude to the Colorado Plateau.

We would slice through this massive plateau for six hundred miles, the river and I, until—in a heightened echo of our passage through the Tavaputs Plateau and our emergence from Desolation-Gray through a gap in the Book Cliffs—we passed through a gap in the Grand Wash Cliffs and emerged at last from Grand Canyon.

Before long I heard echoes within these heightened echoes.

Labyrinth, even more than most canyons, resonates with theme and variation.

(If you feel I'm going overboard on "themes and variations," remember that every river journey is built on repetition. Day after day, evening after morning, camping and uncamping sound the bass line. And the river's sights and sounds, inevitably and up to a point, reprise. The essence of the journey may lie in differences between its days, but the underlying structure remains: themes and variations.)

Above all, Labyrinth was labyrinthine. On the map it writhed with the exaggerated, improbable sinuosity of a sidewinder rattlesnake scaling a sand dune, and in rockbound reality that meant its constant corkscrews were flanked by alternate cliff and flatland. Cliffs on the outside of each sweeping curve, where the swirling river bit into solid rock. Flatland on the curve's inner flank, where at high water the slower-moving current had deposited silt. These deposits now formed elongated crescents of bottom-land, and the river guide showed them stretching out ahead one after the other at irregular intervals: Bull Bottom, Junes Bottom, Tenmile Bottom, Keg Spring Bottom. Because no bottomland was the same as the last, no cliff identical to its predecessor, the river kept playing me variations on these, its current prime themes: sheer red rock faces; then flat green-fringed bottomland. And because of our labyrinthine path the light was al-ways changing key.

The river now ran swift but smooth, broken only by rare, mild riffles, and there was time for me to lean back and look. I floated on down, con-tent—and awed. For the mighty rock walls imposed a new solemnity on our passage. I'm not altogether sure what I mean by "solemnity," but any-one who has moved slowly though such a place will understand.

My contentment owed something to relief. From the earliest planning days, Labyrinth and Stillwater had intrigued me. I couldn't say just why: I knew very little about them. But they'd hung golden in my mind, and as I moved down into Labyrinth I was afraid I'd meet a serious expectancy barrier.

From the start, though, Labyrinth was beautiful. Stillwater turned out to be, if anything, even more magnificent. And for a hundred miles—until I reached the confluence of Green and Colorado—the canyons became my majestic home, through which I floated with delight.

There can be stretches of life that stand out in memory not so much be-cause of the place you lived—pleasing as that home may have been—but because of nearby places you visited. And for all the beauty of Labyrinth and Stillwater, what really moved my journey forward, day after sunlit day, was not so much the canyons themselves as the sidetrips. They echoed the Desolation sidetrips but were longer and more illuminating. Four times they lifted me up out of my canyon world.

The first sidetrip was one I had long planned.

The previous evening I'd landed in Trin-Alcove Bend, at the mouth of a right-bank side canyon, and the camp—my first in Labyrinth—got off to a good start.

As I rowed the last few feet toward the greenery that fringed the canyon's little delta I saw, no more than half a dozen paces up the damp creek bed, framed to perfection by overarching tamarisks and backlit by the low sun, a doe. Just for a moment she stood poised, statuesque, haloed. Then she'd turned and bounded away, kicking up spurts of wet sand. And what enhanced this echo (though this time there was no fawn) and made it a notch more satisfying was that the doe, unlike the pair back in Desolation, had seemed wholly wild—the sharp edges of its instincts unblunted by frequent human contact.

Then there were the footprints. Now, footprints, especially near a place I plan to camp, normally depress me. May even turn me away. But when, before setting up camp, I walked a few yards up the massive trench dug by three converging side canyons and saw fresh prints in wet sand—the footprints of two people—I wondered whether they could have been made by the young couple I'd seen float past as I stood beside the John Wesley Powell History Museum. It seemed entirely likely. They'd had the look of people making a long journey: confident or settled or unhurried or something like that. As I walked back to camp I decided, to my surprise, that it would be pleasant to meet them.

John Wesley Powell's journal reported that he'd climbed to the rim on the opposite bank and found a remarkable view—and this was one Powell sidetrip that, along with another down near the Confluence, I wanted to echo. That evening, in camp, I studied the escarpment opposite. Although it rose close to four hundred vertical feet, most of the rock seemed to slope fairly gently.

Now, it's easy to misjudge a slope when you look directly at it, so I applied a lesson I'd learned from Powell's journal, years before: I turned my head on one side. That way, I could differentiate much more clearly between the slope's varying degrees of steepness. The reason this maneuver works, of course, is that with your head held upright—and eyes therefore displaced laterally—your stereoscopic vision and depth perception work well on a horizontal plane but hardly at all vertically. When you turn your head on one side, though, and realign your eyes vertically, the reverse becomes true. And looking across Trin-Alcove Bend with head tilted sideways I found I could indeed interpret the facing slope more accurately. Before long I'd picked out a seemingly straightforward route. With one exception: a few questionable feet up one short pitch.

After breakfast next morning I rowed across the river, moored the raft and begun to push through a fringe belt of greenery. It turned out to be a far more formidable barrier than it had looked. Deeper, too. For ten sweaty minutes I crouch-and-crawl-struggled through a thicket of intermeshing tamarisk saplings. The thicket had burned, years back, and blackened branches interlaced the new growth. By the time I at last emerged on the far side, my thin river-runner clothing and all skin left uncovered by it were streaked with grime. I stood for a moment, looking back at the dense greenery. A few short, dead-end tunnelways suggested that even the local deer used it only for hideouts and didn't attempt to push all the way through. But I appreciated this modern barrier (in Powell's day, tamarisk had not begun to invade the river): beyond it there was no sign of humanity. For people who value solitude, that enriches a place.

The lower rock slope indeed posed no problem, and the questionable pitch turned out to be surmountable without serious difficulty—going up. But when I'd climbed it I paused, wondering whether I'd be able to get back down or should look for an alternate return route. And standing there in skimpy clothing, carrying nothing, I suddenly felt unprotected, almost naked. Inept, too. Dangerously incompetent.

Solo wilderness travel—if it's your bag—offers priceless bonuses. But it imposes constraints. When you're traveling alone, if you've got any sense, you exercise a tinge more care than if you had company. Any mistake is likely to prove serious; a major mistake will likely be your last. So you try to make no mistakes at all. You exercise particular care when you wander any considerable distance from your mobile home—backpack, raft or whatever. If something goes wrong while you're away you will, with no one to help, have to rely on what you're carrying. You therefore make sure you carry—in pockets or belt-bag or small day pack—a few basics tailored to suit the terrain and the distance you'll be going: water, emergency food, alarm whistle, small first-aid kit. For years I'd routinely taken such precautions. But that morning my guard had slipped. The only change I'd made in normal river wear was to slip out of river-runner sandals into lightweight competitive-runner camp shoes. And now, standing at the top of that short rock pitch, feeling suddenly naked, I resolved that on all but very short sidetrips from the raft—and perhaps on those too—I'd exercise better judgment. Then I turned and went on up the sloping rock.

Before long I stepped up onto its crest—and stopped short. "My God!" I blurted to the space spectacular. "What a view!"

(If you regard my words as sacrilege, remember that I was invoking *my* God. If you think your God would take umbrage, I can offer only sympathy. My God—a hypothesis that remains iffy—is something rather like a Space-Age Pan, and It would certainly not object to my invocation. Would, I'm sure, approve.)

Minutes must have passed, there at the crest, before I did anything but stand and stare.

A lifetime of wilderness walking has made me reasonably blasé about spectacular views from high places. But Powell's report—its details long rusted from my mind—had not prepared me for what I now saw. And there was something else. For more than two months I had lived in the river world. Mostly, it had been a recessed world, enclosed, cut off. It was therefore a shock to come up onto a not particularly high place and discover without warning that after the months of incarceration—delicious incarceration, and voluntary, but still incarceration—I could on that clear day apparently see forever. For long minutes I stood motionless. This, I told myself, is how the world was meant to be.

I'd sensed the same primitive, untouched quality before, on virgin East African savannah. But savannah is "ancient" only if measured on our human scale. And for all its primitiveness, it is clothed. The landscape now spread out before me looked almost shockingly ancient. And it was unclothed. Was rock entire. Naked rock that at first glance seemed to reach out flat and endless to every horizon. Red rock and pink rock. Then interleaving beds of brown rock and rock that was almost white.

Once I had embraced the huge flatness and let my mind accept that there were limits to it, there were other colors, too. Along the horizon that at first had seemed unbroken ran low escarpments—low at such vast distances—that were sometimes pink and sometimes, where shadow fell, a pale, ethereal desert blue. But even when my mind had encompassed these distant ramparts the spectacle remained rock entire. A rock spectacle that seemed to have emerged from the planet's early history, long before land animals, let alone mammals or man, were even a gleam in evolution's eye.

And this ancient panorama spoke with vivid eloquence. Its rocks did not span the vast eons of the Grand Canyon strata; but here, because the landscape stretched flat and layered, I found it easier to picture sand being blown across ancient dunes and deposited in ancient hollows, grain after grain, until the hollows had filled and the level sand was ready for the weight and heat and countless years that would convert it into sandstone. Or perhaps the sand had been deposited in an ancient sea, grain on grain, intermittently, over millions of years. At that moment it didn't matter which scientific story might prove true. What mattered was the huge expanse of rock clasped inert in this blip of time—not just the blip during which I stood motionless but also the blip during which I lived, the blip during which our species had lived. What mattered was this huge expanse of rock that lay clasped—inert, as if dead—in glaring light and echoing time. Only the recessed river, far below, winding brown and green-fringed, seemed alive—and also a giver of life.

I lingered for an hour on the plateau, photographing, moseying. Slowly, I pried beneath my initial impression that the panorama was nothing but flat, unbroken rock. My eyes began to see more than the distant escarpments. Saw scattered red sandstone tablelands, even a few conical red hillocks, smooth and saucy, pert but pimply. And at my feet, as always, the desert leaped into life: once, nestling in an alcove, a pebble collection, each exhibit rounded, each with different texture, each desert-varnished to a distinctive shade of brown, and the cluster vitalized by a single white marble maverick. I even stumbled on two human remembrancers: an inlaid metal marker, "US General Land Office Survey, 1911"; and six inches of rusty wire, undated. But when, just before leaving, I stood and once more embraced the whole wide, pure-rock panorama it still exuded an air of being undiscovered by man. Certainly unsullied by him.

Intellectually, I knew we were present. A mere stone's throw across that immense openness, no more than twenty straight-line miles away, down in one of its major but invisible crevices, ran a highway and a railroad, even the town of Moab. A year earlier, on my 4000-mile reconnaissance, I'd driven along the highway. But I hadn't seen the plateau. Had not been truly aware of it. In such country we moderns tend to operate below the surface, like termites.

On the map, the space between me and the hidden road looked innocent of human intervention. It seemed sad that I found this a merciful state of affairs. I sighed, then surveyed the panorama again, and smiled. That wide, clean world proclaimed, in the clear voice of its innocence and beauty, a confidence that we—this unique spearhead species with breathtaking potential—would not dream of fouling it.

(I should have known better. Even while I stood there, oil interests were

Above Trin-Alcove Bend. The panorama "rock entire."
"Only the recessed river, far below, winding brown and
green-fringed, seemed alive—and also a giver of life."

burrowing in, seeking carte blanche to carve networks of new roads across the pristine desert so that they could drill and extract—and foul the place with industrial detritus. They're still burrowing.

Their advocates see—or pretend to see—such action as sensible, even heroic. Ron Arnold, co-founder of the "Wise Use" Coalition recently said: *"Our goal is to destroy, to eradicate the environmental movement. . . . We want to be able to exploit the environment for private gain, absolutely . . . and we want people to understand that this is a noble goal."*

We are indeed a wonderful and unique species—with stunning potential.)

At last I turned and walked back down, following an easy though wide-sweeping route that my moseying had revealed. Half an hour later I was once more floating seaward.

The river flowed smooth and simple, complicated only by swirls and side currents. Soon, the bounding red cliffs began to grow taller. When I looked up at their glorious, solemn, blue-varnished rock faces, the rims seemed very far away. And above the rims I could see only a narrowing strip of bright blue sky. But my mind's eye no longer stopped short at the rim. My river world stretched wider, now.

Two evenings later I made another sidetrip.

Once again I climbed four hundred vertical feet. But because the canyon now cut deeper, the plateau remained far above me. The star, this time, was the river. It flowed along the wings yet held center stage.

I had camped soon after five o'clock at the pivot of Bowknot Bend, where Labyrinth Canyon outdoes itself: by meandering in two curves so serpentine that on the map they look like the loops of a bow tie, it flows eleven miles yet travels a straight-line distance of barely one. I'd camped at the place you would knot the tie.

After I'd set up camp there was enough daylight left for a quick trip up to the Notch—low point in the isthmus of rock separating my camp from the place, four hundred horizontal yards away, at which the river, after a seven-mile swing around Bowknot Bend, completed the second part of its knot.

A twenty-minute climb up a steep trail, through layered gray sedimentary rocks, and I stood in the Notch. Massive red sandstone now soared up on either side. Scrawled near its base was a "register" of visitors' names; but the panorama swamped all thought of artifacts.

Behind me, low evening sunlight beamed directly down the canyon, along the stretch of river I'd already traveled. It illuminated in whetted detail each curving sandbar, each variation in the river's fringe of greenery. It demarcated with floodlight clarity the sloping gray-brown sedimentary rock from the sheer sandstone laid over it; made the combination look like a gluttonously thick slab of red icing on a crumbly cake.

But the riveting perspective lay on the far side of the Notch, along the river I had yet to travel. I could see very little of Bowknot Bend, off to the left. But to my right, far below, river and canyon for two miles cut straight and true. The river ran silver from the sky's reflection, twisting among sandbars. Low sunlight, slanting across the gorge, left all but the rock's far rim in shadow. Even in the deepest of this shadow the geology was there; but what mattered was the beauty.

In beautiful places, as I've said, thought can be an impediment to pleasure. Can even contaminate it. There at Bowknot Notch, looking down and along the massive trough that held the river not yet traveled, I don't think I did much thinking. It was enough to look. To absorb the colors and lineaments and conformations of rock and river. Then watch them change. For as the sun sank, rock and river underwent transformation. No sudden or drastic conversion. Just subtle shifts of emphasis. A gentle darkening. Slow seepage from day toward night.

All too soon, with the transformation still unfulfilled, it was time to leave. I let my eyes run over it all. The last sunbeams lit only a thin, pale sliver of red rock along the far rim. Below, except for the sandbar-studded river, the shadows held no detail, no color except a profound blue-blackness. But now that there was no more geology, there was more than geology. The blue-black mass of the rock and the silver lanyard of the river not only stood in vivid contrast; they generated an almost tangible tension.

I pried my eyes free, started back down the darkening trail.

Many people, I knew, had climbed to the Notch. Among them, Buzz Holmstrom. I wondered if what he saw from that place contributed in some special way to an entry near the end of his journal:

Sometimes I feel sorry for the river. It works every second of the ages carving away at the rocks, digging its canyons. It carries a million tons of silt a day. And again, I feel sorry for the mountains, with the river gnawing at their inside, but I guess my sympathy doesn't seem very important to either of them.

Buzz climbed to the Notch, from the downriver side, on October 26, 1937. His scanty notes for that day report only superficialities. But he is not alone in such thin at-the-time reportage. Because the big, vivid things hang clear in your mind, and perhaps in your camera, you tend to jot down only specific, easily forgotten details. Besides, it's often not until later that you can grasp what you really felt about the big, vivid thing. And in Buzz's journal, sure enough, his inner thoughts emerge, by and large, only at the very end.

It's doubtful that Archibald MacLeish ever stood at Bowknot Notch, but he knew about the tension I sensed there. In his short poem "What Any Lover Learns" he wrote:

> *River does not run.*
> *River presses its heavy silver self*
> *Down into stone and stone refuses.*
> *What runs,*
> *Swirling and leaping into sun, is stone's*
> *Refusal of the river, not the river.*

Next morning, in perfect weather, I began the swing around Bowknot Bend that promised to take most of the day but would bring us back to the far side of the Notch, barely four hundred horizontal yards from our starting point.

As I rowed unhurriedly downstream, the early sun struck warm on my bare arms. River and rock curled out ahead, unfolding that day's themes and variations—old and new, prime and subsidiary.

Up on the rock walls—each wall different from its cousins yet echoing them—time and manganese and iron had drawn blue washes of desert varnish, some tenuous and delicate, some broad and bold, some exquisite, all stupendous, each distinctive. Then there were the alcoves. At intervals along the rock walls' rims, millennia of rain and snow and frost and wind had gouged notches—each a typical sandstone alcove, each exclusive. Curious little rock spires often rimmed these rim-top alcoves—each spire bent-head-shaped, yet each unique. The shifting light rang changes on all these motifs. And when the light was right, they echo-reflected in the smoothly flowing river.

I floated slowly onward, savoring the strips of greenery and the sculptured rock walls with their varnished blue murals and red adornments, relishing the silence that enveloped them.

That morning, I seemed even more aware than usual of the silence.

It had begun, I think, in camp. Before packing my camp shoes I banged their soles together to remove the dust, and the sound reverberated—and went on echoing, echoing, echoing, growing slowly fainter until the silence flowed back in. My awareness resurfaced almost as soon as I'd pushed off: floating with a gentle downriver breeze, I half-shipped the oars through their oarlocks—and heard the mild rattle echo back from canyon walls. The river's occasional surface whirls made no sound; but when we passed over them I could sometimes, even when rowing, hear whispers along the bottom of the raft. When I rowed, I did so easily, gently, and the oars made only cat's-paw sounds. At one point, while changing film and moving nothing but fingers, I became aware of a faint rhythmic creaking that I felt sure must originate in the raft. I sat very still. The sound did not come from seat or oars or anything else I could pinpoint. At last I realized that it was drifting in from my right. On the bank, a sizable tree trunk had been washed downriver and lodged in a dead bush, and it was moving up and down with the current—constantly, rhythmically, like a grasshopper oil rig—and the creaking came from the rub of tree against bush, wood against wood.

We swung south into the Bend's middle stretch and the sun beat full in my face—no longer warm but hot. I floated on down. It occurred to me why I had heard the faint sounds, inboard and out.

In the five days since leaving Green River, Utah, I'd shared the river with no one. Had seen no one. And I'd traveled companionless. In a group, even a group of two, you're mostly screened off from subtle sounds. Are deaf to the silence. Alone, you can hear.

Solo travel confers other advantages, of course. On a practical level, it eliminates all danger of the bickerings and petty politics and even challenges to leadership that tend to afflict groups. And although group wilderness travel can to some extent bathe away the rush and fragmentation of civilization, solitude works its therapies more quickly, more surely, more profoundly. And its specific rewards reach beyond that. Buzz Holmstrom understood:

> *I know I have got more out of this trip by being alone than if I was with a party, as I have more time, especially at night, to listen and look and think and wonder about the grandeur that surrounds me, rather than to listen to talk of war, politics and football scores.*

Overhead, two ravens kraaaked by, close. A single magpie slanted black and white and silent against red rock. I rowed on, letting my mind run.

There was a flip side to solo travel, of course. A sour side. If you're not careful you can wrap the cloak of solitude too securely. Can wrap it so tight that it constricts. Self-protection may leak over into paranoia.

And not only in individuals. Later, I read in *The Beatles, a Yogi, and the Search for Plants* by Roger Di Silvestro:

> *Psychologists know that individuals who become obsessed with themselves, with their own concerns and problems, are following a hazardous path to neurosis and other pathologies. What is true for the individual is true for the species. As a species, we have through history tended single-mindedly to our own desires and aspirations with little concern for how*

our actions affect the many species that sustain us. We can see where this is leading—we can see the grasslands turning to desert, the polluted waters, the fallen forests. Like a self-absorbed individual, we as a species have become dysfunctional, and we have moved toward collapse. By learning about the workings of the nonhuman world—by learning what a plant really is, and what it needs to survive, and how we help or hinder it—we can better understand and more wisely use the natural systems that support us, and we can build for ourselves a healthier, more enduring future.

As far as individuals go, much depends on your point of view. There are two words we commonly use to describe the state of being alone. "Solitude" and "loneliness" announce the same physical condition. Only subjective attitudes differ.

I pulled in for lunch, snatched a few minutes with the book I was now reading, napped, rowed on. The book had almost certainly helped trigger my day's train of thought.

Solitude: A Return to the Self by Anthony Storr, a psychiatrist of renown, is an antidote to the tendency in our current Western society to label those who delight in solitude as maladjusted. Sigmund Freud proclaimed that you could judge well-adjusted people by their success in personal relationships. Dr. Storr, who once shared this view, suggests that an equally valid criterion of maturity, at least for some people, is whether they're able, even eager, to spend long periods alone. A healthy minority will, I'm sure, embrace his alternative gospel. Count me—how did you guess?—in.

Count me in on many scores. Dr. Storr comments positively on the value of long solo journeys or vigils as means of gaining a sense of unity and harmony with the cosmos. But he also recognizes the ill repute in which loners tend to be held. I know. I've been described, in writing, as "a smug curmudgeon who travels the wilds not because he loves nature but because he dislikes people." Drivel. But conversations sometimes rumble along the same lines:

"So you don't like people?"

"Well, it depends where I'm looking from."

"Looking *from*?"

"Yes. When I'm entirely inside the human bubble—as I mostly am, more or less—then my answer's selective. A few people, I'm very fond of indeed. A fair number, I find overwhelmingly pleasant. And a very considerable number, I find pleasant on the whole and, on balance, valid organisms. But I can't honestly say I go for people in bulk, the way we're routinely exhorted to go for them."

"Oh."

"And when I'm sort of outside the human bubble—when I've been away from civilization on my own for a longish spell and am looking at humanity from the outside, insofar as that's possible, and can see all too clearly what we're doing to the poor bloody planet that's our home, then I confess I have difficulty in saying I like us. As an undifferentiated mass, I mean. We're a fascinating breed all right—apparently unique and riddled with potential. But oh, it seems sad, and tragic, that we're falling so excruciatingly short of that potential. Perilously short. Maybe even suicidally short."

By this time I've lost my audience. I descend from the pulpit.

But the solitude cockpit always squirls. There are those who would say, and also those who like hell would not say, "Keep your eye on young people who spend a lot of time on their own—they may make something of their lives." And some people are simply not suited to being alone for long. Again, a loner can alienate people when he erects what he or she regards as necessary defenses. I know one man who certainly qualifies. Along the shruburban road that leads to his house you pass several "Beware of the Dog" signs and one that warns "Beware of the Cat." In his garden, nailed to a trellis at insistent eye-level for anyone who approaches his door, a sign reads:

BEWARE OF THE MAN!
HE IS PARANOID ABOUT PRIVACY.
Jehovah's Witnesses and other
salesmen will, like all insensitive
intruders, be EMASCERATED.

Below, a black fingerprint bears the label "God."

You'll understand, I'm sure, that this man would object to my revealing the location of his home and castle. His name? I take the Fifth.

The river curved around into the final stretch of Bowknot Bend, and soon I could see, high and right, a familiar red saddle. As we moved closer I kept looking up at a distinctive pinnacle at one end of the saddle and at the little notch between it and the main red cliff—the Notch in which I had stood and gazed down and along the huge, shadow-filled trough of the river not yet traveled.

The Notch was still some way off, but I kept glancing up at it with something suspiciously like instant nostalgia, and during one check my eye caught, up there beside the pinnacle, a flicker of movement. Even before I lifted my binoculars I saw that the creature in the V of the Notch stood upright and was predominantly blue, and although I didn't have my mammal identification book handy I made the identification at once, and beyond reasonable doubt. The binoculars confirmed. Pale blue shirt, gray slacks, broad-brimmed hat. And the figure stood gazing downriver, just as I had. A single hurried telephoto shot; then the figure had vanished and once more I had the river to myself.

The rest of that afternoon, I dawdled. Since leaving Green River, I'd averaged more than my regulation daily ten miles and had forged a day ahead of schedule. Besides, although the canyon was essentially unchanged— no more or less beautiful than before—fresh details demanded copious heed and photography. River-rock siren songs, richly modulated, now seduced me.

A new rock motif, until now heard only faintly, emerged in architectural forms that I thought of as "embryonic arches." The Southwest's canyon-lands—notably in Arches National Park—are famous for their rock arches, and Labyrinth now kept revealing draft sketches. The great curving incisions in the sandstone were shallow, and the spaces that in an arch would have been empty were blocked with solid walls of rock—like theater proscenium arches with their pink curtains still down. But the arches were there all right, in embryo: delicate arcs framing the massive pink rock curtains. I found them curiously alluring. Few if any, I knew, would mature into actual arches. For that outcome you need a thin spur of rock wall, so that erosion can join air to air. Most of my "embryonic arches" would become caves, or simply dissipate. But what mattered was that they were beautiful. One in particular, not far below the Notch, was exquisitely curved and proportioned, its massive pink walls ornamented with black water-weatherings, its form echoed, top right, by a small subsidiary bud-arch.

The river sang, too. It now curved and swung almost metronomically between sandbars, and smooth green swards of young tamarisk often carpeted the sandbars. Once, where the current had transected sand, the sheer vertical bank revealed a graphic lesson in the way tamarisk roots went down three or even four times as far as their slender green saplings went up.

The canyon also established other new motifs. On a steep cliff face that may once have been overlaid with soil, a small but ancient tree clung to life as if in agony, roots clutching for food across bare rock—open to the sun and casual gaze—like a gigantic gray spider. At the foot of a typical chaos-of-amorphous-rock talus slope, two big boulders with explicit shapes lay side by side: a huge inverted heart and a gigantic boomerang.

With so much to see, and time to spare, I floated on with little awareness of where I was. Not until I'd rounded a bend and looked back to see whether the Notch was still visible—looked back and found it was not—

An "embryonic arch," Labyrinth Canyon.

did it dawn on me that for the last hour I'd been passing through the massive trough I had looked down and along when I stood at the Notch. It seemed odd, now, that I had traversed that trough without being acutely conscious of its significance. But there'd been no sense of the tension between rock and river that from above had been so stabbingly clear. Down in the trough, the canyon had, for all its new siren songs, been essentially the same as before. No more and no less beautiful. No more and no less remarkable. Perhaps that was the point. What I had seen from the Notch was not really an exceptional sector of the canyon; I had just been looking at it from a new perspective.

I moved on down, pushing languidly, still taking my time, rowing with body but not mind. Watching the river unfold. Watching it swirl if not exactly leap into sun. And all at once I saw that what kept my journey alive was the daily tension between expectation and realization. That's what any traveler learns. What makes his journey run is not events but events' refusal of his expectations.

Five minutes later, a swirl spun the raft and I found myself looking back upriver. Two canoes were moving down toward me, fast. Soon they pulled abreast, stopped. Four men, open canoes. They paused only for a minute or two: they were taking out next morning at Mineral Bottom, eight miles down, where a road ran in to the river, and they wanted to camp just above it. One of them agreed to take some postcards I'd written and mail them next day.

The canoes moved on down, out of sight. I followed, still taking my time.

So far, the river had been feeding me a digestible diet of human company. Not the almost total lack of it I'd experienced—and enjoyed—on my walk through Grand Canyon, thirty years earlier; more like the sporadic meetings that occurred during my walk up California, five years before that. On balance, just enough to stimulate; rarely enough to rock my emotional raft.

I pulled in at a dry creek mouth and had just decided against camping there—because what flat land existed had been colonized by a dry and aggressively prickly little plant, and because I'd glimpsed slithering away beyond it a snake that might or might not have been a rattler—and was walking back to the raft when I glanced upriver and saw another canoe.

Soon it was close enough for me to detect something familiar about the lone figure paddling it. Up binoculars. Sure enough: wide-brimmed hat, pale blue shirt, gray slacks. Their wearer waved, steered toward me, pulled in, stepped ashore.

We exchanged pleasantries, then names.

"John Joseph," said the stranger. He smiled. "Highly biblical."

He was a New Yorker—a carpenter, apparently an ex-journalist, probably in his mid-thirties, equipped with a curious blend of courage and temerity. He liked, he said, to take occasional long trips in his canoe. He'd cracked it up in white water the year before and spent the winter refurbishing it, and this year was sticking to flat water: he'd put in at Green River, Utah, and had arranged for someone to meet him at the Confluence with a motorboat and tow him back up the Colorado to a takeout point. He seemed without fear of river or sidetrips. But the little town of Green River, he said, "scared the hell out of me. The people I saw there, I mean. I sat and watched television till three in the morning 'cause I was afraid somebody was going to break into my room." Even for a seasoned New Yorker, that seemed aberrantly paranoid.

We talked at some length, mostly of river pleasures. He was an amiable fellow, and—remembering his humorous "highly biblical" introduction— I made no attempt to hide my secular outlook. At the end we spoke of the challenges I'd face in Cataract and Grand Canyons, and just before Joseph got back into his canoe, as we shook hands, he said, very gently, "Well, may God keep you in one piece."

After he'd paddled on downstream, I rowed across to the far bank and found a flat, clear place that, although it faced west and would therefore get no morning sun, otherwise promised a good camp. Before dinner, with *Solitude* now my sole companion, I read a few more pages and tried to deny that I'd been jarred very slightly out of my comfortable cocoon. After dinner I sat and tried to deny that I'd compensated with a half-snoot too much bourbon.

13

. . . STILLWATER

The Notch
Bowknot Bend
Labyrinth Canyon
CANYONLANDS NATIONAL PARK
Fort Bottom/ watchtower ruins
Stillwater Cyn.
Green R.
Colorado River (formerly Grand R.)
One-Mile Canyon
confluence walk
LAND OF STANDING ROCKS:
The Maze
The Doll House
Cataract Cyn.
Colorado R.
The Confluence
The Grabens
0   10
MILES

Mile 679 to Mile 735
September 26–October 2

For six days the river and I wound our way southward, deep and sinuous, between the rock walls of Labyrinth and then Stillwater. The river flowed serene and beautiful. I traveled contentedly, at home.

The river was always there, bearing me along or moating my night castles. Yet it remained a muted, undemanding waterway. Mostly it ran flat and unbroken. Rarely did I have to pay strict navigational attention.

The scarce riverside wildlife generally low-key, too. But one morning, before leaving Labyrinth, I was drifting silently down, oars out of the water, when I saw ahead, on a side-canyon delta, close to the water's edge, a brown shape. The shape stood motionless, body angled away from me. The wind was blowing upstream, from it to me. I drifted closer. Soon I confirmed through binoculars that the shape was, as I'd suspected, the first of its species I'd actually seen on the trip. Then, to avoid a protruding log, I had to dip oars in water. Oarlocks emitted a mild rattle. Down on the side-canyon delta the coyote gave a start, pivoted its head, looked directly at me, melted away.

Occasional beavers still sleeked across the river, but most of the rare wildlife was avian. A raven might case me, low and ravenous; once, a convocation of them swirled high against dark cliffs. Magpies made cameo appearances. A pair of swallows flashed past, tearing the air. Great blue heron sentries still stood guard, but now spread very thin. Near the end of Stillwater, two chukars posed briefly, brown and nervous, on a boulder protruding from green underbrush; when they dove for cover, the brush swallowed them as if it were green water.

So during my six days of floating through lower Labyrinth and then Stillwater, almost all was quiet on the river front; but I made five sidetrips.

On the first I circumnavigated another and younger rincon. This time, for some reason, the walk was no more than mildly interesting. With one exception.

At the apex of the rincon's loop I paused to watch a brown flash that might have been a chipmunk. The flash vanished into a meshed-stick structure that might or might not have been its nest. I was still standing beside the presumed nest when I noticed for the first time that a butte off to my right looked vaguely familiar. Familiar yet wanting. And then I remembered two things.

Floating downriver the day before, I had seen, far ahead and off to the right, a rock formation that was clearly the one John Wesley Powell had christened "The Butte of the Cross." Years earlier, a drawing of it in his journals had left me feeling that it really didn't look much like a cross. Seeing it first-eye from the river had confirmed my skepticism. Yet there was no denying that the stark, thrusting edifice had the monolithic majesty of Squaretop Mountain, back above Green River Lakes—and something more. It had greater complexity, carried heavier overtones. The main pillar seemed to stand on a massive and perfectly proportioned plinth, and together they formed a towering edifice that had an almost holy, transcendental quality. On reflection, it was easy to understand why a dyed-in-the-cloth Christian might perceive it as his prime icon. (Later I rechecked Powell's journal. He had actually written "*in the form of a fallen cross.*" But I still found it difficult to nail the resemblance.)

And now, standing beside the presumed chipmunk nest at the apex of the second rincon and seeing—from behind the scenes, as it were—that the familiar-yet-lacking-something butte was in fact the main obelisk of Powell's Butte of the Cross but that it stood alone, no longer mounted on its massive plinth, I remembered something else. Powell and his party had landed near the foot of this rincon and had climbed out "*to take another bearing on The Butte of the Cross. Reaching an eminence from which we can overlook the landscape, we are surprised to find that our butte, with its wonderful form, is indeed two buttes, one so standing in front of the other that from the last point of view it gave the appearance of a cross.*" No doubt I felt a less profound surprise than Powell that his icon turned out to be an illusion.

Another day, searching for a genuine artifact, I walked only a hundred and fifty yards from the river but moved back a hundred and fifty years.

Thirty-three years before Powell launched his boats on the Green, a French-Canadian fur trapper named Denis Julien traveled it. Whether he did so by boat or on foot remains uncertain, but in the two-hundred-odd miles below the Uinta Basin he left half a dozen rock inscriptions, all close to the river. Sometimes he cut only his initials; sometimes his full name with a date; sometimes he added adornments. Other than a few "marks" in what is now Arches National Park, little else is known about him. His immortality rests on these graffiti.

The two inscriptions farthest downriver have been engulfed by Lake Powell; but three remain above the Confluence. I had looked for and failed to find the first two. Then, the morning I went ashore on a third search, I hit pay rock. Hit it without great difficulty.

Just above the mouth of a side canyon, on a flat, smooth slab of red sandstone interleaved with shale and protected by an overhang, I found a remarkably clear inscription:

The small, masted boat—which seemed to suggest that Julien traveled *on* the river—matched in style the words and figures: simple, almost childish. But the drawing below it had a quite different flavor: primitive and essentially abstract, yet at the same time full, flamboyant. The river guide described it, very reasonably, as "a winged sun."

Now, there seems little doubt about the genuineness of Julien's name or the date. Or of the boat. But the more I studied the inscription, the less I could believe that a man who would draw such a childlike boat also drew the enigmatic sun with outspread wings.

It was difficult, I found, to judge the drawings' relative ages. Most of the lines had been recently touched up, no doubt to make photography easier. A few modern graffiti had also been scrawled alongside—such maunderings as "CA ♥ AT"—but a well-meaning "vigilante" had muddied them over. Not for the first time, I failed to solve the problem of just what, other than the passage of time, distinguishes genuine historical markings from trash graffiti.

When I turned away at last and began walking back down to the river my mind kept worrying away at the sun with outspread wings; kept hearing an elusive echo. As I stepped into the raft, I snared it. Carl Jung had somewhere written about—as far as I could recall—an inmate of an insane asylum who showed him, with pride, a drawing of "a sun with a hanging tail"; and Jung, making certain connections, had later concluded that such a sun was one of the shared symbols of humanity's "collective unconscious." Floating on downriver, I had a hunch that Jung's shaft of insight might cast light on the winged sun beside Denis Julien's inscription.

Next day, soon after crossing the boundary into Canyonlands National Park, I made my third sidetrip.

Around noon, a couple of hours after glimpsing—downriver, on opposite sides of the canyon—a pair of rock spires with extraordinarily eloquent phallic shapes, I pulled in at Fort Bottom. I spent a few minutes on the flat at the remains of "Wild Bunch Cabin"—built by a homesteader but just possibly visited by the gang—then walked up a trail that seemed sure to lead to a clearly visible artifact marked on the river guide map as "Ruins" and described as having "the appearance of an Indian watchtower." The name "Fort Bottom," I assumed, also referred to the watchtower.

The trail—well worn by modern feet, no doubt from boat parties, but perhaps following an ancient route—wound up a gentle slope and then, at the lip of the mesa on which the watchtower stood, crossed a low but sheer rock face. I climbed the little rock face; stood up; stood transfixed.

The mesa rose barely two hundred and fifty feet above the river, and its flat surface remained far below the surrounding plateau. On three sides, rock walls therefore hemmed me in. But here, where Labyrinth eased over into Stillwater, the geology broke. Beyond a protruding mass of the plateau called "Big Horn Mesa" stretched an open basin. And the view that had abruptly opened up across it was a panoramic tapestry of rock surfaces.

A textured tapestry. Red rock—sheer, sloping or flat. Brown rock—pale or profound, eroded either skirtlike or conical. A layer of white rock carved into rows of curving buttresses, or sometimes into bubbles that looked ready to burst. And across this rich but static panorama danced racing cloud shadows.

I stood for a long time above the little rock face, just looking. Once again I'd felt the shock and elation of lifting my head above the day-after-day river world. And felt this joy without having to belittle the river world. It was like surfacing from a dive beside a breathtaking coral reef and appreciating anew its magnificent backdrop of curving white beach and green, rustling palm trees.

I shook myself free of vista wonder, walked on up the gently sloping mesa to its far end, to the watchtower.

The building hardly an impressive structure; yet a certain oddness, even distinction, about it. Perhaps ten feet square. Its walls: flat brown shalelike stones gathered from the mesa's surface. These stones deftly interlaid, sparingly mortared.

The building's layout: rectangular in plan with rounded corners. A single open entranceway, capped by a familiar wooden lintel. Just inside it, four big flat stones angling up from the floor, inclined away from the entrance. The stones clearly man-installed; their purpose obscure. Two window spaces, both with wooden lintels. One window stoned-in, apparently as an afterthought.

The ruin stood open to the sky—though it may once have boasted a roof—and its walls had an uneven and unlikely two-level crest-line, with an embryonic mini-tower at one end. The odd mini-tower effect could have been intentional or could have resulted from the falling away of a few stones. It certainly intrigued me.

The "Watchtower," with echoes.

From the first, I doubted that the structure had been built as a watch-tower. The field of view it commanded was all wrong. On every side, the steep drop-away of the mesa's cliffs created a broad swath of dead ground. Even if some idiot enemy chose to approach in daylight he could easily creep up close, undetected. True, there seemed only one viable place he could storm the mesa: the cliff's low point, where I'd scrambled up. If you were thinking in military terms you could, as someone apparently had, call the structure a fort. But as a fort the structure was in the wrong place. If you wanted to defend the mesa you'd build your main defensework at the vulnerable low-cliff point. Sited as it was, standing out from every side in stark silhouette, all the "watchtower" did was advertise your position. And the four inclined stones inside the entranceway were no last-ditch defense: they sloped away from an intruder, not toward him, and stood slightly to one side, not directly in his path.

Deciding what the structure was *not* proved to be easier than deciding what it was, or might have been. For a long time I stood and looked at it; then sat and looked at it. From where I sat, my field of view extended be-yond it, southward over the relatively flat basin. And all at once I had my answer.

For my eyes detected a resonance. The silhouette of the ruin's odd, two-level roofline, along with the embryonic mini-tower at its left end, echoed the two-level-and-mini-tower silhouette of two buttes and a little spire that, several miles away, formed a protruding branch of the plateau's es-carpment. And when I went back inside the structure I found that the one still-open window space framed, to dead-center perfection, those same buttes and spire.

"Yes," I said to the window and the echo. "Yes, that's it."

Anyone who lives for long in an untouched landscape—especially in wide, stark, dramatic, primitive country—will find that, whether he recog-nizes it or not, the land becomes part of his religion. Probably forms its foundations. Ancient or modern man, it makes no difference. City dwellers, cut off from the land, naturally tend to disagree. Two and a half centuries ago, city dweller Alexander Pope wrote,

> *Lo, the poor Indian! whose untutored mind*
> *Sees God in clouds, or hears him in the wind*

—though Pope did allow the poor Indian, through "simple nature . . . an humbler heaven." A modern, tutored Indian might respond,

> *Lo, poor Alex Pope! whose overtutored mind*
> *Cannot see God in clouds, or hear him in the wind.*

Anyway, for those in touch with the land, its substance reaches deep into their souls. And the moment my eye perceived the "watchtower's" resonance with its landscape, I knew it marked a holy site.

When I cast around for physical confirmation I found precious little to work on. The four inclined stones inside the doorway now struck me as having a vaguely religious aura. And outside on the mesa I found, protruding from its horizontal strata, two clusters of inclined rocks that might be seen as echoing them. Near the main structure stood what seemed to be the beginnings of another—one small corner, only a foot or two high; but its stonework was meticulously laid, and the corner, unlike the rounded corners of the main structure, formed a sharp right angle. It occurred to me that this fragment of masonry might be not the beginning of a major building but a small independent shrine.

The one physical confirmation, I decided, was the structure's location: the isolated mesa seemed an impeccably proper place for a religious structure.

We humans like to perch our religious icons on prominent summits. One prime example: the colossal cruciform statue of Christ, pinnacled 2000 feet above Rio de Janeiro, that shepherds the city from its natural, thrusting granite pulpit. This theme persists around our planet, though the icons vary as our gods change. And they are always changing. God, after all, is what we rather think we detect when we reach the limits of our human minds. So even ignoring the propaganda value of an icon overlooking a city, what better site for a shrine to your particular god than a prominent place from which you can look out over wide spaces? The "watchtower," though apparently perched far from any dwelling place, certainly met the last prescription. But when I turned at last and began to walk back down into Fort Bottom I had to admit I'd mustered precious little support for my hunch.

Only after I was back in the raft and floating downriver did I find what I chose to regard as two independent confirmatory signs.

The first was another echo.

I'd floated only a few yards and was looking back up at the "watchtower"—now a mere pimple perched on its mesa—when I saw that from that angle the silhouette of the structure echoed the silhouette of a distant butte, small and isolated and nestling precisely in the V of a gap between the watchtower mesa and the protruding Big Horn Mesa escarpment of the main plateau. Just for a moment, the echo, though different from the one I'd detected through the watchtower window, was just as perfect, just as arresting. Then I'd floated a few more yards and the V and the resonance had vanished.

By then, though, I'd made my second discovery. Had seen something that was staring me in the face throughout the hour I spent up on the mesa. Staring me too fully in the face to be detected.

From the mesa I'd been looking directly at the protruding spur of Big Horn Mesa. It had presented a solid rock face. But now, looking back and up from an angle, I could see that at the spur's very tip, separated from it by the lotteries of erosion, stood a tall rock spire. And I recognized the spire. From this side it looked very much the same as when I'd seen it, a couple of hours earlier, from far upriver. It was, I mean, vividly phallic.

Now, the word "phallic" is often used loosely to describe any vaguely upstanding shape. But this knobbed spire was starkly, astonishingly, eloquently phallic: a massive and graphic articulation in stone of an erect human penis. And the moment I saw it I knew that somewhere behind me as I floated down the river—no doubt masked for the moment by the same chance full-face disguise that Big Horn Mesa had pulled—was the matching spire I'd seen from upriver. In other words, the "watchtower" stood in a huge space dominated by two striking phallic symbols.

Sex and religion are inextricably intertwined. Religion is an attempt to squeeze meaning out of life. And life begins with birth. And every birth, except in life's earliest forms, originates in copulation. And copulation demands a phallus. The rest follows, with variations. The phallic symbol ruled many primitive religions. It is still central to Hinduism. (Sex-shy Christians celebrate the birth of Christ but skate around the whole nasty initiatory business, on perilously transparent ice, by postulating a "virgin birth.") Anyway, the moment I saw the phallic spire at the tip of Big Horn Mesa I perceived it as confirming my notion that the "watchtower" was in fact a religious icon built on high in a holy place.

I thought I knew who had built this pantheon.

For several centuries spanning the year we call A.D. 1100 (in honor of one of our own gods) there lived in many dry parts of the canyonlands a people we call the Pueblo, or Anasazi. My knowledge of them had been picked up slowly and osmotically in the course of foot trips through other parts of the canyonlands, and it remained scanty. But I'd grasped some salient points. The Anasazi seem to have abandoned their homes and the agricultural lifeway that supported them for reasons that included a long-term drought—signaling a change to a climate much as it now is. Even at the height of their occupation, though, they leaned gently on the land. My limited experience suggested that they tended to live in very small groups—often just a single family in one place—and that their homes were widely scattered. In the course of my travels I'd acquired some feeling for the flavor of these homes. Once, in Grand Canyon—when such an act was not yet illegal or widely regarded as vandalism—I had lived for twenty-four hours in one of their cliff dwelling–granaries. I still carried with me, vividly, the memory of the little wooden lintels with which they always seemed to cap entranceways to their buildings, possibly to warn them in time, as they crouch-scrambled through, that their backs were about to scrape against sharp stonework. Since that day and night in their cliff dwelling–granary I'd also carried around, in an unfocused but still potent way, a sense of the ghosts who had inhabited it. And now, as I floated on downriver, I began to realize that similar ghosts probably flitted around the watchtower-pantheon I'd just visited.

Later, as I set off on my fourth sidetrip, looking for some rock dwellings, I wondered if I'd detect ghosts in and around their walls, too. Cousin-ghosts, maybe.

I found the dwellings easily enough, tucked into two low cliffs, just where I'd been told they'd be. As my informant had said, they were "kinda neat."

(It's no accident, by the way, that I've failed to pinpoint these Indian artifacts. I've exercised similar obfuscations in a couple of places back upriver, and may do so again without notice or apology.

The reasons for such apparently antisocial behavior are highly social: I'm fearful that certain beautiful places may be violated by what I write. Part of such places' beauty lies in their relative freedom from people; and publicity publicizes.

Because a river journey is so uncompromisingly linear, I've had to pinpoint more than I'd like, but I'm hoping you'll recognize that I'm trying to bring light into minds, not onto physical places, and that you'll act accordingly. Or, rather, will refrain from acting.)

There were two groups of dwellings. The first: a small house with annex and, a few feet along the ledge, a larger single unit. The second—a duplex plus a third very small detached unit—stood a couple of blocks away on a lower ledge; at salutary in-laws distance, perhaps. Nearby, the big white flowers of two jimsonweeds—the first I'd seen on the trip—caught my eye. Jimsonweed, of the nightshade family, has been renowned down the ages as, among other things, a narcotic for inducing altered states of consciousness and prophetic visions (possibly, for example, in priests at the Delphic oracle), and I seemed to have heard of its use by Native Americans.

Now, I find nearly all rock dwellings beautiful. But the moment I saw the first of these I detected distinction. They achieved structural balance, harmony. Something like rakishness, too; an almost debonair jauntiness.

That first impression held. A neat wooden lintel capped each entrance-

The main rock dwellings.

way. All walls were built with flat red stones collected from the ledge on which the dwellings stood. The stones, like those up at the watchtower-pantheon, had been deftly interlaid, sparingly mud-mortared. In part because stones and mud were the same pale red as the ledge, but also because the artifacts' lines fit those of the natural rock, the dwellings were Frank Lloyd Wright structures: they meshed with their place.

But they were also very practical residences. Both groups were tucked in, as usual, under overhangs deep enough to qualify as incipient caves. The overhangs would clearly protect you from rain; but this little community seemed to have sited its homes very carefully to keep the sun off and hold summer heat down. In the first group, the room-with-annex dwelling was smaller and less refined than the other. It looked older, too. Perhaps the little community built the fancier and more capacious structure when there was time to spare or when they achieved an advance in building techniques. It happens. Back up in the flatlands of Wyoming and Utah I'd often seen old log cabins still standing beside modern replacement homes.

As always, I was struck by the way the size of the buildings suggested, though hardly proved, that their inhabitants had been small people. Not tiny, but small. Yet when I went inside and saw on one heavily mud-plastered inner wall a clear set of fingerprints that at first looked close to pygmy size, I found when I placed my own fingers over them that they almost fitted.

The mud wall offered two conveniences that any modern man or woman would appreciate, the kind I often construct at camps I expect to use for more than one night. This ancient Anasazi master builder had fashioned— sometimes with flat stones he left protruding, sometimes by scooping out hollows in the mud—small storage spaces for objects he must often have found the need to store. And he had jammed several short sticks between stones, mudded them secure and thereby created hangers for whatever he found the need to hang. Now nothing hung from them. In one mud hollow, though, small black mouse droppings suggested I was not the only modern to appreciate the master builder's work.

But it was when I went back outside that first group of dwellings and sat where the Anasazi family must sometimes have sat, looking out over their own personal world, that I moved closest, or so I fancied, to their ghosts.

By now, under a cloudless sky, it was warm, going on hot. The sun had swung almost to the chockstone of its daily arc, but a cool breeze air- conditioned this place the master builder had chosen. And sitting there in the open, on the red rock ledge where he and his family must often have sat, looking out over what they had looked out over, day after day, year after year, it was impossible not to grasp how rich their lives had been and how lucky they were—whether they knew these things or not.

Below, at the foot of the ledge, stretched what had no doubt been their arable land—still flat, but now overgrown beyond easy identification by an unskilled eye. Eight hundred years overgrown. It was what lay beyond their farm, though, that spoke to me.

From the ledge I commanded a vista out across an enclosed-yet-open space not unlike the space that had opened up when I first stood, trans- fixed, on the watchtower-pantheon mesa: a sunken and segregated realm, blocked off from the wider world by the rock walls of the main plateau. As at the pantheon, this landscape was richly textured. Red rock; brown rock; white rock; rock steeped in jet-black shadow. Rock terraces. Rock escarp- ments, buttressed and unbuttressed. And rock jutting up in a thousand jagged shapes and sizes, including spires.

That sunlit day, no shifting cloud shadows leavened the scene, lifting shapes from obscurity, casting them back into it. Only the unhurried wing- ing of the sun adjusted emphases. And some time passed, as I sat there on the ledge, before the sun's slow passage lifted a jet-black shadow from a distant escarpment standing almost dead center in my vista; but once that shadow lifted there emerged from in front of the escarpment a spire that had until then been hidden, much as the spire at the spur of Big Horn Mesa had been masked by my angle of vision. And this spire, I now saw with something like astonishment, was also—though less strikingly graphic than the Big Horn spire—evocatively phallic.

I leaned back, put my hands down beside me, flat, on the hot, rough rock that the Anasazi family must once have known so well. It was easy, now, to imagine them sitting there in the sunlight just looking out across this same jumbled yet ordered vista of textured rock, seeing the phallic spire that thrust up in the center of their world—not thinking really, just letting it all soak in. Sitting there while the sun winged its slow daily arc across the sky. A man sitting there like that might well find himself recalling a place not too far distant that crystallized, even more than did this home vista, deep reverberations within him. In a surge of emotion—an oceanic inclusion—he might even conceive the notion of building a pantheon in that raised and holy place.

Slowly, I came to understand other things that could have happened during those long, relaxed hours the family sat on this rough red rock. A man or woman or child with the right blend of patience and imagination, sitting there in the desert heat and watching the sun wing its slow arc, might, with or without the aid of jimsonweed, enter an altered state. Might see, rising up from some primitive collective memory, a vision of a flaming sun with a hanging tail. Or perhaps with outspread wings.*

The fifth and final sidetrip did not come until I'd almost completed my sun-filled passage through Stillwater Canyon.

Now, I must not oversell the sidetrips. In a very real sense, it was they

---

* Later, I made inquiries on two levels.

First, I checked with the Park Service archaeologist for that stretch of river. To my surprise and delight he agreed with me about the watchtower-pantheon: "not a defensive structure . . . probably a holy site." He also commented on or corrected several other specifics that I've let stand—because what I imagined at the time to be true seems in these cases more important than what turned out to be sort of objectively true:

a. it's "generally agreed" that the main Denis Julien inscription and the sun with outspread wings were indeed made by different people;

b. the watchtower "is a dry-laid structure. Unfortunately, during recent (20th century) conservation efforts, modern man inflicted Portland cement on the structure. . . . Most 'vigilante' conservation efforts should be discouraged as they result in more harm being done to the resource";

c. Anasazi homes could in fact be "widely scattered or densely packed, depending on the area"; and

d. at the dwellings, "there's a good chance the master builder was a she."

From other sources I confirmed that my recollection about Carl Jung and the sun with a hanging tail had, though imperfectly recalled, been essentially correct. See Jung's *Symbols of Transformation*.

that carried the week forward. Or at least supplied its distinctive imprint. But my basic and enduring world remained raft, river and rock.

The core and focus of this moving world was the raft. The raft with its bulging blue tubes that when I pulled away from camp each morning—most mornings, anyway—were filthy with mud my feet had brought aboard and spread around during reloading. The raft that ten minutes later, after its statutory cleansing with sluiced bucketsful of river water, gleamed in the slanting sunlight. The raft that after another ten minutes had dried out and lost its pristine, false-promise gleam but was still a cheerful, ship-shape companion—a rotund blue oval mate that encircled and enriched and framed to perfection the home that moved along with me: the shining steel frame and dry boxes and the black crossboard at my feet and all the other mundane yet lilting constants.

On the black crossboard stood the medley of household wares that, together with a pair of outstretched legs, formed the constant yet constantly fluctuating still-life foreground of my vision. A foreground that had become, the way such things do, a comfort. Almost a prop. One of those things that from the outside may seem minor, going on piffling, but in fact infuse the long, slow-ticking days and so color your life.

First yet somehow not foremost in that foreground vision—so close and constant, in fact, that I rarely saw them—my now weather-beaten legs and

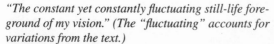

"The constant yet constantly fluctuating still-life foreground of my vision." (The "fluctuating" accounts for variations from the text.)

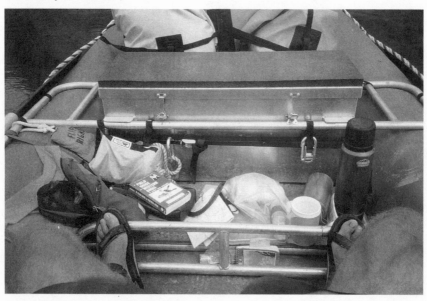

feet: rich red-brown skin glossy with suntan lotion, pale hairs glistening in the sunlight, even through Polaroid glasses. The sandaled feet resting on the black-rubber-covered crossboard.

At one end of the crossboard, propped up against the raft's curving blue starboard tube, the bright yellow waterproof-fabric bucket, full of river water that would spend the day settling toward clarity so that it would clog the ceramic filter less quickly when I prepared it for drinking. Standing on the crossboard beside my feet, selected kitchenware. The gray thermos flask and red insulated cup and blue-topped plastic canteen half full of orange-drink crystals. One of the ziplock food bags—most likely the tea edition, with its small containers holding milk and sugar and vitamin pills (judged necessary on such a prolonged trip because of the lack of fresh food) along with a small spoon and many tea bags. Far left, tucked in beside the bright yellow canvas bag that held the throwline, a plastic bag for garbage. And nearby, if it was late in the day, a couple of used tea bags, drying out before being filed in the garbage bag.

Sometimes, above and beyond the crossboard, on the thick black foam covering of the dry box, more housewares. If it was meal- or snack-time, a small orange plastic bowl and a knife. Often, a dishcloth or cleaning rag or clothing item spread out to dry. And on the flanks, hanging bright against blue tube, a red canvas canteen-holder and a capacious red canvas pouch of emergency items: spare oarlocks, web straps and carabiners.

Completing this still-life foreground of my vision—out beyond the main cockpit, beyond the dry box, jammed in the curving bow so that they wouldn't shift—the three dry bags. Each bag in its right place, so that I'd always know where everything was: yellow bag left, pale blue right, dark blue center. Lying flat on the dark blue bag, tied down by its hanging cord, spending the whole day sunbathing, the black plastic solar shower bag. Ropes added finishing-touch color daubs. Yellow bow line stuffed in its white netting bag. The coiled red climbing rope that was my still-unused lining rope. The blue-and-white-spiral-patterned safety rope that curved around the entire raft like a thin outer frame separating my still-life tableau from the river.

This tableau was always there, hour after hour, day after day. But as my housekeeping evolved, it fluctuated—underwent the kinds of apparently trivial changes that, like the tableau itself, helped weave the journey's underclothing. The small orange plastic bowl and the knife, for example, sat up on the black foam of the dry box much more often since I'd decided, at Green River, Utah, to buy fresh bread: I needed the inverted bowl to lay a slice of bread on when I buttered and honeyed it with the knife. (The first loaf was about finished now, and less than bakery-fresh, but it had been a huge success. So had the fresh fruit and canned beer. And the pouch of wine—which traveled, cooling in river water, in a canvas bucket behind my seat—had me offering daily thanks to Mike and Pom.) The solar shower bag, sunbathing up in the bow, reflected my now-established routine of washing not only myself but my clothes virtually every evening. (Warm, low-humidity nights meant that by morning the thin clothes were bone-dry.) And the red oars strapped along the raft's flanks meant I'd finally decided that although their easily-held-onto rubber-covered handles made them safer for white water, I preferred the yellow pair, with bare wooden handles, for plain flat-water rowing.

Outside the raft's blue frame, new-old river-and-rock scenes perpetually unfurled.

The river, as I've said, was always there, center stage, carrying me along or moating past yet playing a muted role. Unruffled by rapids, it flowed slow and placid, reflective, reflecting.

What it reflected, above all, was rock.

Powell reported that in Stillwater the canyon walls fell so sheer and ran so unbroken that he had difficulty finding campsites. I encountered no such problem—either because of lower water or because a campsite for one demands far less space than for a party. No expectancy barrier, though. The walls, if at first less cathedral than I'd pictured them, were varied and interesting. And the rock itself, though still mostly red, had a new "feel."

To many people, "rock" spells "geology." At the changeover from Labyrinth to Stillwater I'd passed what the river guide called "a striking angular unconformity." It was the kind of event—or, rather, signature of an event—that evokes bliss from geologists, and the river guide's author had blissed out. I dutifully eyeballed the converging rock layers. Now, technical geology can on occasion stir me to genuine enthusiasm. By this time, though, the accumulated weight of hundreds of miles of stunning geology had stunned me into apathy.

But beyond scientific geology lies aesthetic geology.

When I passed the "striking angular unconformity" I think I grasped the broad significance of the scientific evidence. But what I saw as I floated serenely down the last few miles of Stillwater, toward the confluence of Green and Colorado, were soaring red cliffs, buttresses, slanting sunlight, black shadows. And what captivated me was not the scientific geology of this architectural marvel but its beauty, its harmonies.

Beauty and harmony teach you things geology cannot. Teach you in a different way. From them you can acquire, if you're lucky and ready, the kind of learning that builds brick on individual brick, when you're not looking, and by slow accretions may lead, unexpectedly, to the pulling aside of curtains. This kind of learning is not, of course, something you can set out to garner. It's more like happiness, which is—whatever our constitution may imply—not a goal to be pursued but, as one sage has said, something that catches up with you when you're working at the limits of your potential.

Anyway, as I floated on through the final stages of Stillwater's red, enfolding rock corridor there seeped into me a renewed awareness of how much at ease I now felt, how completely at home in this magnificent canyon world. And all at once I saw—as if a curtain had been pulled prematurely aside—that this river journey had already moved up and joined the other two long solo journeys that had been highlights of my life.

I drifted on down, at peace, content. My quiet passage through Stillwater had been virtually flawless. It had been one of those almost achingly perfect interludes that can light, luminously and forever, many kinds of journeys, many kinds of lives. You rarely recognize them at the time, but . . .

Off to the right, something caught my eye. A flash of red in the rock wall's flimsy green skirt. Yes, a cluster of red leaves. The first red leaves of fall . . . Then my eye refocused on the space between the greenery and the raft's blue oval. The river seemed to have picked up speed, as if it knew something was about to happen.

I ran my eye ahead along the right bank to a side canyon now sliding into view. The map showed that it footed into the river barely a mile above the Confluence. As we drifted on down, I studied this side canyon carefully. It looked very steep.

Next morning I climbed the side canyon on my fifth and final Stillwater sidetrip. I knew that if everything went as planned it would be the longest so far and the highest—and I'd taken due precautions.

The afternoon before, as soon as I'd set up camp at the foot of the side canyon, I reconnoitered. Several members of Powell's second party had on September 16, 1871, apparently climbed from here to the rim, more than a thousand feet above, and when I'd eyeballed the side canyon from the raft I'd picked out a plausible route.

The reconnaissance tended to confirm it. For a few yards at the start there was even an embryo trail. And I found a way to avoid a small but sheer cliff that looked easy enough for a party of men—equipped with helping hands—but mildly discouraging for a cautious soloist. (Powell had only half my quota of arms but half my burden of years.)

I went to bed early, and in the morning, around 5:30, watched the brightest meteor I'd ever seen streak across the narrow black strip of sky sandwiched between blacker canyon walls. Had I been superstitious I'd have called the "shooting star" a good omen.

By eight o'clock I was on my way.

Half an hour's steady, uneventful climbing. Then, at the first barrier beyond the upper limit of my reconnaissance, I had to wriggle up a narrow chimney between two rock slabs. The movement was mildly awkward because I'd exercised better judgment than at Trin-Alcove Bend: I was carrying four water canteens, three non-meat "pemmican" bars, a metal cup, tea bags, an alarm whistle, a small first-aid kit and several other items—and to accommodate them I had to wear not only a belt bag but also a pocket detached from the big backpack and attached to my belt. And to climb the chimney I had to stuff the new replacement zoom camera, protected by a plastic bag, into a shorts pocket. Although these impedimenta impeded, I made it up the chimney. I'd walked only a few paces beyond it when a melodramatic jumble of huge boulders—poised as if falling rocks in arrested motion (which in a sense they were)—made me reach into my pocket for the camera. My hand found—nothing.

I knew at once what had happened. Back to the chimney's head; peer down. A couple of feet below, sure enough, perched on a ledge barely wide enough to accept it, lay the camera. Far below, at the chimney's foot, glittered its plastic bag. I knelt, reached down, lifted the camera to safety, gave thanks for a high serendipity quotient: when the contortions involved in wriggling up the chimney had forced the camera from my shorts pocket, the odds against its lodging on that narrow ledge were monumental. And although I'm not superstitious I chose to regard the camera rescue as a second good omen for the day. (Have you noticed how self-declared skeptics still tainted by atavistic illusions tend to say, "Now I'm not superstitious, but . . ."?)

I climbed on up the side canyon in cool and welcome shade: sunlight still touched only the rim, high above. Mostly, I just chose the best-looking route over and through trackless rock, but in one stretch a series of "ducks"—small man-constructed rock cairns—signposted me along. In a couple of minor hollows, windblown sand even bore footprints.

I clambered up another ledge-barrier, moved on without haste. In spite of the extra weight, it felt good to be carrying more than three quarts of water. It removed all time pressure, made the day safer.

An hour or so after leaving camp I swung left up a small gulch. From the raft, the day before, this gulch had looked the most promising exit route, and it still did. Before long I'd climbed—in sunlight now—almost to the rim. Briefly, the route narrowed to a rock ledge barely wide enough for my boots. Good fingertip holds, though, in rough rock, and only a four-foot drop beneath my heels. No problem.

Then I was walking up a shallow, gently sloping rock basin.

As I walked, a plaintive cry from the left. A large bird slanted across my front into a juniper tree. I was still trying to decide if it could indeed be an enormous woodpecker when I came up over the lip of the basin.

The bird flew forgotten from my mind. I'm almost sure I said out loud, as I had above Trin-Alcove Bend, "My God, what a view!"

Above Trin-Alcove, the first-ness of the unexpected vista had heightened its impact; on the mesa above Fort Bottom there'd been rich rock texture and the "watchtower"; but this panorama above the Confluence was, unaided, the most dramatic.

Once more I felt the African-savannah, this-is-how-the-world-was-meant-to-be sense of primitive, untouched simplicity. And harmony. But this time, for all the scene's simplicity, variety ruled.

Northward, back up the Green, beyond the river canyon that from where I stood was no more than a suggestion, my eye coursed for mile after unimpeded mile over naked but intricately layered rock. When I swung my head right I could look down and along the final mile of the Green to the Confluence (which from camp had been hidden). In the far distance, beyond a big desert mesa, humped dark mountains that I knew must be the La Sals. Farther right, my eye leapfrogged the invisible canyon of the combined rivers and became impaled on a startling tract of rock needles that the map called "The Grabens." Then my gaze swung south and onward around the panorama—and reached its climax: a territory that the map dotted with such names as The Doll House, Land of Standing Rocks and The Maze (which Powell called "The Rock Forest"). From where I stood, The Doll House rang truest. What I saw was a land of cupolas and cones and miniature mesas, of humps and pimples and spires squirly as antique chess pieces. Across all these diverse and upthrusting rock forms ran a single horizontal pattern: red-brown layers irregularly interleaved with white. And shapes and pattern together forged fantasy; created a toylike, make-believe, Hänsel-and-Gretel world.

Beneath an immense blue sky the air hung calm. Silence reigned. And space, and peace.

I walked left, across the rocky tableland, to its lip. Far below, a sandbar at the foot of One-Mile Canyon jutted out into the muddy river, then curved back to meet the narrow bush-dotted delta on which I'd camped. I peered at the place sandbar and delta met. My raft should have been moored there. I peered again. It was not. My hand reached for binoculars. The raft was there all right, blue and oval; but to my naked eye it had looked so small that it passed as one of the lesser bushes.

I swung the binoculars right, along the trough that was the Green's final mile. At the Confluence, the other arm of the river—the old Grand, now called Colorado—looked twice as wide as the Green. Perhaps more. Greener, too, though hardly pellucid. The rock layers of its canyon walls, I could now see, slanted at a substantial angle from the horizontal layers of the Green's. The river guide, I remembered, said something about another "angular unconformity," and it seemed to me that the rivers' convergence at this precise point of unconformity suggested something more than co-incidence. But no time, now, for technical geology. The attraction up here was not the Confluence, as I'd expected, but the panorama.

Turning away, I began to explore the wedge of rocky plateau between the two river canyons. Savoring. Photographing.

The camera—as can happen if you use it properly—refocused my attention on the foreground. The varied foregrounds. They were, in their different ways, as dramatic as the background. Clusters of white boulders, rounded and flattish and odd, perched on bare red rock like de-stalked

On Confluence walk, looking back upriver. Far below, my raft at sandbar campsite is invisible to the naked eye.

toadstools. Abrupt cliffs, red and sheer and manganese-varnished. Level rock tables dotted with small, black, roundish depressions. (The depressions, carpeted with red dust were, though dry, clearly incipient rainpockets.) Scattered across the open and apparently bare expanses of rock—though at first you somehow hardly noticed them—gnarled juniper trees. Shallow basins with their windblown red soil already supporting slightly denser but still-skimpy junipers; other greenery, too. These basins rimmed by rounded slopes, often fluted and interleaved in their own little angular unconformities—at that moment of no technical interest but often beautiful enough to stop me in my tracks.

Standing before one such unconformity, I became aware of a need. Caffeine-fix time. (Some people laugh at my compulsive tea brewing. True, my days now tend to revolve around it—and . . . well, all right, maybe that *is* addiction.) A breeze had sprung up, and I looked for a sheltered place furnished with firewood.

I found a small open-ended hollow, began collecting the scraps of dead wood that were all I'd need. The breeze had risen a notch, and as I knelt to pick up some juniper twigs it wafted a faint and fleeting animal sound to my ears; an indeterminate sound, not unlike a human voice. Wondering what species might have made it, I stood up so that my head protruded above the lip of the basin and surveyed the wide landscape. Nothing. Back to the kindling search.

A few minutes later, as I arranged three stones into a hearth for my tea-making ceremony, the basin began to reverberate with another sound. A small plane droned into sight, flying low and slow. I leaned back, stared up: a blue-and-white high-wing monoplane bearing the big-lettered inscription, US AIR FORCE. The plane cruised slowly past, barely a thousand feet above, weaving erratically, as if sightseeing. I tried not to resent the intrusion. The plane passed on, out of sight and sound.

In the hearth I built a miniature wigwam of sticks, set them alight, sat back and watched small flames play around my metal cup, full of water, balanced on the hearthstones.

The fire mesmerized, the way naked flames can. My mind wandered out onto the rockscape and down to the Confluence, then back into my hollow and around the skimpy patches of greenery that clothed it.

Other than the moment I saw the angular conformity at the Confluence, I had not once looked at this naked and dramatic rockscape with geology in mind. Not technical, scientific geology. And this time there was an even better reason than down in Stillwater to eschew science, opt for aesthetics.

In most places, "geology" means making educated guesses based on glimpses of protruding rock features; but in unclothed country you study bare rock. The naked earth. You see not just occasional hints of what the rock is doing beneath the soil that clothes it but its entire, curving, beautiful form. And in such country you need not be scientific to appreciate geology. After all, the average man looking at a naked woman does not, unless he's been emasculated by political correctitude, find his mind running to comparative anatomy. It runs to aesthetics. That is, to pulchritude. With naked rock, too, a mind unblinkered by academic correctitude runs to aesthetics.

Now, the curious fact is that a scantily clothed woman looks, at least in the early stages of delectable experiences, even more seductive than a naked one. Once again, as with women, so with rock. Perhaps that was why this alluring rockscape with its scattering of greenery had, even more than Stillwater's bare rock walls, left me numb to scientific geology, sensitive to aesthetics.

In front of me, the water in the cup boiled. I leaned forward, removed the cup, dropped a tea bag into the water. I swished it around a couple of times, then sat back again to let the potion brew—and saw, to my astonishment, out beyond the open end of my little basin, a walking figure.

I think I hesitated a long moment before I called out, "Well, hullo!"

The figure—a youngish man in shorts—stopped, turned sharply, smiled. "Why, hello!"

He looked back the way he had come and said, apparently to open rock, "Look what I've found!"

A second figure appeared. "Well I'm damned," it said.

The two men walked toward me. Sunburned. Fit. We exchanged small talk. They squatted down on the far side of my hearth. I squirted milk powder into the tea, added sugar, stirred, began to drink.

They were camped, they said, a couple of hours away, back in The Maze. They'd just followed the trail on the topo map out to this point.

"Trail?" I said.

We compared maps. Theirs was a newer edition than mine, and indeed showed a trail leading out almost to the Confluence.

"Frankly, we couldn't often find any trail. Just kept going in the right direction."

"Good," I said. Aldo Leopold had it right: "Recreational development is not a job of building roads into lovely country, but of building receptivity into the still unlovely mind." No problem with my visitors' minds, though.

They were from Detroit, they said. Electricians, with General Motors. Yes, the company had sure as hell gone to hell. No wonder, after years of putting profits before everything. It occurred to me that my little basin seemed a strange place to harvest such insider confirmation of Detroit scuttlebutt.

The electricians were experienced outdoorsmen. Very much into birding, it emerged. And they'd recently canoed Boundary Waters Wilderness in Minnesota: "Good place. You have to camp in campsites, but the rest's untouched. You get to see moose there."

We discussed the moose I'd seen in Wyoming. I finished the tea, offered to brew some for them. Thanks, but don't bother, really.

They tried to come out West every year, they said. Mostly to the desert. The year before, they'd camped all through The Maze. Always found enough water. And precious few people. This year, they hadn't seen anyone for four or five days before meeting me.

"Well," said the taller of the two, "we did see one raft yesterday. In the distance. We'd walked down Water Canyon, and on the way back up we saw this raft pull in there."

"Yesterday?"

"Yes."

"About noon?"

"Yes."

"What color was the raft?"

"Turquoise. Couldn't see much else—except that they had oars."

"Oh, there was more than one person in the raft?"

"Well . . . We assumed so. But all we could see through the little binoculars we had was the flash of oars."

"May I see the soles of your boots?"

The electrician raised an eyebrow but turned one boot.

"Thought so," I said—and explained how I'd landed at Water Canyon around noon the day before, walked up a short way searching for potable water and seen fresh footprints. "Very distinctive prints. Yours—no question about it."

The three of us sat smiling, sharing that meeting too.

We chatted on, about many things. I guess I did most of the talking. It happens.

That short sidetrip up Water Canyon had been simple, I said, "but some of the climbing on the way up here had its mildly hairy moments. For that kind of thing, I can't say I really like being on my own."

The shorter of my two visitors seemed to have been studying me closely. Now he smiled. "No," he said, "a man who spends two months alone walking through Grand Canyon and six months walking from Mexico to Oregon obviously doesn't like being alone."

I stared. "How did you know?"

He was grinning now. "Oh, I've just figured out who you are: the trademark tea brewing—and other things. You see, you may not know it, but you're sort of the reason we're here." Years before, it seemed, they'd read some of my books, and Ed Abbey's, and decided to come out West to see what it was all about. They'd been coming ever since.

We talked on. I explained the solitude misunderstanding: it was solo rock scrambling, or roaming very far from the safety of my "home" raft or backpack that tended to make me nervous. But I'm not sure I'd made it clear before my visitors went on their way.

After they'd gone I resumed my exploration and photography of the little plateau. By the time I'd walked over to the lip of the combined rivers' canyon, the breeze had become a gusty south wind, and although I could look down and see how the Green's murky brown water, at first flowing separate and right, away from the green Colorado, before long overwhelmed it, the wind kept gusting so fiercely that I dared not stand very close to the rim. I moved back into the tableland and set up my tripod for self-portraits: "man walks through convoluted rockscape." I took a couple of shots; then, attempting another, had to stand ten paces away and watch helplessly as a turbo wind gust felled the tripod.

I ran back, checked the camera. Jammed. Useless.

I nibbled lunch, dozed in the lee of a ledge, decided the wind was now too strong for safe lighting of a fire, began to weather-fret. Local lore ran: "Don't worry about clouds unless they come from the south." So far, I could see only a few small clouds anchored over the La Sal Mountains. But a sustained wind like this meant a steep pressure gradient, and that raised questions about the next couple of days' weather. I made a half-hearted attempt to find a way out to the point immediately above the Confluence but kept balking at low rock bluffs. In that wind, you couldn't trust your balance without jug-handle holds. Around three o'clock I quit.

By 4:15 I was back at camp, sipping tea in the first, welcome shadows. It had been beautiful, up there on the plateau. And although there'd been moments when I could have felt more stalwart, by the end I was doing fine. Perhaps I was fitter than I'd thought.

Another sip of tea.

On balance, in spite of blemishes, my fifth and final Stillwater sidetrip had been well worth the effort. It was, anyway, one I'd had to make. From the start, I could now admit, I'd been slightly afraid of the whole thing.

14

BIG DROP

LAND OF
STANDING ROCKS:
The Maze
The Doll House

Green R.

Colorado R.

(formerly Grand R.)

Cataract Cyn.

The Confluence
Spanish Bottom

*Mile-Long
Rapid*

Colorado R.

Big Drop Rapids

0   10
MILES

*Mile 735 to Mile 756
October 3–5*

By mid-morning next day, even before I floated out from between Stillwater's sheltering walls, a south wind ruled the river. And as soon as I debouched onto the open water of the Confluence I felt thankful that, because it was only five miles from camp to Cataract's first rapid, I'd already battened down the raft into whitewater mode.

Out on the open water—much more open, suddenly, than I'd expected—the wind whipped upriver unimpeded. It brawled with swirling currents, whisked racing whitecaps. It sired sandstorms from sandbars and sent them billowing across the river. I found us being twirled like a toy. Even muscular oar work buffered the vagaries of wind and current only enough to keep us moving in more or less the right direction, and when I shipped the oars and took a few shots with my simple Olympus camera, we drifted almost aimlessly. Generally upriver, though. So back to battling with the oars.

Almost before I knew it, we were past the Confluence and heading down the Colorado. Down a river twice as big and powerful as the Green; maybe three times. A river still divided, right and left—in that piquant switch of name burdens—between murky Green and green Colorado. Before long, though, the murk triumphed, right bank clear across to left. It was excruciatingly difficult to believe that somewhere in that turbid expanse twirled even one molecule from my little source basin.

The river and I flowed on southward, toward the sea. But the river had notched up to a new stage of maturity. The Confluence had changed it—

the way a dark experience can, overnight, render an apparently mature person mature in some deeper sense.

If anything, the wind had now intensified. Whitecapped waves. Surging gray currents. I battled the oars. To encourage myself I mouthed out loud, into the teeth of the gale, "Oh well, anything for a change, I guess."

Soon, on the right bank, a huge red-edged wooden sign:

D A N G E R

CATARACT CANYON
HAZARDOUS RAPIDS $2\frac{1}{2}$ MI
PERMIT REQUIRED FROM
SUPERINTENDENT CANYONLANDS
NATIONAL PARK FOR BOATING
BELOW SPANISH BOTTOM

High overhead scudded small white clouds tinged with gray. Their shadows kept shrouding the battlefield in deeper gloom.

I swung us around, began to pull instead of push. Now I sat looking back upriver. But already it was difficult to locate the Confluence: it had blended with the general flow of the canyon walls, had become just another flat in the passing show. I kept pulling, hard. It occurred to me that you'd have difficulty finding a confluence of rivers of this magnitude—in the United States or anywhere else in the developed world—that had remained so free from human impact.

Yet there was no denying that the Confluence had been an anticlimax. I suppose I hadn't given any thought to how it would be when I passed through this place at which my river both ended and continued. This place where the Green died but the river lived on. I rather think I'd expected a mini-pageant, trumpets offstage. Instead, this battle.

The war dragged on all the way to Spanish Bottom. The only respite: when I looked ahead and saw high right, strung along the rim, a cluster of gay, toylike rock pinnacles that I knew spelled "Doll House" and "Land of Standing Rocks." Otherwise I fought wind and current and strove to adjust spirits and techniques to the bigger, more powerful river. A reasonable degree of success. But it was a relief to reach Spanish Bottom, just above the first Cataract rapid, and pull in for lunch.

After lunch I dozed, then sat debating. Should I scout Rapid 1 now, then run it? Or wait until morning, when the wind might have died? The way it was gusting now promised grim whitewater maneuvering. Still, running the first couple of rapids before I camped would be a confidence builder.

For a long time after lunch I sat and ruminated.

I was facing up-canyon and off to my right the wind scourged the river. Until it let up, forget the rapids. And cloud shadows kept plunging the scene into gray gloom. The far bank was a stark line of burnt trees: Dave Stimson, the Canyonlands river ranger, had said the fire was started by a backpacker burning toilet paper. No, if you came to this canyon from almost any other place it might, in its way, seem close to magnificent; but it was not Stillwater.

So, without question now, my peaceful ten-day cruise through Labyrinth and Stillwater was over. It had been an almost achingly perfect time. An idyllic interlude that had built slowly, so that it was all but over before I'd begun to recognize it. That was the way such things tended to happen: they crept up on you. And already the interlude was beginning to radiate a warm, nostalgic, Indian-summer glow.

A gust of wind caught the tethered raft. It bumped against the bank. A mini-avalanche of sand tumbled into the river.

Such a golden interlude could occur in any kind of journey. It might be a physical journey. Down a river, say. Or an individual traveling his life course. Or a civilization unfolding. (Europeans often saw the years just before World War I as such an interlude; Americans were now fingering the 1950s.) Or the journey might be that of a species evolving. Or of life evolving on a planet.

It seemed to me that you could—possibly without stumbling across the twilight zone that separates insight from crap—perceive a certain ancient pageant played out on the East African plateau as just such a halcyon interlude in the evolution of life on this planet. (Halcyon, I mean, if you viewed evolution as a whole: the times may not have looked that way at all to any single species, let alone any individual organism.) For a long and uninterrupted span beginning in the Permian age, just after the dinosaurs had folded their scales and silently crept away, the equatorial East African plateau—already uplifted a mile and more above sea level—was spared two kinds of disasters that often break the flow of evolution: ice-age glaciation and inundation by oceans. The mammals, a previously insignificant evolutionary twig that had just begun to prosper, were thereby given a chance to flourish, uninterrupted. They took it. They branched out; radiated to fill many niches. Eventually they built a rich and complex web across the savannah. Even today, when only tatters of that web remain, glimpses of it can be breathtaking. Human descendants flock from all over the world just to watch.

If we dollied the camera in toward the end of that stable and fruitful span we could view the savannah as the scene of another halcyon pageant of a lower order. (Or higher order; take your pick.) Near the end of that

long post-dinosaur interlude—perhaps four million years ago—the mammalian branch sprouted hominids. (Again, of course, I mean "halcyon"
from a collective, not individual, perspective: the life of an individual
hominid who lived then was, when viewed from where we now think we
stand, "nasty, brutish and short.") But if you accept that we began somewhere in the vicinity of Olduvai Gorge and also—though this demands a
greater leap of faith—that we are indeed the current spearhead of mammalian evolution, even of planetary life, then it seems reasonable to regard
that relatively recent little pageant on the East African plateau as a golden
interval for both planetary life and its mammalian branch.

Out in the present, in midriver, I glimpsed a dark blob that might or
might not have been a beaver's head. The wind had dropped a little but
choppy waves still tended to obscure such matters.

Come to think of it, if we dollied the camera in on that ongoing East
African pageant at a time that was virtually the present, and focused our
lens down to the next life-system level—to individual organisms—and if
we once again zeroed in on the only individual whose life journey I know
and shall ever know in its entirety, we might glimpse scenes in what could
be called, in hindsight, a halcyon interlude for that organism.

Co-managing a Kenya hotel with my wife turned out to be, as I've said,
not my line. Its demands may have hastened the breakdown of our marriage. Anyway, we separated, and eventually divorced. I went into farming,
first as pupil-assistant, eventually as a manager. Farming turned out to be
the first occupation that really satisfied me for any length of time. Yet after
five and a half years in Kenya, I left. (Without, strange as it may seem, having "discovered" the savannah's rich wildlife.)

In later years I had sometimes looked back through rose-tinted nostalgia
mists and seen that spell of farming on the East African plateau as—in
some ways, though certainly not all—a golden pause in the sun, before I
moved on to face new challenges.

I left Kenya for a rainbow of reasons, spread across the human spectrum.
But one purpose I recognized and voiced at the time was a wish to "get out
and see something of the rest of the world." And when I left Kenya I
launched myself into the currents of a much wider river. Even at the time, I
think I understood, if not very clearly, the significance of what I was doing.

Four traveling years twirled me on a journey through Southern Rhodesia (now Zimbabwe), Britain, Canada and sundry waypoints—and deposited me in San Francisco, California. That journey changed my life,
internally as well as externally. Toward the end of it, in Canada, a friend
looked at me and said, "You may not know it, but you're going through a
glorious metamorphosis." I had no idea what she was talking about.

In San Francisco I fell in love with the city and a damsel. Two years later, after an almost achingly perfect interlude, several routine quirks of fate left me standing for the first time beside the Colorado. Left me standing at the Mexican border with a pack on my back, facing Oregon. Facing an entirely new and intriguing challenge.

And now here I was, midway through another Colorado journey, at the end of another golden interlude, poised on the brink of Cataract Canyon, with Grand Canyon looming.

I felt myself shiver. Beyond my right shoulder, the sun had sunk behind the canyon wall. Cool gray shadow, reaching out across the Colorado, had enveloped raft and resting place. Had tranquilized the river, too. Gusts now churned it only rarely, and during the interludes between them the water's surface subsided. Subsided to an almost peaceful calm.

I glanced at my wristwatch: 3:53. I stood up.

For a split second I looked away from the rapidly approaching tongue, checked the watch: 5:11. Then my eyes flicked back to where they belonged—out beyond the left oar.

We were almost level, now, with those first small, wide-spaced rocks. Bisecting them perfectly. And gathering speed. At the foot of the tongue, right, I could now see, clear and unmistakable, that ugly boulder-hump with the horrendous hole behind it. We'd clear it all right, just as I'd planned when I scouted down the bank.

With the hump safely identified I push-pulled the oars, fiercely. We pivoted. Now I ferried bow-left, facing the new danger: a series of holes on the tongue's left edge—and below them, a whitecapped cauldron I couldn't yet identify but that I knew lurked in mid-rapid.

A gust of wind caught the raft. I corrected. No problem. Then we were racing past the series of holes, bow in just the right place, a foot or two clear, and I could see the white cauldron ahead. No need to correct. I spun us bow-first. And then the current had carried us past the cauldron and down the center of the rapid's tail—just as Ranger Dave Stimson had said it would and as my long scout down the right bank had seemed to confirm. Then we were out of the white water.

But not for long.

The second rapid was another down-the-tongue job. Or so Dave and my scouting had promised. Approaching the tongue I ferried, compensating for minor wind gusts, until we were headed dead-center into the drop-away; then, at the last moment, I spun us bow-first and pushed like crazy.

Instant bedlam. Walls of surging white water, tainted brown. But everything straightforward. Just a careening rush. Small oar pressures to hold the raft at right angles to each wave, nothing more. The waves were big, though. As big as any we'd taken. But the bulging blue bow rode up and over them, one after the other. At each wave, water showered us with glistening off-white cascades that were cold, very cold; but the little raft held true. No twinge of danger, only exhilaration. Then we were clear, floating level, and I was scanning the right bank for a sheltered campsite, above Rapid 3.

The freeze-dried Mountain Chili matured in its pot. The wine tasted good. The rare gusts of wind passed harmlessly overhead. A few yards below, the river slid into the first white water of Rapid 3.

I looked back up toward Rapid 2. Yes, it had been important, getting those first two safely under my belt. With the wind gusting like that I wouldn't have fancied tackling anything too demanding, but Rapid 1 had been neither technically difficult nor bum-tingle scary. Just about right. Just enough of a challenge. (It was also called Brown Betty Rapid, after the cook boat of the ill-fated Brown-Stanton expedition that exactly a century earlier had surveyed a possible river route for a railroad through both Cataract and Grand Canyons; but *Brown Betty* was in fact lost about four miles downstream.)

Afterward, Rapid 2 had been fun. And the big waves had renewed my confidence in the raft.

Another sip of wine.

The river had in a sense reassumed its old identity as an overgrown trout stream. Only in one sense, though. In the rapids, things hadn't felt all that much bigger than in the Green; but there was no doubt, really, about the river's new maturity, its new power. I'd have to treat it with even greater respect. Would have to pay attention.

I tilt-slithered a helping of chili from pot into metal cup.

"Paying attention" meant doing what Les Bechdel had recommended in his *River Rescue* book: thinking carefully about "What if?" Above all, "What if I flip?" I knew the rules: getting back to the raft was normally the safest thing, whether it was upside down or not; failing that, get yourself ashore—and hope you can recapture the raft. But I ought to have a contingency plan in case I was separated from the raft. During dinner I decided that starting next morning I'd always travel with a waterproof matchsafe in one shorts pocket and a tiny Swiss Army knife, secured by a cord, in the other, along with a tightly rolled aluminum foil space blanket in a ziplock bag. Also some iodine tablets: I could purify river water in the space blanket. Should have done all this long ago. But better late than never.

I finished dinner, sat watching day dim toward night. Against pale sky, bats swooped and swerved to snare their insect breakfasts. The bats materialized almost every twilight, but until now I hadn't really noticed their extraordinarily abrupt maneuvers. Very different from the swallows' smooth, curvaceous sweeps. Sonar-directed, so the dying light made no difference. But my day-use eyes could hardly follow their dark little sideslipping shapes: they kept flicking into and out of existence. *Twinkle, twinkle, little bat / How I wonder what you're at.*

I looked upriver. Darkness had curtained off Rapid 2. And Rapid 3, just below camp, swamped its sound. But I was conscious, now, that those first two rapids had refreshed my memory about many things, piffling through ponderous.

The one-minute-after-the-hour nonsense, for example. Not until we were actually in the tongue of Rapid 1 had I remembered to check that my watch didn't read 5:01. By then it would have been too late, anyway. At a guess, this foolishness had its roots in my school days. The train that carried us all away at the end of each term, back out into the wide world and to our various homes, was scheduled to leave the local station at 9:01 a.m. So we sometimes used "the 9:01" to signify any ending or departure. For years the metaphor had lain fallow in my mind. But in the last couple of decades, with timepieces gone digital, it had been borne on my consciousness that when I glanced at any watch or clock it seemed to read, on an overwhelmingly unreasonable number of occasions, one minute past the hour. Bedside digital clock-radios, in particular, projected almost echoically vivid messages: their brilliant LED numerals beaconed out of the darkness into the dream-clouded canyons of your mind. Anyway, my clocks and watches had for years now seemed to say, with inordinate frequency, "1:01" or "4:01" or some rhyming cousin. As you know, I'm not superstitious. But I'd come to regard "XX:01" as a potential omen. I'd even offered comic wagers that when I died that's what the clock would read. So back up in Lodore Canyon I'd naturally avoided starting a run down any rapid when my watch proclaimed those ominous figures. Before Cataract's Rapid 1 I'd forgotten to check. Now, though, with memory refreshed, I'd resume sensible precautions. Knowing that the whole thing was a can of paper worms made, of course, no difference at all. (Not long ago, when I explained this drivel to a friend, she exclaimed, "Oh, but I feel the same—except that with me it's been *repeating* numbers. You know, '3:33' or '11:11.' ")

The rapids had jolted my memory about serious things, too. Adrenaline tides, for example.

Back in Lodore and Desolation I'd learned that the scary times were the scouts. As you walked down the bank—ears drumming with the rapid's roar, eyes dazzled by glistening foam—or stood on a rock and pondered and repondered route choices, the adrenaline began to flow. As you walked back up to the raft, wondering if your choice was really the right one, flow surged to rush. And when you stood hesitating before you unhitched the bow line, rush built to flood. That was prime farting time.

But once you cast off and got your hands on the oars and began to peer ahead for markers, peace descended. Now, everything narrowed to specifics. To nitty-gritties. Picking up the marker: that small but distinctive camel-humped boulder right of the tongue. Picking it up early enough to let you ferry onto the precise line that would bring your bow past it very, very close indeed: brushing it would be good, but banging might trigger disaster. Feeling bow brush rock. By then, though, your mind was leapfrogging thirty feet downstream to the narrow gut between those monstrous twin rocks—the racing ribbon of water you had to hit dead center, bow-first, raft aligned arrow-straight. All this time your mind was so pinned to the present, so engrossed in doing what it had to do, that there was no time, no room, for anything you could clearly call fear. Not even when you found yourself plunging down into the maw of the gut and it was steeper and faster and narrower than you'd expected, or when you hit the first tail wave a touch off kilter and had to correct frantically to line up for the second. You were too centered, too busy, to feel fear. And when you came clear at last into flat water you were smiling, grinning, laughing.

I'd learned all this before I got to Green River, Utah. There, I'd discussed the adrenaline pattern with Karen, the Holiday boatman. "That's right," she said. "I think we all go through the same routine. Terrific. No wonder they call us 'adrenaline junkies.' Seems you never get over it, either. Dee Holiday says that after thirty years at the game he still reacts much the same."

Now my adrenaline seemed destined to flow freely. In the next 10 miles we'd run more than twenty rapids, culminating in Lower Big Drop, alias Holy Shit. (Cataract once had fifty-two rapids, spread over 18½ miles, but Powell Reservoir—a.k.a. Lake Powell—had engulfed its lower half.)

Out on the river, night had taken over. Suddenly weary, I washed up, slid down into my sleeping bag. Far to the south, lightning flashed. I bantered around with what had become one of my standard wilderness gags: it had to be lightning, because if it was the start of World War III those occasional winking lights of commercial jets wouldn't still be creeping across the night sky.

The wind was blowing directly from the storm toward me but the lightning looked a long way off. I did put the big blue tarp ready, though, beside my bed.

That night it rained and I dreamed.

When the rain hit I came half awake and pulled the tarp over me and lifted it clear of the sleeping bag by draping it over half-empty dry bags and tucking its edges under them. But all night, every time I felt the wind blow, I came one-third awake and worried about the perfunctoriness of the tucking, and periodically did something about it. In between the caretaking, I dreamed. Dreamed dreams that were as idiotic as most dreams but more menacing and more unremitting. Or so it seemed. Anyway, I suffered one of my rare disturbed nights and woke still halfway weary.

Yet the morning went well.

The wind had died. Most of the rapids turned out to be simple. The rest, no more than interesting. And I felt pleased with the way I ran all but one.

After a long and careful scout of Rapid 5 I knew that the key to avoiding the bad-news obstacles that riddled its foot lay in entering close to but just left of a big submerged rock. Too far left, and I might hit a hole, just below. From above, though, the submerged-rock marker might be difficult to see.

It was. I picked it up late. Very late. Even after a spurt of frenzied ferrying I still passed it too far left and barely had time to straighten up before we hit the hole. We hit it hard, just right of center. The raft spun. I tried to counter. In that swirling white foam, though, the oars flailed. Sudden helplessness; then we were out of the hole—unscathed but spun around. For a moment, the bow faced directly upriver. But now, in less foamy water, the oars worked, and within seconds I'd pivoted us back with bow pointing downstream again, facing danger, facing the bad news ahead. We rode the rest perfectly. But I remembered that moment when we faced upriver.

It was the only time all morning that I felt I did not have the raft under control.

Above Rapid 10 I landed river left to scout. Dave Stimson had warned of one hole that demanded respect—and this was apparently the rapid that sank the Brown-Stanton party's cook boat. Only later did I learn from Robert Brewster Stanton's book *Down the Colorado* that *Brown Betty* was actually lost during an attempt to line her down the rapid.

Stanton's book sheds light on the problems that pioneers faced:

When we were going through Cataract [starting June 1], the River was rising, though it had not gotten to its full high water stage, and that year, 1889, the rise did not reach its average height, so that most of the rapids were full of rocks above the water, and their sharp edges played havoc with our thin cedar boats. It was not any individual rapid, but the eighteen and a half miles of continuous, boiling, tumbling waters among the rocks that wore them out, and so severely tried our powers of endurance.

In my noncedar raft (its design forged from a century of post-Stanton river-running), pampered by a river guide (ditto) and by Dave Stimson's advice, I ran Rapid 10 without difficulty. And its two successors.

Next on the agenda, Mile-Long Rapid.

Mile-Long consists of five closely spaced rapids, numbers 13 through 17, that at high water tend to merge. I landed river right, spent over an hour scouting the first four rapids. As I walked back up to the raft I kept running the sequences over in my mind: a succession of current-and-obstacle details that not only had to be precisely recalled in the right order but would also demand split-second translation of images viewed from the bank into images seen from directly upriver.

Above all, there was Rapid 15, with its endearing name of Capsize: a complicated series of moves, including one in which I'd have to pivot at precisely the right moment and pull across a line of white water. I'd pull rather than push in order to achieve enough momentum to carry us across the barrier line. This technique of pulling hard, stern-first, out of the main current into safer water on one flank—usually through side waves—is today known as "Powelling," apparently because it resembles John Wesley's method of barreling down all rapids.

Back at the raft, adrenaline or no, I felt tired. Could the disturbed night be taking its toll? I brewed my standard caffeine response and then, with juices seeping back, sat in the moored raft and for several minutes applied what I call "an Emmett": a relaxation technique known as Selective Awareness—by self-hypnosis out of Transcendental Meditation—perfected by an M.D. I know, Emmett Miller. Before long I felt relaxed, centered, ready.

The whole sequence went like clockwork. Particularly Capsize Rapid. Halfway down, pulling hard, I looked over my shoulder at precisely the right moment and immediately saw my rounded-rock marker on the barrier line of white water. I Powelled through dead on target. The relatively slack water beyond gave me even more time than I'd expected to pivot the bow so that it faced new bankside dangers. Adjust onto planned line. Ferry on down, under absolute control. Let bow brush, exactly as intended, a triangular-rock marker. Then, as I straightened out to run a final tongue down into the clear—even before we entered the tongue, because I knew we would hit it dead center—I laughed and shouted out loud, "Perfect!"

The elation still swirled as I threaded us through the rest of Mile-Long with the confidence of a pro who'd been at it for years.

Now, confidence can slither undetected into overconfidence. And hubris spells danger.

Just before either Rapid 18 or 19—I'm not sure which, because I hadn't bothered to check the guide—the full flow of the river, confined and swift but without white water, swung across at an angle from the right wall to left. In mid-swing it divided on each side of a huge boulder and dropped away in two smooth tongues. I could see the far tongue, left of the boulder, clear down to the place it leveled off into flat water. Without much thought, I chose the shorter route, right of the boulder, and floated languidly toward it—broadside on, bow left, ready to make minor adjustments to avoid any obstacles in the short stretch of it that lay out of my sight. I was almost at the drop-off when I saw, over the raft's right tube, that this tongue did not, like the other, glide serenely down into the flat water. It poured over into a horrendous hole that spanned the tongue's entire width.

No time to pivot, then pull left. So I pushed, frantically, on both oars. The imminent glassy lip of the drop-off and the seething maw below, now all too visible, goaded me on. Inch by inch we began to ease left, toward the big boulder—away from the lip, from the hole. Very slowly, we gained momentum. For a moment I thought we were going to be swept up onto the boulder and jam solid. But then we'd lifted onto the bulge of water above the boulder's sloping base. We hung there, almost motionless. Then we were sliding down into the safety of the far tongue.

Minutes later I pulled ashore above Rapid 20. The adrenaline was ebbing, fast. Suddenly I felt drained.

Dave Stimson had drawn my attention to Rapid 20 but had remained vague. When I asked for specifics, he smiled and said, "The guide rates it '1,' but . . . Well, you'll see." (The river guide rated each rapid on a scale of 1 to 10. Capsize was a 6; Lower Big Drop, 10.) By now I'd learned to appreciate the way Dave metered his advice: enough information to post warnings and plant signposts, not enough to tarnish expectation; plenty of latitude for me to deal with details. For Rapid 20, he'd left me wondering.

My first impression: a confusion of black boulders and white water. No hint of a route. Second impression: ditto.

By now it was nearly three o'clock. Lunch long overdue. I lunched, siestaed. Afterward, though, even wearier. No doubt now: the disturbed night had caught up with me.

I did walk slowly down and scout the rapid. Close up, it looked horrific. Mostly, a confusion of whitewater obstacles. At its foot, a curving drop-off that blocked all except a narrow channel, left. This channel guarded by a large boulder and its god-awful hole.

I dragged myself back up to the raft. I'd meant to camp that night just above Lower Big Drop. But by now I'd grasped that it was stupid and dangerous to run a "bad" rapid when you were operating at anything short of peak performance. Besides, by morning light the run might look easier. So I camped where I'd pulled in.

Afternoon eased into evening. After dinner I leaned back against my dry-bag backrest. The food had injected enough energy for a reassessment.

All along, I'd known that Cataract posed a test. A test that would last little more than a day but would scan my fitness for the month-long run of Grand Canyon. And ahead, now, lay Cataract's cusp. In the next two miles the river dropped 72 vertical feet—and climaxed in the cusp's cusp: Lower Big Drop. Yet for the moment I felt more nervous about this next rapid.

Briefly, I scouted the lining possibilities. But my heart wasn't in it. I had to *run* this one. If I balked, how could I pretend to be ready for Lower Big Drop, let alone Crystal and Lava Falls in Grand Canyon? (By now, I guess, I'd fully embraced, almost without further thought, the idea that I'd try to run all the river's rapids.)

Dusk deepened. Downriver, the canyon's irregular and crumbly red walls were sinking toward gray. "The attraction of Cataract," Dave Stimson had said, "is the rapids, not the rock."

I closed my eyes. Well, all right, I'd scout Rapid 20 again in the morning. And probably run it.

Close below me, the rapid roared something like defiance. I listened more intently. No, it didn't really roar: this one didn't intimidate with size. It snarled: its threat lay in confusion. But if you failed to sort out the confusion—to dampen the "noise" in its communication sense—and found yourself down at the foot, heading inexorably for that line of holes . . .

I comforted myself with two warring quotes. First, somebody's insight that "life is not a gift but an open-ended loan, liable to be called without notice at fate's whim." Then Nietzsche's edict: "That which doesn't kill you makes you stronger." You had to stomach the Nietzschean machismo and allow the underlying truth. Had to allow that facing physical danger can help raise you up from a condition in which you look out on a bleak world and ask plaintively, "Is this all there is?" Can help lift you back on track and leave you gushing "Oh, what a wonderful life!" Can help you, that is, to achieve just the kind of alchemy that long journeys are—whether you know it or not—often designed to engender.

I reopened my eyes. Downriver, the canyon walls had faded to ghost spaces. Overhead, a star-spangled wedge of night sky.

Now, I'm reasonably accustomed to facing physical dangers. Dangers keen enough to threaten life. And I've always accepted them. But sitting there at the head of Rapid 20 I found myself accepting in a new way. I was aware that the next mile, the next 200 miles, would strain my sketchy rafting capabilities to their limit. Aware that if things went wrong, down at the foot of Rapid 20, for example, and I flipped, out here on my own, with heavy water below, then I might not make it. And I found myself accepting that possibility in a new way. Looking back, I was no longer sure that in the past I'd done so. Not sure I'd faced the reality head-on, eyes open. But this time I felt I did accept. Did so with a certain stoicism. Stoicism of a new kind. I seemed to say to myself, "I've had a good life. And if this is it . . . well, all right."

Night displaced dusk. Down to my right, the rapid snarled on.

Mind you, I wasn't sure I trusted myself. My conversion probably went no more than intellect-deep. If things went wrong I'd fight like hell against extinction. After all, that was how we organisms are constructed. How we have to be constructed.

Next morning, after a good night's sleep, back to the nitty-gritty.

By morning light the run at first looked no easier. But a lengthy scout disclosed a possible way through. When I pushed out into the current, post-Emmett, semi-confidence ruled.

Halfway down the rapid. Ferrying bow right. Still on the chosen line. And the water ahead looking rather less fierce than I'd feared . . . Then we were not on line but being pulled right. Being drawn toward the line of holes across the foot of the rapid. Pull hard, both oars. Pull like mad. At first, no change. Then—painfully slowly—inching back toward the line that meant safety. Moments later we eased in behind and below the big boulder and its god-awful hole. Now ferry in close to the left bank, then spin the bow downriver. Done. We went through the narrow channel dead center, comfortably clear of the line of holes, and slowed into quiet water.

Rapids 21 and 22—Upper and Middle Big Drop, both rated 7—were big water but fairly straightforward. (Though Middle Big Drop at high water is apparently "a terrifying, gigantic river-wide wave that's unavoidable.") No serious problems. As soon as we emerged from Middle Big Drop, I looked ahead. Not far below, the river vanished. Just ended. As if cut off. With a knife.

A respectful distance above the drop-off I pulled ashore, left, tied the raft very securely, and walked down the bank.

Dave Stimson had said, "When you see it, you'll say, 'Holy Shit, am I going through *that*?'" I reached the drop-off, complied.

What I saw, a few feet out from the left bank, was a raging white maelstrom. And I knew my route transected it.

"At higher water you can make a run way over to the right," Dave had said. "You'll see that the river guide says 'scout from the right bank.' But when you're there the river will only be running around four thousand cfs, and you'll have to scout left and run left." He'd gone on to give me more detailed instructions than usual. And now, standing beside the rapid, I read a note he'd written in the guide: "Run is *right* of big mossy rock!" Also a clarification in my handwriting: "Mossy rock is on *left* side of rapid."

I checked. The mossy rock formed the near wall of the maelstrom— which roiled and fumed, white with sustained anger, through a gap or gut between it and two other big boulders. Through a gut perhaps twelve feet wide.

"The trick is to hit it dead center," Dave had said.

If I succeeded, I could now see, there'd be two or three feet to spare on each side. But if I erred either way and hit a boulder while in the grip of that torrent . . .

My eye ran on beyond the gut, across the line of the drop-off, clear to the far bank. A tight, unbroken obstacle course of massive boulders and foaming white water. Unrunnable. Just as Dave had known it would be.

Eye back to the maelstrom. This time, to its approaches. At once, a shock: the maelstrom was not, in itself, the problem. What I had to worry about was getting into it.

So I worried. Worried for more than an hour.

The only way you could enter the maelstrom was down a steeply plung- ing tongue, so narrow that at first I doubted whether even my little raft could squeeze between the rocks that flanked and formed the tongue. Mak- ing it through the gut might be a matter of feet, but at the tongue you mea- sured tolerance in inches. And if you so much as grazed any of those flanking rocks, at the drop-off or in the first few plunging feet, you'd go skitterwise into the gut, wildly out of control. And maybe out of the raft.

I took a deep breath—then realized that the tongue itself was not, after all, the true crux of the problem.

You could not, I saw, float down into it from directly above. A slanting line of small, barely submerged rocks, fringed with white water, guarded the approach like a tank trap. At first that seemed to mean there was no way a raft could reach the tongue. Then I saw that the tongue consumed two bodies of water. One came directly downriver, through the tank-trap rocks. The other angled in below them, from the left. It slanted in smooth and sleek, broken only by one small, white, rumpled flare of foam, no doubt caused by a submerged rock. This flare would persist for a spell, then fade away.

The smoothness was good, up to a point. It would make for easier ma- neuvering. But its very sleekness posed questions. What line down that smooth, slanting run would take you to the tongue so that when you reached it you were in the right place to pivot left and, throwing your raft upon the waters, plunge down it into the maelstrom? And what about a marker to guide you onto your chosen line and let you hold it?

I spent the next hour chewing at those problems. Making decisions, then unmaking and remaking them.

At first I felt sure about the line that would bring me to the tongue: it ran just to the right—that is, upstream—of the lone white rumple-flare in the smooth approach. For ten or fifteen minutes I hung happily with that decision. Then, belatedly, I enrolled a routine river-runner's aid: I threw a piece of wood into the smooth run, well above the white flare. The stick floated down, exactly as intended, just to the right of the flare. But it dipped over and into the tongue much too far right. A raft approaching on that line would be wrecked on the tongue's far-flank boulders. I launched another stick—on a line that would take it just left of the marker. And this time, when it reached the tongue, it plunged down dead center. Several more trials confirmed this line. I stood considering the import of their message.

If I floated down left of the flare marker, the raft's port tube would hang perilously close to the glassy drop-off. Would there be room for the left oar to help hold us back, dead slow? And also contribute to the small ongoing adjustments I'd have to make? What if . . .?

All at once I realized I'd been staring intently at rapidly moving water for far too long. My retinas had retained the shifting images, and when I looked at stationary objects they seemed to be moving. To avoid the risk of distorted messages, eyes and brain needed a rest. (I'd been studying the water longer than I may have seemed to suggest. To keep things simple I've reported the launching of only four or five pieces of flotsam. But I had to keep finding new pieces of wood, then throw them out into the river. And not every piece landed where intended. So the trials took time.)

Below the maelstrom, the bank was a staccato jumble of boulders—part of the "block talus cone" that along with its partner on the far bank created the barrier that was Big Drop. Or so the river guide said. I scrambled over the boulders to the foot of the rapid.

Downstream, a bend hid the last two rapids—all that remained of Cataract before the tentacles of Powell Reservoir began to snuff out the living river. Dave Stimson had told me about those last two rapids: "Just big waves, nothing else. And the waves are great for releasing your adrenaline build-up from Big Drop. Just ride 'em and whoop." But these rapids still lay beyond the bend, out of sight. Besides, although my eyes were now back to normal and I could see clearly enough, anything below Big Drop at that moment hardly seemed real. First things first.

I turned back upriver—back into the roar of the rapid. As the river guide said, "Even the sound of the water is on a different scale: the Big Drop roars a bass to the tenor of the other rapids upstream." I scrambled on. Level with the maelstrom, jammed under a rock, the torn-off lid of an ammo box lay twisted in silent testimony to the river's power.

Beyond the mossy boulder I paused and began trying to imprint the flow of the maelstrom on my mind; then realized that once you were in it there was probably precious little you could do about where you went.

Soon I was back at the entrance tongue, restudying the smooth run that slanted into it—the silk-smooth run with its little white flare of foam that kept fading away. What would happen if that vital marker faded away just when I needed it most? I re-agonized, reached the same conclusion as before: that was just something I had to risk; was part of the package.

Once again I looked out across the whole horrendous rapid. Aside from the maelstrom, it still looked essentially unrunnable.

Checking the guide, I reread a 1960 report that it quoted: "Comparison of photographs taken by E. O. Beaman on the 1871 Powell expedition and the rapid today shows that 10- to 20-foot boulders have been rolled, shifted, and removed from the rapid within the last century." Yes. Time kept eroding this obstacle, the way it did most obstacles, most challenges. If you can wait long enough, things alter, shift, mutate. But mostly you don't have the time. Not the years, let alone the centuries. You're stuck with your day, your hour, your minute; eventually, with your split seconds.

I glanced upstream. For more than a week I'd had the river to myself; but for the first time on the trip—perhaps the first time on any physical journey I'd made—I would have welcomed the sight of someone. Almost anyone.

My eyes swung back to the rapid, to the present, to reality. One last time, I ran through the script I was stuck with.

All easy enough, in theory. Ease down dead slow, paralleling the shoreline, into the start of the smooth run. Just short of the drop-off, angle right, toward the rumple-flare marker. Pray it persisted. Ease forward, still under perfect control, and pass a few inches to its left. Hold clear of the glassy pour-over that would now yawn under the port tube. Reach the tongue. At exactly the proper moment, push with the right oar. Push with the precise force to pivot us directly down the plunging tongue. Plunge straight as an arrow—bisecting to perfection the tongue's flanker rocks with the cascades pouring over them—and hit the maelstrom dead center. Beyond that, probably, back to prayer. Back to invoking Yhprum's Law: "Just sometimes, every damned thing goes right." Once in the maelstrom, though, I'd have to strive to hold us straight—whatever that seemed to mean at any given split second. And through the very maw of the gut it might be wise to lift both oar blades from the water and push both handles as low and far forward as possible so that the oars angled back and up with the blades maybe clear of the mossy boulder and its opposite numbers. Maybe.

Yes, the script was clear enough. I swallowed twice, farted, turned and walked back upriver.

The adrenaline flood peaked at what felt like a record crest. I stepped into the raft, watched the resulting ripples widen out across the smooth river, then sat down in the soft white plastic seat on the black-topped dry box. Check watch: 12:57. I smiled. No problem. Still a lot to do.

First I stowed away in dry boxes everything that might be jolted or washed or ripped loose. Everything. Not just the cameras and food items I'd put away before running other rapids but the binoculars that normally hung around my neck and the water canteen that normally hung in its red canvas holder strapped to the raft frame. I snap-locked both dry boxes and strapped down their lids, then checked the strap securing the dry bags, up in the bow. I slid the toggle on my eyeglass retainer snug against the back of my head, tightened the adjustable strap on my broad-brimmed hat and slipped it under my chin. By the time the housekeeping was done we were long and safely past 1:01.

Then I did my Emmett. During such "trances," time stops. And I don't think I checked my watch when I emerged. But I know I felt extraordinarily relaxed and centered. All but a few leftover crinkles of fear had been smoothed away. I was ready, eager.

I untied the raft, pushed gently out into the current, began to let the script unfold.

We eased down, parallel to the shoreline. We approached the left edge of the drop-off. I was still holding us back without difficulty, and we were moving very slowly. I could see the familiar line of the smooth run now, and I angled us into it. The flaring white marker was there, just where it ought to have been.

Still under perfect control, I let the current ease us forward. The glassy pour-over was already there, beyond the raft's port tube, but we had a bigger margin of error than I'd feared, and enough room for the left oar to play its part in holding us back and making small, vital adjustments to our line of travel. The line still looked good. And the rumple-flare was persisting. We passed a few inches left of it.

Now the tongue was there, just ahead, plunging left, down between its flanker rocks. The angle of plunge looked steeper than before, the flanker rocks more menacing. I suppose the roar must by now have grown louder, but I don't think I noticed it. My eyes monopolized my senses. And my eyes were riveted on the tongue. We inched toward it. I remember feeling elated at the way I still had us under control.

The bow came level with the tongue. Through the oars I could feel the water begin to gather itself. I could still hold us on line, but we were gaining speed. And then the center of the raft, just ahead of me, was moving into position directly above the center of the tongue. I waited another split second, then pushed with the right oar. We pivoted to perfection, down into the tongue. The bow dipped. We began to accelerate. I lifted both oars clear. And then we were plunging as if in free fall and I had a flash-glimpse of the right flanker rocks—bigger and more terrible than ever—and of the Niagaras pouring over them. In the moment of the fall I looked ahead and saw that we were perfectly aligned to bisect the mossy boulder and its opposing cousins. Then we were rocketing into the maelstrom.

All hell let loose. We bounced, bounced again, again, went on bouncing. No sense of air around the raft now, just white foam. Foam that surged and boiled and flung itself in sunlit dervish dances. But this white hell was a heavenly hell, for as we rocketed forward we held line.

The flung foam was all I could see. Or perhaps I caught a glimpse of dark boulders, left and right; I'm not sure. All I knew was that we were holding line, straight as an arrow. I'm not sure I did anything to hold us there. I think it just happened. And then, almost before I'd registered what was happening, before I'd had time to do more than feel the beginnings of exultation, we were through. Through and heading downriver, still arrow-like.

We were clear of Big Drop's last white water before it occurred to me that even during our rocket trip through the maelstrom, when I could see nothing but churning white foam, high and all around me, we had shipped little or no water. I checked body and clothing. Not even damp. We floated on downriver. Floated on air, it seemed, not water.

We eased into the first bend. Now at last the two remaining rapids were real. The reservoir below them, too.

We rounded the bend, entered Cataract's penultimate rapid. As advertised, a straightforward roller coaster. We bounced joyfully through it, hitting every wave head-on. Minutes later we were in the last rapid of all. This time I knew I could let go. As we lifted over the crest of each huge white wave I put my head back and whooped. Whooped and whooped again in celebration of Yhprum's Law. I hoped Dave Stimson could hear me.

The waves diminished, died away. The last white water flattened out. A huge, familiar silence began to build between the canyon walls. We moved slowly into it.

By degrees, the current slackened. Soon, the river was no longer pure river.

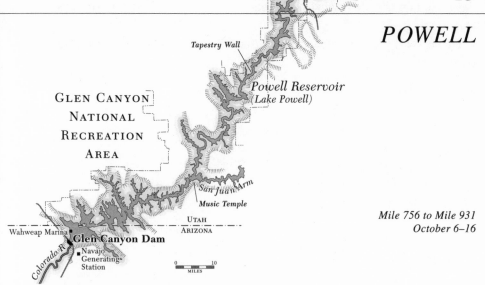

15

POWELL

Mile 756 to Mile 931
October 6–16

For three days I rowed noncompulsively through lower Cataract Canyon and its successor, Narrow Canyon.

On the second day my river finally died. Along its rock walls, reservoir stigmata began to appear. They would persist, I knew, all through the 180-mile hiatus that lay ahead, and the best I could do for the crucified and buried river was to concoct a creed that had it still flowing along in some ethereal form, deep in the dead water, awaiting resurrection and the plunge into Grand Canyon.

The third morning, thirty miles below Big Drop, we emerged from between the rock walls of Narrow Canyon into wide water. I welcomed the new openness. The canyons had captivated me; but toward the end I suppose I'd begun to feel enclosed, hemmed in—a captivated captive—and coming out into open water was something of a release. Also, once again, a change that reenergized.

I turned left, rowed into Hite.

The original settlement of Hite—on the river's right bank, at the site of a ferry crossing—today lies full fathom fifteen. Modern Hite is a utilitarian and unlovely lake-shore marina, six miles "upstream" of the submerged ferry. At Hite Marina I picked up my little outboard motor and in mid-afternoon motored away southwestward toward Glen Canyon Dam.

Powell Reservoir, that massive distension of the Colorado River induced when the dam blocked its flow—that body of desert water successfully public-relationed on us as *Lake* Powell—is a beautiful, sad place. Superficially beautiful. Profoundly sad.

The reservoir is judged and proclaimed to be beautiful partly because it provides near-epic spectacle; partly because it affords boat-access to many innocent human eyes from which such sensational desert scenery would otherwise remain hidden; partly because promulgating its charms suited and still suits the dam boosters' agenda; and because a lot of people now make a lot of money out of it.

Harbor no doubts about the place as spectacle.

Red cliffs soar sheer from bright blue water. Everywhere, encircling you, gigantic natural sculpture. Red rock eroded into abrupt, battlemented buttes. Or into beehive humps and crumble-tipped cones that hint at coconut cookies. Or into a series of smooth ridges that bulge along in sinuous near-parallel until sheered off at lakeside in stylized, hoopla simulation of a line of covered wagons parked side by side. Some mornings and evenings, for magical interludes, the whole exhibit bathed in desert alpenglow. You sit at ease in your boat, floating on the wide blue water, and marvel.

As I motored steadily southwestward in perfect weather across the open, sunlit water I reveled in the rock themes and in the variations played on them by light and shade, time and weather. Embryonic arches mouthed embryonic messages. From time to time, huge boulders hung poised on impossible slopes, suspended in a different time dimension.

And desert varnish kept working its wonders. At the massive cliff called "Tapestry Wall," its patina formed curtains of thin vertical lines that indeed suggested the weft of a warpless fabric. I lingered in the silence of the wall's shadow, relishing the beauty and grandeur, trying to see only what lay beyond the reservoir's most insistent stigma. When I motored on again, the broader red rock concert resumed. And always, out beyond my bulging blue raft, I had the wide blue water.

You could be excused for imagining that, in spite of the river's absence, my passage down the reservoir became a peaceful interlude rich in stimulating contemplation. After all, I putt-putted along, freed from demands for major physical effort, surrounded by mutating spectacle. But you would be very wrong. Every mile, fell the shadow.

The shadow lay in many tones, pale gray through black.

For one thing, I no longer traveled in either silence or solitude. My little motor, though demure by outboard standards, prattle-roared. And I had fellow travelers.

Small boats attached to enormous outboard motors kept rocketing past. They drew white lines across the water, wounds across the silence. Once, a gargantuan powerboat sliced by dangerously close. Perhaps the two pygmy figures standing high and stiff on its bridge, detached and sun-glassed, did not even see me. From the lowly elitist perspective of my tortoise raft I chose to guess that they were out on the water because they'd been too long in city penthoused, and I doubted that they'd broken free.

Not that I cast a jaundiced eye on all fellow travelers. Sometimes my empathy went beyond mere acceptance that people who did not understand what had happened to this place would find it beautiful.

Some visitors moseyed around in rented houseboats—bulky boxes that look like floating RVs, and are—and once I found myself daydreaming about a romantic week aboard such a comfortable and sequestered sanctuary. When I watched water skiers execute wide side sweeps and send spray arching white and high and beautiful against the sun, memory revived the slashing fun of it.

Most fellow travelers ignored my little raft puttling along at three miles an hour, but one boat that had raced past then circled back and pulled up astern. The people aboard shouted words. I killed my motor. Was I all right? What was I doing? Eight hundred miles in three months? Really? Didn't I feel seasick in such a small rubber raft? Did I need anything? How about an apple? Some water? Kind people, but inhabiting a different world.

Even the best of company, then, intruded. And always, behind the surface of my passage, lurked deeper shadows.

The blackest of them hung in the background, the way most deep shadows lurk. But one dark element stood clear and constant. Concrete. Livid.

The reservoir's most obvious stigma is its dirty-bathtub ring.

Except on those rare occasions when the reservoir fills to capacity, this band always hems its shoreline. From a distance you see only a narrow white strip separating blue water from red rock. At that range, if your mind can block out the meanings, it remains unintrusive. Even mildly decorative. But as you move toward a cliff the strip becomes a dirty white band, then a thirty-foot-high blank wall; and when you move in close, you register reality. Now you confront the stigma I had striven to ignore back in Flaming Gorge Reservoir and, here, at Tapestry Wall: a thick white scabrous crust that coats the cliff's skin like desiccated fungus. The rock is sick. It has leprosy. And in this zone of sickness nothing lives. Or almost nothing. If you look long enough you may detect an occasional insect and even one or two small lizards that no doubt subsist on the insects. But otherwise you have moved into a Death Zone. And every time I saw or even thought about the Zone, fell the shadow.

It fell most regularly and heavily at nightcamps. Because I could camp only on gentler slopes, the Death Zone might extend back for two hundred feet, and each night I lived in a ghastly white, desiccated-fungus mausoleum.

Nightcamp, Powell Reservoir. "Because I could camp
only on gentler slopes, the Death Zone might extend
back for two hundred feet, and each night I lived in a
ghastly white, desiccated-fungus mausoleum."

Only dusk and dawn brought relief. For brief spells, twilight masked the grossness; even disclosed a simplicity of structure that echoed, faintly, the glorious nothingness that lures me to the starkest kind of desert.

The camps, then, were the worst of it. The camps and other close-ups.

Although I had not seen Glen Canyon before the reservoir drowned it, my memory carried images of its glories from Eliot Porter's elegiac book of photographs *The Place No One Knew*. Sometimes I almost felt as if I had traveled down the peaceful, swirling river and visited its glens and grottos, stood in wonder before their carvings and varnished draperies. A framed print from Porter's book that had hung in my bedroom for years was a close-up taken in a place that had become my sweetest and saddest Glen Canyon remembrancer.

John Wesley Powell had camped in that place on August 1, 1869, and reported

> . . . *a vast chamber, carved out of the rock . . . [It] is more than 200 feet high, 500 feet long, and 200 feet wide. Through the ceiling, and on through the rocks for a thousand feet above, there is a narrow, winding skylight; and this is all carved out by a little stream which runs only dur-*

ing the few showers that fall now and then in this arid country. . . . The rock at the ceiling is hard, the rock below, very soft and friable . . . and thus the chamber has been excavated. . . .

When [a crew member] sings a song at night, we are pleased to find that this hollow in the rock is filled with sweet sounds. It was doubtless made for an academy of music by its storm-born architect; so we name it Music Temple.

I had not intended to visit the Music Temple's grave. During five days on the reservoir, in fact, I rarely pulled close inshore—except to camp or to travel sheltered from wind—partly because I wanted to make good time but also because I wanted to minimize the pain of seeing the reservoir's vandalism, close-up. But the third day below Hite a headwind blew. Steep whitecapped swells bounced the raft like a rubber ball and showered me with spray, and out in open water I found it impossible to change film or even cope with food more complicated to prepare than a pemmican bar. In mid-afternoon, looking for a sanctuary from whitecaps, I saw from the map that we were approaching Music Temple Canyon.

I angled inshore, turned left through a narrow channel into calm water, killed the motor, rowed slowly forward.

What I saw was not what Powell had seen. But the deeper I ventured down a gradually narrowing channel the more hints I detected of the glory now buried 500 feet deep. Only faint hints, though, and grievously impaired.

I saw massive rock walls carved not into caverns, true, but into curving antechambers, into cirques and alcoves, embryonic arches. Delicate patina tapestries often ornamented the upper walls. But always, close and brutal, for thirty vertical feet above me, the rock was sick; bore the leprous white shadow of the Death Zone.

When I'd changed film and poured tea from the thermos I rowed back to the channel entrance and motored out into windswept open water.

Even there, though, the shadow might fall.

The "new spalls" that the Lake Powell recreational map identified— apparently as tourist attractions—turned out to be huge peeled-off sections of cliff. It was as if the living rock had been skinned. In hundreds of miles of canyons I'd seen nothing remotely similar, and I assumed that dead water, soaking the rock month after month after year, must have done more than induce the leprous Death Zone; must have impregnated the rock's outer skin like a fungus and forced great sheets to slough off.

As I motored on toward the dam I remembered that the reservoir had filled for the first time only nine years earlier. How would the place look, I wondered, in a century or two?

In this massive distension of the river, of course, we should expect widespread sickness. A distended artery is a pathological condition, dangerous to any patient's health. Here, no lack of symptoms. Back upriver, almost every sandbar had been a library of mammal and bird tracks. But now the mud flats stretched mute, dead. And these empty libraries spoke, if you knew how to listen, of the underlying loss this beautiful place had suffered: the loss of natural landscape's natural harmonies.

An untrammeled river melds with the land it flows through. That is hardly surprising, for the river is the instrument that has carved the land; has, essentially, created the landscape. The margins therefore fit. Earth and water mate, merge, coalesce. Everything connects. All is harmony.

But a reservoir lies awkward on the land. The alignment of its Death Zone—laid late and flat and unheeding—contradicts the land's natural contours. In rolling country this disjunction screeches. In canyon country it may be less obvious, but if you look with a discerning eye you'll see that land and water challenge, clash, grapple. Nothing fits. Nothing connects. All is discord.

That is why, at Powell Reservoir, if you look and listen the right way, you know something is wrong. Something beyond the sham of beautiful red sandy beaches that turn out to be soft red mud in which you sink ankle-deep. Like Los Angeles within odor of Hollywood, the place is not real. It lacks that interlocking background harmony built into any whole, healthy, undisturbed landscape. This lack, and the subtle but constant tension it generates, throws a black shadow across the reservoir. And to lack add loss. Add the underlying knowledge that the reservoir's dead water is a pall spread over the glory that was once Glen Canyon. Together, lack and loss signal the profound sadness of the place.

Against that sadness, the superficial beauty is tinsel. The reservoir has disfigured its landscape. It may indeed attract—but in the superficial and poignant way a strikingly beautiful and charming woman may remain attractive after she has suffered an accident that injures her body only slightly but throws her mind out of kilter, leaves it deranged. She may still appear beautiful from a distance, but the wonderful, vibrant person has died.

On the fifth day I motored the last few miles to Glen Canyon Dam under an overcast sky. But the wind had died away and left the water once more mirrorlike; my progress a cruise, not a battle. The reservoir, now more than 500 feet deep, filled the canyon almost flush with its rim and the plateau, so you got the impression the land had flattened out. Off to the left, over open terrain, I could see Navajo Generating Station belching a plume of dirty, yellow-gray smoke across the desert airscape.

From above, the dam did not look impressive: just a low gray wall, dwarfed by the background steelwork of a highway bridge and power station. I motored four miles back to Wahweap Marina, checked into a motel. It was Friday the thirteenth. The Bureau of Reclamation, helpful as ever, had arranged for a commercial river-running outfit to transport my raft to the foot of the dam for relaunch. But not until Monday.

So for three days, amid flossy delectables, I fiddled with administrative chores and took TV-filtered samplings of the outside world. Friday, the Dow plunged 190 points. The Pope was visiting Mauritius. The Middle East remained a seething indictment of organized religion. Elephants had been declared an endangered species. In Moscow, Western entrepreneurs using sod imported from Sweden and Finland had opened the USSR's first golf course. Saturday and Sunday, in the first two games of the first Bay Bridge World Series, the interloper A's humiliated my Giants.*

Monday, I checked out.

---

* "My Giants," that is, before major-league baseball became so base that its name changed: after the strike I swore, solemnly, to boycott major-league greedball.

Once a pennant race started, mind you, I resuccumbed—with diluted fervor—to the radio lure of a game that is best played, as someone has said, "in the canyons of your mind." I also told myself that major-league proceedings were worth keeping an eye on because they're a telling metaphor for events in a wider world—where the money boys' sour dominanace has rotted the fabric of modern society, politics through publishing. Still . . . the toy department of life?

16

MARBLE CANYON

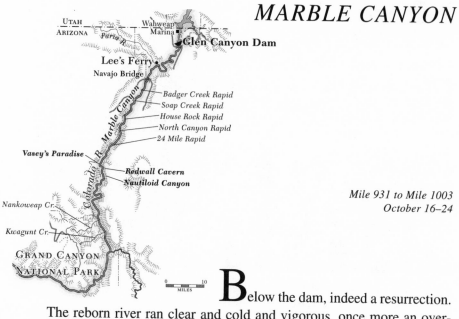

UTAH
ARIZONA
Paria R.
Wahweap Marina
Glen Canyon Dam

Lee's Ferry
Navajo Bridge

Marble Canyon

Badger Creek Rapid
Soap Creek Rapid
House Rock Rapid
North Canyon Rapid
24 Mile Rapid

Vasey's Paradise

Redwall Cavern
Nautiloid Canyon

Colorado R.

Nankoweap Cr.

Kwagunt Cr.

GRAND CANYON
NATIONAL PARK

0 10
MILES

Mile 931 to Mile 1003
October 16–24

Below the dam, indeed a resurrection.

The reborn river ran clear and cold and vigorous, once more an overgrown trout stream—a broad, swirling, blue-green waterway that tantalized, sure enough, with glimpses of hovering trout. Big trout. A steady trickle of fishermen now motored past, intent.

The dam, seen from below, was—like it or loathe it—impressive. A 600-foot-tall wedge of curving pale pink concrete jammed down at an angle, tight and immovable, between the canyon's red sandstone walls. A softly humming marvel now framed by the arcing steelwork of the road bridge.

I launched, began to float downriver.

The three fleshpot motel days had left me in threadbare touch with the natural world. At first I could only grasp that the resurrected river ran bigger and stronger than when it died below Big Drop. Colder, too: its 45-degree water was drawn from the bottom of Powell Reservoir. After an hour or two, I began to appreciate the canyon's restored integrity: the way land and water fit, everything connected. But I think I remained no more than sketchily aware that these dozen final miles of Glen Canyon, though said to have been its least dramatic part, spoke vividly of what we had lost. By now, anyway, as I floated on down, my mind was peering ahead to Lee's Ferry. There, I'd have to make an important choice.

John Doyle Lee, "a loyal but excommunicated Mormon," established his ferry service across the Colorado in 1871, using a boat discarded by

*Looking over my disassembled raft at the relaunch
point below Glen Canyon Dam.*

Powell. He was arrested in 1874 as one of the alleged leaders in a massacre
of non-Mormon pioneers almost twenty years earlier and was executed—
apparently a scapegoat—in 1877. The river guide noted that "Emma, the
seventeenth of Lee's nineteen wives, operated the ferry from 1873 to
1879." Other owners carried on until 1928, "when three men drowned during an attempted crossing and the ferry was shut down. One year later,
Navajo Bridge was completed."

Today, Lee's Ferry is the put-in point for Grand Canyon river-runners.
(Fifty-mile-long Marble Canyon, immediately below Lee's Ferry, is sometimes regarded as part of Grand Canyon, sometimes not. It now lies within
Grand Canyon National Park, but at the time of my 1963 foot trip the park
ended at Nankoweap Creek, where Marble melds into Grand, so I tend to
award Marble Canyon autonomy.) At Lee's Ferry Ranger Station the National Park Service checks all river-running permits. There's a heavy demand for permits and the Park Service has to ration them, then control
entry tightly. People who want to make a noncommercial river-run through
the Canyon normally go on a waiting list and it may take years for their
names to come up. I managed to short-circuit the procedure—but one condition of my permit was that I explain why I got special treatment. So you
are hereby advised that because I had in 1963 become the first man known
to have walked the entire length of the Canyon in a single journey, and be-

cause my book about it was still in print, the Park Service felt I'd shown I could both take care of myself and also produce something worthwhile, and that they could therefore bestow on me an immediate permit for "literary research."

I was and am truly grateful for this NPS dispensation. But I must explain that phrase "literary research." It will surely provoke somebody into saying, "Ah! So he went down the river just to write a book about it!" I did not. On the other hand, I knew I'd write a book if the journey generated one—which not every long wilderness journey I'd undertaken had done. Things have to be right.

If you doubt my word, reflect on the gap of twenty-six years between my Grand Canyon walk and this river run. During those years many people had urged me to undertake another such journey: along the Continental Divide, say, or the Great Wall of China. But in the end, none sat well enough. They were ideas, not dreams. Then, at its proper time—and there can be improper times—this one surfaced. It fit both my lifelong pattern and my needs of the moment. So I went.

Another condition of my Grand Canyon permit was that although I could travel alone in my raft I must run all rapids with another party. If I flipped I wouldn't last long in the frigidly cold water, and the park superintendent felt I needed someone on hand to help, just in case. Which suited me fine. In the end I managed to retain control over which party I accompanied: I didn't want to pin myself down to arriving at Lee's Ferry on a specific date, as the superintendent originally demanded; and if I found one party was going too fast I wanted to be able to wait for the next. Traveling with a group of strangers through Grand Canyon would be a gamble, anyway. And now, as I floated on down toward Lee's Ferry, I knew that the traveling companions I chose there would profoundly influence my days and weeks in the Canyon. If, that is, I had a choice.

The beautiful red, curviform-sculptured sandstone walls of Glen Canyon ended. Two cows and a calf, foraging riverside, marked the change. I rowed on between duller, more crumbly cliffs. Once, a brief break of black lava laced with a glaring tongue of sand. Before long, new red escarpments. Then, below them, the basin that signaled "Lee's Ferry."

No choice needed. I just seemed to fall on my feet.

A party of ten rafters and kayakers would leave in two days. Their leader, Jack—bearded, stalwart, amiable, relaxed—was not only willing but eager to have me tag along. An ex-professional boatman who'd run the Canyon several times, he clearly knew his stuff. He'd assembled this party by mail, and the seven men and three women were still getting to know each other. We arranged that I'd travel sort of semi-detached—and that next morning I'd solo on down for eight miles, camp just above the first big rapid and await their arrival the following day.

Next morning, when I pulled out into the broad river, the sun beat down and the swirling river glistened. Almost at once the Paria River flowed in, right, and although I couldn't see how much water it added, if any, the main river seemed suddenly bigger, stronger, more serious. But still manageable. Maneuvering into the first riffle and riding the big waves at its tail were fun. In daylight.

A year earlier, during my 4000-mile, seven-state logistical-reconnaissance drive, I'd mostly taken pains to avoid seeing the river; but when I left NPS headquarters at Grand Canyon it remained uncertain whether I'd get a permit on acceptable terms, and I'd detoured to Lee's Ferry to scout the riffle just below the ranger station. To avoid detection, I might have to run it at night. Now, it felt good on many counts that I'd been able to avoid that thief-in-the-night ploy.

I floated on down. The dark walls of Marble Gorge began to engulf us. Soon, spanning the gap between them, almost 500 feet overhead, a graceful white girder arch: Navajo Bridge. Four more miles and I came to Badger Creek Rapid.

The run looked straightforward enough. But heavy water. Very heavy. As I pulled in to the right bank and camped I knew that by the time we ran the rapid next day things would look different.

The rejuvenated river might now run cool and vivacious as a mountain stream but it had lost even the diminished freedom it still enjoyed below Fontenelle and Flaming Gorge Dams. It ran under man's hourly control.

Glen Canyon Dam is the prime "peak-power" electricity provider for a vast area of the American Southwest. By controlling water flow through its turbines, operators can raise power output to meet, minute by minute, the peak midday demands of its customers; and can then taper off in reverse lockstep to a nighttime low. The river therefore rises and falls in a daily tide. Its typical weekday range: 3,000 cfs to 20,000 or even more. Weekends, rather less. This artificial tide imposes heavy restrictions on such river dwellers as willows, carp, beaver and river-runners.

(These daily tide limits, and the flow's dependence on power demands unmitigated by other considerations, were how things then stood. But many people were pressing for change. And they've succeeded. The needs of river dwellers will in future be factored into the dam's computers. The daily tide will be buffered. Willows and other riverside vegetation will revert to something slightly less divorced from natural cycles. Carp will offer thanks to squamous gods. River-runners will camp a little more easily, sleep a little less uneasily. Beaches will no longer be swept away without some restoration of sediment.

All this makes a worthwhile stopgap measure. The only real solution, though, remains removal of the dam—in some slow, sensible, non-Hayduke manner.)

When I secured the raft at my Badger Creek Rapid camp I made due allowance for overnight tide flux: left enough slack in the ropes; considered how the raft might swing. It would, I knew, be like that all through the Canyon.

Once I'd set up camp I began preparing for big white water.

First I deflated the raft's floor almost completely: that way we'd be more stable, even if a touch less maneuverable. Then I reloaded the gear. Every last item that did not have to be readily available went into one of the dry boxes—though I now had a small waterproof camera that could travel slung around my neck. I'd phoned the Sextons from Hite with news of the second zoom camera's demise and they'd chosen this more suitable replacement and expressed it to Wahweap.

While I was reorganizing the raft a couple of backpackers came down the side canyon on the far bank and filled their canteens. Young fellows. Mid-thirties, perhaps. In the prime of life. Backpacking had long been my bailiwick, yet at that moment, as a temporary river rat, I felt more than the river separating us.

Later, cooking dinner, I let my mind run downriver. Things looked good. Jack and his party seemed to promise everything I'd hoped for, and I looked forward to getting to know them. The last commercial trip of the season had launched that morning, too, so there'd be no raucous outboard motors, no big groups of nervous tourists, only a scattering of private river-runners. And maybe a few backpackers.

Across the river, a small fire flickered into life. The two young fellows had apparently camped halfway down the rapid.

After dinner I sat listening to the river, acutely aware of being poised on the brink of the journey's big physical challenge.

The outlines of that challenge stood clear. More than 200 river-miles laced with white water. Much of it formidable. Three acknowledged high-points. First, a concatenation of rapids, one after the other, between about Miles 20 and 30: "The Roaring Twenties." (In the Canyon, "Mile" figures indicate river-distance below Lee's Ferry.) The river ranger at Lee's Ferry had warned me, specifically, about 24 Mile Rapid: "The guide rates it '4,' but there's a big new rockfall that blocks the whole center of the river, and it's now at least an '8.'" The second highpoint, Crystal Rapid—almost 100 miles down, also relatively new, and rated 10—was one of two that provoked awed comments from experienced river-runners. The other, also rated 10, and famous even beyond river-running circles, came not far from the end of the white water: Lava Falls Rapid. I once stood beside it, in backpacker mode, so I understood people's awe. When the river ranger tendered some technical advice about Lava he'd smiled ruefully: "Last time I ran it, I broke a rib."

I was also very conscious, that evening above Badger Creek Rapid, that the challenge came with a deadline. I still didn't yearn to chip ice off river-side boulders and therefore still wanted to be out of the Canyon by mid-November—just over a month ahead.

Across the river, the backpackers' campfire had died down. I slid into my sleeping bag. Yes, Badger Creek Rapid had a steady, deep-throated voice.

Somewhere in Powell Reservoir the river had, though existing only in abeyance, passed the halfway point of its journey. So you could regard it, controlled or not, as being well into solid maturity. As being in the prime of its life . . . I was struggling to complete some kind of emerging connection when I slipped off into sleep.

In the morning I woke late. No hurry: Jack had said his party wouldn't be down until around noon. The river's voice sounded less strong now, and my raft had been left tilted high and dry, as I knew it would, by the morning's "ebb tide." But the river still had that heavy, serious air of maturity about it. . . .

You could say the same about my journey. In that linear sense, as in many others, river and journey were the same thing. They had evolved, as most things do, not along preordained lines but in response to unexpected events. In an unpredictable yet not random way. Had evolved in response to dams and other obstacles; to events' refusal of a traveler's expectations.

I rolled over and, still in the sleeping bag, began preparing breakfast. Across the river, the backpackers had gone. Had vanished from the scene as completely as had, in a different sense, a certain man bearing my name who twenty-six years earlier had backpacked the length of the Canyon. Then, I'd been forty-one. My mind slid back half a dozen more years.

When my erratic four-year journey from Kenya to and through the New World came to its unexpected end in San Francisco (I seemed to remember I was heading rather vaguely for Mexico, though I was damned if I knew what I expected to do there), I was thirty-four. In the prime of life. Almost exactly halfway to where I now stood. And as my friend had said in Canada, undergoing a metamorphosis.

Now I understood what she'd been talking about. During those four years I'd learned to fend for myself in a new and rougher world, without servants, with even less money than before. (To a modern American, the idea of having had servants but very little money may sound like a fairy tale; but trust me.) The new experiences had eroded some of my notions about how things should be done, sir, and had undermined certain ossified values I'd generally accepted even though I'd often felt uncomfortable with them. Some of the new values had rubbed me the wrong way, and still did, but they'd cleared away a lot of old crap. I don't mean, of course, that all the old values crumbled. I still honored the most basic of them.

In due time, I . . . well, I don't want to suggest that I ceased to be self-centered, but I became aware, intermittently, of that condition. When an acquaintance asked me, testily and out of the blue, "What are you going to do about your self-centeredness?" I snapped back, "Glory in it." But bravado aside, I believe I became rather more capable, on occasion, of comprehending someone else's needs, and trying to meet them.

I finished breakfast, got up, did chores, ruminated.

There were other things that had evolved during that pivotal four-year passage halfway around the physical world.

In a sense—a limited, rather man-controlled sense—I had always been in touch with the natural world. But in Canada, working as a geologist's assistant in the Northwest Territories and then as a prospector on Vancouver Island, I wandered, often alone, through miles of virgin rockscape and forest. I saw the impact of mining and, above all, logging. Long before I read or heard tell that such acts were crimes I felt it, deep and hot.

When my four-year journey north-beached me in San Francisco many such maturations may have been stirring. Perhaps they went an inch or two toward explaining why two years later, after an idyllic interlude of conjugated bliss with the damsel I'd met there, I decided that the way to find out whether I really wanted to marry her was to walk from Mexico to Oregon. (Not even half an inch, you say? Oh, well.) Anyway, within a month of that decision I stood for the first time beside the Colorado River, at the Mexican border, pack on back, Oregon bound.

Five years later, aftermaths of those events launched me on another Colorado walk.

By chance, I visited the rim of Grand Canyon. I stood there in a state of ecstatic shock—then grasped that the way to escape the pit into which those echoing aftermaths had plunged me was to lift myself up once more by my own hiking bootstraps. I duly walked from one end of Grand Canyon to the other. And it worked. Both walks had worked, in fact, in ways much more profound than I'd expected.

Both times, physical challenge had been a core element. And now, here I was, back on the Colorado, poised to face the prime challenge of this third journey.

As at the source, I wondered how those earlier walks would echo. Would memory turn out to be a mirror that enriched or a screen that obscured? Or might my different means and direction of travel quash all echoes? Answers should soon begin to emerge. Less than fifty miles downriver, at Nankoweap Creek, where Marble Canyon ended, we'd enter territory I knew. Territory that had been known, anyway, to a certain backpacker who had existed a quarter of a century earlier.

Meanwhile, camp chores.

After an early lunch and siesta I rowed across to the far bank and pulled in at the point that seemed the logical place for Jack to land and scout the rapid. It was a few minutes before noon. I sat waiting.

Jack and his party arrived at five o'clock.

They ran Badger without scouting. I followed. The run was indeed straightforward, and my little raft rode the big waves perfectly. Jack's three rafts and four kayaks promptly pulled out left and set up camp at the head of a beach. We'd pre-arranged that I'd mostly camp separately, and I chose a site a couple of hundred feet down the beach—a sort of addendum to their group, yet on my own. They seemed to understand.

Tucked privately into the darkness, remembering the way the raft had ridden our first Grand Canyon rapid, I felt newly and surprisingly confident.

Next morning, soon after a late start, we came to Soap Creek Rapid—where Frank Brown, parsimonious president of the Stanton Survey Expedition company, who had refused to buy life jackets, was washed overboard and drowned. The rapid had a 6,5,5,5 rating. (The excellent Grand Canyon river guide rated most rapids "for four different water stages: *Very Low* (1,000–3,000 cfs), *Low* (3,000–9,000), *Medium* (9,000–16,000) and *High* (16,000–35,000). At flows exceeding 35,000 cfs many rapids wash out," but several increased in severity, and these were marked with a "+." Crystal, for example, rated a "10,+." Sometimes the "elevational drop" was also given.)

Soap Creek dropped 17 feet. We ran it with no scouting, no problems.

Next, House Rock Rapid (9,8,7,7). The river now near the peak of its daily tide. As we approached, another raft rode close to mine and the oarsman called out, "We'll probably stop here and scout. Should have plenty of time to do everything." The lid of one of my dry boxes was no more than loosely strapped down and both hasps were open, but I put off making any last-minute, big-rapid adjustments.

We moved closer to the rapid. Jack and the other kayakers, just ahead, didn't even pause. One by one, they vanished down the tongue.

For a moment I hesitated. So did my neighbor raft. Then it pulled ahead. The oarsman yelled, "Oh, you start left and pull right." Then he was in the mouth of the tongue. He'd run the Canyon once before, and I assumed he knew what he was doing. By now, anyway, it was too late to pull ashore. Even to check the dry boxes and other gear. I took a deep breath, eased forward along the line the other raft had taken.

The tongue flowed fast but smooth. I ferried down, bow left, pulling right as instructed, but without urgency. Ahead, the white water dropped away and the other raft had vanished. Lateral waves loomed close, right. I pivoted bow-first, pushed hard.

At once, white water. Big waves. And steep. We rode them well. But then the waves were huge and then enormous and then they were no longer simple waves but a confused mass of churning white foam, bigger than anything we'd been in. Then an even bigger wall of foam was surging in from the left and we were riding up on it, slewed around almost broadside,

I approach the crux of House Rock Rapid.

bow right, and no matter how I strained at the oars we were still broadside and lifting up and up and up on a massive pale green wall of aerated water that had materialized from behind the foam; lifting higher and higher on this green wall with its startlingly clear inset of dancing air bubbles; lifting and tipping toward vertical, left tube above right. I like to think I leaned left, over the upper tube, to help counteract the tipping tendency. Perhaps I did. But there came a millisecond at the apex of this breathtaking two- or three-second climax to the roller-coaster ride when I think we hung truly vertical. The raft seemed to quiver, as if undecided whether it should flip. As we hung there I thought, "Have I left it too late to jump clear?" Then we were lifting onto the crest of the green-white wall and the raft was easing back from the vertical and I was thinking, "Thank God I didn't jump!" And then we were riding in relative safety over waves no more than big, or perhaps huge—and off to the right human voices yelled indecipherables.

Before long, back in flat water and sanity. Now the voices were yelling "Well, how did you like that hole?" and "By God, I thought you were going to flip!" and I was recalling a tidbit of river lore: "There are two kinds of river-runners—those who've flipped and those still waiting to flip."

That evening, as we approached North Canyon Rapid—at Mile 20, the brink of the Roaring Twenties—Jack kayaked up alongside my raft and told me that his party would pull in just below the rapid and would lay over. "We'll be leaving," he said, "at ten o'clock, day after tomorrow."

They camped right. I chose left. The rapid separated us.

The morning of the layover day, I checked the contents of the dry box that had been no more than loosely strapped down while we careered through House Rock. All things considered, remarkably unsoggy. But if we'd flipped . . . I should have stopped and scouted. On my own, no matter what.

The rest of the day it rained.

Next morning, just after ten, I ran North Canyon Rapid. Rated 5. No problem. Off to the right, one or two of Jack's party waved friendly greetings. Nobody looked very ready.

I floated down half a mile, scouted 21 Mile Rapid—also a "5"—and waited. The layover day's rain had cooled the air, but I now had thick neoprene wetsocks under my sandals, polypro longs under my shorts and a pile jacket under the life jacket, and although the raft's deflated floor made us ride lower, so that even in flat water my feet mostly traveled awash, I felt comfortable enough as I sat reading.

Around eleven-thirty a three-raft party pulled alongside. We chatted.

Would I like to join them? They seemed a very cordial group. I hesitated. But if I did, I said, Jack's party would worry about where I'd gone.

"True enough. Any time you feel like it, though." They went on down. I watched them go: two small gray rafts and one big white job.

Time passed. At last, just as I'd decided on an overdue lunch and a siesta, whoops and yells drifted downriver, echoing off the canyon walls. Soon, Jack's flotilla drifted into sight, tossing a plastic football around, raft to kayak to raft.

From his kayak, Jack saluted me with a beer can. I mentioned the other party's offer, explained why I'd refused. "Oh, we'd have guessed," said Jack.

The raft crews had reshuffled. I'd already detected signs of internal tension, and one raft had now been taken over by the three women. They seemed to exude a steely determination.

Three miles down, we approached 24 Mile Rapid. I happened to be the lead raft, but well behind the kayaks. In warning me that 24 Mile was now at least an "8," the river ranger had said, "Scout it left." By now I really needed lunch. And a siesta. I'd be glad of the pause.

I'd almost reached the bank when I saw Jack standing at the left edge of the rapid, signaling me through with lofted beer can. I pulled ashore.

The party with the big white raft were there. They'd stopped for lunch and a careful scout, and we chatted again as we walked down to the rapid.

Sure enough, a long and horrendous hole blocking the freeway. One narrow funnel, extreme left; another right. Jack stood beside the left funnel, beer-waving his party down.

The first raft swung sideways, caught the edge of the hole, swirled as if veering out of control, then righted itself. The second did marginally better. The women's raft made it, just. All three had taken a bashing. Then, over on the far side, the other party's big white raft approached that funnel. I watched. No problem at all: through and out.

I made up my mind.

"But that white raft's bigger than yours, you know," said Jack. "This side's the way to go, I promise you."

As I walked back up to my raft, I wasn't thinking too clearly. No lunch, no siesta. Other things, too. And at the raft, no Emmett. I guess it seemed unreasonable, with all the spectators. Or maybe I just didn't think of it. Anyway, I got in, cast off, pulled across to the far side.

Soon, I had us aligned above the narrow funnel. Well above. Through binoculars, a small protruding marker rock, extreme right: pass close to its left edge and we should stay clear of the hole.

Bow-first, we eased down toward the lip of the funnel. The smooth, narrow lip. Pull hard with both oars to hold us back; peer ahead for the marker rock. No rock. Pull harder, both oars. Peer harder. Still no rock. We began to gather speed. Nothing left to do, now, but try to hold us straight.

The bow dipped. Now, down at the foot of the smooth, narrow glide, the edge of the hole. The huge, white, churning edge—perilously close to our line of travel. Then, before I'd really evaluated the danger, we were plunging into it.

We hit the white wall of foam that was the edge of the hole and in the same moment, it seemed, were spinning right and being held broadside and were tipping the way we'd tipped in House Rock and water was cascading over me, cold and close to solid, and I was falling because there was nothing to hold on to. The cascade of water eased. I began to struggle back up toward my seat. But then another cascade came flooding down, and this time, because there still seemed nothing to hold on to, it swept me onto the lower tube. As I slithered overboard my right hand grabbed the braided blue-and-white life line that encircled the raft, but the rest of my body was out in the raging, air-filled water and everything was cold and chaotic and all I could do was hold on, hold on.

Entering 24 Mile Rapid. "The bow dipped. Now, down
at the foot of the smooth, narrow glide, . . ."

I held on until the air-filled foam around me became more normal water. The raft seemed to be riding on even keel, and I knew we must be out of the hole. I began trying to climb back aboard.

But I'd tucked the binoculars and waterproof camera inside my life jacket and they kept jamming against the bulging tube. I struggled to pull myself up; failed. Struggled harder; still failed. I could feel that my polypro pants had been dragged halfway down my legs.

Then I saw that we were swinging toward the face of a big black boulder. The water was calmer now, and slower, but there seemed some danger I'd be sandwiched between raft and boulder. I leg-kicked, trying to swing the raft around. It pivoted—either by accident or because of my leg-kicking, and I was safely on its upriver side when I felt it give an unnatural lurch and at the same moment heard a voice call out a warning about the rock. Seconds later Jack was giving me a push up and into the raft. One finger of my right hand poured blood; otherwise, only my pride seemed hurt.

By now we were idling in an eddy, and I sat and watched the kayakers—Jack and others—as they picked up the pieces and brought them to me. My hat and water canteen. Also an oar that must have jumped its oarlock when we hit the hole, snapped its line and been wrenched from my grasp, leaving me nothing on the right side to hold on to. Perhaps I'd even leaned down to try to reclaim it—and so been easy prey for the cascades of water.

Oar and hat back in place, I thanked the kayakers. And meant it. Thanks to the polypro pants and pile jacket, I didn't feel cold.

"You OK?" asked Jack.

"Sure. Let's go." I had to make sure my confidence hadn't suffered. Maybe there were other spurs too: bruised pride, anger, bravado.

Almost at once we came to 24½ Mile Rapid (6,6,5,5,+). Here, in July 1949, three weeks short of his eightieth birthday, Bert Loper, "the Grand Old Man of the Colorado," rowing one of two boats in a seven-man party, suffered an apparent heart attack and was lost. His remains weren't found until twenty-six years later.

The river guide recommended scouting left, but just before our party's kayaks reached the rapid, Jack paused, yelled back, "Run right," and waved a hand in that direction. Then he was gone.

I pulled in left.

So did the women's raft, and its oarsman walked with me to a cliff overlooking the rapid. Several of the white-raft party were there. We all discussed the rapid, agreed unanimously on a run close to the left bank.

By this time my finger, which I'd allowed to bleed so as to clean out the wound, had ceased to be totally numb. It throbbed. Blood was still gushing, and two of the white-raft party helped me bandage it. A cut thumb, too. As we finished, the women ran our route. Ran it perfectly. Far down-river, the rest of Jack's party were almost out of sight. I stood watching them go.

I was still standing there, watching, when one of the white-raft party again invited me to travel with them. I warned him of my solitudinarian quirks: semi-detachment and so on. He repeated the invitation.

"That would be great," I said.

After that, things changed.

First, the Roaring Twenties were muzzled. We scouted three of the five remaining rapids—notably 25 Mile (7,6,5,5), where Peter Hansborough and Henry Richards of the 1889 Brown-Stanton railroad-scouting expedition capsized and drowned. And we ran them without real difficulty. Without crisis, anyway.

The scouting helped me get to know and appreciate my new traveling companions. There were eight in the party. Mostly men, but two wives. Everyone thirtysomething. No one nearly as river-experienced as Jack: Dave Knutson, the party's leader in river-running matters, had run the

24 Mile Rapid: my only washout. Dave Knutson watches.

Canyon only once; the others, never. One of their rafts had flipped in House Rock Rapid. But this party understood their own limitations. So they had no trouble understanding mine. And at scouts, Dave Knutson, though the undoubted leader, was wide open to discussion of possible routes.

His forty years made Dave marginally the oldest of the group. He was slight, bespectacled and wall-eyed, with a drooping moustache and—here on the river, at least—a stubbly black beard. But he led. On the other hand, he had a remarkably low bullshit quotient. He said what he thought, and if it turned out to be wrong, readily admitted it. I quickly began to relax.

Below Mile 30 the river flattened out. In twenty-two miles, only two minor rapids. So time for other things.

My second day with the Knutson party we paused at Vasey's Paradise, where twin torrents gush from a cliff face. We replenished our drinking-water supplies. And while we admired and investigated the astonishingly lush riverside oasis that the torrents sustain I began to recognize, through snatched conversations, members of the party as something more than life-jacketed figures associated with certain rafts.

They came from clear across the country, Arizona to North Carolina, and included an electrician and his architectural draftsman wife, a carpenter with a yen for cabinet-making, a freshly graduated computer scientist and a part-time college instructor. But blood or friendship linked each member to at least one other. So they were no random mail-order mob. They cohered.

That first full day together we stopped for lunch on the sandy floor of Redwall Cavern. The serene, vaulting vastness of that beautiful red hollowing-out of rock went at least some way toward softening the loss of Music Temple. And I chatted with the oarsman of the party's big white 18½-foot raft. Painted on its bow was a toothy shark's jaw, and I'd already christened it *The Great White Shark*—and its commander "Captain Ahab." Ahab was an Arizona photojournalist, recently gone freelance. An amiable, somewhat scatter-gun sort of guy.

Dave Knutson, I soon discovered, could always pinpoint our position, geologically, along the river. And he knew the places worth seeing. Less than two miles below Redwall Cavern he pulled us in at Nautiloid Canyon. We clambered up its smooth white rock sculpture and found and photographed some strikingly clear fossils of nautiloids—simple ancient mollusks, up to three feet long, ancestors of modern squid and octopi. This Knutson party, I began to see, regarded the Canyon not as a playground but as a remarkable place, worth experiencing to the full. Serious need not mean solemn, of course. Now I heard much more laughter. Laughter of a relaxed, unforced kind. And no hint of bitchiness or even tetchiness.

With my new companions there was, from the first, plenty of give and take. Mostly, they did the giving.

Our second day together we did not stop for lunch and I had no siesta and, sure enough, found myself in the kind of semi-zomboid pit I'd sunk into before 24 Mile Rapid. That's a dangerous condition when you face the split-second decisions demanded by rapids. A condition that might also explain why, back at 24 Mile, I'd given way to an angry and childish determination to be independent. Eventually, that third day with the new party, I got a late-afternoon chance for a three-minute nap and cup of tea. Afterward their co-leader—Dave Knutson's brother, Jerry—said they'd sure as hell noticed the difference. And later he told me they'd decided that stopping for lunch each day made sense for them, too. Jerry— a solid, seemingly unassertive environmental engineer from Pennsylvania—seemed to make an effective social leader.

Late that afternoon we floated down toward Nankoweap Creek, where Dave planned to lay over.

Nankoweap, at Mile 52—Mile 1000 of my journey—marked the end of Marble Canyon and the start of Grand Canyon proper. Also the start of familiar country. There, twenty-six years earlier, on my walk through the Canyon, I'd finally cut away from the Colorado toward the North Rim, toward the outside world. Before doing so I'd climbed up to and lived overnight in some Anasazi cliff dwellings or granaries. I found myself looking forward to seeing it all again.

But when we reached the head of Nankoweap Rapid we saw Jack's party camped at its tail. Below the rapid I swung into an eddy and took a long, slow look at the deep-cut side canyon up which I'd climbed to the North Rim; then at the cliff dwellings. It was all there, I suppose: immense; red and shadowed. But my eyes saw only surfaces. Saw only Jack's party waving at us, and behind them a now-foot-trampled trail angling up the talus to the cliff dwellings. The whole scene lay flat. Inert. Nothing echoed.

I swung the raft back out into the main current.

We camped three miles downriver, at the mouth of Kwagunt Creek, and lay over. Near our campsite, I knew, must lie the flat, open place where I'd taken a supply airdrop on my 1963 foot journey, then lingered several days. Now, I explored the Kwagunt delta, listening for echoes. Almost total silence.

GRAND CANYON

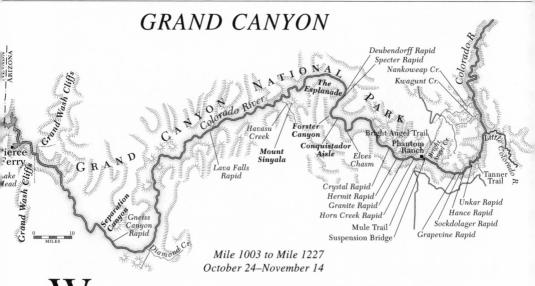

Mile 1003 to Mile 1227
October 24–November 14

We moved on down into Grand Canyon and the rapids dominated our days. The rapid we were scouting or running. Or the one we knew lay just ahead. Or perhaps the big one at the end of the day. And always, in a lesser yet looming sense, the two monsters, far downriver.

The challenge took time to build. In the first twenty miles, only three rapids. Highest rating: "6." But the evening after our Kwagunt layover we camped opposite the Tanner Trail (another place that should have stirred memories but did not); and next morning three of Dave Knutson's friends walked down the Tanner Trail (just as a friend of mine had, to join me twenty-six years earlier). One of the three, Dan, was an expert rafter, familiar with the Inner Gorge. For four days he would take over as technical river leader. Not that Dave lacked as a leader; only in experience. It was he, apparently, who had asked Dan to take over for most of the big Inner Gorge rapids.

The first day, because the newcomers arrived late and we didn't launch until early afternoon, we ran only seven miles. The one major rapid, Unkar (7,7,6,6), turned out to be a straightforward run through big waves. But it demanded attention. I'd intended to look for a certain ledge at the foot of the sheer red left-bank cliff. A tapering ledge that at one point narrowed to barely four inches. A ledge that in 1963, as I edged along it at extreme low water, had generated a suspended, memorable moment. But now, at the crucial point, roller-coasting through steep waves, I caught nothing but a snatched half-glimpse of a red rock face above churning white water.

A Grand Canyon beach. In spite of the physical
challenge, moments of beauty and tranquillity.

Below the rapid I pulled into an eddy. Looking back, I could see that the cliff indeed dropped sheer into raging water. No ledge. No echoes. Everything buried, now.

I swung the raft around, rowed on downriver.

It seemed a pity. Even, for some reason, disturbing. But I might as well accept the facts. My mind was riveted on the physical challenge. Time only for the present. No room for echoes.

Next day we ran seventeen miles: eleven riffles and eleven rapids. Four of the rapids rated "8" or higher.

First: Hance (10,9,9,8,+; vertical drop 30 feet). A rapid with a reputation.

We scouted left. Dan, the new leader—tall, pleasant and competent—chose the route the Lee's Ferry river ranger had recommended and sketched in my guide: to avoid the tumultuous lower rapid you skirted the left edge of a big midstream boulder then pulled hard left behind a triangular rock and moved into quieter water.

I ran last. As far as I could see, when each of the Knutson oarsmen tried to pull in behind the triangular rock, the current's force simply skidded his raft away from it and down into the tumult. Then it was my turn.

As soon as I saw over my left shoulder that we were almost level with the rock, I began to pull. To heave with all my might. For a moment the current seemed to be carrying the raft downstream, just as the others had been carried. Then I felt us begin to ease across the current. A few more strokes and we slid in behind the triangular rock. The rest, relatively simple.

Below the rapid I joined the other rafts. They'd had a rough ride through the tumult but Dave Knutson was smiling. "Yeah, I saw you'd made it, in behind that rock. Good run! You and your *Water Strider*!" This was the party's new name for my little raft: it sat high in the water, they said, and I could pivot it on a dime.

Below Hance we moved down into the Inner Gorge. Ancient Precambrian rocks plunged steep into the river. Their dark, forbidding walls enveloped us. The water heavy, too. But the rapids uncomplicated.

In Sockdolager (8,8,9,9; 19 feet) the waves towered gigantic and steep but *Water Strider* rode them with ease and grace. In such waves there's none of the bang-and-shudder you get when you hit a wave below a hole. There, you slam into water that seems to flow back upriver. In a simple-wave rapid, as you push downriver with all your might to maintain momentum, you ride a belly-churning series of roller coasters. Each wave sends you soaring; slows you down and angles you up and up and up until the bow towers overhead. The sound track: a swishing of water along the raft bottom; perhaps a more staccato fusillade of white water beating down onto the raft. Then you're over that wave's crest and careening down the far side into its successor.

Next: Grapevine (8; 18 feet). Near the start, as I pushed through the edge of a hole, my left oar popped out of its oarlock. We bucketed on through huge, rearing waves. But I found that in spite of my bandaged and still sore right hand I could with the one remaining oar still hold us head-on, and eventually I managed to wrestle the left oar back into its oarlock. Its rubber stop had been pushed far up the shaft, though: close to useless. Then the right oar popped. We plunged on through slightly lesser but still huge waves. Now, two almost useless oars. Yet nothing terrible happened before I had the right oar back in place. But its rubber stop had shifted, too, and for the rest of the rapid, as the waves slowly diminished, it was a battle. A battle I somehow won, with surprisingly little disorder. A battle that left me impressed with the way I could, single-oaredly, hold us head-on to the biggest waves.

We raced on through the Inner Gorge. Three more rapids, then we pulled in, river right, at Bright Angel Creek.

"We'll have to leave in an hour," said Dan. Any later, and we'd catch the day's tide all wrong at Horn Creek Rapid, a couple of miles down.

I hurried up the trail toward Phantom Ranch. At Bright Angel, well-traveled trails from North and South Rims cross the river on bridges, and half a mile up the creek stands Phantom Ranch, the Canyon's current human metropolis: food, cabins, even a pay phone. In 1963 I'd paused there for a week, mid-journey, doing things that had to be done. Now, again, there were things I needed to do. And many more that I'd have liked to do. But I wanted to stay with the Knutson party.

At Phantom, even the rustic central "canteen" provoked only faint memory echoes. I located and picked up the food and stores the Park Service had been holding for me, along with some forwarded mail, phoned a message to the Sextons' answering machine, got back to the river with minutes to spare, loaded the new supplies, cast off.

Out on the river, the first two Knutson rafts were well ahead, Captain Ahab in his *Great White Shark* some way behind, and I found myself floating down on my own in fading light. I ran a couple of riffles and 4-rated rapids. In the soft gray light the river was big, impressive, humbling, good. The sudden solitude made it all even better.

Then we were ashore, all of us, on an outcrop overlooking Horn Creek Rapid (9,10,8,8; 10 feet; not recommended between 4000 and 10,000 cfs).

"Oh, a piece of cake," said Dan. "Look, you enter so that you pass just right of that big boulder up at the head, and you pull in behind it and then you've got a clear run that'll keep you left of the main flow. A lot of stuff down there we don't want to mess with. Yeah, a piece of cake." The stuff we didn't want to mess with was a raging white turmoil.

Remembering Hance, I said, "Might it help to get some momentum up beforehand, to help slide in behind that first boulder?"

"Sure," said Dan. "If you can do it."

I had a clear view of the others' runs. Saw each of them pull, madly, as he approached the big boulder. Saw their rafts move across the current hardly at all. Saw them, one after the other, swept down into the white turmoil, almost into a black right-flanking cliff. But remembering Hance, I still felt confident.

I came down exactly as planned, just right of the big boulder, and before we reached it established a little leftward momentum with two or three strong pulls. Then I was pulling madly. Then madlier. But our momentum died. We swept past the boulder, plunged down into the raging turmoil.

No doubt I followed much the same route as the others. At one point we were certainly careering through monumental waves, perilously close to sheer black rock. But *Water Strider* rode it all like a duck. Below the rapid, safely out in flat water, I wasn't really sorry we'd messed with the turmoil.

A mile below Horn Creek, another layover camp. Among my catch-up chores: gooping oar stops firmly in place and organizing the new, rat-damaged supplies from Phantom. Next morning, at the foot of Hermit Trail—after we'd run Granite Rapid (9,+)—Dan and his two companions left for the outer world.

We ran Hermit Rapid, hurried on. The earlier we reached Crystal (10,+), the first of the Canyon's two monsters, the lower the water would be and the less awesome the obstacle. (Here, more than a hundred miles below Glen Canyon Dam, the daily tides had flattened a little, and they hit high and low points roughly twenty hours later than at Lee's Ferry.)

We arrived in mid-afternoon, scouted right.

"Hm," said Dave Knutson. "Looks quite different from the time I went through. Must have been close to twice this much water."

All three Knutson rafts elected to run left, down the main current—the route the river ranger had recommended. But because you couldn't ferry in such heavy water you ran serious risk of hitting a cavernous mid-run hole, and I decided to run right. I'd face three huge holes, staggered one after the other. Hit any one of them and I'd almost certainly flip. But after a roiling approach run the tongues between the holes were relatively flat and I felt I'd be able to ferry accurately through narrow openings. I spent a long time memorizing markers; then I walked back up to the raft, did a brief Emmett (the Knutsons had by this time made successful runs), and pushed off.

The roiling whitewater approach, no problem. Now, ferry in behind the

Negotiating Upper Crystal Rapid.

first hole . . . Perfect. Straighten up. Done . . . Time to spare. Carefully, I lined up on the steep, narrow tongue between the second hole and a barely submerged boulder. Then we were plunging bow-first down the tongue. Out of the corner of my eye, just beyond the left oar, a glimpse of a gaping white cauldron that was the hole. Here, I'd meant to pivot bow-left, then pull clear of the third and final obstacle, but the force of the hole's side wave pushed the bow right. I glanced downstream. Plenty of time to push rather than pull. I began to push. We moved across the current. All at once I was aware of Dave standing on the bank and gesticulating toward the hole that was the third obstacle. I smiled, nodded, went on pushing, moved clear of the hole, swept safely past it.

Then we were all standing on the bank and whooping it up. It was some time before the elation ebbed enough for us to think about going on down. I could see white water ahead.

"Oh, you just keep left of that island," said Dave. "No problem."

One by one, the other rafts launched, moved down out of sight, left of the island. I followed, still riding the elation. Soon I was riding big white water, too. The water grew whiter, angrier. The waves mounted higher. Grew steadily, progressively, relentlessly steeper. At first the flow held straight; then, without warning, it had swung right and we were swinging with it and the waves were huge and hostile and they encompassed us in a way we'd never been encompassed and there seemed no clear distinction between the raging whiteness outside the raft and inside it, and suddenly I was yelling out a question to the encircling white-foam universe—literally yelling, though I could hardly believe it. What I yelled was "Holy Christ! Where now? There's nowhere to go!" Something like that, anyway.

Then we were dropping. The white chaos still rampaged around us but now the raft angled steeply downward and the pit of my stomach said we were dropping and my mind was filled with the thought that there must surely be boulders down below and that any minute now we'd crash-land onto them.

Then, without explanation, we were out beyond the white water and Dave was sitting there in his raft. His grin suggested a sort of bemused triumph.

"What the hell was that?" I asked.

"Well, I guess that was Lower Crystal. Funny, last time I came through, it didn't amount to much."

Below Crystal the physical challenge slackened.

Lava Falls always hung there, ahead. But now, floating down long stretches of flat water, there was time to look around. And gradually I began to recognize that ever since Badger Creek Rapid, below Lee's Ferry, I had in a sense been traveling behind a curtain. Had been cut off from the realities of this place that in 1963 had enraptured me at first sight; this huge, echoing rift in the earth's crust that down the years had continued to enthrall. Yet ever since Badger, only the Canyon's distinctive, familiar patterns and colors had been there. Nothing more.

Much the same had happened, of course, back in Cataract Canyon. Sheer physical challenge had dominated my horizons. Day after day I'd lived only in the present, only on the surface. It had been the same at the start of the 1963 walk, too. So nothing new. There are stretches of everyday life down which you float in touch with no more than surfaces.

Now, even the notes I jotted at nightcamps reflected the way my thoughts had, since Badger, tended to skate along mundane practical surfaces: One good thing about running big water was that it kept washing the raft clean. If you wore clip-on sunglasses and they got splashed beyond reason you could flip them up and, with luck, regain a clear view through your main glasses. Down in the largely sunless Inner Gorge, constantly showered with spray, I'd begun wearing a semi-dry suit over polypro and pile clothing, and it kept me comfortably warm. The exception: feet. They mostly wallowed in water, and even wetsocks worn under sandals often failed to keep them warm.

This time, though, physical challenge wasn't the whole story. At Badger I had, like the river there below Glen Canyon Dam, lost my independence. Once Jack's party arrived I could no longer, at my sole pleasure, dawdle or dash. Could no longer pause above a rapid while time ticked beyond one minute after the hour. Could no longer even launch or pull in when a moment glittered. The journey had slipped out of my control.

Even after valencing across to the Knutson party I'd not regained control. But things had improved. Radically. Progressively. Thanks largely to them.

Like most solitudinarians, I am not a good group man. For me, perfection is a party of one. Two can be enchanting—but may also tear a trip to shreds. Three is pushing things. Beyond that, count me out. It's not that I haven't tried wilderness travel with groups. I have. And I simply don't like it. Such traditional delights as squatting around a flickering campfire and swapping eternal truths, eternal lies, tend to leave me unenthralled. I can generally cope, in a detached sort of way; but I'm rarely at my best. Nowadays, I at least recognize the failing. Before accepting John Sexton's offer to accompany me to the source I'd warned him that as a wilderness companion I was a dubious prospect—especially now, in my declining years, when as a rule I declined to do things I didn't want to do. Our approach march had turned out very well indeed—but I knew John, he'd been alerted, and we were a party of only two. Traveling through Grand Canyon with any group of strangers was bound to be very different.

But after a few days with the Knutson party I recognized that I could hardly have fallen in with better companions.

Dave Knutson, as river leader, was the one I came to know best. He taught personnel management at the university in nearby Flagstaff, and it was clearly no coincidence that his group operated so harmoniously. When, during two stressful episodes, I eventually did see small puffs of discord, Dave handled them with quiet precision. And for all his lack of river experience, he impressed me with his technical acumen. Or, rather, his judgment.

Not far below Crystal, a torn floor in Dave's raft had delayed us and made him acutely aware that to meet his takeout deadline at Diamond Creek, still more than 120 miles downriver, he'd have to maintain a 15-mile daily average. (I hardly had time to waste, either. The date was November 1. To keep my journey a pleasure and not an icy penance I needed to clear the Grand Wash Cliffs, marking the end of Grand Canyon, by mid-November. And the Cliffs still lay 180 miles ahead.)

When we launched next day, Dave aimed to cover twenty miles before nightfall.

Within an hour we were scouting 104 Mile Rapid. It was rated only 7,6,6,5, but we had hit it at a water level that created a line of horrendous holes, bank to bank. Dave must have been tempted. After a prolonged scout, though, he shook his head. "I've never seen a rapid unrunnable before, but I think we should wait an hour." An hour later the river had risen enough to give us a relatively easy down-the-middle run.

Gradually, I'd also come to a deeper appreciation of Jerry Knutson as social leader. A few days into our co-travels I'd taken him aside and said I was very grateful for everything they were doing but like hell didn't want to be a burden; if they felt I was becoming one, then I'd hang back and join another party. Next morning Jerry quietly advised me that he'd put the proposition to the whole group. The vote had been unanimous: they wanted me to stay.

Brief one-on-one conversations at scouts and stop-offs and even night-camps slowly taught me more about other party members.

John, at twenty-nine, was the "baby" of the party. A quiet man, and private. He liked to go off and read or wander around on his own. When I asked him what he did he muttered something about cooking for somebody. Later I learned he'd recently graduated from computer school.

One night, as I sat in the dark in my segregated camp, a hundred yards from the Knutson party, I was startled by a flashlight beam sliding along a nearby rock face. It swung around, reached me, stopped, went out.

"Oh, sorry to intrude," said John. "But I've got to have a look around."

Several days later the two of us happened to be standing alone near the rafts. "John," I said, "would I be right in saying that you're still searching for the answer to what to do with your life?" He smiled and nodded. "Guess so."

As the days passed I grew to feel more and more comfortable with the Knutson party—and they, I think, with me. They made me feel welcome, yet respected my need for solitude. I began to enjoy their presence, to feel almost a part of the group. Once or twice I shared their camp. When I camped close by I'd often wander over to socialize.

At most nightcamps I managed to get some reading done. Once, tucked away on my own, leaning back against a smooth boulder with the river talking away to the darkness, off to my right, I read the last pages of Edward Abbey's *Journey Home*—and found myself regretting our non-relationship.

In 1968, when his *Desert Solitaire* and my *Man Who Walked Through Time* were both published, and sometimes reviewed in tandem, I'd sampled his book with curiosity and hope. But I'd quickly pigeonholed Abbey as an inept wilderness traveler, replete with bull. Years later, out of the blue, he'd written me a letter clearly meant to be friendly; but something in it—I could no longer remember what—had rubbed me the wrong way, and I'd sent a brief, peevish reply. We'd had no further direct contact. Then, just before I'd started this river journey, on my birthday, Ed Abbey had died. Perhaps that had had something to do with my deciding to read, at last, *The Journey Home*. The river seemed a fit place: after all, the canyonlands were Abbey country.

I'd liked much of what I read. Abbey was indeed, as he himself had written and other people had confirmed, a swashbuckling, bullshitting extremist. But he'd reveled in it, had fun. Now I was sorry I'd never met him. My fault, too. And gnawing away at that wound were three handwritten lines I'd found on the title page of my copy of his book. The brief message, addressed to me and signed "Ed Abbey," was professional and generous. This copy of the book had been given me by a friend—a longtime Abbey admirer, from a distance—who'd gone on a commercial raft trip he led. When she gave me the book I'd presumably read the message; but I'd forgotten it. And now it was too late.

I closed the book. Five years younger than me, as well . . . I leaned back against the cold, smooth boulder. Off to my right, the river that carried us all along was still saying something to the night.

Nightcamps also revealed some revealing wildlife. Not always of the flashy kind.

One evening, at a camp tucked into an overhang so overhung that it verged on cavedom and so encapsulating that the flame of my unprotected candle did not so much as flicker, I was digesting dinner when a small green insect fluttered into my world. It landed on the ammunition-box dinner table and, as far as I could make out, began to imbibe a mini-lake of wine I'd spilled. It was an extraordinarily fragile little creature—perhaps half an inch long, diaphanous to the verge of translucence. It perched on the white ammunition box for several minutes, bibulating, and when it tried to depart it flew into difficulties. The erratic course left little doubt. No breathalyzer needed: FUI. Then, in the flick of a wingtip, from comedy to tragedy. The delicate little creature swerved into the candle flame, singed its wings, fell. It fluttered briefly on the ammunition box cover, then tumbled off the far edge, out of sight. I sat still. Should I put it out of its misery? But it might be only slightly injured; and I could make no informed judgment about its chances of recovery. In the end I decided that the only ethical course was to leave it alone. I did not have the heart to get up and look at it.

Next morning, by chance, I saw it fly up from beside the ammunition box. It settled on my sleeve. Gently, I blew it off. It fluttered away, back out into the Canyon world, pale and fragile against dark, solid rock.

Another nightcamp. After dinner, a rustle in the dark, close. On flashlight. Bulging and moving as if windblown, a big black plastic bag in which I kept food and wine. But no wind stirring. For a moment I sat and stared. Then I reached out and began to lift the bag. From it emerged a ringtail—sometimes called "ringtail cat," though "squirrel-like raccoon" comes closer. Without undue haste, the animal disappeared into a rock crevice; almost at once, reappeared. It moved forward, stood peering down the flashlight beam. Now I had a clear view of the sharp, intelligent face with its black-and-white markings and perked ears, of the low-slung body with its soft brown-gray fur, and of the long, bushy, black-and-white-ringed tail. For a brief spell, ringtail and I counter-inspected. Then I shooed. It went.

Later we played a game. Before going to bed I balanced empty cook pots on a basin that held various snacks, including chocolate. The ringtail kept coming back—and being scared away each time it clattered the pots down. Once, I was fairly sure I got a good flash picture. Afterward I heard the thief snicker, back among the boulders. Next morning, the chocolate gone.

Then there was the chip-loving, equally human-habituated intellectual.

Another nightcamp. Moonlight. Close by, once again, an unexplained rustling. This time, a crisper sound. On flashlight. Impaled in its beam, the bushy black-and-white tag end of a ringtail whose body was rustling away inside an opened aluminum-foil bag of chips. The flashlight beam must have bounced warning glitters off the crinkled foil, for the ringtail promptly emerged. It looked me over. Then it walked unhurriedly past, no more than two or three feet away—soft, elegant—and vanished among rock ledges. I went up, flashlit the ledge crevices. For a moment it was crouching there, peering back, still elegantly beautiful; then it had squat-scurried off into the night. I went back and battened down every item of food, tight. In the morning, somebody had purloined the paperback *Origin of Species* I'd begun reading but had carried it only a few feet before tearing out the title page and dropping the rest.

Perhaps the intellectual ringtail's evening performance had helped quieten me. Anyway, at this same nightcamp I pulled aside, just for a moment, the curtain that had been cutting me off from the Canyon's roundest realities.

I was lying back looking up at moonlit canyon walls when from high on the cliff behind me came the sound of a very minor rockfall. A few seconds later several rocks tumbled down a nearby gully and came to rest about thirty yards away. The event barely caught my attention—until I realized that in all the months I'd spent in the Canyon, spread over many years, I had until then only once heard a stone fall. A single stone. And as I rolled this thought around my mind there emerged the notion of a movie that told in computerized graphics the story of the canyon's creation. Lying there, I could see it, wide-screen. Reality speeded up, so that every second meant a thousand years—or perhaps ten thousand, or a hundred thousand. The river cutting relentlessly down, revealing progressively more ancient strata. Above all, the blurred erosion of the side walls. An almost constant hail of falling rock: pebbles; boulders; slabs; very occasionally, huge spalls peeling off. Creation before your very eyes! And then perhaps, at or near the end, a freeze frame showing the canyon as it is today, with all the currently falling rock fragments (taking the long-term view) suspended on crumbling cliff face and arrested talus slope.

Lying there in the shadow of the real cliffs, I was running this instructional movie through my mind for the second time when I felt myself beginning to sink toward sleep. Then I was thinking that perhaps the time would come when we no longer needed such a toy. Once we'd mastered time travel, all we'd have to do would be to scuttle back down the few tens of millions of years that it took for the Canyon to be excavated, photograph what we saw and . . . I slid down the final slumber slope.

A̲lthough the physical challenge had slackened below Crystal, it never died away.

At first the rapids averaged more than one a mile. Later, one every two miles. They presented, by and large, few technical problems, just heavy water. At first the only routes seemed traditional "straight-down-the-middles." But by now I'd begun to understand that in such rapids it was often better to run bow-first down the tongue and then, once it looked safe, pivot into ferry mode and Powell—that is, *pull* with all my might— through the flank waves into easier water. And sometimes there was another alternative. Thinner water on one flank might let me avoid the rapid's maw by weaving intricate routes among obstacles the other boatmen felt they couldn't negotiate. I christened such bypasses "Colin's Chicken Runs."

But between the rapids, that week below Crystal, often time for other things.

Time for brief stop-offs. For snatched samplings of interesting places. Of people, too.

At Elves Chasm, as we rock-hopped up toward a slim, recessed waterfall, I happened to be just ahead of Jill, Dave Knutson's petite and attractive wife. "Well," she said as we approached a pool at the foot of the waterfall, "I must say you still nimble around the rocks pretty well."

"Not the way I used to. And not like Spiderman, that's for sure." I nodded forward and up.

Kevin, the carpenter with a yen for cabinet-making, was revealing how he got his nickname. He'd already climbed the first big slab beyond the pool. John followed. Spiderman moved into the waterfall's shadowy, deep-cut cleft, high above the pool. Spray kept the recessed rock rich and beautiful with moss and maidenhair ferns but slick and treacherous for climbers. Before long Spiderman was peering out at us, mock-elfinlike, from a small natural grotto.

A couple of days later, Spiderman would confirm that he was, like John, a quester. He'd again make me envious—in a residual, previous-existence sort of way—when he left early on a layover morning, backpacked around a trail loop and rejoined us a day and several miles downriver.

At Elves Chasm, though, I barely knew Spiderman. Jill did. She nodded at him, high in his grotto, and smiled. "Trust him to be up there."

Jill and I sat beside the pool for some time, chatting. She and Dave lived near Williams, just south of the Canyon, and she worked out of their home as a freelance graphic artist. She seemed to know, as clearly as any of us do, what she wanted out of life.

Spiderman and John rejoined us. We trooped back to the rafts and floated on down the wide and swirling river, sometimes sunlit, sometimes shadowed, that was always the same, never the same.

We also had time, that week between Crystal and Lava, for snatched daytime glimpses of wildlife.

Once, just below Elves Chasm, a lone bighorn sheep, alert on a bare rock ridge, watched us pass. At stop-offs or even afloat we might see little brown canyon wrens questing among the rocks; but they emitted only subdued squeaks and twirps, not the ringing springtime territorial calls, with distinctive tumbledown cadence, that I remembered from 1963. Two or three times we saw great blue herons standing in shallows, as inanimate as if sculpted from blue-gray rock, peering optimistically down and seeming, like all their kind, hopelessly dependent for a living on herondipity.

The daytime wildlife may, like the nocturnal ringtails, have helped. And one evening as we drifted gently downriver in fading light—over everything, a gray mantle of nebulous uncertainty—I again pulled a curtain corner aside and moved, just for a moment, beyond the thin, mechanical notion of a computerized virtual geology.

In 1963, my excursions into the Gorge had been brief and mostly static. Now, the river carried us past every foot of its walls—often so slowly that I had time to appreciate details. Mostly, I'd failed to grasp this opportunity. But that evening I'd floated close to several crystalline white seams, or dikes—were they marble?—that thrust up into the dark mass of ancient, twisted rock. And all at once there flooded over me the kind of understanding I'd achieved in 1963: an almost on-the-spot awareness of how these dikes had been created. A comprehension of how it must have been when the molten white material thrust up into the black rock and split it with a deafening WOOH! WOOH! WOOH! that must have sounded, in its way, as cataclysmic yet creative as Stravinsky's *Rite of Spring* percussions.

The insight moment didn't last. But afterward, floating on down, I found I'd reestablished contact with the Gorge's grave magnificence. Could see the soaring beauty with new eyes: the gray-black nitty-gritty of immediate rock walls; the pink and almost dreamlike folding-back world of upper, sunlit terraces.

Throughout that week of floating down toward Lava, though, I could rarely forget the rapids. Several posed problems.

In Specter (8,7,6,5) I hit the key waves perfectly and with momentum. But the biggest wave of all snuffed out the momentum and stood us up so straight that for a moment I thought we were going to flip, bow hurtling backward over stern. The little raft shuddered—then teetered forward over the wave's foaming crest. Beyond that, no Spectral crises. For me. But Jerry got washed out of his raft. He never lost contact with it, though, and was quickly pulled back aboard. "Well, I flipped, back up at House Rock . . . and now I've been washed out," he told me. "And hell, there's a difference."

Then, Deubendorff.

We arrived at lowish water. A churning, drawn-out maze of holes and huge waves. Rating: 9,8,8,7,+. We scouted left. I think we were all impressed.

While we stood staring, a white dory—part of a small raft-and-kayak group we'd passed just upriver—came barreling down. The boatman, running solo, entered the tongue right of center, ferried, began to pull right, toward less tormented water. But big waves made him straighten up prematurely and head bow-first down the main current. We watched as he bounced like a cork through a series of horrendous holes. He made it. But I began looking for alternatives.

Close to the right bank, a run that would call for complex thread-needle work among crowded boulders. Looked feasible though, through binoculars. I shared the idea with Dave.

He studied the route carefully. "Looks kinda doubtful," he said. "Even for your *Water Strider.*" And in the end he elected to chance the main run, more or less the way the dory had gone.

When the Knutson rafts pulled out above the main run I kept going, crossed to the far side, and aligned us above the small subsidiary tongue. Careful, now. No hurry. Ease down into the tongue. Hold us back; ferry slightly to adjust position. The run still looking possible. Ease on down. Soon, the last moment for mind-changing. A deep breath. Fine-tune our line past the first boulder . . .

Three or four minutes later we floated clear of the final tail wave. Perfect. No boulder so much as grazed. Not a glimpse into a hole. And raft and I still bone dry.

The Knutson rafts had all made it. But each had had its moments. And Dave told me later that although he'd shared his misgivings with no one before they ran it, he'd thought Deubendorff at that water stage "looked worse than Lava."

By now I'd grown resigned to the idea that the passage of twenty-six years had, with assists from the present, sandbagged my 1963 Canyon memories.

That moment of surprise and disappointment at Nankoweap had set the tone, when side canyon and Anasazi cliff dwellings lay flat, inert. At Kwagunt I'd failed to locate my exact airdrop site. At the confluence with the Little Colorado—another 1963 milestone—the lineaments of the place looked right and I could recall events that had taken place, but the thin memories stirred no emotion, no spark. (In this case, demographics hardly helped: we arrived to find my former companions pausing there too—our final meeting with the party led by the man I've called Jack—and the twin-assemblage crowded a place I'd hoped to resample alone.) Later, more of the same. I passed, without even noticing them, several sites I'd mentally tagged for reexamination. And other places plain failed to resonate. Nadir had come a few miles above Deubendorff Rapid.

We'd camped at the mouth of Forster Canyon, on a long sandy beach. I'd photographed the rafts with a pleasant upriver view as background before I checked the river guide—and found two words leaping out at me.

No name from the Canyon walk had echoed down the years more surely and sharply than "Conquistador Aisle." My first stupendous view of it from a ledge almost three thousand feet above the river—a view down a long and arrowlike corridor of a tremendous gorge, a view filled with unexpected space and silence and the witchery of desert sunlight—had stopped me in my tracks. The memory of that moment had been imprinted vividly enough to last, unaided. But it had been reinforced countless times down the years: a self-portrait I took, standing there pack on back and looking down the length of Conquistador Aisle, became the jacket cover of *The Man Who Walked Through Time.* And it was a shock, now, standing at the mouth of Forster Canyon, to realize I'd floated the length of the Aisle and then photographed it before recognizing where I was.

Places look different, I told myself, from different viewpoints. The same thing had happened back in Labyrinth when I floated through the massive trough that had so impressed me when I stood at the Notch. But there at Forster it was still a shock. And my memory of how it had been twenty-six years earlier when I first looked down and along the Aisle remained remote, unreal, curtained off.

Then, on the morning of our sixth day below Crystal, a chink in the curtain.

Soon after leaving camp, as we floated downriver, I happened to look up a shadowed side canyon. High above, framed by the side canyon's black walls, the startling, sunlit silhouette of a red butte. A butte with a distinctive molar-tooth shape. Check guide. No question.

In 1963, Mount Sinyala had been an early highpoint. A turning point.

And now—resting on my oars and floating slowly on through the somber, still-shadowed gorge—I found myself hearing an echo. A faint, attenuated echo. But still an echo of how it had been for a forty-one-year-old backpacker, three thousand feet above and twenty-six years back, as he walked in a snowstorm across the broad red-rock terrace called the Esplanade. An echo of the way he'd been walking tentatively, uncertain whether he'd find enough water to sustain him during the next few days, when he'd looked back between snow squalls and seen—faintly, as if through a lace curtain—Mount Sinyala's blurred but still thrusting molar shape. An echo of how, soon afterward, when the clouds lifted and he looked back again, Mount Sinyala stood out sharp and clear, like a floodlit castle, and all around him the sun was flashing celebration signals from a thousand little pools in the red rock—and he made a momentous decision: those rainpockets should be enough to sustain him across the Esplanade.

Then the raft had floated on down and the molar shape of Mount Sinyala had been withdrawn.

At ten o'clock that morning, four miles downriver, we pulled in toward a cleft in the left-bank rock wall. Havasu Creek.

In 1963, during my journey's reconnaissance phase, I came down the trail that ended at the mouth of Havasu Creek and got my first sight of the Colorado River within Grand Canyon. That moment still reverberated. So did another from the same day.

I'd steeled myself, as a weak and timid swimmer, to swim upriver from the creek across a back eddy and so bypass a somber black overhang that barred my way to the start of a rock ledge that might offer an upriver route. The swim had been slow, painful, anxious. But I'd landed triumphantly on a shelving sandy beach, then made a half-hour trial trek along the narrow ledge. The route ahead looked possible, but highly uncertain. By the time I got back to the creek, heavy rain was falling. But I'd not only proved the route was worth attempting; I'd faced and passed a trial of the spirit.

Minutes later the rain eased. I looked up and saw that the storm clouds had parted; and also saw, high above, rock detail softened by a thin, uneven coating of white. Almost at once I grasped that snow on the Esplanade, around Mount Sinyala, meant a good chance of life-sustaining rainpockets up there. If so, I could forget the problematical rock-ledge route. And that moment of prophetic understanding had also remained imprinted on my mind.

Now, on our sixth day below Crystal, as I pulled in toward the mouth of Havasu Creek, I knew details would have changed. For one thing, the river now ran much higher. But when I drifted slowly past the back eddy and the shelving sandy beach that marked the beginning of the rock ledge, they looked much the same. So did the dark overhang, though it now seemed less somber, far less threatening. We pulled ashore. This time, everything was there, just about as I remembered it.

I moored alongside the Knutson rafts, already tethered in the blue-green waters of Havasu Creek.

"We're all going to hike up for a look at the falls," said Dave. "Except for Jerry. He's staying with the rafts. We'll be away an hour or so. You coming?"

I made my excuses, wandered downstream along a broad, tapering rock shelf.

Three years after the 1963 journey, this shelf had been my launching place for a two-week walk-and-swim trip down seventy miles of the Lower Canyon to Diamond Creek—an enclosed stretch that no one seemed to have attempted on foot. A thorough reconnaissance downriver from the creek mouth had convinced me that I'd have to take to the water immediately, complete with heavy pack, and swim across to a narrow strip of sand that would—for a while, at least—allow me to walk down that bank. The river was running at twelve times its 1963 volume, and the pin-prickly time I spent on that rock shelf just below Havasu Creek, preparing gear for a river crossing of a kind I'd never attempted before, and then screwing my courage tight enough for the actual launch, had imprinted the place indelibly on my memory. Or so I'd thought.

After the Knutson party had left I stood for a long time on the shelf. First I let my eye follow its rising line: it tapered to a narrow sill, high above the river, before vanishing into a cliff face—the face along which I'd inched my way until convinced there was no alternative to swimming. Then I pinpointed as accurately as possible the place from which I'd finally pushed off into the river, with courage fairly firmly screwed to the sticking-place, wearing a small inflatable life vest and towing my carefully waterproofed backpack. Now, I let my eye float down and across the tail of Havasu Rapid, following the route I must have floated, dog-paddling hard, on what turned out to be the first of four such river crossings. . . . And as I stood there on the rock shelf I at last felt stirring within me a Canyon memory echo no more than mildly muffled. I don't mean I remembered everything with certainty, let alone in granular detail. But for a moment I remembered the essence of how it had all been. And for the moment that was enough.

I lingered on the broad, tapering rock shelf. At last I turned away.

It was quiet, back at the mouth of Havasu Creek. The rafts idled, beautiful against gray rock and blue-green water. In one of them Jerry sat playing his recorder. At a guess, Handel.

It would be good to report that the gap in the curtain widened, there at the place I'd waded across the mouth of Havasu Creek and pulled myself up a seven-foot gray rock wall—only to face, just beyond it, the somber overhang that had forced me to swim across the eddy. But barely two feet of the rock wall showed, and deep, swirling water altered the feel of the place. The rafts, for all their attractiveness, intruded, too. And Jerry, about as harmonious and unintrusive as a human could have been, was a time-trespasser.

Once I knew he'd become aware of my presence I eased down near his raft, then sat and studied what little I could see of the gray rock wall. Faint echoes, perhaps. But very faint.

I tried to explain to Jerry what I was doing. He seemed to understand; but my verbalizing got in the way, too. Jerry came ashore, we chatted, and for the first time I learned he was an amateur vintner. As we talked we stood looking down at a monarch butterfly lying on its side on cold gray rock, alive but almost inert.

Monarch butterflies occupy a small but special niche in my memory. I once visited the mountain forest near Mexico City in which congregate, each winter, all American monarchs that spend their summers east of the Rockies. They congregate on towering conifers in huge pendulous clumps, black and inert, like gigantic bee swarms. Once you've seen them, you do not forget. And you marvel that some of these fragile creatures started out, six months earlier, from a point more than a thousand miles away—and will probably return to that same point, perhaps to the same tree. Or, rather, their children or grandchildren may do so. For no single individual ever completes such long double migrations. We humans do not yet know how a family pulls off this collective trick, but the key could be magnetism: imprinted in the genetic code of each monarch may lie a magnetized map of its personal migration route to and from Mexico—or, in the case of those that summer west of the Rockies, to and from localized winter homes along the California coast.

Jerry and I stood looking down at the lone monarch lying motionless on the cold rock.

"Poor thing," said Jerry. "I'm afraid it's lost its way. Probably had it, too. After all, we're into November now and it ought to be in California."

"Not the only one," I said.

The rest of the party came back from the falls. Before we went on down-river, Dave asked me to take him and one member of his raft crew across

The Inner Gorge, near Havasu Creek.
Two Knutson-party rafts.

the few feet of water that separated us from the gray rock wall I'd scrambled up in 1963: he wanted to line Captain Ahab and his *Great White Shark*—which handled like an oil tanker—upstream of the creek mouth and so give him a better start line for entering Havasu Rapid over to the right; and in order to do so Dave needed to be a few yards farther up the bank, and free of the need to control his own raft.

I ferried the two men across. They scrambled up over the narrow strip of visible rock, carrying Ahab's stern line, and went about their business. I held position, tight against the gray rock. For a few moments I was almost as aware of its texture as I'd been when I scrambled up it twenty-six years earlier; was even aware, fleetingly, of how I'd felt as I scrambled. Then Dave and his companion were back, mission accomplished. As I ferried them the few feet to their own raft it occurred to me that they were my first passengers.

We ran Havasu Rapid, floated on down. After a while I spun the raft around, looked back up at the mouth of Havasu Creek. Like the confluence of the Green and Colorado, above Cataract Canyon, it had already blended with the general flow of the Canyon walls; had become just another flat in the passing show. I spun us back, began to push downriver. The other rafts were well ahead and I was essentially on my own again. The noon sun beat down, filling the gorge.

That day we ran twenty-two river-miles.

Not until evening did I realize that I'd hardly ever cocked an ear for echoes of my seventeen-day 1966 backpack-and-swim trip. That trip had been a monotonous, slogging affair—all alongside or actually in the river—with only two clearly memorable highpoints: a swim through Lower Lava Rapid, then a tricky airdrop. So echoes might have been diffi-cult to detect even had my mind not been sitting serenely in the present.

That long day below Havasu Creek went as roundly as any since we en-tered the Canyon. Sunlight set Redwall cliffs glowing. The Gorge, though still magnificent, became less gravely so. I ran all rapids well. And that evening I dined alone in moonlight and a mellow mood.

The Knutsons' camp was across the river, slightly upstream. My inten-tion had been to set up on the fringe of theirs, semi-detached, but the beach they chose was too small and I'd moved across the river.

After dinner I sat in the dark, surveying my river world. Downstream, a delicious curve of Redwall underwent slow alchemy as moving moonlight modified its textures. Upstream, beyond a riffle, the Knutsons' camp sent a stream of signals. The white halo around a big rock meant that behind the rock stood a pole with a small Coleman lamp on it, marking their kitchen. On the open beach, around their campfire, sat a circle of black figures. At that range, most of the figures were unidentifiable. But they were no group of strangers now; were much more than just shadows that passed in the night.

The flickering firelight reflected in the river, illuminating along its un-stable line the swift and constant tongue of the riffle and the white waves on its flanks; then one of the figures stood up and masked the firelight and I could see the river differently—less explicitly, more generally—and feel something of its power.

The riffle's rumbling monotone raised a screen between the Knutson camp and mine. But it was good, I found, being able to look across and know more or less what was happening over on the far side of the river that now separated us. A small white light bobbed away from the fire and kept going, erratically, questingly: John, making his rounds.

I leaned back, closed my eyes. Once we'd run Lava Falls—now only five miles downriver—the going should be easier, and in four days we'd reach Diamond Creek, where the Knutsons, like most Canyon runners, would take out. Would return to the modern world. I began to wonder whether I should wait at Diamond for another party or go ahead and run the last ten miles of rapids above Lake Mead on my own—and all at once it hit me that I'd be profoundly sorry to leave the Knutson party.

I reopened my eyes. Beyond the dark and swirling river, their camp was still flashing its signals: Coleman rock halo; flickering fire with its circle of squatting figures; John's questing flashlight beam. I sat looking across the river that separated us. Separated yet united. Even here on my own, I felt a member of the group. I sat silent in the darkness and there surged through me a flood of something remarkably like affection for them all.

Next morning, four miles downriver, black lava flows doused the glow of the Gorge's red walls.

Several major volcanic eruptions poured this lava into the Canyon very recently, geologic time: during the last million years or so, when the river had already cut down to roughly its present bed. Today we see only residual lava traces that time has not yet brushed aside.

A mile above Lava Falls we approached a big black basaltic rock that thrust up from the river. "Vulcan's Anvil," said the river guide. "A *volcanic neck*, the core of a volcano."

As we floated down toward it, Dave called out, "Hey, Colin, you can maneuver better than me. As you pass Vulcan's Anvil, could you put this on one of those little ledges?" He rowed over, handed me a coin. "It's my unlucky penny. Better get rid of it before we run Lava."

Half an hour later we all stood clustered on the right bank above the thundering white cataract that is Lava Falls Rapid—the quintessential "10" rapid, with a 34-foot vertical drop. Each of us, I'm sure, felt somewhat awestruck.

But disappointed, too. We'd been banking, that Monday morning, on catching Friday's water from Glen Canyon Dam. The normal wide weekday fluctuation would give us, at high and then low water, a choice between running left or right of the huge and horrendous central hole. But we'd miscalculated: the water ran weekend-low. And that annulled our options. Mine especially.

I'd long ago decided "highwater left." It sounded my kind of route: precise maneuvering, lesser waves. But the left run now looked, at first glance, horrible. At second glance, impossible. Boulders everywhere. And one buttress of a rock blocking the run near its start, black and baleful under the water cascading over it.

While I was reevaluating the right run the boatman of the Deubendorff dory joined us. He was the group's leader and he'd kayaked down from their camp a mile or so upriver to photograph our runs of Lava. Another Dave. Dave Bassage.

Yes, he said, the left run was impossible at this water level. Interesting, though, at high water. He and his party were laying over a day because they wanted to run it when the Monday water came. I was, he said, more than welcome to join them.

The Knutsons couldn't lay over: they had their Diamond Creek deadline. But much as I regretted leaving them, making up my mind didn't take long.

"Yes, I know you'd set your heart on that run," said Dave Knutson. "And with your *Water Strider*, it makes sense."

So we said our goodbyes.

The night before, I'd begun to consider what I'd say when we separated at Diamond Creek. Something genuine, to convey my gratitude. I hadn't got very far. And this kind of hurried farewell wasn't what I'd visualized.

While everybody was still grouped together on the rocks above the rapid I grasped the chance to say a collective "thank you." The words that emerged from my mouth could have been worse. And as the group made preparations for their runs I fitted in tête-à-têtes. First, Captain Ahab—struggling with bad vibes about the run, and for once not taking even more photographs than anyone else, but still utterly amiable. Then the rest, one by one. Given that they were grappling with the trip's supreme challenge, the responses surprised me. Genuine warmth. Almost embarrassingly appreciative. Somebody, I think Jill, said, "It's been a privilege traveling with you." Jerry murmured, "A most hospitable guest." When I thanked Dave I said, "Look, I know you teach personnel management . . . Well, I give you an A." And by God, the man hugged me.

Then they ran Lava. Dave first, with brother Jerry as passenger. A good run. Captain Ahab—whose "bad vibes" had almost made him decide against trying—got his *Great White Shark* through, but like a true oil tanker, climaxing at an inelegant broadside. Finally, Jerry in his small raft, Dave as passenger. Jerry had had his problems back upriver but had learned fast, and now said he felt confident. "Don't worry," Jill told me. "Jerry's a very determined man." He ran it to perfection.

Dave Bassage, sitting on a rock beside me, nodded. "If you feel good about a run, chances are you run it well. And if you feel bad about it you don't."

For a moment I felt tempted to follow the Knutsons down. But I hadn't really scouted their route. It would take me time to get ready, too. And they were in a hurry. Besides, we'd said our farewells.

Then their rafts were floating on down, together, and I was waving and everybody was waving back. They ran Lower Lava, swung out of sight.

That evening, camped very much alone, just above Lava, I let my mind

Lava Falls Rapid. Dave Knutson, with brother
Jerry as passenger, in mid-run. Captain Ahab's
Great White Shark *about to enter*

ramble back up the Canyon. Three weeks since the put-in below Glen Canyon Dam; two weeks since I'd switched to the Knutson party. It didn't seem that long. Check notes. Yes, two whole weeks.

I looked downriver, at the place we'd said goodbye. In the past, such wilderness partings had almost always left me grateful for solitude restored. Now, I felt a poignant sense of loss.

The layover day, I took it easy.

There on the brink I might reasonably have expected to be nervous, going on fearful. It wasn't like that at all.

After the Knutsons had gone Dave Bassage had moored his kayak at the place I planned to camp; then I ferried him across the river. Dave was forty-one—my age when I walked through the Canyon. A schoolteacher who'd come to find teaching in public schools unrewarding, he now made a tenuous living as a professional river-runner in West Virginia. Most years he managed to make a trip out West and run the Canyon.

Over on the far bank, before he walked back up to his camp, we strolled downriver to scout the left run. We stood about where I'd stood in 1966—

furnished with landlubberly eyes—and had wondered, vaguely, how the hell anyone could run a boat through that pounding maelstrom. But my prime concern that day had been waterproofing the pack again for what turned out to be an interesting swim through Lower Lava Rapid.

Now, from that bank, I could see a great deal more about where to go on a left-side run. And what to avoid. The important thing, said Dave Bassage, was to fix the markers in your mind. "Once you get out there it's all horizons. Falls away at such an angle that as you approach the drop-off you can see nothing beyond it."

I rowed back across the river to set up camp, remembering the Lee's Ferry ranger's advice: "If you run left, it's very easy to get disoriented. Last time I ran it I broke a rib. So make sure you go with somebody who knows what he's doing." On that score I now felt entirely confident.

Back on the right bank I set up camp just above the rapid, in a sheltered patch of sand among tamarisks and black lava flows. And for most of that day and the next I sat there in my private little camp and read *The Origin of Species*. Once, at lowest tide, I did walk down the right bank and scout the far run. Snaggle-toothed, now, with black boulders. But they taught me fresh lessons about the run's hazards at low water. The new knowledge boosted my confidence.

Next morning Dave Bassage's six-man party—three kayaks, one raft and the dory—arrived on schedule at nine o'clock. I rowed across to the far bank. We scouted again. Everything looked just the way it should at high water. We walked back up, embarked.

The kayaks went first, then Dave in his dory. Like the kayaks, he quickly dropped from sight. But he'd looked well under control. Next, the Bassage raft. Ditto. I let myself begin to ease down toward my first marker, a small, barely visible boulder.

No problem. I picked it up in plenty of time and moved down well right of it, holding back, following the line I'd amended a little when I rowed over because this time the tongue between the first and second marker had looked broader. My second marker was a curl of white water at the edge of a submerged ledge. I planned to pull in behind the ledge, and even before I'd passed the first marker my eyes were searching for the second.

At first, no curl. I stood up, oars in hand, and peered. It was there all right, farther ahead and farther right than I'd expected—the only white curl with anything like the right shape. I sat down, pivoted into ferry position, bow right, and floated on, almost broadside, safely right of the line that would take me to the curl.

The tongue seemed longer than I'd expected. But now my eyes saw only the curl.

The tongue began to drop away. We gained speed. In plenty of time to establish momentum so that I'd slip easily behind the ledge that the curl marked, I began to pull, gently. We moved toward the curl.

The angle of drop increased. So did our speed. I continued to pull gently on both oars. And then, just before we reached the curl and I was getting ready to pull with all my might so that we'd slide in behind the ledge, something was wrong. The curl no longer looked like the curl I'd memorized—and there was no ledge, only a churning white chaos. At the last moment—almost before I registered what I'd seen, only that something was wrong—I pivoted us bow-first. Just in time. We plunged down into the white chaos.

Then the raft was rearing up and all I could see was seething white frenzy. Then the right oar popped from its oarlock. For a moment, as we plunged and bucked on down the tumultuous white mountainside, I thought of trying to get the oar back in place; then I remembered that a long stretch of chaos still lay ahead and that the one thing I just had to do was hold us head-on to the waves. So I let go of the right oar—or perhaps it had been snatched free—and used both hands on the left oar.

It worked. We held straight. Rode one monster wave after another. And except perhaps in the moment of helplessness when the oar popped I don't think I felt any great sense of danger. What I felt—I think this is true—was surprise and anger. Surprise that things had somehow gone wrong when I'd had it all figured out and was loaded with confidence. And anger at my failure. Anger tinged with embarrassment, even shame,

The white frenzy eased. Became mere tumult. I got the right oar, still held by its safety cord, back in the oarlock. And then we were flouncing on down, more or less under control. The waves began to subside. Became white-bordered swirls. Became swirls. My anger began to ebb; the shame surged.

I pulled in right, behind a rock spur. Dave Bassage was there.

"I know how you feel," he said. "But one way we judge a river-runner is how he handles it when things go wrong—and I'd have to say you did pretty well, keeping her straight after that oar popped. Sure, it wasn't a great run, but you shouldn't feel too bad about it."

(Two years later, in a letter telling me about a run through Grand Canyon in a new dory, Dave wrote: ". . . it went well with the exception of a near miss in Lava. I was attempting the left side again and was perhaps a bit overconfident after doing so well in '89. After a brief scout we set out into the current and I found myself completely disoriented. I was further right than I should have been, totally filled with water in the first crashing wave, went sideways over the big boulder downstream and nearly flipped, bending an oar in the process. . . ." The run reminded him, he said, of "the difficulty you had with your line.")

For four days the rapids continued to challenge. But without daunt. My new companions proved as congenial and hospitable as the old. By the time they took out at Diamond Creek Wash, where my 1966 foot journey had ended, I knew that if I'd traveled with them for two weeks I'd have found saying goodbye as poignant as it been with the Knutsons.

At Diamond, there were no potential new companions: I'd have to run the last few rapids solo. As Dave Bassage and I shook hands he glanced downriver, nodded. "Yes, from here on it'll be different—again."

Ten miles, eight rapids. None rated above "6"—and after each, my pulse soon back close to normal. Then, where Gneiss Canyon Rapid should have been, no rapid. Before long, reservoir stigmata beginning to disfigure the Canyon walls.

But the river took three days to die.

That first evening alone, I camped just below Separation Canyon, where three men had left Powell's first expedition, only to meet their deaths beyond the rim, at the hands of either Indians—the accepted story—or Mormons. After dinner I sat and watched moonlight flood the Canyon. Watched it illuminate, one by one, the Canyon's building-block strata. Dominant Redwall. Sloping, multicolored Bright Angel shale. Abrupt, pie-crust Tapeats sandstone. Finally, the dark, contorted walls of the Inner Gorge. All familiar now, from way back. Way back down the years. And all, in spite of the pale light, with a new, round, uncurtained reality.

I sat still, doing nothing. The moonlight had not yet touched the river, but from out in the darkness came a quiet, ongoing gurgle.

Less than forty miles, now, to Grand Wash Cliffs. Three day's easy travel. To all intents, I'd met my mid-November deadline. For the first time since I walked away from the source spring, no pressure to push ahead. I leaned back, all at once aware I'd shed tensions I'd barely known existed.

Out in the blackness that was the river, the ongoing gurgle changed pitch. It was difficult to accept that there'd be no more rapids, no more white water. I took a deep breath. It was like starting a vacation after a long spell of hard work. Ridiculous, maybe, but that's how it felt. And that made a difference. No big physical challenge; and solitude—so no surprise, really, that the curtain had begun to lift. The two curtains.

Moonlight began to flood the river.

Yes, that was it. What I'd been thinking of, though not very clearly, as two separate curtains were in fact one. The curtain that had shrouded the memories of my earlier foot journey was the same as the one that had shrouded my appreciation of the Canyon's round realities. The same or a wholly owned subsidiary. Now, it or they were lifting. And with them removed I could look back and recognize that although Grand Canyon had lived up to expectations as the journey's physical-challenge highpoint, it had turned out to be perhaps the appreciation lowpoint.

For three days I moved steadily on down toward the Grand Wash Cliffs.

Mostly, the languid water barely murmured. A single toad croaking on the far bank, a hundred yards away, could sound thunderous. A beaver tail-slap was a bomb burst. And the new silence helped.

I found myself alert to changes, omens. Talus slopes now supported ocotillos and creosote bushes and other "low desert" vegetation. Late the second day, a monarch butterfly, fluttering bright orange against black rock—alive and well, fragile yet determined—drifted downriver with me, toward California.

On the third day, which I knew would be my last in the Canyon, I floated placidly, taking my time.

Mid-morning, windless, warm. A stretch of canyon no different from a thousand others. Nothing particularly beautiful. The bathtub stigmata, in fact, now deeper and dirtier, more disfiguring. Otherwise, just rock walls and talus slopes and sandbars framing an elongated mirror of green-black water.

Then the raft had swung broadside and I was looking at a nearby cliff. Was staring at blocks of dark rock. Staring at indentations on their surfaces, scooped out like shallow saucers. Staring at their smoothly rounded edges and the rough, granular texture that stood stark in slanting sunlight and cried out for fingertips to brush them, gently, sensuously. Then the sun was hot on my flesh and its light had honed everything into vivid focus and crystallized the morning into one of the desert's magical, fleeting, suspended moments.

I closed my eyes; reopened them.

Above the dark riverside blocks, now, soared a bright red rock face and in its crevices clung tufts of green grass and a rotund barrel cactus and a single yellow flower. And then all the rocks of ages were plunging down, without moving, into the glass-smooth river, and beyond the river stretched a golden sandbar dimpled to perfection by that lost river; and then the present river was mirroring the whole canyon—dimpled sandbar and squared-off blocks of dark-textured cliff and bright red rock face and cloudless blue sky—and at the center of this double world I sat knife-edge aware in my blue raft, knowing that although nothing had happened, everything had happened.

The moment lost its edge. I glanced at my watch. Monday. So also Monday out in the other world that presumably still existed—where people were returning in droves to their shafts, ready to start grubbing about again, the way we grub about in cities; and most of those harassed, harnessed people didn't even know about this wonderful world pulsating around me.

Something else, too.

I'd moved beyond country I knew, but an echo from the past had crept up on me. Thirty-one years earlier, on my walk from Mexico to Oregon, just such a magical desert moment had, one sunlit Monday morning, triggered in my mind the same elitist, compassionate thought. And this echo, though attenuated, had sounded clear, eloquent.

I rowed on. The last curtain had lifted.

At the start of that third day below the final rapid, my loose intention was to dawdle on down and float past the Grand Wash Cliffs before nightfall. Once out of the Canyon—precisely on my November 14 deadline—I'd either camp or, if enough daylight remained, row across to Pierce Ferry and pick up my outboard motor that would putt-putt us across the dead water of Lake Mead's seventy remaining miles.

I dawdled too well. With barely an hour's light left, the Cliffs were still eight miles away. I began looking for a campsite. But the rare patches of flat land were all mud. I sampled two. Not true quicksand perhaps, but verily not slowsand. Back in the raft after the second sally, cleaning feet and sandals as we floated on down, I knew what I had to do.

I put on warm clothes, began to cook dinner on the dry-box lid: the kitchen must be out of the way and decks clear and my hands free for navigation during the dark interregnum between last twilight and first moonlight. The river was silty now from swirling over sandbars, and although I guessed it would soon flatten out it could at some point tumble instead of swirl over a sandbar. If worst came to worst, though, I'd beach the raft and sleep aboard. By the time twilight faded I had finished dinner, stowed the cooking gear away and semi-battened everything down.

We floated on into the night.

The canyon walls were black now but stars flagged the breach between them. There was no wind, no sound. Everything dark, shadowy, uncertain. No sense of distance. So no sense of movement unless you looked up and watched the cliff tops long enough to detect their slow passage against the stars. We drifted on down into the dark uncertainties. Changed water pressure on the oars alerted me when we swung out of the main current.

Somewhere ahead, subdued duck quackings. On flashlight. Frenzied splashing backed by loud quack-protests. Wings beating air. Then silence flowing slowly back.

Once, the sound of turbulence ahead. I eased on down, holding us in check. But no problem: just a bigger swirl than usual over a long sandbar. At least, I think so.

Soon, twilight a memory. Just a residual brush of palest sunwash still tinging the western sky—but faint eastern hints of moonrise. Before long, moonlight on the western rims. Below, still nothing definite. Yet sometimes, intimations. Clues and glimmers.

The moonlight gained strength and territory. Still no real sense of distance. But everything beautiful. Before long, moonlight flooding deep into the canyon. A huge black point Gibraltaring out of the night.

An endless, floating interlude. At last, river left, a possible falling away of the canyon wall. But still, all around, uncertainty succeeding shadowy uncertainty. Then, much later, much deeper into the night, there could at last be no doubt. We were out in open water. It occurred to me that I'd been spared the spectacle of the river's slow, muddy crucifixion and burial.

I rested on the oars, looked back at the intimations of shapes. Everything huge, blue, magnificent.

"Well," I said, "Goodbye, Canyon." Then, after a pause, I added, "Again."

And as we moved on through the night across the flat black water I found myself wondering if I'd said my last goodbye to that vast, reverberating place.

18

MEAD . . . AND MEN

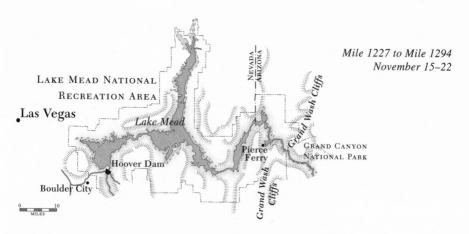

Lake Mead is an older, much duller Lake Powell.

Four noisy, beeline, blinkered days of outboard-motoring. Three night-camps in the leprous Death Zone. Then, in tribute to Buzz Holmstrom, I bumped the soft blue bow of my raft into the huge, gray, unyielding, Berlin Wall bulk of Hoover Dam before backtracking three miles to a rendezvous prearranged with the Bureau of Reclamation. There, we loaded the raft onto a trailer they provided and drove to nearby Boulder City. I checked into a motel, switched on the TV.

In El Salvador, six Jesuit priests had been brutally murdered. In Angola, Western-supported guerrillas were killing thousands of elephants to help finance their war against the communist government. Meanwhile, the Berlin Wall had fallen. And Romanian president Ceausescu had proclaimed that his country would pursue neither democracy nor capitalism but would, as long as he lived, remain communist. In testier moments I find it tempting to dismiss politics as irrelevant, but they seem as necessary to collective humanity as sewers are to cities: important things pass through them.

For three days I motel-hunkered, catching up with things that had to be caught up with. And there in Boulder City I met for the first time, face-to-face, a man who had done much to make my journey possible and even more to lubricate it: Julian Rhinehart, Public Affairs Officer for the Lower Colorado Region, Bureau of Reclamation.

Now, the human condition almost seems to demand that we view the opposition—in whatever enterprise—as ogres, and that we define the opposition as anyone who thinks or acts other than in strict accordance with our own convictions. (The way "strict" is construed separates relatively reasonable people from True Believers.) And a corollary of this very human condition is a tendency, even a compulsion, to assume that we will like people who think as we do and will dislike people who don't. The problem lurks in that word "think." If you take it to mean "*what* they think," then you erect specious barriers. But substitute "*the way* they think," and you unveil new and more accurate perceptions. You'll be less surprised, for example, to discover that Ron Arnold, co-founder of the "Wise Use" movement—that same Ron Arnold who has said, "Our goal is to destroy, to eradicate the environmental movement. . . . We want to be able to exploit the environment for private gain, absolutely"—was once a gung-ho Sierra Club member. But then, True Believers were no doubt reversing their stripes long before Saul of Tarsus, hell-raising down the road to Damascus, made his historic U-turn toward Christian sainthood. Know them, therefore, under their skins. If you do and if, like me, you're a dedicated environmentalist but find many environmentalists acute pains in the arse, you'll understand the apparent paradox. What's more, you'll learn to scrutinize all stripes with skepticism—and a tinge of tolerance.

Most environmentalists have for decades viewed the U.S. Bureau of Reclamation as a monster with a souped-up Ogre Quotient. You could count me in. And when, early in my planning for the Colorado journey, I approached the Bureau about how I might get around their many dams, I did so delicately.

My first contact was Julian Rhinehart. By phone and mail, he did all he could to make things easy for me. That was no doubt his job, but from the start he lavished a concern and understanding that suggested deeper tides. When I called in at Boulder City on my seven-state reconnaissance swing, a year before the journey, Rhinehart was out of town, but he'd already put me in touch with the Bureau man I wanted to see next: Blaine Hamann, Project Manager in charge of Glen Canyon Dam, 300-odd miles upriver.

A few days later, when I drove up to the dam to keep an appointment with Hamann, I harbored no great expectations. Although I like to assume that inside every bureaucrat lurks a human being, just waiting to emerge, I also recognize that most bureaucracies are organized along the lines of a septic tank: the biggest pieces tend to float to the top. I'd just had a meeting with a National Park Service superintendent—a meeting that had not been warm or satisfying or even conclusive—and when I walked into Hamann's office I think I was expecting to meet a lean, cautious, pursed-lip bureaucrat with a rigid engineering mind-cast.

The man who greeted me was a rotund, relaxed guy wearing a gaudy Hawaiian shirt. He exuded joviality. On a wall of his office—there inside the dam that Edward Abbey's fictional character, George Washington Hayduke, had sworn to destroy—hung a bumper sticker–size sign: HAYDUKE LIVES!

Precise details of our talk that day now elude me, but I know everything was good, going on great. When we discussed the logistics of getting my raft around the dam after I'd floated down Lake Powell, Hamann was all business. Brisk, efficient, helpful. He gave me—or, rather, offered—everything I'd hoped for, and then some. We began to talk about the river and my journey. On important matters, we agreed to an astonishing degree. On a few we were content to disagree, without rancor. Long before I left I understood that I was dealing with a warm, aware and broad-minded man with a keen sense of humor and an imperceptible Ogre Quotient.

First impressions held up. Much later, Blaine Hamann told me that when, sometime during the week that Ed Abbey died, a long crack had appeared in the dam—a superficial, cosmetic affair, in no way dangerous—the staff christened it "The Ed Abbey Memorial Crack," or simply "Ed's Crack." And months after I'd finished my journey Blaine wrote, following an extremely friendly, euphemism-free phone talk, "Dear Colin, I was struck dumb by your reference to Glen Canyon Dam as an abomination. . . . I had never seen it through your eyes. I am less comfortable these days. . . ." And he enclosed a poem he'd written about looking down and along Conquistador Aisle. Phrases in his poem suggested the remnants of a modern dam, centuries ahead: *"Whitened convexity. .Vaguely disquieting . . . Harsh lines blurred by the ages . . . Anachronism."* The last stanza read:

> *Slowly.*
> *Drop by unyielding drop,*
> *grain by implacable grain,*
> *Hayduke lives.*

When I mentioned Blaine's letter to John Sexton—whose photography often takes him through the same pastures I graze—and we began to discuss OQ's and the difficulty of separating good guys from bad guys, individually and organizationally, John nodded. "Yes, I know. I mean, who would you rather have to deal with—the head honcho of a national park or of a Bureau of Reclamation dam? . . . And the Park Service is meant to be on our side, preserving."

From the start of my journey, the Bureau's local head honchos—all of whom went out of their way to help—had successively surprised me. The lean and lanky new supervisor of Fontenelle Dam looked like a Montana cowboy, born and bowleg raised; and that's what he had been. The area manager in charge at Flaming Gorge had a less colorful exterior but during our brief contact flashed gleams of insight, sensitivity and tolerance. These qualities, I came to see, were shared by them all.

And not only by head honchos.

Several of the Flaming Gorge Dam maintenance crew had shared the van that took me to the Bureau's guest house at Dutch John. On the way we chatted about stretches of river I'd floated through.

"And how d'you like our lake?" asked one of the group. His voice was amiable, full of quiet, expectant pride.

I pussyfooted. "Well, I'd have to say I prefer the river."

They pressed. I came out into the open—bearing olive branches. "Look. I find myself in some difficulty over this because . . . well, you guys have all been bloody good to me. Gone out of your way to help. And I'm really grateful. But that doesn't mean I agree with everything that's been done here."

They remained altogether cordial—and about as movable as their dam. "But look what the dam's done. It's opened up this whole country. Down below here you'll see hundreds of people fishing—and thirty years ago there'd have been maybe ten."

"Sure. The question is, is that good or bad?"

"But you've got to rule by the majority."

I sidestepped the politics. "But you can't only consider people."

That brought us up short.

I did my best. "Well, the world wasn't made just for man."

"Isn't it?"

We never did really get around that difficulty. At one point I said, "But all the wildlife around here's been destroyed."

"Oh, but cattle will produce more per acre than all the wildlife ever did."

The van pulled up outside the guest house. We went our separate ways.

Later, I kept thinking about that conversation with the maintenance crew. They might live in a different world from me, boundaried by different guidelines, hounded by different imperatives, having to operate within a gigantic bureaucracy that was controlled, perhaps even more than most, by the political winds of the Washington moment, and all this might stick in my craw; but I still liked them. Above all, their generosity impressed me, their genuine liberalism—the way they'd responded when faced with an opposing, more or less incomprehensible view. There'd been none of the shrillness you all too often get from us conservationists.

Trouble was, I understood the shrillness, too.

The dam crew stood secure in what they believed. Man is the hub.

Progress means "development." Things could and would go on like this forever. No matter that I thought they were wrong; they believed. But we conservationists, having seen the light, stand aghast at what such people are doing to the world. We know it can't go on like this without tragedy. And we know there's precious little time left to avert the tragedy. That's why a certain shrillness tends to creep in. One reason, anyway. It was one reason environmentalist literature about the controversy then raging around control of the river below Glen Canyon Dam sometimes shrilled with such drivel-claims as "13-foot swells" and daily flow changes "flushing out and then stranding fish . . . [that] die by the thousands."

All very difficult. On the battle lines, I knew where I stood. But when it came to people, things grayed up. Stripes changed color. And now that I'd come to know a few Bureau people I had to admit, reluctantly, that they'd taken some of the sting out of the dams. Emotionally, I mean. Not intellectually.

On my way downriver I'd remembered from time to time who had set in motion the Bureau's uniform cooperation; and now at last, in Boulder City, I met Julian Rhinehart.

He turned out to be a quiet man with none of Blaine Hamann's flamboyance, but in person he confirmed my conviction that the care and understanding he showed for my needs ran deeper than the demands of his job as Public Affairs Officer. I wasn't surprised to learn that he'd once held a similar position with the Audubon Society. At our first meeting he assured me that in order to move my raft around the first four of the six dams between Hoover and the Mexican border he'd have someone drive down each time from Boulder City with the boat trailer, and that whenever possible he'd do so himself. (Bureau staff at Yuma, near the border, would get me around the last two dams.) Diplomacy is something I'm rarely accused of; but although I did not hide from Julian my feelings about Lakes Powell and Mead, I found myself striving to be as tolerant and civilized as he and all the Bureau people had been.

My last evening in town, Julian and his wife took me out to dinner and afterward we drove back to their home. First, as we'd arranged, Julian and I talked business. He felt it was incumbent on him to spell out for me the Bureau's new and radically changed policy.

It was rather ponderous stuff, but important to the river—and I suppose mildly encouraging. Times had changed, Julian said, and the Bureau felt it must also change. Up to a point it would still be a construction agency— but with the emphasis now on management of existing resources. In the case of the Colorado, the Bureau had to balance the needs of all the twenty-five million people who depended on the river as a resource. These people's needs and the nature of their dependencies were very different, often conflicting, even competing. No matter what the Bureau did, nobody was going to be entirely happy. And the agency now felt that more important than the hows and whys of the past was finding pragmatic answers to the questions of today and tomorrow—given that today's demands were already set in concrete.

We rattled ideas around for a while, more to clarify things than debate such matters as whether today's demands are indeed set in concrete. Then Julian smiled and said, "I know that from your point of view I'm a sort of Devil's Advocate, but . . ."

I nodded. "Sure. But then, in a sense you could say I'm now almost an attorney for the river."

"Yes . . . And not unreasonably so. I guess there's a sense in which you know more than anyone about the river. The whole river, I mean. The river as a whole."

His wife rejoined us and we spent a long evening listening to and discussing music in their notably ogre-free home.

Next day Julian drove me—with the little blue raft bouncing along behind—down to the foot of the huge and impressive but vaguely disquieting whitened convexity that dammed the river, its harsh lines not yet blurred by the ages, its existence not yet widely recognized as an anachronism.

19

MEMORIES AND . . .

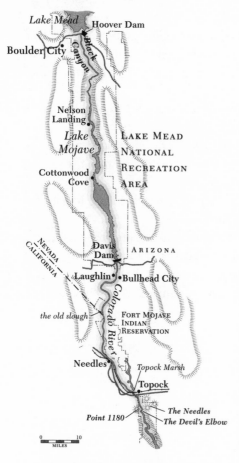

•Las Vegas

Lake Mead Hoover Dam

Boulder City

Black Canyon

Nelson Landing

Lake Mojave

LAKE MEAD

Cottonwood Cove

NATIONAL RECREATION AREA

NEVADA / CALIFORNIA

Davis Dam

ARIZONA

Laughlin• •Bullhead City

Colorado River

the old slough

FORT MOJAVE INDIAN RESERVATION

Needles•

Topock Marsh

Topock

Point 1180

The Needles
The Devil's Elbow

0   10
MILES

Mile 1294 to Mile 1400
November 22–December 4

At seven minutes before three o'clock, Nevada time, November 22, I once more began to float downriver, toward Mexico and perhaps the sea.

It was good to be back. The Boulder City break had been just right: a half-tad too long spent languishing among the fleshpots. And now, liberated from the bondage of luxury, I found my river-eagerness rehoned.

The river that bore us southward between the dark walls of Black Canyon had been reborn yet again—though not freed. Here below Hoover, the water flowed even clearer than it had below Glen Canyon Dam, but less swiftly and ten degrees warmer and therefore less dangerously. There was also something more caged about it. At intervals along the shoreline stood garish mileage markers. Black Canyon's steep and somber rock walls already bore a thin but glaring white Death Zone.

Ahead, I knew, lay the first in a string of reservoirs; and when after a few miles the current began to slacken, it occurred to me that the river had, like any living entity that endures, moved into the autumn of its days.

We were still 500 miles from the sea, yet less than 1000 vertical feet above it. Nine-tenths of our elevation already lost. So a little autumnal resting on laurels seemed justified—for river and journey, both. Also some reassessments.

Passing Grand Wash Cliffs had dissolved the bonds of schedule. No more tension, I hoped, between the need to cover miles and my urge to linger. But I knew that the journey, stripped of its major physical challenges, could lose focus. Besides, I'd been traveling for five months; any day now, the monkey might appear on my shoulder and start whispering, "Go home!"

Other things, too. The night before, Julian had said, "So far, you've been passing almost entirely through public lands. Down below, it'll be different. Mostly private property—and that means development. You'll see a big change from when you walked through, thirty years ago."

Normally, I went on wilderness journeys so that the wildness would replenish me: I tried to avoid the works of man, or close my eyes to them. But I knew that below Hoover, traveling among human artifacts, I ought to keep my eyes resolutely open. At a place called Laughlin, for example, casinos were now rumored to be strung along a stretch of the river's Nevada bank I remembered as more or less virgin. . . .

Up popped the old, recurring question: Would my memories act as a mirror that enriched or a screen that obscured? Or would they lie dormant, as in Grand Canyon? There, they'd been sandbagged by lack of solitude, by ongoing physical challenge and insistent deadline. Across Mead, the outboard's racket had drowned them out. But here below Hoover I'd broken free of all these constraints, and the next 300 miles of river, clear down to Mexico, should resonate with memories. The right bank, anyway.

Almost twenty years earlier I'd backpacked the northern half of this stretch in two separate two-week trips. And the southern half traced, in reverse, the first leg of my summer-long 1958 walk from Mexico to Oregon. That walk had been my maiden experience of both desert and solo backpacking, and its images had burned deep.

I knew the old dictum, of course: "Never go back . . . Things will not be as you remember them." Along the river, physical elements would surely have changed; and I'd look at things differently now. But that wasn't all.

Memory can be a curious cuss. It's tempting to think of it as a simple record—imperfect perhaps, but reasonably immutable and accurate. Rather like a movie print. Events peel off the hidden spool of the future, pass before the lens of the present and undergo momentary illumination by the direct beam of consciousness, then roll firmly onto the spool of the past. There they lie in storage, concealed more and more deeply as your personal spool fills, subject to slow erosion and less and less easily available for recall, but essentially stable.

As you age, though—that is, as you gain experience—you recognize that time edits. Edits two ways. It removes dross. And it tidies up.

This is where you have to be careful.

Memory tends to eliminate almost immediately routine matters of no importance. (Can you remember which sock you put on first this morning?) But it tends to retain events that cause great pain or pleasure. (If you're old enough, you can probably still remember what you were doing when you learned of John Kennedy's assassination.) On the other hand, you may encyst—rather than "repress"—profoundly traumatic events: the images are sure as hell there, vividly recorded, but in self-protection you tend to avoid bringing them up into awareness. Most adults acknowledge this kind of elasticity in our memories.

We find it less easy to accept that memory, our sole subjective source of history, our personal librarian, is also a liar. A consummate liar. But research has confirmed that deceit is memory's standard *modus vivendi*.

A decade ago, psychologist Elizabeth Loftus wrote, *"Our memories are continually being altered, transformed and distorted."* Recently, in a technical paper, she quoted the case of Jack Hamilton, California Angels pitcher, who on August 18, 1967, in Boston's Fenway Park, effectively ended the potentially brilliant career of twenty-three-year-old Tony Conigliaro when he *"crushed the outfielder's face with a first-pitch fastball. More than 20 years later, Hamilton (now over 50) can't forget: 'I've had to live with it; I think about it a lot. . . . Watching baseball on TV, anytime a guy gets hit, I think about it. . . . It was like the sixth inning when it happened. I think the score was 2–1, and he was the eighth hitter in their batting order. With the pitcher up next, I had no reason to throw at him. . . .' [In actual fact,] it was the fourth inning, no score, two out, nobody on. Tony C. was batting sixth. . . . Hamilton remembered that it was a day game because he recalled trying to see Tony C. in the hospital later that afternoon. The truth is different: The game took place at night."*

That such errors commonly occur in what one might expect to be vivid "flashbulb" memories is confirmed by Ulric Neisser, an Emory University psychologist.

The morning after the explosion of the space shuttle *Challenger* in 1986, he asked the students in a freshman psychology course to fill out a questionnaire: Where were they when they heard the news? What were they doing at that time? Who were they with? And who first told them the news? Almost three years later, when the students were seniors, he got them to answer the same questionnaire—with one extra question: How sure were they of their answers?

Dr. Neisser's technical paper on the experiment reports that, of forty-four students who completed both questionnaires, *"none of the enduring memories was entirely correct . . . Only three subjects (7%) [remembered the details correctly but] with minor discrepancies. . . . Eleven subjects (25%) were wrong about everything. . . ."* What's more, the students who got everything wrong were just as likely as the others to be confident of the accuracy of their recall. And no amount of prodding would convince any of them that the "phantom" memories were false—even after they'd seen the original questionnaires, in their own handwriting.

In other words, our brains not only lie: they often emit smoke screens.

As I floated downriver below Hoover Dam I didn't know if there were yet any established scientific verities about the way memory can routinely—not because of damage or disease—delete whole layers of events and then lie about the deletion. But I did know that scientific research, for all its weight, carries nothing like the conviction engraved by vivid personal experience. And the only human memory to which I have wide and ongoing access had recently provided me with some relevant and compelling instruction.

At a nightcamp back in canyon country I was listening to the pocket tape recorder on which I sometimes took notes—listening in order to check the sound quality of what I'd just recorded—when the background to my voice changed abruptly and the voice was talking about something quite different. Or rather, it *wasn't* different. The tape was a used one, carrying no-longer-needed material, and after a moment of surprise it dawned on me that the spool had run past the end of my recent notes and was now playing an interview a magazine editor had done with me in my home several years before. What my voice from the past said—apparently in answer to a question about dreams for the future—was: *"I want to do the whole length of the Colorado. . . . I'm not particularly interested in it at this moment . . . but someday I may want to . . . I wouldn't necessarily do it walking. I might, as a change, want to do it by boat, or a combination of them. . . . At the moment it isn't strong enough, but I might do it. . . . I think you should have a store of these [kinds of projects]. Life should be an unfinished business."*

There in my canyon nightcamp, I had switched off the tape recorder and leaned back, astonished.

Five months earlier, as I lay in my tent that stormy first day at the source, spooning soup from a cup and running over in my mind the origins and evolution of the journey, I'd recognized that the germ of the idea had come close to surfacing a dozen years before when I wrote, seriocomically, of wanting "to complete a piecemeal walk along the entire Colorado River." There in the tent—and before that, while planning—I'd thought of this seed as springing into full, rounded, unexpected life as I stood in my shower one spring morning, only three years earlier. But this tape, made long before I took that shower and surfacing by accident during the actual journey, provided irrefutable contrary evidence.

(That evidence now carries a remarkable footnote:

Two years after completing the journey I unearthed some forgotten notes in my own handwriting—not just isolated scribbles but ten now-faded and mildly tattered sheets—that bore witness to preliminary research I did in the mid-1960s for a passage of the Colorado, mostly by boat, from source to sea. These notes record not only general ruminations on the project but distances involved, projected elapsed times for various stages of the journey, even possible alternate types of boat. And although I'd later felt sure my 1987 decision was made before I heard the news that no one seemed to have traversed the whole river, one notation showed I learned it back then.

All this astounded me. It still does. Rereading the 1960s notes did trigger a vague, faint-tinkling memory of that early emergence of the river idea; but the fact remains that twenty years later, when it resurfaced in my mind, I'd perceived the new manifestation as virgin. Somewhere down the years, the old manifestation had slipped between the boards, into oblivion. Alternatively, you could say that the germ had lain there gestating far longer than I'd realized.

Anyway, I now know, in spades, that memory is quicksilver stuff.)

Below Hoover, as I floated on down the reborn but slowing river and peered ahead, pondering the fickleness of memory, I remained unsure whether the 300 miles to the Mexican border would turn out to be a novel and resonant leg of my long journey or would peter away into bland anticlimax.

I needn't have worried.

The first half of that 300-mile leg generated only one major echo from the past. And it came near the end. But after a quiet start, the present throbbed.

Not far below Hoover the current began to taper away. We moved on down together—river, raft and rider—out into the dead headwaters of the first reservoir. And for a week—down all 60 miles of Lake Mohave, to Davis Dam and beyond—my days were ruled by the wind.

It began gently. A mere breeze. But this breeze blew from the south, directly uplake—and without the outboard motor I'd have been helpless. (I planned to use the motor only when forced to; but I'd keep it aboard all the way to the Gulf, for the string of reservoirs and the final ocean lap.) By late on the third afternoon the breeze had built to a wind and the wind had boomed to a steady fury. I pulled in at Cottonwood Cove marina to phone Julian Rhinehart and tell him the wind meant I'd be a day late reaching Davis Dam. I'd visited the marina briefly on the backpack trip, but my mind was now so focused on the present that I failed to look or listen for the past. Just beyond Cottonwood I camped, early, in a sheltered cove. After dark, the lights of Las Vegas built a dome in the northern sky.

Next morning my little weather radio, which back in canyon country had been mostly mute, issued a warning for Lake Mohave boaters: "Stay in port. Or if you must go out, exercise great care. Gusts of fifty miles an hour expected." Out on the lake, racing whitecaps ratified this forecast.

Around noon the wind began to back: the low-pressure system's center had passed through. By two o'clock the radio had for some reason fallen silent again, but the wind had eased a little and now blew almost directly from the west. It should, I figured, leave a band of comparatively calm water along the lee shore. A quick rock-ridge reconnaissance. Yes.

A few minutes after two o'clock we eased out of shelter into open water.

The astonishing thing, now, was not the water. Under the lee shore, indeed few whitecaps; but off to the west, a brown, diaphanous screen was advancing across the desert, fast. As I watched, the screen enveloped first distant mountains, then foothills, then rolling plain. A line of peaks to the north faded, vanished. Before long the whole landscape hung fuzzy, indeterminate, tentative. A sort of natural-world virtual unreality. Low winter sunlight suffused the pale brown haze with a strange and vaguely disturbing warmth—and triggered an unexpected echo.

Once before I'd seen just such a desert sandstorm. During the Mexico-to-Oregon walk, while I paused for a day at the mouth of Death Valley, ready to start through it next morning, a west wind had sprung up, intensified, built to gale force. By late afternoon a great wedge of suspended sand, funneling through a gap in the mountains, thirty miles away, had spread out in a dense brown haze across the huge trough that was the Valley. Soon, it enveloped me, dimmed the sun. The storm threatened to disrupt my fine-tuned plans for the physical challenge ahead, and I watched the haze intently. Perhaps that was why I remembered the way sunlight had suffused its pale brownness with a strange and vaguely disturbing warmth—and why, putt-putting south along the lee shore now, I heard the echo across time and space with surprising clarity. After all, that storm had happened thirty-one years earlier, in a place far removed from . . . All at once I realized that Death Valley lay due west. And perhaps a hundred miles away. Not far at all, as the dust storm scuds.

All afternoon, as we motored south, haze and wind persisted. Around four o'clock, prematurely, the light began to fade. I swung right, into the setting sun's almost level rays, began to look for a sheltered campsite. The sunlight reflected from the particles of suspended sand and I found myself edging along the shoreline, peering at indistinct shapes through a brown, gauzy, barely penetrable screen. It was a frustrating, eerie business. But at last I found a protected cove, camped.

The night laundered my world. Beneath a pristine morning sky, in champagne air, the laundryman north wind drove streaks of foam dancing before him down the bathtub lake. At 8:20 I ventured out semi-intrepidly into his realm.

At first I ran before the wind. Close to shore, the whitecaps were less than mountainous. And I could sail true with them. But my scheduled rendezvous next morning with Julian Rhinehart lay on the far side of the lake: at some point I'd have to cross open water, exposed to the wind's full force.

An hour passed. Then I swung left, struck out for the far shore. Now the whitecapped waves reared taller, steeper, more daunting. We angled across them, pitching and yawing. Sometimes, when we nosed down into a trough, the motor lifted clear of the water and I'd hear and feel the prop race dangerously fast. Otherwise it was rather like running, slightly off-true, an endless succession of big waves at the foot of a rapid. And yet not like that.

Not like that, for one thing, because of the diametric difference between these wind-generated waves—their water essentially stationary while the forms moved—and river-rapid waves—with their water racing through while the forms stayed essentially stationary. At the time, though, I don't think I dabbled with theory. Practics ruled. My mind had all it could cope with in holding the raft at a safe angle to the waves yet at the same time on a course that would eventually take us, with luck, into friendlier water behind a promontory on the far shore. And at last we did ease into its partial lee. Time then, to feel pleased at my foresight in lashing the big blue tarp around the gear stowed in the bow; it had shed all the showers of spray that kept slashing inboard. And time to ruminate, warmly, about the decision I'd made before leaving camp to wear waterproof and windproof jacket and pants over my normal blue pile jacket and polypro pants; otherwise I'd have faced the prospect of struggling to put them on out there in heaving, hideous mid-lake.

Before long I pulled into a sheltered cove; lunched; dozed. Then I read for a while, hoping the wind might drop, telling myself that if there'd been a war on I'd have motored on down.

By two o'clock, still no rumor of war; but the water maybe a little less wind-streaked, the waves a shade less threatening. Sometimes, anyway. Worth a try.

Once I'd launched, conditions at least seemed no worse. An hour later, they were. Either the wind had risen or it had a longer reach of open water to work on. Or both. But we were now within striking distance of the protected landing that was my rendezvous with Julian; I plowed ahead.

All day, I realized, I'd seen nobody else on the lake. Then, just before the cove that was the rendezvous, I glimpsed—intermittently, because they kept vanishing in troughs between the whitecaps—two wind-surfers scudding at implausible speeds across the horizon and then skimbling back again, the masts of their rarely visible boards canted over at unthinkable angles. Around 3:30 I pulled into the cove in which nestled our rendezvous marina.

Next morning the wind raged unabated. Still no reports of any war, and I discarded my plan to motor the mile or so down to Davis Dam and back—the way I normally did at dams so that at the end of the journey I'd be able to feel I'd indeed traveled every travelable inch of river. Instead, I walked down almost to the dam, returned to the raft, found a relatively unwindswept place nearby and sat waiting for Julian Rhinehart. Sat looking out across the gray, wave-corrugated lake to its far shore—and beyond.

On my two backpack trips northward along that shore, rough terrain had often forced me to travel some distance inland; but during the last few southering days, a few places should have echoed. Mostly, they had not. When I landed at the mouth of a side canyon down which I'd come for water, twenty years earlier, while living for a week in an old-timer's cave, nothing looked familiar. Cruising downlake, hugging the western shoreline and looking for the sheltered marina called Nelson Landing, at which I'd ended one backpack trip, I somehow managed to miss the inlet. The passing mountains had raised no echoes, either. Nor had a pair of rounded, nipple-tipped brown hills that the map, following a traditional western euphemism, called "Squaw Peaks." Odd. But the present had been more than enough.

That afternoon, below Davis Dam, when I rowed on down a sluggish and niggardly river, the north wind still blew.

For a while the dam acted as a baffle. So did tall, leveelike banks. But the shrunken, sunken river was gray, wind-streaked, sad. Even without the garbage, it would have had an exploited look.

I floated slowly down, eyes on the right bank, unsure what memory should be resurrecting.

Twenty-one years earlier, before my two-week backpack trip upriver from the town of Needles, I'd known that the country I'd be traversing would pose no great challenge, and in order to inject an element of uncertainty, even mystery, I'd eschewed the USGS topo maps I normally use in unknown country and had taken only a four-by-nine-inch section cut from a large-scale, backpackingly uninformative road map. I no longer had that scrap of paper. But I remembered standing back, perhaps half a mile inland, and looking down at Davis Dam; and I had no recollection of other significant man-made structures. The topo map I now carried was dated 1950 and showed, not far below the dam, a small cluster of buildings strung along the river, labeled "Mike's Camp." Probably a fishing camp. A place that would blend with the landscape. That might even be invisible if you stood half a mile inland.

But that had been two decades ago. And I'd heard rumors.

I floated on down the sad, gray, wind-streaked, victimized river.

They were there, right enough. First, just one. A huge slab, stark and bleak in the thin afternoon sunlight. Soon I could see the rest: a strip of them strung along the right bank, one after the other, each determinedly different, each fundamentally identical. All stark, gaunt, repulsive. But magnets. The bright, satanic mills of Vegas had metastasized.

Now, I can't list gambling as one of my vices. Not, I mean, gambling for money. No claim to virtue implied: I just find I'm rarely interested. But when I'd floated down level with Laughlin's first casino, I pulled in to the floating dock at its foot, moored the raft securely in as wind-sheltered a place as I could find and walked up a steeply sloping wooden ramp.

At its head, barring the way to the casino, stood a small stall: tourist brochures and a shelf of paperback books. Absent, I think: *The Poverty of Affluence.*

In the stall sat a woman, reading.

"Is it OK to leave my raft down there?"

The woman put down her book, smiled. She had an air of confidence, an assurance of self-worth, that transcended her current niche. "Sure it is. With the river this low, nobody's using the dock. Usually we have ferries coming over all the time from the Arizona side, but they're all beached now. Well, all except one. And the dam says there'll be no more than one unit—that's forty-seven hundred cubic feet per second—coming down for the next few days. But then, the dam often lies to you."

"And my raft'll be safe?"

"Sure. We don't get any trouble." The woman glinted. "Except maybe from river rats." But barely a breath of malice.

She'd been working at the casino for almost a year. "Interesting place, in its way. Don Laughlin started this one around twenty years ago. Bought out a little fishing camp. And now there's nine casinos along this strip—not counting the one going up next door. That's number ten. And twenty-five more planned in the next five years. Looks like next week we'll get approval for a new sewage system."

Over on the Arizona bank, she said, Bullhead City didn't exist until work on the dam began. Late thirties, early forties. For years it stayed small and quiet. Then Laughlin sprouted—and Bullhead City became the bedroom community for casino employees and tourists, both. Incorporated 1984. Already over twenty thousand. And growth projections prodigious. Yes, an interesting place, in its way.

I walked up another ramp, clutching my hat against grabbing wind gusts, opened a small door, stepped into the casino world.

Acre on acre of gleaming machines. Clusters of heavy, glistering glass. Huge, echoing mirrors. Green tables creating miniature urban parks. A pretentious, gorbacious, self-indulgent, would-be-comforting middle-class womb. Smug yet edgy.

Flitting cocktail waitresses in tight black outfits that sometimes concealed as much as two-thirds of each buttock. Milling customers in all shapes and sexes and sizes. Predominantly Anglos: no minorities beyond one possible Asian. Mostly oldies, but a smattering of youngies. Driven-looking people, smoking. Gaunt people with the down-turned mouths of politicians and the flat, unleavened faces of those who live bereft of horizons beyond the dollar. A sub-smattering of the sort of people the desert tends to support: lost-looking losers, trashed by life, wasted by alcohol. The only viable faces: the croupiers'.

I browsed the main paddock, strayed beyond. Above a buffet, a sign echoing Vegas's one genuine attraction: "Breakfast, 69 cents, 24 hours every day." At 3:30 P.M., a long, long waiting line. I strolled down a mock-paneled corridor. Inmates exhibited the same Promethean tolerance as at Vegas airport: no matter how you were dressed, no one gave you a second glance. Or perhaps, in this case, it was just that they didn't want to meet your eye. I walked on, filled with a glowing, Pharisaical sense of superiority.

Coming back down the mirror-rich corridor—I think it was at a corner between two doors labeled in identical overwrought script, "*Paradise Bingo Room*" and "*Linen Chute*"—an approaching figure caught my eye.

I stopped. He stopped. The big battered hat was his most respectable clothing item. Below it came a dirty blue pile jacket, half-unzipped, with a
green shirt showing through; then rough red pants, patched at one knee,
tucked into thick gray socks. Scuffed hiking boots. The man himself
largely sequestered behind dark glasses. Longish hair, unkempt. White
beard.

I raised my right hand. The superannuated river rat raised his left hand.
I walked on past the mirror. Yes, an effective disguise for a Pharisee. In
that context he'd likely pass for the sort of man who loved to snarl out
into the wilderness with nothing but a jock strap, a blunt knife and one
condom.

On the way out I paused at an alcove with a big sign proclaiming a game
called "Megabucks": you had to come up with four triple sevens or something, and the current jackpot total flashed overhead in lights. No human in
the immediate vicinity: you apparently harvested your triple sevens or
whatever someplace else in the acreage, and the current running total of
your potential winnings was flashed at this remote advertising snare. It
rose a dollar about every twenty seconds. When I paused it was a million
and change, and the odds seemed sure to be so long that just for a moment
I was tempted to dabble. But the madness passed. After all, what would I
do with a million and change? Sure, it would be convenient. I could invest
in some new tennis balls and maybe stop buying shampoo. But my hand
stayed safely clear of my wallet, and my mind had barely begun to weigh
the delights of realpoo when I came to my side door and opened it and
stepped out into the wind.

Down on the dock I relaxed my vigilance just long enough for a sudden
gust to whip the hat off my head. The hat bowled away along the wooden
planking. Halfheartedly, I made as if to run after it; but I was no match, I
knew, for that wind. And then, just as the hat helter-skeltered merrily toward the end of the dock, toward open water, its chin strap caught in the
last of a line of mooring stanchions—the one my raft was moored to. The
hat hung there, waiting to be picked up. I walked forward, picked it up,
hooked the chin strap firmly sub-chin, untied the raft, rowed out into the
river. If you go to a casino, of course, it pays to be born lucky. Otherwise
you're likely to lose the shirt off your back. Or whatever.

I did lose one thing, though, in Laughlin.

Below the casino I drifted on down the gray, wind-streaked, still beleaguered river. Left, above and beyond its encapsulating, raw-rubble levee,
neon motel signs and urgent motor sounds signified Bullhead City. Right,
the Laughlin strip. One blockbuster high-rise after another. The Colorado
Belle, mocked up as a paddle-wheel steamer. A mock–Middle Eastern ed-

ifice. A mock something-or-other else, unclassified. Then an embryo plain-Hilton slab, still being delivered into existence by a pair of storklike cranes. But all, behind their stripes, the same.

The flatland ended and the casinos stopped and desert rock began. I rowed around the first bend, camped inconspicuously in a protected place where the rock swung back, on the edge of what seemed to be a golf course in the making. And it was then, off-loading gear, that I discovered I'd lost one of two cream-colored plastic buckets that served many purposes. The bucket had been there, I knew, when I left the dam—tucked in its usual place behind my dry-box seat. Somewhere in Laughlin, it seemed, the wind had swiped it.

After dark the wind let up enough for me to hear—over on the Arizona bank, beyond the Bullhead City levee, in among the motel signs—a couple of gunshot blasts and a police siren and the screech of tires.*

A sad and dreary day of rowing down the windswept river. Down a river that on my topo map sang with islands and lagoons and seductive curlicues but in present truth remained a beleaguered waterway encapsulated by almost endless levees. By blank, raw, rock-rubble, straight-line levees. A river no more. A mere canal, rising and falling at the whim of remote men.

Then the start of another day. A day I felt dismally sure would turn out to offer nothing but a reprise of the encapsulated, emasculated river. As I pulled away from camp that morning, only one auspicious element: the wind had waned.

Thirteen minutes later I happened to glance shoreward—and saw at the foot of the right-bank levee, high and dry on the edge of a little bay that had formed in one of the few places the shoreline was flat enough for the low night-tide to expose a narrow band of mud, a cream-colored object. The moment I saw it, I was almost sure. The closer I rowed, the surer. Soon I was floating downriver again with the cream-colored bucket tucked in once more behind my dry-box seat, and with my spirits—which I'd hardly recognized as being depressed—now uplifted by the mundane incident; boosted sky high in a way that was all the sweeter for being so unexpected, so unreasonable, so absurd.

---

* Remember, I reached Laughlin in late November, by raft, toting memories—and therefore with an attitude. Much later, back home, a friend would say to me: "Laughlin? Sure I know it. You drive forever across godforsaken wilderness with the mercury at a hundred and twenty and no shade, and suddenly there are these modern high-rises standing out in the middle of nowhere, and you go inside and it's amazing—all air-conditioned and *civilized!*"

It was therefore through freshly rose-tinted glasses that I began looking ahead along the right bank, peering back twenty-one years.

Near the start of my backpack trip north from Needles, I'd been walking along the top of a levee when it came to an abrupt end. Just dropped away. I found myself looking down into a hollow that reached back four or five hundred yards, blue-laked, green-bordered. In the lake stood five white herons, tall and elegant and statue-still. Below me, in the channel that formed the mouth of the slough, fish tumbled, backs breaking the water's calm surface. Beyond, in green trees, birds bustled and chattered. The only sign of man's hand was a line of stepping-stones across the narrowest part of the channel—and even they were incomplete, reassuringly inefficient. Nowhere a straight line. Everything soft and curving, natural.

I walked down to the water's edge, found a shady place under a bush, and rested for at least two hours in that blue-green slough-world lying countersunk in the harsh, flat, gray desert. My star visitors: two coyotes, courting. But birds also came and went. The dorsal fins of carp continued to break the water's surface. And always there was the silence—heightened by the brush of water past stepping-stones. The silence and the blueness and the greenness and the harmony and rightness.

Now, as I floated southward, peering ahead and back, the slough hung green and gentle in my memory. But did it still exist? And could I find it, or its site, somewhere along the featureless levee that was now the right bank?

North of the slough—where the California-Nevada boundary met the river, and an Indian reservation began—there'd been no levee. When I walked on along the natural riverbank, integrated patterns of humps and hollows and gullies had injected meanings. Flowers softened the desert; and shrubs, even trees. But that had been then.

The rough sportsmans' map that was now my only guide for this reach of river promised little help in pinpointing the place. There were certain signs I remembered, though. Or thought I remembered.

I rowed on southward. Mile after mile, only bleak, ungiving levee. But after two hours, a candidate.

The raw-rubble levee gave way—though less distinctly than I'd expected—to one that time had clothed with a scattering of greenery. And—just the way I'd seemed to remember—the river deflected. Not a bend exactly; but a definite though minor kink.

I pulled ashore. The suggestion of a little bay. No more than a couple of small indentations, really; but the first I remembered since finding my bucket.

I tied the raft to one of several sawn-off logs lying half-buried in the sand and walked up a long, sloping bank toward the levee. The bank seemed different from any I'd been floating past, and hope flickered. Perhaps the changes indeed signaled "mouth of old slough."

I stepped up onto the crest of the levee.

An expanse of pale brown sand. Scattered brown arrowweed bushes, dead or dying. No actual bulldozer marks; but the unnatural, unrelieved flatness that bulldozing begets.

For a long moment I stood looking. At last I walked across the sand toward another levee, thirty paces away, that cut inland at an unfamiliar angle: now I was ashore, might as well find out what kind of desert lay beyond it. I reached the foot of the inner levee, began to climb. Thick bushes made for rough going.

Then I was out on the crest—and what met my astonished eye was not desert of any kind but green, well-tended farmland. Flat, rich, irrigated land, plowed clear across the floodplain to brown desert foothills.

Out in this huge cultivated expanse, a quarter of a mile away, a pickup was moving toward me along a raised dirt road. It reached the edge of the plowed land, off to my left; turned toward me along a track that paralleled an irrigation ditch at the foot of the levee. I waited. The pickup came level. I waved. The driver stopped, got out, walked toward me. He was shortish, square. No longer young but still active, strong.

"Say, can you tell me how far it is down to Needles?"

"Oh, 'bout nine miles." He had a warm smile.

"Hm, that's about right. There used to be a slough, somewhere around here."

"Sure did. It's just up there, on the high ground." He pointed over the levee on which I stood. "But it's all dry now. Dried out when they let the river drop. "

"Or maybe when they put the new levee in, north along the river?"

"Could be."

I took a few steps down and forward, to the edge of the concrete-lined irrigation ditch. The man moved forward too, so that we stood just a few feet apart. The ditch was narrow, with only a little water moving slowly through it, and the man and I talked across it without raising our voices, as if there were nothing between us.

His name was Milos Russell. He'd leased the land from the Indians, fourteen years earlier. Yes, it was all brush when he came. Now, he had almost 4000 acres under the plow. Alfalfa, cotton and wheat. Sudan grass, too.

"D'you get two crops of wheat?"

No, he rotated the wheat and the Sudan grass. But he got eight cuttings of alfalfa a year.

"Sure looks good."

"Yeah, thank you. But it's been a financial disaster. Farm prices went all to hell."

Russell, now seventy-four, seemed interested to hear I'd once farmed in Africa. "Had a friend who was a deciduous fruit expert who went out to Rhodesia before it was Zimbabwe. Not sure just what part, but he said it was good farming country."

As we stood there in the warm winter sunlight, our conversation flowed on over other fields. My long walks, especially the one up California. Briefly, World War II. I doubt if either of us was very aware, at the time, that as we leafed idly and pleasingly through our collective memories we were in a sense reshuffling the cards in two decks that together covered almost a century and a half of living. In the end, our reshuffling brought us back to the current tops of the decks.

"You say you lease your land from the Indians. Would they be the Fort Mohave Indians?"

"That's right. They've got a village in Needles now, and another over on the Arizona side. Yes, I guess you could say they've sort of given up on the reservation, for themselves."

"Yesterday I went for a walk, back upriver, and found a big slice of floodplain staked out, with lines cleared on some kind of a grid. The stakes had MOVADA printed on them. Was that in the reservation?"

"Sure was. MOVADA's a combination of Mohave and Nevada. They only staked that out a few months ago. Thinking of putting in God knows how many more casinos, clear down to the California line. I dunno . . . Laughlin's bad enough. There's talk about 'em dumping treated sewage into the river. Well, maybe it'll work. But if something goes wrong . . ."

"Am I right in saying that the old slough was inside the reservation?"

"Yeah. Just on the edge."

"And maybe that's why it hadn't been spoiled, last time I was here?"

"Very likely. Back then, they weren't into development."

Finally, I nodded back behind me, over the levee, and asked exactly where the dried-out slough lay. Russell explained. Then we reached out across the shallow stream of water flowing slowly down the little irrigation ditch. It was a long reach, and as we shook hands our palms met rather awkwardly. We both smiled. Then Russell turned and walked back to his pickup in the warm winter sunlight and drove away down the dirt road, and I turned and walked back up over the levee.

The remains of the slough were there, right enough. Not readily recognizable, but clear enough after I'd walked a few yards up this inner levee that hadn't existed when the slough lived. Now I could see a considerable expanse of tules. For the first time in days the wind had died, and not even the tops of the dry brown tules moved. Their whole counter-sunk world lay becalmed. Lay desiccated, dead, finished. A couple of bright green trees, tapping deep-down moisture, accented the desolation.

I didn't stay long, there on the levee. Didn't even define the limits of the lifeless slough. But as I walked back to the raft I saw in soft sand some tracks that could have been a dog's but which I chose to believe were a coyote's; perhaps even those of a descendant of my courting pair from back when the slough was still alive. At the river, it occurred to me that this was the first California soil I'd set foot on since the journey began.

Lunch, tucked in among some bushes. Then I dozed—and woke to see a pair of Canada geese, the first in several days, flying past, low. Just for a moment they seemed to be responding to old memories and turning in toward the slough; then they banked away, flew downriver, out of sight. Almost at once, two military helicopters roared over, nearly as low as the geese had flown. They clackered on upriver, nose to tail, unswerving; vanished from sight; from sound.

I untied the raft from the sawn-off log half-buried in its sands of time. There were other logs, too. Perhaps they were the bones of the trees that had once lived green and healthy on the natural bank, beyond the stepping-stones. I cast off, pulled away, looked back. One comforting thought: the slough might be dead, but the shell of the place was still there, waiting; waiting for the time when the interfering animal had broken away like a great boulder from the side of a mountain, making a great noise, before it rolled away into the desert leaving only a little trail in the dust before coming to a stop, and Coyote could sleep on it at night—until the river washed it away and reclaimed the earth.

I rowed slowly southward. Still no wind, and I looked back across the river's mirror surface at the place the slough had been. The slough that had hung in my memory, green and almost luminous.

A few more pulls on the oars. Another glance back. No denying the sense of loss . . . And then, without warning, I was reliving my first and therefore most traumatic loss of such a kind.

It happened in England, mid–World War II. Probably in '42. So I'd have been twenty. I must have been temporarily detached from my unit, on a course or something similar that left me with a free afternoon not far from the school I'd attended between the ages of eight and twelve. It had been a day school, but I was one of half a dozen boarders who lived in the headmaster's house, across the road from the school. The house was called "Brandwood," and that wartime afternoon, as I walked down a vaguely familiar road, it occurred to me that the name fitted, in a thin suburban way, the memory I had of a comfortable old three-story brick house—probably of no great architectural merit but with a certain charm—set in a rambling garden, all shrubs and trees. I'd never been back and had rarely thought of the place, but as I walked toward the bend in the road that I halfway knew would bring Brandwood into view, to my surprise I felt rising within me a warm and embracing sense of affection for the place. Or perhaps I just mean nostalgia.

I came around the bend.

Brandwood had gone. Been erased. Canceled. So had its garden. In their place towered a bleak, blank, impersonal, multistory apartment building. I glanced across the road. The school looked unchanged. But in memory, I realized, the headmaster's house had been the thing. Had down the years been my eternal verity of that place, that period.

After a while I went on down the road, past the impersonal, usurping apartment building. But the still stunned young man who walked away from it, on the school side of the road, was no longer quite the same person as the one who had come around the bend in the road. He had, I understood later, been shocked into acknowledging, or at least beginning to acknowledge, the verity of impermanence.

Half an hour later I called at the house of a former school friend of those Brandwood days. His parents looked much as I remembered them—except that they seemed stunned by an overwhelming sense of loss. Ken, their only son, a fighter pilot, had a few weeks earlier been killed on a training flight.

A new north wind gusted down the river, shattering its mirror. I let the wind sweep me on southward, back into the present.

Next day, a glitch.

I'd camped a couple of miles below the slough, river left, on a beach below a stark, raw-rubble levee. Next morning the river had dropped drastically, and when launching time came I had to ease the raft down a long, gently sloping stretch of rubble-strewn sand. I moved it the way I'd often done when low water left it stranded: pulling on safety rope or D-rings, first at one end, then the other—bow, then stern—so that the raft swiveled around its center and each pirouette left it a little closer to the river. By now I'd become so confident the raft could stand up to rough treatment that I did no more than clear away some of the beach's bigger rocks. We were a

Repairing the journey's only raft puncture.
Note low water, confining levees.

couple of feet shy of water when there was a sharp crack; almost an explosion. Then a long exhaling sound: a sad, drawn-out sigh. Even before one side of the raft began to sag, I knew what had happened. I knelt, examined the beach. Some of the scattered pieces of levee rubble had knife-like edges (and later, on other beaches, I found shards of broken glass).

While I was preparing the two punctures for patching, a northeast wind sprang up. A wind that came angling in over the freshly plowed fields I'd seen that morning from the levee's crest. A wind that was soon gusting savagely over the levee and dropping dust from the fields in its lee—sprinkling this dust, liberally, onto adhesive that had to be left for a spell to get tacky. And this turned out to be only the beginning. It was that sort of day. Details don't matter, but one way and another, by the time I had the punctures as satisfactorily finished as conditions permitted, sunset was approaching. I waited out the mandatory twenty-four-hour curing. Then—glitch-time over at last—we floated on southward.

Still the engineers' levees, protecting farmland, converting river into canal. At intervals, irrigation pumps vampiring the waterway's lifeblood to feed the farmland. Then culverts dribbling salinized dregs back into the canal. Occasional sentinel herons; otherwise, a dearth of wildlife.

We floated on toward the town of Needles.

Because Needles marked the point at which I had on my summer-long walk up California angled away from the river, I'd now begin retracing, in reverse, the first two hundred miles of my 1958 land route. Well, not really "retracing." That implied duplication, continuity. I'd be listening for echoes, though. And already my mind's eager eye kept leapfrogging twenty miles ahead into the next stretch of wild country, to a dramatic river bend. This bend—the Devil's Elbow—lay deep in a jumble of sharp-pointed, red-rock pinnacles, The Needles, that gave their name to the town.

We floated on, past the town. At least, the town must have been there, off to the right, though I didn't register its presence until I saw southern suburban development. But confirmation, then, from junk now littering a lifeless gravel riverbed: beer cans, plastic bags, oil cans, road markers, tires, more tires—all painfully visible in the clear, shallow water. I found myself recalling a verity from *Sensitive Chaos: "a river that has been artificially straightened out . . . indicates the inner landscape in the souls of men who no longer know how to move with the rhythms of living nature."*

Below Needles, people had kept warning me, powerboats swarmed. Yet I still had the river to myself. Since leaving Laughlin, as far as I could remember, I'd seen no other vessel of any kind. And before long the world began to heal.

Levees still corseted the river. But behind the left-bank barrier, now, a wildlife refuge. Once, a gap in the gaunt California bank revealed rolling desert slopes, unspoiled except for a railroad line that ran close to the river.

Memory stirred.

In 1958, on my last leg beside the Colorado, I'd come singing into Needles along the Atchison, Topeka and Santa Fe. Once, a train had thundered past and I'd waved and the engineer had waved back.

Now, floating down, I heard a train rumble, then hoot. In the dry box at my feet were the topo maps I'd used in 1958—all marked, clear down to Mexico, with routes and camps and interest points—and after checking the first of them I pulled ashore, walked inland and stood on the railroad track.

No doubt about locus. But I'd been hoping to recapture the feel of a different place and time.

Then another train approached, thundered past. Just before its huge, inhuman wall of wind hit me, I waved. I couldn't see whether the engineer waved back. In fact, I don't know whether there *was* an engineer. This modern machine was huge and enarmored, and if humans existed aboard they were too high above me and too cut off from the rhythms of the living world for us to establish contact.

I turned, began walking back toward the river—and found myself reading chronicles of recent natural rhythms.

Inscribed on a smooth, gently humped beach, etched deep and clear, illuminated by slanting sunlight, a sandscript report on conflicting fishery
rights that two very large birds, probably herons, apparently claimed in
one small oxbow pond. Other bulletins, too. A member of the subspecies
Homo insapiens dunebuggiensis, probably a juvenile, had driven onto the
beach and cavorted briefly and without apparent purpose, crisscrossing the
heron tracks. Later, a beaver had dragged a sizable branch of some kind
from back near the oxbow pond down to the river, pushing its tail at an angle against the sand, repeatedly and hard, for leverage. The unbroken
brush mark left by the branch had crossed the dune-buggy tracks twice, as
if to begin the process of wiping them away; of cleansing the beach.

Late next day, my fourth below the old slough, I saw the first of the several big steel structures—bridges and pipelines, clustered close together—
that span the river at Topock. I knew that once I'd passed them and moved
into wild terrain, I would at last feel I'd truly begun the second, 1958-
echoing half of the three-hundred-mile stretch between Hoover and Mex-

On a sandy beach, south of Needles "a beaver had dragged a
sizable branch of some kind from back near the oxbow pond
down to the river, pushing its tail at an angle against the sand,
repeatedly and hard, for leverage. The unbroken brush mark left
by the branch had crossed the dune-buggy tracks twice, as if to
begin the process of wiping them away; of cleansing the beach."

ico. Already I could see, beyond the stark steel structures, a cluster of red, needlelike pinnacles. Deep in the sinuous gorge the river had cut through them lay the Devil's Elbow. I began to row with new energy.

Then, diversion.

The levee guarding the Arizona bank ended. And when I looked up behind it I saw, beyond a scrawny marina and restaurant, a reed-fringed slough. I hesitated only briefly.

At first, beyond the marina, nothing but open, unspoiled slough. I rowed slowly forward. The slough narrowed. Then it abruptly ended—or, more accurately, began—at the mouth of a small creek. The creek—less than twenty feet wide and far too shallow to accept even my little raft—snaked and swirled toward me between flat, reed-fringed mudbanks. Beyond the reed beds, only a couple of distant desert mountains, low and hazy. Yet the place had magic.

Late-afternoon sunlight italicized the water's swirls and ripples. Threw into startling relief each curve and curlicue of the moist mudbanks. Their dazzling track-script, too—raccoons, coyotes, mice and other minor mammals, small birds, large birds . . .

But what I'm saying is, somehow, beside the point. Perhaps the key to the scene's magic lay in the nature of the light, not its angle. The slanting sunlight had an astonishing clarity, an almost unnatural purity; yet was soft, warm, sympathetic. It had the quality that can leave you breathless at the apogee of a desert morning or . . .

I have still missed my mark.

Perhaps that quiet interlude in Topock marsh drew its magic from the way place and light combined to defeat time. Water and mud, the reeds and distant mountains, the patterns and slanting sunlight—all were things of that moment; but they embraced the past. Not a shadowy past lurking in my memory. A firmer reality: the old, natural river. Floating there at the mouth of that little creek, I was reading a page of history written when the waterway I'd been traveling was still a living river. I also had a three-dimensional realization, at last, of the curlicue patterns—the delicious islands and lagoons and oxbow lakes—that my maps had all along been promising.

For almost an hour I sat there at the head of the slough, letting eye and mind roam over the silent, singing scene. Shadows lengthened. Patterns of water and mud, reeds and distant mountains, shifted and sidestepped.

At last, the shadows drained away. The light began to fade. And because there was nowhere to camp, there in the marsh, and also because the Devil's domain still beckoned, I rowed slowly back down the slough past the penny-pinched-into-ugliness marina, pulled out into midriver and began to float down toward the Atchison, Topeka railroad bridge that was the first of the stark steel river-spanning structures.

The light had almost gone, and I hesitated. If I was to camp before dark, in unspoiled desert, I'd have to move faster than I could row. I lowered the outboard motor into the water, pull-started it. Din. Vibration.

Maneuvering between the bridge supports demanded concentration. But at one point I did read the big-print messages on a line of markers: NO SKIING, CAMPING OR FIRES. It hardly seemed a place anyone would want to camp, but the caveat confirmed my need to move on down. Almost at once, another line of markers: NO WAKE OUT OF MAIN CHANNEL. No problem: my little outboard left no discernible wake.

We eased clear of the last steel structure. The shoreline lights ended, slid astern. We moved on down into the gloaming.

A few minutes, and I killed the outboard. Din and vibration died away. The sounds of Topock were faint now, and fading. I picked up the oars, began to push on their handles. I peered ahead, searching for a place to camp along the dark and silent shore.

20

...MEXICO

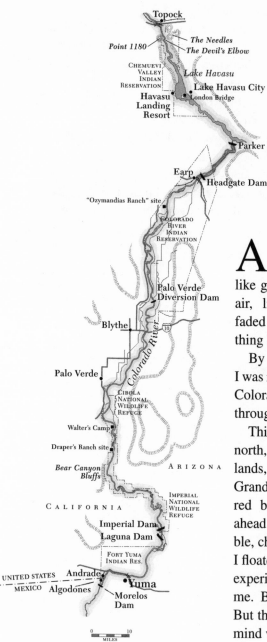

Topock
The Needles
The Devil's Elbow
Point 1180
CHEMUEVI
VALLEY
INDIAN
RESERVATION
Lake Havasu
Lake Havasu City
Havasu
Landing
Resort
London Bridge

Parker Dam

Earp
Headgate Dam

"Ozymandias Ranch" site
COLORADO
RIVER
INDIAN
RESERVATION

Palo Verde
Diversion Dam

Blythe

Colorado River

Palo Verde
CIBOLA
NATIONAL
WILDLIFE
REFUGE

Walter's Camp

Draper's Ranch site

Bear Canyon
Bluffs
ARIZONA

IMPERIAL
NATIONAL
WILDLIFE
REFUGE
CALIFORNIA

Imperial Dam
Laguna Dam

FORT YUMA
INDIAN RES.

UNITED STATES   Andrade
MEXICO   Algodones   Yuma
Morelos
Dam

0   10
MILES

Mile 1400 to Mile 1611
December 5–January 1

Abeckoning vision that glisters like gold can melt into air, into thin air, like an insubstantial pageant faded or a snowflake in hell. Something like that, anyway.

By noon of the day below Topock I was in the heart of the gorge that the Colorado has carved, deep and red, through the Needles massif.

Thirty-one years earlier, walking north, I had never seen the canyonlands, had never stood on the rim of Grand Canyon; and when the stark red bulk of The Needles loomed ahead I'd found it startling, formidable, challenging, wonderful. Now, as I floated southward laden with desert experience, the place failed to excite me. Barren beauty, yes. Definitely. But the scale too small. Besides, my mind was already zeroing in on a reenactment.

The main Needles massif stands on the Arizona bank, and in 1958 that had made it a different world, segregated behind the river barrier. But on the California side there thrust up a single outlier peak (which the map labeled only with its elevation, 1180) and I had camped at its foot, at the funny-bone point of the bend in the gorge known as the Devil's Elbow. I'd climbed Point 1180, and from its summit had commanded a magnificent northward view into the red gorge. Beyond, flat and ominous, stretched the beginning of the Mojave Desert—the huge and arid expanse I must soon cross. That vista had burned itself into my memory.

Now, I pulled ashore at the Devil's Elbow, into a reed-backed bay. Above loomed Point 1180.

By the time I'd searched for the cave in which I'd camped—and failed to find it because reed beds now grew dense against the flanking rock walls—it was too late to climb the peak that day. I scrambled high enough to pick out what seemed a viable route to the summit, then set up camp on an open beach.

Next morning, in spite of a queasy stomach, things at first went well. I climbed slowly but steadily. No dire obstacles. Ahead, the summit cheerfully close. After forty minutes, perhaps halfway up, I scrambled onto a broad terrace. And all at once, without warning, my energy had drained away. Drained beyond dregs.

A brief doze: no improvement. As far as I could make out through a gauzy veil that seemed to have fallen over everything, the summit now stood a very long way off. Stood strangely unattainable. And the route to it now questionable, going on impossible.

Ridiculous, I told myself. Must be that queasy gut. The day before, I'd scrambled longer and faster. A few weeks earlier, the climb above the Confluence had been much more demanding. And I remembered no 1958 problem in reaching the summit. Sure, I'd been backpack-fit. Well, all right, also thirty-one years younger. But age, I told myself, should make no difference. Halfway convinced myself, too. After a while, though, I went back down.

I'm still not sure just what happened that morning, to mind or body. Was it indeed the queasy gut? Or age? Or yet another flu relapse? Or, as later events hinted, something entirely different? But my notes report that when I got back down to camp I still felt "crummy, pretty deathly"; and the gauzy veil must still have hung thick enough to obscure common sense, for instead of holing up at my overnight camp I loaded the raft and relaunched. I'd intended to leave as soon as I got back, so perhaps motivational momentum carried me forward. Anyway, I floated down for several

*Partway up Point 1180, a pause. Looking
downriver, beyond the Devil's Elbow*

miles before camping on the left bank just before the river faded away into
Lake Havasu. There, I lay over for a day.

When I relaunched, a residual veil may still have lingered. I know that
during the four days' travel down to Parker Dam we often seemed to float
on more than water. And much of that time I felt imperfectly positioned in
the present.

Early on the first day, there was a notification that I had, with merciful
innocence, been positioning myself improperly in space.

We were motoring through a channel between shore and an island.
Strung across the channel, a line of south-facing markers. I throttled back,
swung the tiller, cruised past them, close. They advised me—in big print,
then small—that I'd made several illegal nightcamps: "NO SKIING,
FIRES, CAMPING next 17 miles." In sunlight, the small print was emi-
nently readable. I swung us away, offered thanks for the gloaming back at
Topock.

Beyond the wildlife refuge boundary, we angled in toward what memory
and my old map called Needles Boat Landing, in the Chemuevi Indian Reservation. For the moment, I ignored the far side of the lake; that could wait.

The little cluster of Boat Landing buildings—now "Havasu Landing Resort"—was simple, unwrecked and unlittered. No 1958 echoes. Unexpectedly, though, one short-term reverberation.

The Indian woman in the general store pleasant and helpful. Exuding a quiet pride, too. "Oh yes, the tribe has put garbage cans along the beach."

At the grocery store, a part-Indian woman equally cordial. "Yes, you're right—thirty years ago there was nothing over there across the lake. Just an old Quonset hut out on the peninsula, beside the airstrip."

"Hm, I seem to remember seeing the airstrip, and wondering what . . ."

"Oh, it had been an R and R place for the Air Force. But when they built the city they dredged a channel through the base of the peninsula, you know, so's they could put that bridge in. Used to be you could see the bridge from here, but it's hidden by trees now."

I walked back toward my raft, remembering the Fort Mohave tribe who'd handed over their reservation for thirty pieces of casino silver. These Chemuevi, weighing silver against substance, seemed to have emerged richer.

I camped a mile south, on an open beach, barely two hundred yards from the place I'd met the fourth rattlesnake of The Walk, of my life. And early next morning I walked inland from camp, across the eroded plain.

Failure. Even with my marked 1958 topo map, no way I could be sure in which of many gullies that rattler had been sunbathing, out of the wind, when I stomped into its world and provoked a defensive rattling. But all at once, standing on a level mesa, I moved back thirty years.

I'd had to walk, hour after hour, day after day, across the grain of the land. Down into deep-cut wash. Up the far side onto flat, rock-strewn mesa seamed with small gullies, bare but for scattered creosote bushes. Then down into another wash. This pattern repeated, with variations, day after day. And now, standing on one of the mesas, I remembered just how it had been. Remembered the clouds and sunlight and windswept silence. The toil and the crunch of my boots on sand, on stone. Remembered the rhythm, the frustrations, the joys. I stood there for a time, smiling across the plain at distant mountains, now comfortingly familiar.

Back at camp I loaded the raft and motored east, across the lake.

With the morning sun behind it, the far shore would have looked like almost any stretch of sloping desert plain—if sunlight had not kept bouncing off pale squares that I knew were walls; had not kept torching windows into fireballs.

The evening before, sunlight slanting across the lake had ignited the red mountain behind the blanket of buildings into near-incandescence. For a long moment, with lake and city and mountain all floodlit pink, the scene had been breathtakingly beautiful. Then lake and land darkened. The lights came on, one by one, jewel by jewel—creating at last a star-spangled coronet that echoed in the lake as a shimmering pattern of gaily painted organ-pipes. "We really are an astonishing animal," I'd thought. "What promise! If only we'd take the right steps . . ." My sermon broke off; skepticism surfaced. "From here it's beautiful, all right, but how will I feel about it tomorrow, up close?"

Now, an hour's steady motoring brought us to the base of the old airport peninsula. We putt-putted up the new dredged channel and under the solid bulk of "London Bridge"—dismantled stone by stone, transatlanticated, then meticulously reassembled, minus one arch. I landed, walked across the bridge. Although unsure which Thames-spanning bridge this once was, I seemed to detect faint tinkles from youth. Maybe.

The "English Village"—closed to traffic, and at this time of year pleasantly uncrowded—was less blatantly bogus than I'd feared. A man and his wife, sitting on a bench beside the lagoon-channel, offered a sight-seeing tour of their city. We got in their pickup, went. The man had worked for the local power company since 1969, five years after the city began. Got his "twenty-year pin" the previous day. Beneath an understandable pride in the place lurked unease at what he had helped them do to the desert. I spent almost all day in Lake Havasu City and found myself, on balance, unenthralled but unappalled.

By the time I puttered on southward out of the lagoon-channel, pink evening light once more gilded the city. It flushed the clouds that now hung over it with warning red. We headed out across the lake. What was it Julian Huxley had said? "Change is inevitable, progress possible."

Camp that night was Number 150: a milestone of some sort. Next night, the calendar disclosed another: December 10—five months since John Sexton and I set out from roadhead above Pinedale. December 10 . . . Only fourteen shopping days left . . . Out in the "real" world, malls already seethed with scurrying flocks of advertising's frenzied victims. Unreal.

These last few days, though, realities had kept piercing my mind's residual veil. The usual, softly wild realities.

At the layover camp, moonlight and silence. Lying encooned in my sleeping bag, I wonder what woke me. I turn my head. Five paces away, near the bow of the beached raft, something. I lie still, watch. A beaver, breathing heavily. No details, only shape. And the raft mere bulk, black against silvery water. Then, from just beyond the raft, a second beaver schmoos up from the water. It too is breathing heavily. A labored, rasping wheeze. It advances on the first shape, its body making definite yet ill-defined movements. Was its intent hostile or amatory? For a moment the first heavy-breather holds its ground. Then it schmoos around the bow, still only a black shape, but so close to me as to seem almost touchable—and schlides back into the water. Its lover/enemy/co-patient hesitates, rasps a few more rasps, follows. Once again, only the bulk of the raft, black against silver. Back to sleep.

Another camp, in a reed-fringed bay. Birdlife for breakfast. Out in the silver lake stands a slim white statue: great egret. Beyond the reeds, a covey of coots coot stubbily at apparent random. A common grackle, dark and iridescent and probably male, chuck-chuck-chucks around camp, close, soliciting alms. He despairs, departs.

A whitecap afternoon. I drift before the north wind, broadside, oars tucked under knees, outboard tilted up clear of the water. A quiet, noisy, exhilarating world. The first boat I've seen in two days motors uplake. Its fishermen stop, ask if I'm OK. I drift on in a brown study, studying distant brown mountains. Overhead, a black-fleck cloud of cormorants spins slowly, tentatively; I think of them as fellow solitarians, so it's probably migration time. A great blue heron flaps past; herons rarely offer comment, but this one emits a hoarse craaaking croak and manages to infuse it with a profound distaste and contempt for my presence.

My last morning on Lake Havasu, the north wind still blew. Again, sunlight and whitecaps. We scudded broadside toward Parker Dam, motor tilted clear. I sat caught in the rhythm of the waves, listening to the silence behind the wind.

Space. Open sky. Distant mountains: jagged spines of bare brown rock. Long desert slopes furrowed with harmony and meaning. The lake's narrow bathtub ring rarely visible.

At last, the brown mountains began to close in. Between them, Parker Dam's superstructure. In its pseudo-Colosseum way, impressive.

I looked back northward. Lake Havasu was another pathological distension of my river. But this time I seemed to have developed a tolerance for the place. Even an affection. Something like that, anyway.

Since early planning days I'd been fed warnings about what had happened to the stretch of river between Parker Dam and Headgate, a small dam that diverts water for agriculture. This 12-mile reach, I'd been told, was now the core of Crazy country.

"A madhouse," said one friend. "Powerboats everywhere, piloted by idiots."

Later, a Nevadan elaborated. "Yes, we call 'em the California Crazies. Alias *Homo oblivius*."

"How d'you tell California Crazies from Arizona Animals and Nevada Nuts?"

"Oh, they've got more money."

The Crazies, I gathered, had contaminated much of the lower river, and between Parker and Headgate they slammed their powerboats and appendaged water-skiers up- and downriver and into each other even more crazily than elsewhere.

The river below Parker seemed more stillborn than reborn: a shrunken, sluggish waterway. Urbanized, too: its banks lined with the second-home winter quarters of "Snowbirds," as refugees from northern winters are locally known. But the place deserted. Few Snowbirds. And the river too shallow and narrow for Crazying. All day, I met only two other vessels.

One, womanned by a figure in a gold-band-peak cap, indeed slammed past at full throttle and left me rocking in her wake. The second, an Arizona Sheriff's Department boat, pulled me over. The dour deputy who manned it complained from behind sunglasses that my raft bore no state stickers. I produced them, explained that they had peeled off.

"They ought to be on boards, up on the bow, where I can see 'em, quick. That's where everybody carries 'em."

I suggested that boards could be dangerous in white water.

The deputy ran a shaded but sour eye over the raft. "D'you have a fire extinguisher?"

"A *fire* extinguisher?" I think I tried to suggest that if I somehow succeeded in kindling a fire aboard the raft it would soon blow the tubes and sink us—neatly solving the problem.

"I won't cite you this time," said the deputy. "But these are navigable waters, subject to the Coast Guard, and *they'd* cite you. So read this, carefully." He gave me a thick booklet, powered away.

I filed the booklet in a dry box. Some summer when I had TB . . .

A time constraint had made me motor rather than row this inter-dam stretch. The Bureau of Reclamation man who'd trailered us around Parker (this time, Julian Rhinehart couldn't spring himself free) would do the same at Headgate. He'd been accommodating beyond the call of duty, but he had to drive back to Boulder City that evening and courtesy demanded I make haste. There were also places I wanted to revisit.

It turned out that time had washed over all three of the old-timers I'd met along this stretch in 1958. Their haunts, too. And I found myself approaching Headgate Dam well within schedule.

By now, the map said, we'd moved into the Colorado River Indian Reservation. River right, less Californicated; left, less Arizonked. The waterway began to slow, widen. Along the right bank, reeds growing thick.

Soon, at their edge, thatched with their cut stalks, the first traditional, bee-hive-shape beaver lodge I remembered seeing since before the canyons began.

We putt-putted on.

Then, protruding above the reed beds, hanging there in the sunshine, suspended between two worlds—between soft pale foreground reed heads and dark distant mountains, between fact and fantasy—what looked like the turret of a medieval castle: a square wooden turret (though "turret" wasn't quite the right word) equipped with a flagpole. The turret seemed to be mounted on another and larger one that was almost hidden by the pale reed heads. Both turrets had windows. Big windows, all around, so that the turrets' sides were mostly glass.

I cut the motor, drifted down level with the apparition. It still hung there, still essentially unreal, still barely believable. Near it, a gap in the reeds.

Recheck watch: still plenty of time.

I rowed slowly toward the gap, passed through it. The reeds began to open up into a small lagoon. And all at once, as I glided around the last reed bed, there stood on the lagoon's far side—totally real now, but still barely credible—a tall, tapering, solidly built three-story structure. The wooden "turret" I had seen from outside was the topmost of three progressively smaller rooms mounted one on the other. Each room was indeed mostly windows. Around each ran a veranda, and the flat summit formed a railed lookout post with, at one corner, the mastlike flagpole.

The immediate effect: nautical. Battleship-solid. Yet the structure still radiated a floating, wraithlike, otherworldly quality. I rowed a couple of strokes closer. Yes, it was floating all right. A houseboat. Of sorts. And then, as I began to feel like an intruder, a man and woman appeared on the lowest veranda.

"Oh, I didn't mean to intrude."

"Not at all," said the woman.

We chatted. Soon, they invited me aboard for tea. Attractive people, with flair yet simplicity. At a guess, early-baby-boom vintage. Terry, who hailed from Cincinnati, proved amiable but reticent; Kathy was "a Californian, all the way," and communicative.

They'd lived there for seventeen years, she told me. "We're the last of the squatters."

"Literally squatters?"

"Oh no, we pay our dues for the houseboat, and it's registered and so on." They'd rigged solar power; and a trail and then a dirt road connected them with the nearby highway.

We sat overlooking the calm, reed-enclosed lagoon. Along one edge snaked a floating, weathered-wood landing stage. Moored to it, a couple of small, modern, low-tech boats. Otherwise the encircling reeds hid everything but the tops of distant mountains. The warm winter sun beat down.

"This is how life used to be," I heard myself say. "How it ought to be."

"Yes," said Kathy. "We couldn't stand it the other way."

They worked, it seemed, at various visitor-oriented jobs. "I guess you could say that in summer we subsist on the Crazies, in winter on the Snowbirds." But they did other things. In a couple of days Kathy would be driving up to Laughlin to protest the planned dumping of reprocessed sewage into the river. "What if something goes wrong with the reprocessing? I clean my teeth in this water."

They showed me around their home. Stout timbers on massive uprights. But everything unpretentious, practical, comfortable. From the second floor, a diving chute curved down into the lagoon. Faded sofas lined the verandas. Indoors, each room windowed out onto greenery. From the railed and flagstaffed lookout post you commanded the world: lagoon, reeds, river; a band of rolling desert plain, speckled with man-things; then brown desert mountains, wide blue sky.

As we came back down, a pair of mallards paddled into the lagoon. On the pontoon, a grackle glittered. Overhead, a skein of pelicans staged an elegant flyby. "The pelicans shouldn't be here this time of year," said Kathy. "That means something's out of synch . . . but I sure like watching them."

By now the sun was grazing the reed heads. I remembered that a mile downriver, at Headgate, the Bureau man would be waiting. It was difficult, though, to leave a reed-fringed, change-resistant time tract within which both beavers and people built old-style, harmonious homes. Difficult to leave this couple whose simplicity had nothing to do with naïvety. They'd achieved a complex, pared-down elegance; and if I sometimes seemed to detect a mildly smug self-satisfaction . . . well, I knew at least one solitudinous, Pharisaical river rat who could be accused of a kindred hubris.

An hour later I camped below Headgate Dam, river right, in a backwater. Beyond the backwater ran a road, invisible but certain.

Next day I revisited Earp. Leaving the raft moored in its backwater I walked inland to the nearby road and turned south.

In 1958 I'd walked northward into the village. But memory—that rich though slippery historian—had been reinforced by what I'd written afterward in *The Thousand-Mile Summer:*

Two highways met. Together, they crossed a railroad and the river. A dozen trees commemorated these events.

As I walked down the railroad tracks I saw a gray water tank floating blimpishly above the trees. On its side was painted:

WYATT

EARP

HOME

The water tank dominated the village. It was strategically sited to attract the eye of every northbound motorist, and appreciably increased his chances of misjudging the curve and crashing into the corrugated iron

EARP TRADING POST
Cold Beer—Ice   Live Bait   Fishing Tackle   Groceries

The motorist's final prospect as he pierced the wall of the trading post would be the legend that ran its entire length:

WELCOME TO EARP, CALIFORNIA

Beyond the trading post, the garage lurked behind a pageant of billboards. The biggest proclaimed:

THIS TOWN NAMED

FOR **WYATT EARP**

EARLY FRONTIER MARSHAL

of TV series.

Another sign added, just to make sure:

EARP, CALIF

Beyond the garage stood the post office and a line of frame cabins collectively labeled "Motel."
Earp slept.

Now, as I walked southward, the image of how things had been hung graphic in my mind.

But at the road junction, instead of a dozen commemorative trees, an open space on which squatted a modern gas station and taco stand. No problem, though: the village was what mattered. It began, as far as I remembered, a couple of hundred yards ahead, just beyond the first bend.

I approached the bend. To my surprise, the image had now moved slightly out of focus. I no longer felt sure whether I should expect to find the village immediately beyond that first bend or around a second one. I kept walking.

I rather think I'd just seen enough, beyond the first bend, to grasp that no buildings stood there, when my attention switched to a small, square, not-at-all-familiar pillbox of a building on the left of the road. A narrow black board on its front bore the subdued inscription:

UNITED STATES POST OFFICE
Earp, CA. 92242

It seemed odd, having the new post office so far outside the village; but because I was carrying a small parcel to mail home—and also, I suspect, because I felt vaguely unsure of the way things seemed to be turning out—I went into the post office.

A customer was being served, and I had a chance to look around. Sure enough, nothing rang the faintest bell. When my turn came I said to the friendly postmistress, "So you've moved the post office since 1958?"

She smiled. "Not far. It used to be just next door."

"Oh, I thought it was in the grocery store. . . ."

"That's right. But it burned down. You can still see the cement foundation, just outside our door there."

"But . . . but I remember the post office as being right in the middle of the village."

"That's right."

"Then . . . was the whole village burned down?"

"Oh no. The village went before that. It was privately owned, you see. Rented. On the Indian Reservation. And the guy fell behind on his payments and they dunned him and he made off. Just left. The Indians were going to restore it and keep it up, but they couldn't get it up to county codes and eventually they bulldozed it all out—except for the post office and store, next door there."

"When did all this happen?"

"Let's see. We moved here in '64 . . . so it must have been around '68. And then, a couple of years later, the store and post office burned down—when it was being robbed. This place was built in '70."

We talked about the old village.

"Yes," said the postmistress, "I remember the Wyatt Earp signs. All over. Even up on the water tower. When they bulldozed the village they left the water tower up. Stood there for years. A guy put some advertising on it . . . And then, just three or four months ago, somebody crashed into it. It's lying on the ground now, over across the road, just a few yards up."

Minutes later I stood beside it. The tank lay on its side in the lee of a big creosote bush. The advertising, red and black on white, still hit you in the eye:

MIKE MACK'S
SKI SHOP
EMERALD COVE
RESORT, 9 MI.

But the base of the tank had rusted. Between it and the road, fragments of charred wood and pitch lay black, forgotten. Around it stretched the flat gravel of a typical desert wash, supporting only creosote bushes, one distressed tree, a couple of telegraph poles and a spreadage of litter.

By the time I walked northward out of Earp again, I'd begun to recover. Discovering the village's obliteration had hardly been a cataclysmic experience. The place had been no Brandwood: unlike the headmaster's comfortable old Victorian house and garden that had without my realizing it stood so solidly in childhood remembrance, it had not commanded any deep affection. If anything, the shock came closer to mild Ozymandias effect. Even that was stretching it, though. Earp had been no colossal statue raised by a mighty king to impress generations of men, century after century. Just an amusing tin-pan bric-a-brac. An oddity, quirking away, pleasantly enough, at the back of my mind—a nostalgic engram, superficial even by nostalgia's easy standards.

I turned off the road, angled across open desert toward the backwater and my raft. No denying the sense of loss, though: the knowledge that behind me—and finally, this time—Earp slept.

Two evenings later I camped on the right bank beneath a low mesa that held the promise of another thirty-year echo—potentially Earpian, yet different. But I did not immediately climb the short and easy slope behind camp for a look out across the mesa. It seemed better, for some reason, to wait till morning.

At the edge of camp, a recently bulldozed road wound along the foot of the mesa. Even in failing light the road's rubble embankment looked raw and ugly: pale, angular chunks of quarried limestone, out of harmony with everything. Then I noticed on the face of one foot-long chunk, recently cracked open by brute force, a network of black etchings. I kneeled, looked closer.

Fossil images. Long-dead foliage, flat yet unwithered, like delicate flowers pressed in a book. Mostly, a confused whorl of fronds, heads toward the stone's center. But two plants stood out with astonishing clarity, like a sharp-focused black-and-white photograph of seaweeds caught in mid-sway. I carried the chunk of limestone a few feet and set it beside my bed for photographing in morning light.

After breakfast next morning I photographed the fossil fronds, then walked across the road and began to climb the slope that led up to the mesa.

In 1958 I was taking a ten-mile shortcut across this barren brown mesa when, about four o'clock, I saw a line of brilliant greenery quivering low in the heat haze ahead. That memory, too, had been reinforced by what I'd written:

"A mirage!" I thought. "A genuine mirage!"

Half an hour later I was walking beside a field of very tangible barley, green and thick, that rustled like taffeta. . . .

Beyond the barley, outside a row of big new barns, I found the ranch manager. "Six years ago, this was just another stretch of mesa," he said. "Flatter than most, maybe—that's why we bought it. But no different otherwise. And now we've got three hundred acres of the finest citrus and barley and alfalfa along the Colorado."

The ranch seemed too high above the river for ordinary irrigation.

"Wells," said the manager. "All from wells. We pump every drop of it. Makes it expensive, of course; last year was the first time we showed a profit. But now everybody's sitting up and taking notice. All the land 'round about has been bought up and they're just waiting to see what happens. If we make a real go of it we could change the whole face of the desert. That's about the size of it—change the whole face of the desert."

I walked on through an orchard. The air felt cool and moist. My feet sank into soft earth. In untilled corners, grass grew thick.

Then the trees ended and I stepped back into untamed desert.

The breeze hit me like the blast from a hairdrier. My feet crunched over stones and gravel. The sunlight bounced up like something solid. Ahead, creosote bushes shimmered endlessly away to blue hills.

Twenty minutes later I stopped to look back. The ranch had sunk to a quivering line of green along the flat brown horizon.

Any man in his senses would have dismissed it as a mirage.

Now, thirty years later, as I climbed up the slope leading from river to mesa, I knew the ranch site lay less than a mile inland.

I stepped up onto the mesa. My line of sight ran across it without interruption. I felt almost sure: no citrus, anywhere on that mesa.

Almost sure: the desert, for all its apparent openness, has a gift for concealment. The only thing I could see, though, anywhere near the place my 1958 topo map pinpointed as the site of the old ranch, was a small group of buildings.

I began to walk toward these buildings. Sometimes the flat, open mesa I moved across was beautiful virgin desert, stony, dotted with creosote bushes; but mostly it was desert deflowered by motorcycles, dune buggies.

I approached the place my map said the citrus trees should be. Except for scattered creosote bushes and snaking man-spoor, everything bare and open. No sign of any hidden fold in the ground—the secret-concealing kind that deserts delight in. I had stopped and was standing still, wondering if I could somehow have botched the direction-finding, when I noticed a pattern of parallel lines stretching out left and right from below my feet. The lines were indisputable, but very faint. If I hadn't been scanning the sand for some kind of sign I'd have missed them. I retraced my steps and found I had walked, unknowing, for almost a hundred yards across the ghostly parallel lines.

I stood surveying the mesa. No sign, anywhere, of the row of big new barns beside which I'd met the ranch manager. The only nearby buildings—those I'd seen from down near the river—were of a very different kind. But they stood just beyond the line pattern. I walked over.

A modern desert residential cluster, purpose obscure. Two shoddy permanent buildings. Sub-clusters of five or six old mobile homes, up on blocks. Someone clearly in residence, but nobody at home except one friendly cat, one distrustful dog.

I reconnoitered. A fringe of disenfranchised automobiles, dune buggies, bicycles. Supplementary consumer detritus. One newish red Wilson golf bag, sidepocket unzipped, supine on stony ground; three of its clubs spilled haphazard. Other than one rusty item, just possibly a tine-harrow, no farm implements.

I walked back to the orchard's pale ghost, spent an hour wandering around, clarifying.

The faint parallel lines—no doubt fine sand filling old irrigation and tillage depressions between citrus trees—defined the orchard limits. The oat and barley fields had reverted to desert indistinguishable from the rest of the mesa.

I went back to the place the orchard had ended and I had stepped out of a lush green world into harsh sun-blasted desert. Now, in every direction, nothing but that second world.

I began to walk back toward the river. After a few yards I stopped, looked back. Nothing that even hinted at what had once grown in that place. My "sensible" impressions, all those years ago, had been right: in the long run, the shimmering green oasis had indeed been a mirage.

I turned back toward river and present.

Once again, a sense of loss. Because I'd known as soon as I stepped up onto the mesa that the ranch probably no longer existed, there'd been less shock than at Earp. But the echoes from this artifact sang in a different key; carried deeper overtones. "We could change the whole face of the desert," the proud ranch manager had said. "That's about the size of it—

change the whole face of the desert." But now, at the place we'd stood to-gether, nothing but lone and level land stretching far away. This time, a true Ozymandias effect.

Back at the raft, I was about to push out into the river—was actually aboard, looking back at the campsite and making a routine last-minute check that nothing had been left behind—when my eye fell on the chunk of fossilized limestone, still lying on the sand. I hesitated. Then I stepped back onto the beach, hefted the rock, carried it to the raft and stowed it aboard, jamming it tight so that with luck it wouldn't damage the fabric. I'm not sure that at the time I knew why I'd changed my mind.

Later, I understood front and fairly clear. The fossils in that piece of limestone can be seen as having something to say about time and persistence. About chance and survival. Something to say about events that had taken place a mile inland on the mesa as well as about the long and complex and unknowable chain of events that had left the stone lying on the sand, cracked neatly open to a very legible page, where he who river-runs might read.

This morning that stone lies on my desk—one of only two artifacts I brought home from the river. I have just renewed the pleasure I get every time I inspect its whorl of delicate black etchings, suspended mid-sway down the eons. Beside the stone, a book lies open at Shelley's poem:

> *I met a traveller from an antique land*
> *Who said: Two vast and trunkless legs of stone*
> *Stand in the desert. Near them, on the sand,*
> *Half sunk, a shattered visage lies, whose frown,*
> *And wrinkled lip, and sneer of cold command,*
> *Tell that its sculptor well those passions read*
> *Which yet survive (stamped on these lifeless things),*
> *The hand that mocked them and the heart that fed;*
> *And on the pedestal these words appear:*
> *"My name is Ozymandias, king of kings;*
> *Look on my works, ye Mighty, and despair!"*
> *Nothing beside remains. Round the decay*
> *Of that colossal wreck, boundless and bare,*
> *The lone and level sands stretch far away.*

The river had since Headgate flowed fast and shallow—and empty. Frequent shoals and barely submerged boulders and logs—and other snags, too—spelled danger for any boat. Even rowing, I had to stay alert. The day below Ozymandias Ranch, it occurred to me that since the sheriff pulled me over, back above Headgate, I'd not seen a fellow traveler.

Fossil fronds, below "Ozymandias" Ranch.

Slowly, though, the river changed.

At first the levees persisted. But once, on the Arizona side, a gap. I pulled over and found myself looking up a cut-off. An echo of Topock marsh: peace and beauty, curves and harmonies. The winter sun beat warm on my skin. Two black-crowned night herons surveyed me without trust from a tree snag. Far up the cut-off, a gleaming and perfectly placed white egret created a Cezanne-Utrillo focal point for the soft blue-green riverscape.

A few more miles, and the main channel wriggled free from the engineers' grip. There were still levees, but they stood well back. The river, once more a living entity, twisted through reed beds, sprouted beckoning side channels.

In tandem with the river, the tempo of my progress changed. Grew richer. Quickened.

I don't mean that the final hundred and forty miles to the Mexican border became a race. Nor even that my average daily mileage soared. But now the days unrolled serenely, unchecked. Still no human fellow travelers. And few wild companions—except birds.

Thirteen geese clustered uneasily on a sandbar, snow white until they took flight; then, big black wingtip wedges. Consult birdbook: snow geese—the birds Paul Gallico had long ago hung in my mind as almost mythical creatures.

A nightcamp, sunrise. I opened my eyes to see, high above me on a levee, sharp in the fresh and slanting light, the trip's first roadrunner. It looked down on me and mine, long and carefully; disapproved; vanished.

In some ways I now had greater freedom to float languidly southward, taking my time. Yet that final two-week run to the border left me, at least in retrospect, with a sense of gathering momentum.

Some of the perceived acceleration may have been due to my sense of being drawn more and more strongly toward the place that promised a culminating echo from 1958: the border post at Andrade. But there were other things too. And they acted in unexpected and roundabout ways.

The river now ran soft and varied. Reed banks. Scattered islands. Intriguing route choices. Once, choosing a swift and narrow channel that twisted between an island and tree-fringed shore, I found myself negotiating what amounted to a small and intimate waterway—and realized that the place reminded me of the journey's early, virgin days, back in Wyoming.

Soon, more Wyoming echoes. The main river now flowed between banks furnished with tree curtains that cut off the flat land behind. The current pendulumed bank to bank, and the raft and I swung along. As in Wyoming, I found myself delighting in the raft's elegant choreographics. Relishing its slow oscillations and random pivots—bow, stern, port, starboard. Then a caressing puff of wind would fatten into gentle zephyr and modulate our rhythms. And within these dances the raft often performed a subtle internal motion—a soft swinging to and fro, barely perceptible unless you paid attention, like the bass line in a restrained quartet.

This series of small events—near-end harking back to near-start—created a pleasing symmetry.

Then a more graphic echo, with sound track.

I had camped river right, on a grassy, tamarisk-fringed ledge at the brink of a sand-and-pebble beach, and was sitting quietly, looking out across the calm river and watching it fade with the day, when I became conscious of a drawn-out, almost querulous sound, strange yet strangely familiar. I looked up. Outlined against the pale evening sky, a confused mass of huge gray birds was organizing itself with unhurried wingbeats into rough line-ahead formation. As I watched, the birds readjusted—smoothly, by almost imperceptible degrees—into an immense and balanced and intensely beautiful V. They wheeled south, headed downriver. I scrambled to my feet, watched them go. Sandhill cranes. No doubt making their evening move to favored roosting places, just as they had back in Wyoming. Perhaps they were even the same birds. Snowbirds wintering south, like me.

The cranes disappeared, far downriver. I stood for a long time in the fading light, looking at the place they had vanished, still seeing them, still hearing them. At last I sat down and began preparing dinner.

You might reasonably picture my nightcamps as the one element that, every day, brought the sense of gathering momentum up short. But even they did not always elude the new southward tug.

At root, the camping process remained much as it had been since I established a viable routine back in Wyoming. With ongoing adjustment, of course. And this long, echoing stretch between Hoover and Mexico imposed its own distinctive permutations.

Whenever possible I now camped on the California bank—to catch the warmth of the rising sun's first rays. Although the days remained almost summerlike, most of the clear winter nights had by dawn dragged my bedside thermometer below the freezing mark. The morning before I saw the sandhill cranes, it read 11 degrees Fahrenheit.

Yet in bed I always remained deliciously warm. Weeks earlier I'd switched back to my warm sleeping bag. Its Gore-Tex cover kept out dew and frost, and now I rarely pitched a tent: it would cut me off from the world and also slow each morning's repacking of gear. So the first rays of morning sunlight to hit camp began to warm the air surrounding me. It felt like embrocation being rubbed into the skin. Within minutes the outside world became habitable.

The long hours of evening darkness had imposed another significant camping change. By now I'd added to my gear a Sexton-sent pressure lantern and collapsible table. Heaven-sent. The lamp, standing at waist-height on the table, made each camp much more comfortable, even civilized. On balance, the benefits outweighed the way the lamp's hiss and glare cut me off from the night.

After dinner that sandhill-crane evening I wandered down to the raft to get something and found myself standing at the raft's bow. Slanting light from the almost-full moon, just risen beyond the far bank, dug reservoirs of shadow behind the bulky dry boxes. I ran my eyes over all the familiar shapes—and remembered how, back in Wyoming, I'd stood looking down at the raft and felt the first stirrings of affection for the little blue vessel that for six months would be my home. To my surprise, I'd never christened it. Except for the Knutsons' "*Water Strider*," which somehow failed to stick, I had not found a satisfactory name. Just "raft." Odd. But now, without question, it was my familiar home that fitted like an old shoe. A home on which, without quite realizing it, I'd come to lavish that comfortable form of love the Greeks called *storge*.

I turned away—and found myself looking across the sand-and-pebble beach at the camp that was also my home, wherever I set it up. It made a neat little enclave, nestling there among the tamarisks, with its local lamp-lit dome overpowering the moonlight. The lamp illuminated every detail: blue table cluttered with brown cooking stove and semi-shiny pots and red foil AlpineAire freeze-dried food packages and other kitchenware; beside it, the brown tubular folding chair and two half-empty dry bags, pale blue, dark blue; also one cream-colored plastic bucket and two washing bowls; a couple of feet away, my blue-mummy-bag-on-maroon-foam-mattress-on-black-groundsheet bed laid out on gray-green grass. Nothing new in any of that, of course. It was essentially the same every night.

But now, looking back across the beach at my camp, appreciating its neatness and convenience and even beauty, I found myself seeing beyond it to the more elaborate camps and homes we have built in the course of our history—Babylon, Paris, Tenochtitlán, Lake Havasu City. And in the same instant I became newly and knife-edge aware of what an extraordinary species we are—adaptable and resourceful and imaginative to a degree that outstrips, as far as we can discern, every other animal. Outstrips, yes. That was the problem. *Homo hubrisiens.* If only . . . Just in time, I quit my pulpit and walked up the moonlit sand-and-pebble nave, back into the lamplight.

As happened most nights, I made good use of the lamp's prime benefit. After sunset the cold had as usual crept quickly in; but I knew that there beside the lamp, snug in down jacket and pants and heavy boots, I could sit and read for as long as I cared, without discomfort to eyes or body.

That evening I finished Christopher D. Stone's *Should Trees Have Standing?*, which I'd read fifteen years earlier during a three-week Alaska backpack trip. Then I opened a book I'd read soon afterward: Julian Huxley's *Religion Without Revelation.* Not at all a bumpy transition. *Should Trees Have Standing?* explored an unusual legal case argued before the U.S. Supreme Court, and one passage near its end had in Alaska roused me to a kind of mental orgasm:

> *What is needed is a myth that can fit our growing body of knowledge of geophysics, biology and the cosmos. In this vein, I do not think it too remote that we may come to regard the Earth, as some have suggested, as one organism, of which Mankind is a functional part—the mind perhaps; different from the rest of nature, but different as a man's brain is different from his lungs.*

The passage had hung in my memory. Danger lurked, I'd come to see, if you took the notion as license for "the mind" to manage the whole shop. Still . . . When I suggested to a good friend that here might lie the seeds of the next major religion, he shook his head: "I doubt it. For one thing, there's nothing in it for the average man." But I'd remained unconvinced.

Now, reopening *Religion Without Revelation*, I riffled through it, reading those seminal passages that I had, in my usual sophomoric way, underlined. They still made sense. *"[T]he objects of religion . . . are in origin and essence those things, events and ideas which arouse the feeling of sacredness." ". . . obscured by symbolic vestures . . . throw away the veils." "The enjoyment of the beauty and varied wonder of the natural world [is] one of the indispensable modes of human fulfillment . . . involving something essentially religious or holy."* I turned off the lamp. Another Huxley aphorism skirled into my mind: *"Man is nothing else than evolution become conscious of itself."*

Freed from the lamp's hiss and glare, I began to see and hear the night. Moonlight and silence flooded land and water. I leaned back in my chair. Yes, the sound and spectacle of big birds wheeling in concert against pale evening sky could indeed beget something sacred. . . .

And then, looking up at the moonlit sky, I saw with sudden, unexpected clarity that this life that had been mine for almost six months—this life of blue raft and sunlit days and tail-slapping beavers, of lamplit camps and hushed moonlit nights, this life that embraced distrustful night herons and roadrunners and huge wheeling birds and all the pageant's other players, this life I'd come to take for granted—would before long come to an end. I don't mean that I felt the journey was over. Certainly not that the little monkey had appeared on my shoulder to whisper, "Go home!" I mean only that for a moment I saw, very clearly, that the end of my journey lay not far ahead. And the glimpse only glinted—the way your headlight beam reflects just for an instant from a parked car as you swing around a bend. I think my premonition of journey's end was already gone—except for its lingering memory—before the coyotes began their song.

The first coyote yowled close, just across the river. Far downriver, another answered. Their dialogue arced across the night silence, yowl to yowl, yowl to bark, question to answer. At least, the rhythms suggested specific communication. Things like "Meet you an hour from now . . . East side of Main, two blocks north of the post office"; or perhaps "Meet you when our star has moved three yips up . . . at the slough where the river . . . oh, you know, where we always meet." After a while I tried yowling and barking into their conversation. I'd like to report that we conducted a truly great conference call, but I remain prey to doubts.

When the coyotes fell silent I cleaned my teeth, slid down into the mummy bag, slept.

Events soon confirmed the gathering momentum I had sensed at that nightcamp.

Three days later Julian Rhinehart made his final contribution to my physical journey by trailering us around Palo Verde Diversion Dam, and below the dam the river flowed sadly diminished, severely canalized. By the time I floated under the Interstate 10 bridge at Blythe, a dozen miles down, it ran more strongly—but still hemmed in by tall levees. Harnessed. Uniform. Dull. And the uninspiring surroundings may have helped urge me on. Anyway, the journey's new tempo held.

The day below Blythe, I traveled 31 miles. And that day, though exceptional, set the tone for the two-week run to the border.

The only diversion came next morning, when I made a minor sidetrip. A necessary sidetrip. The 31-mile day had been planned catch-up: back upriver, I'd phoned my contacts in Mexico and at last confirmed that they would take my raft around by land to a put-in point below the 60-mile stretch of dried-out river below the border; and I'd said I'd phone again as soon as I knew if I could be at the border town of Yuma before New Year's Day. By the evening of that long day's run, when I camped river right at the mouth of a lagoon that formed the first major levee break, it seemed reasonable to assume I'd reach Yuma in good time. And next morning I rowed half a mile up the lagoon to a resort called "Walter's Camp."

On its pay phone I assured my Mexican contacts that I'd be in Yuma by New Year's Day—then lingered just long enough to confirm a reverse-Ozymandian story. As I'd suspected, the flourishing resort derived from a single riverside cabin, ramshackle and deserted, that I'd paused beside in 1958. Then, a sign upended against a cement mixer announced "Fishing and Hunting in Colorado River." It had seemed wildly optimistic.

Below Walter's Camp the levees soon petered out, and before long the river swirled and sang between banks that curved green and varied and unpredictable. From raft-level, though, my horizons limited. So the scenery still rather dull. Certainly uninspiring. And for the rest of that week we moved steadily southward, sometimes swept along by the current's flow and always, now, by the journey's.

The nights clear and cold. But growing less cold. At successive camps, as the light-glow dome built by Blythe in the northern sky diminished, so the southern Yuma-built dome dilated, brightened.

The days sometimes sunlit, sometimes clouded, always balmy. Off to the right, familiar chocolate-brown mountains and crenellated foothills—sometimes distant, sometimes close. But the flat riverside desert held at

Near Draper Ranch. The river no longer channeled.

arm's length by thick tule beds—those same tules that thirty-one years earlier had kept me largely screened off from the river. Even when I managed to get ashore, notably at Draper Ranch and Bear Canyon Bluff, the echoes from 1958 were pale, pianissimo. In many ways, I decided, I wasn't really traveling through the same country. Or perhaps it was just a different traveler.

The country still largely unpopulated, though. Once, wandering along an Arizona sandbar, a blasé coyote. Then, on the California side, pawing away at something, the first fox of the trip. But very few humans. Ashore, none. The day below Walter's Camp, one other boat. Next day, one less. Then, next mid-morning, briefly and at some distance, a couple of fishermen in a dinghy. What they saw when they looked my way was, I guess, a white-bearded old guy driving a strange blue-nosed water sled; because the only words I heard come floating across the open water that separated us were "Santa Claus!" Then the men started their outboard and motored off downriver, presumably back into a world where this day was a shining star for children and where most everyone would for the second time in a month attempt to move closer to God by overeating.

Back in my world, we moved on down together, river and raft and rider, toward Yuma and Mexico and perhaps the sea.

 Three days later I checked into a Yuma motel.

Situation normal. U.S. forces had invaded Panama, and when President Noriega sought refuge in the Vatican mission had blasted him with rock music. In Romania, communist president Ceausescu had been deposed and executed, Balkan-quick. Poland had taken "a bold leap into capitalism," and next day the price of bread jumped 38 percent. Here in the West we were trying not to gloat over the collapse of the Soviet Union, and failing. Everyone was saying, "There goes the only other superpower"; no one said, "There goes the first of the superpowers." Pundits were punditing on the downfall of a faulty economic creed; few suggested, in public, that the canker might lie in the worship of any human-bubble Economic God. In the opiate-of-the-crasses department, "The Dow" had hit an all-time high, above 2800. Samuel Beckett and Billy Martin had ended very different lives with very different deaths.

When I'd readjusted I began to grapple with chores.

The doubts about my Mexican travel plans had from the first centered on Morelos Dam, just south of the border. There, most of the already depleted Colorado was diverted into a network of irrigation canals that nurtured the delta's farmland, and I'd been told that below the dam the river rarely amounted to more than a trickle, often disappeared; but that 60 or 70 miles south it met the Rio Hardy—a waterway created by the diverted water after it had done its farm work. My plans depended on the state of the main Colorado below Morelos Dam. If it still flowed, I'd keep rafting south. But if, as seemed likely, the river petered out, I had three options: attempt to raft to the Rio Hardy through the irrigation system; walk to the sea along the delta's eastern edge; or walk in or near the old and mostly dry riverbed until I could relaunch my raft in the Rio Hardy, 60-odd miles south.

Some weeks earlier I'd learned for sure that below Morelos Dam the river indeed petered out. I'd also become convinced that the first two alternatives posed major problems. So I'd made plans about as tight as you can when confronting a mirage.

I would backpack along the line of the old riverbed to the Rio Hardy. There, at a place called Campo Mosqueda, my Mexican contacts would reunite me with my raft. Beyond that, new uncertainties. Above all, continued doubts about whether I'd be able to raft clear down to El Golfo de Santa Clara, a fishing village at the head of the Sea of Cortez, or Gulf of California.

But first, here in Yuma, logistical details. For several days I battled the phone system from my motel room. Finally we arranged that my Mexican Good Samaritans would drive over from Mexicali, where they all lived, collect my deflated raft and drive me to the border post at Andrade. Earliest possible D-Day: January 4.

Meanwhile, a permit problem. Back home, I'd been told I need not carry my passport: I could pick up a Mexican travel permit in Yuma. But now, no joy in Yuma. Nor from a barbed and murky phone conversation with a Mexican border official. And on New Year's Day—after making the same New Year's resolution I'd made for decades, and always kept: "This year I will under no circumstances make a New Year's resolution"—I rented a car and drove across the river to the border post at Andrade, where in 1958 I'd taken the first step northward on my six-month walk to Oregon.

As I drove, there lay beside me on the car seat a book I'd just borrowed from the Yuma library: *The Thousand-Mile Summer*. Mainly, I wanted its photograph of the first-step scene. But my description of The Walk's start helped refresh memories of the old, semi-colonial border crossing:

On the Mexican side of the customs gate, a phonograph blared music down a dusty, sun-drenched street. A man who might have been planted there by a travel agent slept on a broken adobe wall—head and shoulders eclipsed by a huge sombrero, body fitting the jagged wall like a model's in one of those fatuous mattress advertisements.

California had gone Spanish, too. The U.S. customs officer lolled on his patio in a wicker chair, and at his feet squatted a Mexican boy. The boy was a craftsman. He buffed and polished and burnished the customs officer's elegant knee boots until their radiance threatened to set the dry scrub on fire. The boy sat back at last, and the customs officer inspected his boots. He rotated them slowly, first one, then the other, like a mannequin. Finally he nodded approval and tossed down a coin. "The kid's a good polisher," he said, and you knew his day was made.

The customs officer stood up, stepped to the edge of his patio, and shook hands with me. Somehow, he managed to make that a solemn little ceremony too. "And the best of luck, all the way," he said.

I swung the 50-pound pack onto my back, walked to the customs gate, and put one foot in Mexico. Then I turned and took my first step northward along the dusty road.

Now, driving, I knew when I was still a mile short of the border that the crossing would no longer be a relaxed backwater. Already, instead of a quiet dusty road, a paved thoroughfare thronged with people, beetled with cars. Even allowing for a local New Year's Day fair . . .

I came to the border.

At the place the U.S. customs officer had lolled on the patio of his rural cabin, a parking lot. Across the road, set some distance back from the border, its replacement: a suburban-bureaucracy-style office building labeled "ANDRADE, CALIF." Outside it, plastic orange highway cones herding cars into a line that filed slowly past its impersonal glass windows.

At the border line, no laid-back, hand-operated gate. No casual wooden "TRANSITO >" sign a few feet farther on, nailed askew to a wooden post, that drew your attention to a diffident roadside adobe building. Instead, the angular Mexican customs and immigration edifice bridged the road—smaller than its U.S. counterpart, yet managing to look blockier and more cumbersome, even uglier. Across the front of the high roof—the edifice turned out to be mostly roof, shading a small kiosk—ran the legend, big and black on white: ALGODONES B.C. MEXICO.

I parked the car, penetrated the dim official interior of the U.S. building, obtained gruff and indifferent permission to proceed, went back outside.

A few paces, and I could see beyond the bridgelike Mexican structure. No jagged adobe wall mattressing a sombrero-shaded siesta. Instead, a crouching modern rabbit-hutch store: DENTISTA—DENTAL OFFICE. The road still sun-drenched—but paved, "canalized," filled with the sight and sound of traffic.

The library book now fulfilled its primary function. The 1958 photograph delighted the Mexican officials. Between us, we agreed that no man-made structure had survived the years. But two trees still stood: a leaning roadside eucalyptus, fifty yards inside Mexico, virtually unchanged; and a tamarisk, marginally visible in the old photo, that now spread in green cascading elegance over one side of the ugly edifice's roof. When we had finished comparing past with present and the fully defrosted officials had finished sharing the splendid news with each other, they assured me almost as an afterthought that no matter what their fellow functionary might have said on the phone, if I was going no farther than El Golfo then there was no way I needed a visa. We parted with mutual expressions of pleasure that in three days we'd meet again.

I went back to the car and drove about a third of a mile up the road. There, I pulled onto the right shoulder, parked. After a moment or two I got out and walked across an old bridge over a roadside canal, toward the river. Ostensibly, my target lay firmly in the present: as always, I wanted to make sure I closed the gap between the point I'd taken the raft out and the place I'd restart my southward journey.

Beyond the old bridge, no paved road, no streaming crowds. Just a dirt track winding through brush. And silence. Soon, dense undergrowth barring my path. No way I could get close enough to look across the river and see exactly where I'd taken the raft out. I went back over the canal bridge, hesitated beside the rented car—and made a halved-heart decision. Then I began to walk northward along the road.

Half my heart said I was walking northward to make sure I'd close the spatial gap. The heavier half now admitted the existence of a second target that had all along lurked among the shadows.

In *The Thousand-Mile Summer* I'd implied that at the border I waved goodbye to the friend who was driving my old Plymouth "woodie" station wagon back to San Francisco *before* I began to walk north. What had really happened seemed irrelevant to the story and cumbersome to inject in its proper place. Besides, later events had by that time made the subject painful to discuss. What had really happened was that about a third of a mile from the customs station my friend had, as arranged, pulled the woodie up alongside me, on the shoulder, and I had stopped and taken off my pack and set it down beside the deserted dirt road and we had said goodbye. And my friend was the damsel who had brought me to this place in more ways than one.

Her name was Thelma, but her initials were TIM—and "Tim" was what everyone called her. Tim and I had, as I've already told you, lived an idyllic two-year interlude of conjugated bliss in San Francisco before I decided that the way to find out whether I really wanted to marry her was to walk from Mexico to Oregon. Given these things, it's hardly surprising that our roadside *au revoir* was, for both of us, soul-wrenching. And when, afterward, all that was left of Tim was a faint cloud of dust hanging over the road, I reshouldered my pack and struck blindly away from that road. I struck away left, walking instinctively, neither knowing nor caring just why I did so nor exactly where I was going—just pounding through silent sand and brush, seeking solitude and solace. Seeking to escape the pain and desolation.

And now, walking northward from my rented car, thirty-one years later, I once again turned off the road, left. I followed my 1958 route meticulously. Followed, that is, the line I'd drawn then on the topo map now held in my hand.

The inked line skirted a small side-road circle marked "Andrade." I had no recollection, I found, of passing through such a place. No surprise there, really. Or to find that even if Andrade existed in 1958 it had now been supplanted by SLEEPY HOLLOW RV PARK. I passed beyond the parked RVs. At once, escape. Just silent, deserted scrub. I offered brief thanks that our human infestation tends to be linear and very thin.

My ink line on the map reported that I had followed a Southern Pacific Railroad embankment, and after what seemed a long trek through dry scrub I found the embankment. Again, no spark of recognition. And up on the embankment, no railroad track. I stood for a moment, asking myself whether there'd been a track in 1958. No response. I turned right, walked along beside the embankment. Soon, a gap that had been cut in the embankment. Cut long ago. A jeep track angled through it. My inked route crossed the railroad line at exactly that point, and at once I remembered that I'd chosen to pass through the gap because the going on the far side looked easier. Or was I imagining that memory? Perhaps concocting it from the superimposed present? I walked on, still retracing the marked route.

As far as I could see and remember, nothing in that dry and dusty desert backwater had undergone radical change. But no certainty in my mind. I followed the inked line onto the top of the disused railroad embankment. Still no clear, unambiguous recollections—just ghostly hints of memories that might or might not have been figments of my imagination.

I walked on, along the top of the embankment. Soon, it crossed a road. The road along which Tim had driven away. In 1958, by the time I'd reached that road—that dirt road—the pain and desolation had lessened. At least, I think so.

Now, thirty-one years later, I paused beside the paved road and looked back along the railroad embankment. Two surprises. First, I'd remembered almost nothing of the terrain; perhaps nothing at all. Second, although I'd long believed that time had healed all scars, I could once again feel, deep and quick, the pain of that day's parting—and of later events.

Those later events had left the greater scar. Far greater. The Walk's superficial consequence had been a "Yes" answer to the question that fathered it. In due course, Tim and I had married. Ludicrously short of due course, we separated. And now, standing on that paved road beside the railroad embankment, the pain of those later events for a moment overwhelmed me.

I turned away, at last, began to walk back toward the border.

The miles between Hoover and Mexico had kept throwing light on the way years wash over the past and convert it into present. Convert it in disparate ways. The passage of time might obliterate old patterns that made up the physical world. Or freeze them almost intact. Or change them, subtly or severely. Or let them metastasize. As for the patterns that built in our minds . . . well, they turned out to be much the same. Now, I heard more clearly the truth behind psychologist Elizabeth Loftus's words: "Our memories are continually being altered, transformed and distorted." And also behind Federico Fellini's when he mused on filmmaking: "We don't own our memories. They own us."

I reached my rented car, unlocked it, got in. Yes, memory was a curious cuss. I turned the ignition key. But it was time, now, to leave all that behind and step out into uncharted territory.

21

BYPASS

Mile 1611 to Mile 1676
January 4–12

T hree days later, at the new Mexican border post, under the old tamarisk tree, I took my first step south toward Campo Mosqueda—and perhaps El Golfo and the sea.

In fact you could say I took that first step three separate times.

My band of Good Samaritans from Mexicali had arrived at the motel early that morning, and from the start they made the day a fiesta. It began when we loaded the deflated raft onto their trailer and continued while we shopped in Yuma for a couple of last-minute items. Hardly sounds like fiesta material, you say? That's because you don't know my Samaritans. In particular, you don't know Anita.

Anita Williams was my original and entirely serendipitous Mexican contact. The moment I phoned her, before leaving home, she'd been enthusiastic. She had, it seemed, a real love for the river. And she got things done, too. It was she who'd finally confirmed from the Mexican bureaucracy that rafting through irrigation canals to the Rio Hardy was probably impractical. Once I'd decided to walk to Campo Mosqueda, and needed the raft ferried there, it was Anita who found a friend with the requisite van, trailer, time and generosity. And it was she who in Yuma infused our merry band with the fiesta spirit.

Now, our brief shopping trip was, on the surface, a normal, sedate affair. I don't want to suggest that we whooped it up. Nor that Anita was a sort of whirling Carmen. In her youth, maybe. But now she was a mature and subdued yet glowing presence who energized all around her: Charlie, her quiet, self-effacing Anglo husband; Alberto Gruel, the friend who contributed van, trailer and generous spirit; and Fernando, his strapping compadre who did more than a fair share of loading gear onto the trailer.

Shopping accomplished, we drove across the river to Algodones.

New officials now manned the Mexican border post, but my bilingual Samaritans quickly smoothed us past them. Alberto—a professional photographer and trip guide—took a shot that duplicated, as near as we could manage, my 1958 first-step-northward, pack-on-back photograph. Then I about-faced, paused, took my first ceremonial step south.

Because a scattering of curious passersby now stood watching, that first step was a public act with a faint theatrical overlay, and at the moment of happening it became not so much an event as a pseudo-event. The kind of counterfeit that can curdle journey into exploit.

Fortunately, I knew it was a false start. As I began to walk down the paved and canalized main street of Algodones past the leaning eucalyptus tree and then a double string of tourist shops, my Samaritan van-and-trailer pulled into an open construction site, a hundred yards ahead. By the time I joined them, the Samaritans were waiting to minister tea as a prelude to formal farewells.

There in the dusty construction site we had a final, low-key, stand-around-and-chat mini-fiesta. By now we were six. At the border, another friend of Alberto's had joined us. Alfonso Cordova was a sturdy, bearded young man who had recently spent five months making a thousand-mile walk from the southern tip of Baja California to San Diego along the old route of the *misioneros*. Although I tried to share something of his experience, we at first foundered on language and perhaps reticence. But as I finished my tea and the caffeine circulated, I found myself stretching and saying, "Jeez, it's good to be out on the road again. I feel . . . oh, I dunno, I feel . . ."

". . . free again," said Alfonso Cordova. "I know."

And our eyes met.

I reshouldered my fifty-pound pack, shook hands all around and reconfirmed yet again that, eight days ahead, the Samaritans would bring the raft to Campo Mosqueda. Then, for the second time, I took my first step southward toward it.

This time it was better. But at the start I still had the paved road and its traffic, even some Samaritans snapping last-minute mementos. That was enough, at such a moment, to disturb any dedicated solitarian. But then a side road angled off left and I turned down it and there was no more traffic. Not even pedestrians. Only quiet and sunlight.

Before long I'd walked clear of the last buildings and was out in scrubby

The start of the backpack leg, southward from the border into Mexico. For a few hundred yards, on the main street of Algodones, "I still had the paved road and its traffic. . . . But then . . ."

desert and could see the river ahead, broad and blue. Off to the right, though, it came up short, blue against gray, at the stonework of Morelos Dam. Beyond and above the dam hung blue sky and the promise of deeper silence.

I paused, put down the pack, readjusted its harness. Then I shouldered it again and, a little before noon, for the third and final and real time, took my first step toward Campo Mosqueda.

Soon, I stood beside the dam. Sure enough, it diverted the river's lifeblood westward into a broad irrigation canal. The canal struck off at a right angle, then curved south and out of sight. To my left, below the dam, almost lost in the wide sand-and-scrub riverbed, lay all that was left of the river after its bypass operation: a pathetic little waterway perhaps twenty feet across. A breeze crimpled its surface and I couldn't be sure it was as shallow as it looked, or even if it lay stagnant or still flowed feebly seaward. But there was no doubt that the patient looked close to the end of its tether.

I began to walk southward along the overgrown right bank of the old riverbed. After a mile I could still see, down in thickets, a hint of water.

Another mile, and no longer a hint. I stopped for a long lunch. Afterward, because the going was rough and the dry watercourse sad to see, I cut back across irrigated farmland to a dirt road. The road paralleled both the river and a big, swift-flowing, concreted irrigation canal. Around 4:30, at one of the canal's take-off sluices into an irrigation ditch, where it was possible to get down to the water and wash my feet, I camped.

That first afternoon set the pattern for the week. For a week that passed in an oddly featureless blur.

The pattern, once established, followed a rhythm so repetitive that it seemed to mesmerize me. Even as the days unfolded, they tended to coalesce. At any given moment the "now" was clear and present; but whenever I looked back I found that the hours and days had already begun to fuse. Individual events might remain clear, but their order had blurred. In sharp contrast to my last weeks north of the border, present and immediate past rolled along in an almost homogeneous doughball, cut off from the distant past.

The physical challenge templated this pattern. By the time I camped that first evening, my fifty-pound pack weighed seventy-five and my feet were crying out to be washed in the irrigation ditch. As the days passed, the apparent load eased somewhat, along with the real one. (The food, of course, steadily diminished; but the water—up to a gallon and a half, weighing a dozen pounds—had to be regularly replenished.) And my feet, along with the rest of me, gradually got more used to walking long hours with a load. Not that I ever walked for anything that I would once have called "long hours." But although I disliked admitting the fact, it turned out that—as I'd half-feared—it was all I could do to keep up the daily eight or nine miles, without the luxury of a rest day, that seemed necessary if I was to reach Campo Mosqueda on schedule. (The exact mileage still remained unclear: beyond a couple of excellent photo-based topos that covered the first stretch, I had to rely on a faint fax copy of a very sketchy road map.)

Now, I don't mean that I ever came close to defeat. But each morning I knew that in order to make my day's stint I'd have to pin mind and body tight to the task. So each day's routine followed the same pattern. Up early. Foot-slog, with pause for caffeine-fix, until around midday. Lunch and siesta. Relax through the heat of the day (never very hot). Then, well rested, slog on for another hour or so in the cooler evening. Even under this mild regimen, incorporating brief rests every half-hour, it was always a relief to shed the pack and set up camp.

Naturally, I attributed the physical struggle to lack of conditioning. After all, it was five months since I'd carried a load on my back. And I could hardly expect my feet to be boot-bashing-tough after months of sandals and soaking. I think I still rejected the notion that age might have anything to do with it. Dammit, I'd done well enough at the start, backpacking in the Rockies.

That first afternoon of walking resolved one unexpected issue—by leaving it fundamentally unresolved.

My unfocused intent had been to follow "the line of the river." But the husk of the old river, which on photo-based topo maps had looked intriguing, continued to be a sad, discarded place, used only by scarce wildlife and a very few human hunters, and walking beside it depressed me. Its overgrown bank made for tough going, too. In contrast, the parallel irrigation canals often had easily traveled levee-roads along their banks. And although the canals were artificial and sterile affairs they offered open space and sparkling water. So I tended to repeat the first day's pattern: following a canal rather than the dry watercourse, or striding out along a dirt road that ran south between them.

It seemed a reasonable compromise. After all, the canals were where the water now was, and in that sense they were now the river. In a broader sense, the whole country was the river's: the silt it had deposited formed the entire delta—dusty desert and plowed farmland, both. So no matter where I walked, I told myself, I was following the river. When convenience presses, it's touching how deftly we humans can rationalize.

By this time I'd also convinced myself, beyond shadow of doubt, that my decision to walk this stretch had been the right one: was the only possible decision, really, for anyone facing the question of what to do when he found that non-navigable irrigation canals bypassed the living river. As with earlier problems of schedule and vessel, once I'd made apparently successful choices there seemed to have been no reasonable alternatives.

Not until nine months later, back home, did I learn how wrong I'd been.

Out of the blue, then, came a letter from a man who had read a brief magazine mention of my journey and was interested in sharing memories of the experience—because he had made the same journey at about the same time. Details in the letter authenticated his claim.

We communicated, by mail and phone, and I learned how each of us, facing the many options our almost identical journeys presented, had been steered toward different decisions by our different backgrounds and outlooks. I also learned the answer to a question I'd posed only casually and had long ago filed away as unanswerable.

Jon Barker was a twenty-six-year-old professional rafting guide from Lewiston, Idaho. Summers, Jon worked for his father's river trip outfit or for others; winters, he freelanced, widely. One of his letters came from a winter ski job in France, another from the banks of the Zambezi. Jon had long dreamed of a length-of-Colorado trip—"I sort of felt that it just should have been done, not that I should do it so much"—and had refused several Grand Canyon rafting jobs so that the whole river would be a new experience. Because of work commitments, he'd had to complete his trip in seventy days.

Comparing notes, we agreed from the start that we were in no sense "in a competitive mode." We had, in any case, achieved slightly different things.

There was no doubt about who finished first: Jon reached the sea November 11, 1989—the day I passed Parker Dam. And he had always traveled under his own power, without a motor. But he started six miles and two thousand vertical feet below "my" source. Much of the way, he had not traveled solo. And his responses to certain problems had involved some loss of continuity.

At different times he'd used three different vessels. He backpacked upriver from Green River Lakes carrying an inflatable kayak and looking for the highest navigable point. He put in at Three Forks Park on August 25—forty days after I passed through—and kayaked down, making several early portages, to Kendall Hot Springs. There, he switched to a hard-shell kayak. And later, below Flaming Gorge Dam, to a gray 17½-foot inflatable raft. His response to the impossibility of rowing a raft down the big windswept reservoirs was a switch back to the hard-shell kayak. Because he was always kayaking when he came to the big dams, portaging around them proved relatively easy. (On the few occasions he had to deal with Bureau of Reclamation people he found them "fantastic . . . I mean it, beyond helpful.") Below the dams he'd switch back to his raft—"because I cannot whitewater kayak." Either he or a girlfriend ferried the boats between switching points in his pickup truck, which also carried backup food and supplies. This logistical leapfrogging, said Jon, tended to break the continuity of his experience. The girlfriend, Catie Casson, traveled with him in the raft for 600 miles—through most of the canyonlands—and another friend, a fellow professional boatman, shared the raft with them for 175 miles. So for all the similarities between our journeys, there were marked differences, too.

When Jon and I compared notes we decided that our paths must have crossed somewhere near Green River, Utah. And eventually we pinpointed the precise time and place.

Jon and Catie floated into the town of Green River between eleven and noon on September 19. On that day and about that time I'd been standing beside the still-empty shell of the John Wesley Powell Memorial Museum, watching the river flow, as it were, out of the museum's sidewall, when without warning there materialized from this masonry, out in midriver, a raft. A gray raft, rather bigger than mine, carrying a young man and woman. The pair had a relaxed and competent air that suggested they were at home on the river. And as I stood there wondering whether they too were making a protracted journey, the woman looked up, directly at me. I waved. She waved back. Then the raft vanished under the big road bridge. Later, at Trin-Alcove Bend, I'd wondered whether footprints near my camp might have been made by this couple, and had decided—remarkably for a solitarian—that it would be pleasant to meet them. Almost before I'd formulated the question of whether the footprints were really theirs and whether we would indeed have found we had something in common, I'd dismissed it as unanswerable.

But now, a year later, it all looked clear-cut. Everything fitted. For at least thirty miles above Green River, Utah, Jon and Catie had seen no other boats. The morning after they arrived they'd gone on downriver—two days ahead of me. And they had camped at Trin-Alcove Bend. Unfortunately, Jon and Catie have lost touch, and I've not been able to contact her and add the final neat confirmation of our near-meeting: that she remembers waving, that September noon, to a man wearing shorts and broad-brimmed hat as he stood at the edge of the John Wesley Powell Memorial Museum.

In November, Jon reached Morelos Dam with an even hazier notion of what happened to the river below it than I would have in January. Facing similar options, he made a different choice. But given his background and viewpoint—river-runner rather than backpacker—and the time pressure and available truck support, his choice made sense.

What he did was launch his hard-shell kayak below the dam. After a day of struggling through stagnant swamp water, often with the kayak rubbing along the bottom, he "finally came around a corner and it all just sank away into the sand." From that point he and Catie drove south in his pickup, stopping half a dozen times to check the dry streambed before they reached the Rio Hardy. There they relaunched the kayak at a fishing camp, probably about a mile below Campo Mosqueda.

In other words, Jon had at all stages of his planning and execution faced options much the same as mine but had made very different choices. And the differences belatedly opened my eyes to the falsity of the hidden assumption I'd made, there below Morelos Dam: that not only the decision to walk but also all the journey choices I'd made appeared to be the only reasonable alternatives.

Making such assumptions is a hideously human trait. When we look back at the way something has unfolded we tend to assume that events were more or less preordained to unfold the way we know they did. The level of entity makes little difference. The unfolding can be of a journey or river, or the life of an individual or community or nation or civilization or species. Or the life-web of a planet. Some otherwise acute people still regard *Homo sapiens* as the inevitable climax of unfolding evolution—a preordained summit, its glorious crown still obscured by swirling Wagnerian clouds. But alter a couple of minor gene mutations or chance extinctions or climatic swings—or effect a slight deflection in the path of a big meteor that dropped, or did not drop, among the dinosaurs—and things could have turned out very differently. Cast the die again and you'd probably not produce anything even remotely like *Homo sapiens*. In other words, evolution, at any level, is not a matter of steady forward progress toward a goal but a cauldron of events and potentials emitting thunder and unpredictable lightning bolts—a steaming brew that grows steadily more complex as it lurches along toward God knows what.

I knew all this when I made my week's walk below Morelos Dam. But learning about Jon Barker's journey, nine months later, clarified my thoughts. A salutary process, handy for deflating hubris.

After that first canalside camp below Morelos I sometimes rolled out my sleeping pad and bag in farmland, but as the week wore on I more often chose the old watercourse. Mile after mile, impenetrable vegetation would block access to the sunken riverbed; then I'd find a clearing on its flank, or even down in its bed, that would let the first morning sunlight warm my camp. (Dawn ground temperatures sometimes fell as low as 16 degrees Fahrenheit.) Once or twice, as the week wore on, I even found clearings furnished with pools of water in which I could wash my feet.

In the old riverbed I had privacy. And less dust than out in the farmland. Close up, the husk of the river somehow did not depress me the way it still did when I looked out over its wasteland expanse of scrub and sand, and the little world around my camps in the carefully selected clearings had a good, clean feeling. They were natural, in their deprived way: free from straight lines, rich in harmony of form. At one early camp I scribbled in my notebook, "Something rather pleasingly restful about this lost riverbed. Not really sad, as I'd expected. But please don't ask me what I mean by either of those statements."

Among the blurred-together string of days that unreeled during that week's walking below Morelos, my nightcamps formed the best markers. When I looked back and tried to identify a certain day I'd say to myself, "Oh, yes, that was the afternoon I camped on the edge of a plowed field,

beside a small irrigation ditch, and a farmhand who was clearing weed out
of the ditch and checking the sluice-gate at its head asked me for a ciga-
rette, which I didn't have, and where after dark I lay listening to the water
pouring through the sluice gate, out of the canal into the ditch, and realized
it was weeks since a nightcamp had provided the sound of plunging water—and then found myself struggling to believe that somewhere in that
little irrigation ditch cavorted at least one molecule from 'my' source." Or
perhaps I'd say, "Yes, that was the evening I camped in the old riverbed beside an elongated puddle, and some time during the night heard the drumming of animal feet, scared, and almost at once there were coyotes
yowling and wailing and barking so close that although I was barely half
awake I could detect nuances of feeling (notably distrust of the intruder)
that I'd never been able to detect at a distance—and soon after sunrise
a herd of domestic goats shambled down through the tamarisks to the
puddle."

The other highlight events of that week tended to be isolated cameos
that I could remember clearly enough but could not assign a time slot.
Mostly, they featured people. And most of them took place when I stopped
to ask for drinking water.

Because neither canals nor the rare river pools seemed safe sources, I
kept stopping at ranches or other buildings—bypassing my lack of Spanish with canteen sign language. As the week wore on and the ranches became less frequent I jury-rigged from my residual schoolboy Latin and
French, through trial and error, the vital question, "Altro rancho—quantos
kilometer?"

After a few days, the people-cameos at watering places tended to merge
one into the other. A few stuck in memory, though. The nubile damsel, stir-
ringly beautiful and with a knowing eye but surrounded by family. The elderly man who spoke fair English and who listened to the story of what I
was doing with apparent gravity and appreciation but who, as I walked
away, began telling his cluster of womenfolk about this traveler in a
"*panga*" (or boat) who had come all the way from "Wyoming"—and told
it with such obvious merriment that the whole group dissolved into cack-
les of laughter.

Not all the cameos came at watering places. Once, a slightly sodden
group of men seated outside what I assumed was a *taverno* invited me, in
friendly pantomime, to sit down and drink beer with them, and I had to
refuse—partly because we could not share a verbal drop but mainly because I knew even one beer would drown my resolve to complete the day's
mileage quota. Another morning, as I walked along a bleak levee-road be-

side a canal, a boy of perhaps ten accompanied me on his bicycle for twenty minutes while he tried to improve his English and I my Spanish, and although neither of us made much linguistic headway the interlude made, I think, a pleasant break in both our lives.

Nonpeople highlights were rare. A dry overgrown ditch, six feet deep and a dozen feet wide, provided the most memorable. It was late afternoon. I'd left my pack tucked in under a levee and beaten a way through tules that choked the ditch, then made a longish sidetrip to a ranch for drinking water. When I came to the ditch on the way back I remembered that the first time, as I brushed through the thick growth, I'd knocked a cloud of seeds onto my head and shoulders. To avert a reprise, I reached out with my walking staff and hit the stalks ahead of me. At once the air was filled, miraculously, with delicate white thistledown. Each thistle head—or whatever the seeds were—hung white and aery, backlit by the afternoon sun. Haloed. And the entire suspended troupe moved in unison before a barely palpable breeze—floating one way, eddying back, hovering, then wafting forward again. I stood still, there in the dry and dusty ditch with the full canteens in my hand, watching the solemn yet festive seed ballet and remembering two moments in my life—in the Deep South, then in East Africa—when dancing fireflies had also suspended time and held me spellbound for long and magical moments.

As the week wound down I became aware that both the country and its arteries were undergoing slow, almost imperceptible changes that in the end begat transformation.

For many miles south of the border, the old watercourse off to my left had remained essentially dry. Its bypassed lifeblood flowed through broad, concrete-lined irrigation canals, and water drawn from these canals nurtured well-tended arable fields, plowed so that they utilized every corner of land. Dirt roads snaking through this farmland supported occasional hamlets: strings of small and often ramshackle houses. Many of these humble homes had rich little gardens, and were beautiful in their way. They looked satisfying places to live, even though they might not offer "all the comforts" and would be routinely dismissed as poverty-stricken by people enmeshed in the industrialized world's consumer treadmill.

By the fifth or sixth day, balances had shifted. The broad concrete-lined irrigation canals had become narrow concrete-lined irrigation canals and they in turn had softened into even narrower green-fringed ditches. The arable fields that their water sustained were now less meticulously tended, less stewardly of space. Soon, swaths of desert scrub began to separate them. Now there were no more hamlets, and the ranches stood farther apart, looked less prosperous. And as man's grip eased, so the moribund watercourse began to revive. Occasional small puddles became occasional ponds in deep natural holes. Became frequent and bigger ponds. And just before my seventh camp below the border—half a dozen miles from Campo Mosqueda, with the mountains beyond it no longer a faint and colorless line along the distant horizon but an imminent presence folding rich and blue-gray beneath the sinking sun—as I walked along a levee road with the old watercourse at my left hand, there was a big outlet pipe beside the road and through it a steady stream of water gushed back into the riverbed. Below that point, the river began to breathe again.

When I camped for that seventh time south of the border I became aware of another transformation.

Dense vegetation choked the riverbed and blocked access to the water that probably now ran, or at least trickled, somewhere below, and I chose a campsite on a flat and open place at its edge. As I slipped off my pack, a mosquito investigated me. It was only the second of the week. For a moment I wondered about Campo Mosqueda—then remembered Anita had told me the camp got its name from summer infestations; in January there'd be no problem. After I'd set up camp and was sitting down and leaning against my pack I realized that the air felt much warmer than had been normal just before sunset. That lunchtime I'd had a comprehensive wash at an accessible pool, but now I felt hot and sweaty, and I stripped off and sat naked in the last of the sun's rays. I sat there for long and luxurious minutes, letting the air clean and cool me. Then the sun slid behind the mountains and I slipped into some clothes. But the air still felt warm. Almost balmy. And no longer desert dry. That day, I'd moved a quantum walk closer to the sea.

Next morning, as I strode on toward Campo Mosqueda along a levee road raised high above surrounding land, I watched the resurrection of river and countryside gain momentum. Soon, to my left, in the old watercourse, a steady if tentative channel of water. To my right, no more farmland. Instead, more and more frequent waterways winding intermittently through tall green vegetation so dense that often you couldn't see where water gave way to land.

By the time the road swung westward, away from the old riverbed, on the last leg into Campo Mosqueda, I knew I was going to make it. On schedule, too. I relaxed, let my mind wander.

It roamed south, into the mirage-land of the delta.

That I knew anything at all about what lay ahead was almost entirely due to one man. Steve Nelson had during the mid-1980s been an Outdoor

Recreation Officer with a Bureau of Land Management unit in the Southern California desert. While there he discovered the largely uncharted
lower Colorado—uncharted, that is, since floods in 1983 had spun the
river on a radically new course—and for three years had spent as many
free days as possible in kayak-and-foot-explorations of the lower delta.
Early in my planning I was lucky enough to get in touch with him, and although he now lived in Washington State he had by phone and mail poured
out for me without stint the rich results of his delta research. He'd put me
in touch with others who might help—most notably, with Anita Williams.
His knowledge, more than any other element, had guided me in choosing
between the four travel options below Morelos Dam. A map he provided
was the one I'd been depending on for the last half of the walk to Campo
Mosqueda. And he'd never stopped contributing. In Yuma I'd found waiting for me a series of meticulously marked maps that proved invaluable
and a long letter rich in last-minute thoughts—including the suggestion I
buy a toilet brush for scrubbing off the thick delta mud I was sure to bring
back aboard the raft every time I went ashore.

During his delta travels Steve had become fascinated with the river's ongoing evolution, and his maps showed the new main channel and the principal dead-end backwater channels. Something more, too. The river's new
channel was actually its former channel, abandoned since major floods in
1950. For thirty-three years the old riverbed, receiving little or no river water—water that, at best, petered out short of the sea—had slowly silted up
with soft mud. Since '83, when the river resumed its old course, the renewed river current had been scouring out that recently deposited mud,
and Steve said that once I got down into the "cut channel" I should have a
clear run to the sea. Should have. Hazards still lurked, though. Notably,
tidal bores. The bores—particularly in the half-dozen miles upriver of
Punta Invencible, where the estuary narrowed sharply into river—could be
five- or six-foot walls of water traveling at twelve miles an hour. But they
occurred only a day or two each side of spring tides. At neap tides, no danger. In Yuma I'd checked tide tables and found that if I took it easy beyond
Campo Mosqueda I should hit the danger area during the neap.

There was one other potential problem. For three years, Steve had
watched the renewed current progressively clear the sediment upriver for
some twenty miles, and his maps showed the limit of "cutback" at various
dates. The "point of backcutting," he wrote me, "is often a series of
rapids." A Steve-connected informant told me on the phone that they could
be "falls with maybe twenty- or thirty-foot vertical drop-offs"; one hunting party, he maintained, had gone downriver in heavy boats before dawn,

and without warning had shot out into open air, been thrown clear and nearly drowned. Steve called this "good storytelling." But at times, he said, rapids existed. And his maps showed that in late 1987, when he made his last observation, the cutback point had been only a mile or so below The Bend—a dramatic double-bend in the river near Yurimuri, a fishing camp that was the last human riverside habitation.

Steve saw The Bend itself as the biggest obstacle. There, he said, the river became so shallow that even a raft might not be able to get through. Much depended on river flow and tidal backup—and whatever changes there'd been since his last visit. I should be able to get up-to-date information at Yurimuri: the camp custodian there, known as "The Captain," was a good man. If necessary I might be able to portage over a couple of hundred yards of semi-dry land, across the neck of The Bend . . .

Far ahead down the long straight levee road, a cluster of roofs. Campo Mosqueda. Legs and feet approved. I slogged on, letting my mind wander again. . . .

I couldn't honestly say I'd enjoyed the week's backpacking. Not much, anyway. Still, I was glad I'd done it. And just as I'd hoped, there was a good feel to the way it counter-balanced, here near journey's end, in satisfying symmetry, the week of walking at the journey's birth.

It was early afternoon when I walked into Campo Mosqueda. Into the tropics.

The last mile down the levee road had been sweaty work, and I was glad to slide the pack off my back. After a few minutes an elderly man ambled up, accompanied by two elderly, ambling dogs. None spoke much English, but I gathered that the man was the camp custodian, and that, yes, it would be fine if I used a pair of wooden picnic tables that stood under a pole-supported reed-thatched roof.

I moved my pack into the shade of this shantylike structure that looked as if it might have been imported intact from a South Sea Island beach, sat down on one of the tables' bench-seats, leaned back.

Before me lay a waterway perhaps sixty feet wide. A calm, unmoving, canal-lake-backwater that I had for the moment to accept as the Rio Hardy, as my river. One end of its blue mirror fitted into a stonework flank of the levee road's extension. On the far side of the road a big, scruffy, forsaken-looking pump house stood silent. The air felt softly moist. There was no wind.

Near the far bank of the slumbering backwater a great blue heron stood sentry duty. A few somnolescent coots paddled about in slow motion. And the water was blue and deep. After the week's bypass, it felt good to be back. The river might still languish in a weakened state but it had survived the operation.

(Five months later I understood much more about bypass operations. Knew how at first they leave you feeling as if you've been hit by a Mack truck—or if you're a river, a Mexican irrigation system. But also how, if all goes well, you can within a remarkably short span be back playing in tennis tournaments or backpacking—or flowing serenely on toward reunion with the sea.

And five months later I regarded the arterial blockage that led to my coronary bypass as a reasonable explanation for the way I had during the weeklong walk down to Campo Mosqueda struggled to put in eight or nine miles a day. Also for the way I'd failed to climb Point 1180, above the Devil's Elbow. This explanation, my doctor said, was medically unprovable, but tenable. Comforting, too.)

Westward, beyond the river, the mountains rose close and steep, brown and desiccated. Desert mountains, quivering in the sun. Southward, their peaks tapered endlessly away into the distance, into the delta, into the unknown, like stepping-stones to nowhere.

For a decent, dozy interval I sat at peace in my wall-free shanty shade. Then I took the canteens from my pack and walked on down the levee road to a group of small houses. Outside one sat a white-haired Anglo. He was amiable, helpful. When we'd filled my canteens, I asked my burning question.

"No, afraid I can't help you there. Not anymore. I been hunting this delta for twenty years, and I figured I knew it inside out. But since the floods of '83 I get lost down there. Get lost every time. So I don't go anymore. Same with my wife. I could go ask her—she lives two houses down—but she wouldn't know, either. At a guess, I'd say, yes, you'll probably get around The Bend. But don't take my word for it."

Next morning the Good Samaritans arrived on schedule.

Our working mini-fiesta occupied most of the day.

The raft had to be inflated and rerigged. Stores repacked and loaded. The outboard installed and checked. (As usual, I didn't intend to use it in the flowing river. But I knew I might need it lower down, where incoming tides and wind could combine to make rowing impossible; certainly on the last lap to El Golfo, out in the ocean; perhaps even earlier if I found the way blocked and had to backtrack.) By the time we had the raft loaded and its picky owner satisfied with every damned detail, the sun had swung down almost to the crest of the western mountains.

The departure from Campo Mosqueda. Afloat
again, I ham it up for my Good Samaritans.

We shook hands all around. I climbed aboard, pushed off. Anita took last-minute photographs; I brandished the Steve Nelson toilet brush and proclaimed, "Onward!" Anita put her camera away. I stopped hamming it up, spun the raft around and began to row southward on the last leg of my journey, toward Yurimuri and The Bend, and perhaps El Golfo and the sea.

22

REUNION

Around its first bend, the backwater on which I had relaunched raft and journey soon merged with a broader waterway and together they flowed gently seaward. Behind slanting sunlight, the mountains rose close and steep and gray-blue. I rowed toward them.

The river continued to gain strength. Several small feeders augmented it. Some ran turbid with agricultural runoff, and the water out beyond the bulging blue raft margins grew murky. I rowed on, taking my time. Dawdling down the dozen miles to Yurimuri and The Bend reduced the risk of meeting a tidal bore later on. At least, I think that's what I told myself. But it felt good to be back in the raft-world, and although a certain sickroom melancholy still hung in the air, I wanted to savor everything the convalescing river had to offer.

The patient's pulse, even after more transfusions, remained weak and sluggish. The river grew wider but its depth and flow remained uncertain. For a long stretch I could detect no current. Then a primitive Indian fish weir spanned the river and its protruding stakes incised faint downstream V's in the water's surface.

Before long I camped, river right, at the edge of an abandoned gringo fishing camp.

Next morning I drifted on down in bright sunshine. Big birds—pelicans, herons and others—floated and glided by. For half a mile the river hugged the foot of the mountains and their stark black folds injected life into the landscape. Then we swung back into flatland and I could no longer deny that a forlorn air hung heavy over both land and river. A sense of abandonment.

The river attempted to resist. At first it remained canal-like. Sluggish, artificial, dull. And grayly morose. Then for a brief spell it sprang to life.

Abruptly, at a cut through an old earth dam—about the place the map said the Colorado riverbed merged with the Rio Hardy—the channel narrowed to barely fifty feet across. The current quickened. For a couple of hundred yards, as we careened through swirls and eddies, I had to steer with care—and noted how, even with the outboard tilted clear of the water, its weight on the protruding stanchion made the raft respond sluggishly. No longer a Water Strider.

Soon we were once more floating down a broad and lazy river. On my Mexican map, its name switched back from Rio Hardy to Rio Colorado. In reality, no change. Still more canal than river. Still sluggish and artificial. Still forlorn, abandoned, sad.

But the pervading melancholy lay even more heavily on the land.

Now only the riverbanks were visible. The left bank was all bare mud or natural vegetation: brush, reeds, tamarisks, an occasional tree. But along the right bank clustered man-made structures. Sporadic strings of trailers, cabins, houses: gringo fishing-and-hunting camps. Some two-eyes-on-economy scruffy. Some with pretensions.

All the camps had been largely or wholly abandoned. One or two showed signs of recent care, even habitation. But the general impression: human retreat. Adobe walls cracking, tilting. Plots being colonized by tamarisk. And many structures jilted in mid-construction. The floods of '83, I'd been told, had so changed the river and its wildlife that few Americans now found it worthwhile to build vacation homes or even maintain existing ones. The whole string of riverside communities had died, or was dying, as surely as if condemned by a new dam. But more slowly, more painfully.

Still signs of human life, though.

Now, remote, sick places tend to harbor individuals who run to extremes. Taciturn souls, for example, and turbo-motormouths.

A swarthy young Mexican, intent on laying out the duck decoys piled in his red canoe, paddled past. He gave me a cursory nod. At least, I think it was a nod.

On a landing stage in front of one of the more inhabited-looking houses sat an Anglo woman. Even from a distance she exuded loneliness.

As I rowed within range, her voice floated across the calm water. "Why, hello! We don't see many folks down this way. . . . My husband and I have just retired here . . . permanently, you know . . . just us and our dogs . . . so

it's quiet, I can tell you . . . the dogs don't bark, even . . . they're African
. . . oh, what's the name? . . . you know—wrinkled foreheads . . . never
bark . . ."

By now we were only a few yards apart.

". . . When we came here there was no electricity in our house, so I paid
this guy fifty bucks to run it in because I had to keep going out to the trailer
. . . and . . . What's your name?"

I floated past.

"Really? My name used to be Collins . . . but now it's Hill . . . Esquiline
Hill . . . Have you ever heard a name like that? . . ."

An upstream breeze scattered a covey of words. Then . . .

". . . we've got dead bolts on the house now, but when we came there
were only key locks, and I had this guy come and put dead bolts in, so
now . . ."

I pulled out of range.

Birds buttressed the general mood of abandonment. Once, a great blue
heron sat solemn sentinel on the crumbling adobe wall of a half-built
house. A flock of white pelicans preened themselves along cracked and
tilting stone steps. Dense white streaks on the stonework proclaimed their
squatters' rights.

Most local birds seemed singularly unfearful of human presence. As I
drifted downstream toward a floating brown pelican—a seabird rarely seen
inland—it posed, unmoving, in the morning sunlight. We moved closer.
Up binoculars. Details jumped out, and for the first time I grasped the
complexity behind the words "brown pelican." Some plumage black. But
mostly gray, flecked with white. And the huge fleshy bill sack, green. But
the showpiece was the long upper bill: pink shading to red, then blossom-
ing into scarlet; its tip a sudden, jabbing yellow, bordered black. We
moved even closer. The bird's one visible eye, big and blue, watched me.
We had recently driven his species close to extinction, I remembered, with
our human DDT. Soon, only a few feet between us. Down binoculars.
Well, a few yards. But still closing. Now, maybe a dozen feet. Then, as I
passed, the pelican put his head back, opened his massive bill, let the huge,
loose bill sack hang clear—and held that startling pose long enough for me
to glimpse the tiny tongue, pale and vibrating, far back in the gaping cavern. At least, I think it was the tongue. Just for a moment, I wondered if the
whole memorable performance had been intended to daunt me. I rowed
on. In Hitchcockian mood you might see the birds as taking over this de-
caying place—with grim and sardonic glee at the fall of their erstwhile
masters.

But the new lords of the local animal farm remained vulnerable to life's old uncertainties. On the riverbed, barely covered by shallow water, the body of a large bird, probably a cormorant. A layer of pale dust, or perhaps fungus, coating the partly decomposed carcass. I held the raft above it. The still-murky water had cleared somewhat, and I could just make out, clamped around the bird's neck, remnants of the gill net that had strangled it. Soon, a brown pelican corpse stretched out on bare mud. I pulled alongside. No indication of foul play. But the bird's vivid and complex color patterns already fading toward extinction. The one visible eye glazed, vacant, unseeing.

It was late afternoon when I pulled in for the night, a couple of miles short of Yurimuri, at a fishing camp the map called Los Amigos. But los amigos had split. And time and dust had laid a pall over their deserted village—over their patioed cabins and over their trailers with wheels sunk hubcap-deep in sand. The door of one silvery trailer hung brown and open from its upper hinge, tilted despondently. Beside my camp, a brick structure of some pretension and considerable ugliness stood half-complete, long forsaken, fading fast. Its unglazed windows and gaping doorways were empty sockets. Even delicate pink sunlight could not veil their vacant stare.

Next morning I slept late. Soon, heavy cloudbanks began to squat along the mountaintops. But still no hint of any monkey whispering on my shoulder, and it was past noon when I rowed down the final stretch to Yurimuri. By then the clouds blanketed the sky and a gusty upriver wind was blustering the river's gray surface into hammered, dull-yet-glinting pewter.

Halfway down the string of deserted riverside cabins that Steve Nelson's map labeled "Yurimuri" and the official map called "San Miguel (El Capitán)," a flicker of movement. I pulled in, walked up to the suspect cabin. Sure enough, two gringos, my age, grumpier.

Yes, they admitted, the custodian was known as "The Captain."

Could they tell me where he lived?

"Third house, that-a-way. Can't miss it. Lotsa kids outside."

The Captain turned out to be a solid Mexican citizen equipped with flimsy English. I confirmed that there were no phones at Yurimuri, but we failed to make much progress down either of my question lines: Could I get through the shallows at The Bend? And could I get a message out by some means to John and Victoria Sexton, who were planning to come and meet me wherever the journey ended, and therefore needed to know where that would be?

The Captain proposed an answer to our language problem. He nodded over my shoulder. "Two hunter guys speak Spanish. Will translate."

We walked back the way I'd come. It was difficult to say whether the gringo pair or I was less happy to find ourselves meeting again.

The translation moved slowly, erratically. One roadblock: a discrepancy in interpretations of "the main river." The hunters regarded The Bend as a backwater. Yes, they'd heard the "thirty-foot vertical drop" boat accident story but had drawn no tidewater conclusions. To them, the main river was a waterway that still flowed south, then swung west to dead-end in the Laguna Salada. When I reiterated that a man who clearly knew what he was talking about had said I should be able to get through the shallows at the head of The Bend, particularly when the water was backed up at high tide, the older hunter snorted. "Listen, I been coming here since 1958, and I tell you, you won't get around that bend. As for high tide . . . I tell you there's no tidal water within thirty miles of here, let alone just around that bend. A good thirty miles. No, take my word for it, there's no way you'll get around that bend."

When the Captain finally retreated, he left me with two vague and unconfirmed impressions: He thought I should be able to get through the shallows; and a portage to below the tidal cutback did not, for some reason, seem possible.

By this time the hunters were thawing. They'd apparently arrived only just before I landed, after a bad day's travel, and had begun to recognize their own grumpiness. One of them said to his partner, "Let's go out and get us some ducks. Once you've killed something, you'll feel better." But rain was now falling, and they made no move.

Would it be all right for me to camp in a half-completed cabin near theirs?

"Sure. Old Joe wouldn't mind. He'd just got the roof on when the floods came, and he never did finish it."

I moved into Joe's place.

After dark, by lamplight, I pored over Steve Nelson's maps and written advice, then studied tide tables. On paper, it all looked very simple. But Steve understood the confusion that reality imposes. Talking to him on the phone in Yuma, I'd quoted Philip Fradkin's assessment: "Down there in the delta, everything's a mirage. Physically and emotionally. Nothing's what it seems to be." "Yes," Steve had said. "That's right." Even over the phone, I could hear his smile.

Before going to bed I went out to check the raft.

The rain had stopped and the air smelled fresh. I ran my flashlight over the tether ropes. Everything shipshape.

Beyond the raft, blackness curtained the river. I peered into it, picturing the reeds that I knew lined the far bank. The answers to my questions remained hidden by that veil of blackness; lay a mile or so beyond the reeds, where the river, after looping back on itself, swung south again, around The Bend. At least, I hoped it did.

The day dawned cloudless, cleansed. By nine o'clock I'd floated down to the point at which the river, after swinging eastward, angled abruptly north and began its looping two-mile backtrack to The Bend.

I shipped oars.

For several miles above Yurimuri the river had been reviving; had moved closer to being once more whole and healthy. But now its flow had slackened. Mudbar-shallows began. Then the river forked, and I faced choices.

The map was no help at all. But Steve Nelson had said that where the shallows began the river "split into several channels," and that he'd "always had the best luck keeping right." I could see only two channels, and the leftmost looked both wider and faster-flowing. After considerable deliberation, but with no great conviction, I eased into it, pushing on the oars rather than pulling, so that I could see what lay ahead.

From the start I liked what I saw. The channel clear and well defined, perhaps two hundred feet across. Its current, if anything, gaining speed. But there was more. The breeze had died, the water stretched away mirrorlike and the sun beat warm on my skin. I stopped rowing. The current carried us forward into the silence.

In a vague, unfocused way, I think I'd expected a tense, nose-to-grindstone morning. After all, I was facing what promised to be the journey's last major physical challenge, its last big question mark. But now, floating serenely down this clear and mirrorlike channel in sunlit silence, I felt as if I were on holiday, making subdued whoopee. Consciously and gratefully, I disengaged my nose from its grindstone.

Before long the channel swung almost due west and we were heading back toward the brown desert mountains. Another Indian fish weir spanned the river—a rough affair of protruding stakes with no pouch net filling the gap at its center, the way I'd seen one above Yurimuri. There was just room for the raft to pass through the gap where the net would fit. Nearby, small fish rose. Off to our right, black-necked stilts stalked the shallows. An osprey cruised by.

We eased on toward The Bend.

Then the mountains had skewed off to the left and the sun and its shadows had shifted, and I knew we'd swung right and were northering into the shallows' last leg. Ahead, busy as coots, a flock of coots. Once, back among the reeds, a great blue heron taking a long and distrustful gander at me and mine. It hesitated, departed. But still, surrounding us all, only blue-mirror water and the green double line of reeds, sometimes backed by darker hints. Away to the left, the brown mountains. And hanging over everything—lighting and lightening—a wide blue sky.

The water shallowed. Delicate route-picking now. Twice I scraped bottom, gently. But we glided on. Such scrapings didn't really count: both happened because my attention had wandered to birdlife living it up along bankside shallows. Watching the birds, I noticed how the reed beds encroached on the water, concealing any dry-land bank there might be. It occurred to me that the reeds looked perfect for restraining the raft while I drank mid-morning tea. They were.

Afterward, as I moved on again in mid-channel, the water abruptly muddied. Suspended silt now concealed the water's depth. I investigated. Here, away from the reeds, no vegetation grew, and the bare-mud river bottom was so soft and so remarkably shallow—as I discovered when the oars kept grabbing it—that the gentle current continually lifted its top layer and held the granules in thick-soup suspension.

A glance at my watch. Pushing eleven. Difficult to believe that almost two hours had passed since I'd made my choice of channels. Or that I'd holidayed so successfully that we'd traveled barely two miles.

Still slowly, I eased us on through the shallows. At the very shallowest part, another Indian fish weir spanned the channel. This time I could see not just the tips of its converging lines of stakes but the whole six or seven feet of the small, branching trees that had been cut and impaled in the mud. Beyond this weir the water began to quicken again, to run deeper and clearer. Mountains and sun and shadows rotated once more, and I knew we were turning into the final lap.

Along each bank, a thin strip of bare wet mud now glistened. Mud so wet it must very recently have been covered with water. Mud that therefore spelled "tides." Soon, sun and shadows signaled that we were swinging southward. I began to let my mind fondle the idea that perhaps we'd made it.

The right-bank greenery had now switched from reeds to tamarisks. Dense tamarisks, growing on solid soil. Perhaps even on an old levee. In that flat, restricted world it was difficult to be sure. Difficult to be sure of anything.

The current ratcheted up another notch. Now every midriver snag cut a sharp V in its downstream water. The snags grew more frequent. Small sandbars surfaced.

Then the river was gathering itself for something.

And then it was accelerating and had swung so far south that I was looking directly into the sun, and the light was reflecting off water and wet mud—was reflecting so brightly and blindingly that I could see only that we were approaching yet another fish weir and that beyond it something was different. Then, abruptly, we hit a submerged sandbar. Snagged on it. Were held. But no damage done. No real problem. And the pause let me snatch a look at the whole vivid and splendid scene that lay ahead—a dancing, floodlit, hammered-silver world of water and glittering mud—and allowed me to discern, despite the bouncing glare and rush of information, that the river raced safely through the fish weir with no horrendous drop, and that beyond it lay the remains of another weir and that this second weir, and perhaps a third, reached across open mudflats with only a narrow channel winding down their center.

Then we were off the sandbar and picking up speed and I was peering into the scintillating radiance and lining us up for the gap in the first fish weir and the air was rich with the sound of water—not white water, quite, but rushing water that was alive, alive, alive—and we were gliding dead center through the gap in the weir with inches to spare on each side and the bow had tilted and we were sliding down the sloping tongue of smooth water and I knew we'd made that part all right and that now I could look ahead again into the shimmering reflected light and see that the suddenly narrow channel—ridiculously narrow after the wide waterway above the weir—seemed to split into two branches; but almost at the moment I began to grapple with the question of which branch to take I knew there was no way I could make a decision in time—and we were scudding down the right branch into a new world.

The new world was all water and mud and light.

The water raced down a narrow channel. The mud spread wide on both sides of it. The light filled them both, filled everything.

The mud—flat or very gently sloping—lay only a few inches higher than the water, and out at its far limits stretched dark green bands of vegetation. At least, I can't honestly say I remember seeing them, but I know they must have been there. And far to the south, where mud and river tapered away to infinity, there must have been a line of desert mountains. But I'm not sure I saw them yet, either, for they lay outside the reflected light, and it was the light that transmuted the mundane water and mud. I know this was so because when I looked back up toward the fish weirs the scene was earthbound, dull. Then I turned back and looked ahead into the light and the world once more shimmered.

I floated down into it.

At first the channel was so narrow that I barely had room to get both oars in the water at once. So narrow that I thought, "Can this really be the

*Below the last fish weir, into tidal waters: mudflats and
a new world, "all water and mud and light." The channel
was "so narrow that I thought, 'Can this really be the
mighty Colorado, flowing out to sea?'"*

mighty Colorado, flowing out to sea?" But before long the current slowed
and the channel widened and I could halfway ignore navigation and just
drift on down and examine this new world that surrounded me.

The mudflats still lay a few inches below my eye level and I could look
out across their gloriously smooth and gleaming surfaces that stretched
back forty or fifty yards to wedges of thick tamarisk. I acknowledged the
tamarisks, now. When I looked ahead down the sparkling channel I could
also see and openly acknowledge the distant desert mountains.

Nearby detail began to register.

At water's edge, a sloping mudflat gleamed green. I pulled alongside.
Algae. Green, seminal algae. I drifted on down. Ahead, one great blue
heron chased another away from the river. From where I sat watching them
long-leg it out across the radiant mud in competing yet conjugal tandem,
they looked elegant, symbolic. And as I drifted on, sitting enthroned in my
bulging blue enclave at the moving center of this bright new world, I found
myself marveling at the persistence and pugnacity and labyrinthine pulsa-
tions of the phenomenon we call life—our anti-entropic blip within an entropic world. Found myself marveling at the way its early and simple

forms are always waiting, given a sliver of a chance, to grab new footholds by creating—apparently from nothing but water and mud and light, in such unpromising and seemingly hostile places as primeval ooze—green patches of basic life-stuff that encompass within themselves the seeds of much more complex lifeforms. Found myself marveling at the way the descendants of such basic stuff, down one bloodline, may at that same moment of apparent creation be defending their temporary territories on those same mudflats. Marveling at the way another descendant, down another bloodline that has drifted toward at least a modicum of self-awareness, may by chance be floating past at that moment in a bulging blue enclave on the last lap of a long and unnecessary and maybe crazy journey, and be made aware—under the influence of the same water and mud and light, and the presence of the two fellow lifeforms—that his journey had just vaulted into one of those rare but soaring intervals that can, thank god, illuminate for the long blink of a magical eye almost any journey, any life.

The high didn't last, of course. You can't hold long at apogee. But I did not foresee that within a couple of hours the monkey would clamber up onto my shoulder at last and whisper, "Go home!"

You could probably attribute the mood swing, in part, to backwash from the sense of achievement that had helped build my elation. Now, all that lay between me and the sea—assuming no tidal bores—were fifty-odd miles of sluggish river. And with the journey's last major challenge overcome, a letdown may have been inevitable. But what weighed more heavily, I think, was yet another transformation in the riverscape. A change that began slowly but became a metamorphosis.

By degrees, the channel widened. The broad mudflats vanished. Soon, steep banks sloped up to tangled vegetation, high above my line of sight. The magic light had long since faded, died.

I rowed on down the now sluggish, muddy, mundanely canal-like waterway. Once, downstream, a small flock of Canada geese took off. Two parallel rusty hawsers, mostly buried deep under the mud but tide-excavated for a few feet at the river's edge, confirmed the improbable map report of an old ferry site. Otherwise, just a dull and muddy canal.

Now, delta country fascinates some people. Steve Nelson for one. Anita Williams for another. My mind acknowledges delta-land subtleties and accepts the richness of natural life at this edge where land meets ocean, but even when I can see for mile after open mile my spirit tends to be flattened by the flatness. And now, imprisoned in a sunken canal, my eye came up short at the muddy banks.

In mid-afternoon the tide turned. Rowing became useless. I suppose I could have tried to find a campsite somewhere along the inhospitable shore and waited for the morning's outgoing tide, but I don't think I seriously considered doing so. The monkey was there on my shoulder now, whispering.

I started the outboard.

That made a difference, even beyond the loss of silence. It was a truly monotonous business, now, plugging on down the canal with few physical demands and no tricky navigation to engage me. The banks grew higher, even duller. Once, river left, a great blue heron stalked its shallows. My mind drifted.

Back at the source, if you'd asked me which animal would in the next six months be my most constant river companion, I would certainly not have said, "Great blue heron." But there was no doubt the herons had it. Earlier, there'd been competition. But weeks had now passed since I'd seen a beaver. Coyote had persisted—but he'd never done much more than lurk in the wings.

The six months had generated other unanticipated constants—minor in themselves yet fundamental to my journey. The way the raft's bulging blue tube had marked the boundaries of my moving world. Most days, when wind and water permitted, the surprisingly pleasing interlude after pushing out into the river when I washed the raft and did other necessary chores as prelude to serious rowing. Lunch-napping on the bank with my life jacket as pillow. The old gray thermos flask, refilled with boiling water at breakfast, always waiting near my feet at one end of the rubber-covered crossboard, ready to bring a tea bag and me to life.

My mind drifted on, selecting at apparent random from the past months little incidents that should not have been important and probably weren't but that came popping up anyway. A memory grab bag of the kind any long journey generates.

A canyon-country nightcamp with a nearby girder bridge—the one Hayduke and his friends had been set to monkey-wrench—that spent all night adjusting to the temperature and emitting strangled and most unmetallic snorts, like an inhibited dragon that had decided to roar, then suppressed the notion. The way the sound of the oars changed when I rowed under a low bridge. Somewhere, an ordinary domestic cat walking along the lip of a concrete ramp, silhouetted against brilliant sunlight. The collapsible plastic toothbrush that in a moment of sanitary zeal I decided to sterilize in boiling water—and converted to a grotesque Salvador-Dali-molten-clock exhibit, corkscrewed and useless. The member of a Grand

Canyon raft party who asked, "Do you find soloing growth-forming?" On a beach, a rounded and reddish stone object, bumpled and bubucled and barely three inches across, that I assumed was an accretion of small pebbles until I noticed certain swirling patterns that suggested a lifeform—perhaps inside a mammalian cranium of limited capacity—and jotted in my notebook, "fossilized brain of stockbroker?" Below Headgate dam, a man's voice wafting from a trailer camp across the quiet and empty river: "We got a boat a-comin' down"; and after a pause, the voice of the woman now standing beside her man: "That's the way to go!" The Bureau of Reclamation employee at Yuma who trailered me around two dams and who had just been more or less terminally ill but had recovered and was now joyously ganging up on an unexpectedly sunlit future.

Off to my right, the sun slid below the riverbank. We putt-putted into shadow. Before long I managed to find, river left, a section of bank a shade less repelling than most. I squelched ashore, labored up a twenty-foot mud slope, secured one line to a skimpy tamarisk bush and the other to a folding metal kedge anchor—a sterling Steve Nelson suggestion—and saw that the mud indeed held it securely. Carrying gear up the slope got meaner every trip, but eventually I had camp established, up on the flat.

From there I could see, beyond the river, the line of desert mountains. Otherwise, nothing but sickly, encircling tamarisks. Immediately underfoot, mildly firm mud, deeply cracked. Rotting reed stalks. And clamshells. Clamshells everywhere.

The day seeped away. Grayness fell. I opened a bottle of California Cabernet, leaned back, took stock.

A slew of relevant factors. If this was delta camping, it was a pain. If the weather forecast held and rain came, it would be a royal waterworks pain. After the long morning's row, an incipient soreness in my left arm had become a clear and present pain. The monkey, now camped on my shoulder, had begun to screech. It was maybe fifty miles to El Golfo—and if I started early next morning and pushed hard and made it in one day and found a phone there, I could call the Sextons and maybe they could drive down right away. Conclusion: "The time has come. Let's get it over." Corollaries: "Maybe this is my last camp; the end is nearer than I'd thought."

Now, when we become aware of an approaching end we tend to look over our shoulders. Any kind of end. When we slide at last into prime dying time and get ready to relinquish tenure and pick up our black slips we begin, tradition says, to review our lives' follies and fulfillments. A community doomed by a dam often waxes historical, nostalgic. Ditto a nation or civilization that senses decline. Or even a species, tinged with self-awareness, that recognizes the tilt beyond apogee. Anyway, at my mud-clam camp, sure enough, I continued the process I'd begun, untidily, that afternoon. Under cover of darkness and Cabernet I sat and looked back, still sketchily and only a touch more tidily, at river and journey.

Now that we were at last about to reunite with its mother-lode sea, I felt glad to have the river firmly under my belt in a single piece. In a single piece . . . that was the big deal. The time had not yet come for partition and analysis; but a couple of things stood out. I was glad I'd lingered long enough at the source to imprint it on my mind so that, just as I'd hoped, it still hung there vividly. Hung there the way the earliest days of your life stand out in memory. Other starts, too: in a new job or country or love affair.

And now that I'd slept with the river for six months I understood her better. Although it was clear, for example, that Philip Fradkin had in one sense been right when he called the Colorado *A River No More*, I could see that in another sense he'd been wrong. The river was still there, was still alive. And what I'd seen had convinced me that in the end she would reassert herself.

There might be no need to wait for the reservoirs to silt up or the irrigated land to be salinated out of production. The dams wouldn't last forever. When they went there'd be a period of destruction and readjustment, sure. Just how much destruction would depend on whether they and their peripherals disintegrated in a slow and sensible, non-Hayduke fashion. But once the falling boulder of mankind hit the earth at the bottom of the mountain and came to a stop and Coyote could sleep on it at night, the river would be all right.

Another sip of Cabernet. Around me, the grayness had edged over into black. Only the river showed, pale and imprecise.

As for the journey I could now feel tapering away—this journey down the Colorado and down other rivers, too—I wished I'd been able to take it more slowly. Had had more time to stand and stare. But that was a minor and anticipated wart. All in all, things had turned out remarkably well. Mostly, I'd managed to keep my progress quiet and unostentatious, free from the artificiality and distortion that the presence of outside observers is bound to impose. Had succeeded in keeping it a journey, not an exploit.

As I'd felt sure would happen, the six months had changed me. Just how, I might not recognize till later. But perhaps the richest reward of any long wilderness journey is the way it allows you, insofar as such a thing is possible, to move outside the human bubble and look at the world free from the bubble's refractions and its incestuous and even more dangerous reflections. Given enough time outside the bubble, looking in, you gain perspective—as well as risk a new arrogance.

You can move outside the bubble much more easily if you travel alone. And only twice had anyone been in the raft with me. At the mouth of Havasu Creek I'd ferried Dave Knutson and one companion a few feet so that they could help Captain Ahab. Later, near Blythe, I'd pulled ashore and was checking tube pressure and other things when three wide-eyed Mexican boys, perhaps ten or twelve years old, materialized from nowhere and began asking questions; and when I was ready to go, one of them said, "Could you take me out a little way in the raft?" At first I said, "I'm afraid not. Nobody comes in this raft." Then I saw his face and remembered what it would have been like. The oldest boy looked afraid and refused my offer, but the other two clambered aboard and we went for a short row-around. Watching their faces, I'd been glad I changed my mind. I was still glad. But the point was that both sharing occasions had been so brief they hadn't even touched my solitude.

By now the paleness that was the river had almost fused with the night. The water made no sound.

Yes, solitude had been vital. Without it I would not have come to know the river. Would not have come to recognize, more surely than before, that a river, like most entities, is less a thing than a pattern, a process. You could see it as a cog, a pivotal cog, in the endless wheel of existence. Or as one element of a cycle that could be regarded—if you chose to look at it that way—as beginning at a certain spring in high and often snowcapped mountains where drops of fresh water began a long and tortuous journey through unknown lands until in the due course of time they, or their now-separate molecules, flowed into and merged with the vast salt sea—where, in the due course of more time, the sun's heat drew them up for temporary storage in clouds that, given the right winds and arrows of chance, might drift over certain high and possibly snowcapped mountains where cold air would force them to decant these molecules of desalinated water back near the same source spring from which—if you still visualized the never-ending cycle as starting there—you could say they had brought forth the river.

A final sip of wine. Yes, a river, even more than most entities, never died. It just folded back into the whole.

A coyote yowled for breakfast, close. By 8:30 I'd reloaded the raft and unkedged the Nelson anchor and squelched down through the mud for the last time. We drifted downriver with the barely perceptible current and within half an hour the toilet brush and I had managed to remove almost all the goo from sandals and raft. Standing up ceased to be a hazardous operation.

As I completed the other morning prelude chores I saw, not far ahead, a small metal dinghy. The two young Mexicans lifting their gill nets were the first humans I'd seen since before The Bend. They were friendly, spoke fair English. I sought mirage-land confirmations. El Golfo? A hundred kilometers. Yes, there were phones there, said one netter. No, said the other, no phones. But they agreed that down in the estuary, at Isla Montague, I must keep left or I'd find myself out in "the big ocean." We waved goodbye. I started the outboard motor and swung the tiller around and headed downriver, toward El Golfo—and a reunion, sooner or later, with John and Victoria Sexton.

Soon, two more small gill-net boats. I waved at their occupants; wondered, presciently, if they were the last humans I'd see on my river.

The river widened. The banks rose taller, steeper. The unfolding prospect grew steadily duller. But once, where the left bank sloped more gently, an old coyote ambled down it, a little stiffly and perhaps a little sadly, and stood watching me pass—no problema—then lowered his head and drank. Once, on a sandbar, sure enough, a great blue heron. The sun came out and I traveled in shirtsleeves and it was warm and pleasant. An invitation to dawdle. But the weather forecast still whispered in one ear, the monkey in the other, and all morning and on into the afternoon I kept rivering relentlessly toward the salt sea. Then the river had widened again and I was traveling through yet another and more open and radically different world. The channel now averaged half a mile across. Once, improbably, it narrowed to barely forty feet and the whole flow ripped through this bottleneck. But then we were back out on a wide and featureless waterway and there was nothing but monotony.

We motored on. The river grew still wider, the banks even taller, steeper, bleaker. Now, a bush was an event. Then the tide turned. Soon, an upriver wind allied itself with the tide. By hugging lee shores I still made some headway. Some. But the river grew yet wider, the banks even bleaker. No interesting bush events now. Wind and waves increased.

By the time we approached Punta Invencible I knew it was no good. Forget El Golfo that day.

Beyond the point, according to my map, the estuary would flare suddenly wide. For incoming tides, this was the bottleneck that generated tidal bores. For me, the place would rewrite options. In the open water beyond the point, the southerly wind would probably kill all hope of useful progress. Might even spell danger. And short of the point, with both banks sheer mudwalls, there was no place I could camp. Just beyond the point, though, the map proclaimed a slough, river right.

We pulled clear of Punta Invencible. The wind indeed wilder. The waves bigger, steeper. But over on the far shore, barely visible yet hinting at sanctuary, the slough. I motored across, pulled into its mouth.

The high banks indeed gave shelter from the wind, and along their rims I could see green grass. I squelched up the least daunting mud slope and took the photographs I'd promised Anita Williams of this "Indian wheat" that might offer rich food potential for low-rainfall, alkaline-soil lands. Then I paused, just looking.

The grass formed a green border along the river, twenty or thirty paces wide. Beyond that, bare mud. Flat, featureless mud. The day's last sunlight angled across it and the wind had momentarily eased, and under different circumstances I suppose the place might have enchanted me. Well, interested me. But the monkey was now yelping. And dark upriver cloudbanks corroborated the weather forecast. Westward, clouds were marshaling along the mountaintops, too. Problema.

So it came about that at Camp 188—if all went well, my last of the journey—I at last did what I'd had vaguely in mind for six months and had consistently put off: I nightcamped in the raft. It worked just fine—though around midnight I came half-awake to find we had settled on the dry bed of the slough.

The alarm sounded, small but shrill. We were afloat again. There was no wind. Eastward, stars studded the sky. North and west, though, nothing but blackness.

By the time I'd finished breakfast the eastern sky hinted at creeping dawn. When I rowed out beyond the slough's mouth, into open water, the night was dying and I could just about see where we were going. Still a flat calm. But the black cloud blanket creeping across the western sky.

At sixteen minutes past six o'clock on that morning of January 17, I started the outboard, swung the tiller, began to motor down toward El Golfo and the sea.

At first, hugging the western shore, no wind. And the ebb tide picking up. Then, a light easterly breeze. I angled across to the eastern shore. Good shelter. Stronger current, too.

Peering ahead now. Trying to pick out the head of Isla Montague, that final big island close to the left bank, so that I could slide into its shelter.

Only one problem: the approaching storm. The storm that continued to build. The storm that menaced, exhilarated.

*The last day. "At sixteen minutes past six o'clock on that
morning of January 17th, I started the outboard, swung the
tiller, began to motor down toward El Golfo and the sea."
Lowering cloudbanks "left only a thin pale strip along
the eastern horizon. Into it, the sun came up like thunder."*

I motored on, still peering ahead. Slowly, the daylight gained strength.
It made the lowering cloudbanks look thicker, blacker. By now they left
only a thin pale strip along the eastern horizon. Into it, the sun came up like
thunder.

Like lightning, too. Level sunbeams shafted out across the gray estuary,
struck the western shoreline. That shore, which had been a brown mud
wall far off to my right—a mundane divider of grim gray waterway from
lowering black cloudbank—ignited. Burst into flame. Transmuted into luminous orange-red cliffs glowing with an unearthly incandescence. I sat
still, eyes riveted to this ethereal vision.

And then, double-arcing down, radiant against black cloudbank, two
rainbows. Rainbows that did not curve down parallel, the way normal double rainbows do. They converged—and intersected at the very lip of the
glowing, incandescent cliffs. For long moments the vision held. A glorious
barrier, incorporeal yet impregnable, fit to protect the Holy Grail.

Then, behind me, the sun must have lifted into the cloudbank. The light snuffed out. All around, river and land and sky once more stretched gray and dead.

I motored on.

Overhead, now, the clouds black, solid. A few big raindrops. And back to the north the storm clouds looming as black and threatening as those that had filled the mountain pass just after I said goodbye to John Sexton. A pleasing symmetry there, too. "Well, see you in six months," John had said. With luck, about right.

But one merciful difference between this storm and the one that had ushered in my journey. So far, no wind. Still a flat calm.

Soon, just visible in the murk, the low shape of Isla Montague. Yes, easy to miss, all right. I swung the tiller. We eased into the sheltered channel between island and shore, away from the gray space that indeed had the blank and open aspect of "the big ocean."

We motored on toward El Golfo.

The channel between island and shore felt like a river again. But everything gray now. The island's shoreline, drained by the tide, incised by muddy sloughs, wet-gray and mournful. Yet each slough, in its somber way, beautiful. One of them guarded—improbably, predictably, reassuringly—by a great blue heron.

Slowly, almost imperceptibly, the storm backed off. Retreated northward. No more rain fell. Soon, far ahead, a hint of slanting sunlight. We motored on, motored on.

An hour, and the hint of sunlight a veritable band of sunshine. Up binoculars. Mudflats and water tapering away forever. Their boundaries tenuous, trembling. Indeed a mirage. An insubstantial pageant, fading.

The island's shoreline began to swing away, right. Swung wider. Wider yet. Then we were no longer in a channel but out on an open gray expanse. Ahead, nothing but gray waves and sky. Left and right, low and dark, twin tapering lines that were land. But this expanse of water, was it river or sea? Had the last freshwater molecule really merged with the salt sea? The evidence seemed inconclusive, and if . . .

Close ahead, out in the gray waves, just for a moment, something appeared, vanished. Something solid and curving and black. Before I was even sure of what I'd seen, let alone drawn conclusions, the shape rolled again. This time, a black back and triangular fin, clear and undeniable. I smiled. Symbolic evidence, surely. A dolphin, it seemed to me, was a sea mammal, not a river creature.

I looked ahead again, beyond the place the dolphin had surfaced. On either flank, the thin dark lines of land tapered away to nothingness. Between them, only a vast and open grayness. Yet off to the left, at the edge of the grayness, that band of slanting sunlight.

I motored on, letting my eye roam over it all.

So that was the way the journey ended. With neither a bang nor a whimper. But at last, beyond shadow of reasonable doubt, the final freshwater molecules had achieved reunion. My river had ceased to be. Had closed its cycle. Had come home to our salt-sea mother.

I held the tiller steady. If that's how dying was—well, all right.

Garlands and Accolades

No solo journey is truly made alone, and many people helped make mine possible. Some were central to the project. Others passed like rafts in the night, but glinted. And although there may be a few who've escaped my wide backward-sweeping net, I want to say "thank you" to everyone who contributed, in all categories:

NAMED IN TEXT *(in order of appearance)*

Above all, John and Victoria Sexton, without whose nurturing—before, during and after the journey—this book might not exist.

Also Philip Fradkin; Dale and Frandee Johnson; Rex Paulson; Martin Litton; Bill Arnell; Bill Russell; Brian Rasmussen; Michael George and Pomeroy Collins; Dave Stimson; Karen Nelson; John Joseph; Dr. Emmett Miller; Dave and Jill Knutson, Jerome (Jerry) Knutson, Allan Duncan (Captain Ahab), Dan, John Whitescarver and Kevin Campbell (Spiderman); Dave Bassage; Julian Rhinehart; Blaine Hamann; Milos Russell; Houseboat Terry and Kathy; my Mexicali Good Samaritans—Anita and Charlie Williams, Alberto Gruel, Fernando, and Alfonso Cordova; Jon Barker and Catie Casson; Steve Nelson; and "The Captain" at Yurimuri.

APPEAR IN TEXT BUT REMAIN UNNAMED

Dr. Ron Chaplin; John Vail; Robert E. Harding, Refuge Officer at Brown's Park National Wildlife Refuge; Adrian B. Sanford, my camping-incognoscenti friend; Glade Ross, NPS Ranger at Lodore Ranger Station; Mark E. Bailey, Area Manager, and Terry Humphrey, Recreation Planner, Bureau of Land Management, Price, Utah, and Deborah Gigliotti, volunteer BLM ranger, Sand Wash; Mike Whelan, manager, and David, of Holiday River Expeditions at Green River, Utah; Janet Steinberg, who also suffers from digital clock drivel; Tom Workman, NPS river ranger at Lee's Ferry; "Jack" and all his party; Keven and Polly King of the main Knutson party, and Dan's companions, Greg and Warren; Dave Bassage's companions—Tom Counsellor, Phil Davis, Randy, Greg and Blake; Annette

Rhinehart; Charlie Workman, who detected civilization at Laughlin; Bill and Mary Jo Bursleis, who showed me around Lake Havasu City; Howard Carver of the Bureau of Reclamation, who ferried me past Parker and Headgate dams; Steve Cuddy, who accompanied Jon Barker for a spell; Leighton Robinson and John Roberts; and Jerry Power, of Yuma, Arizona.

Rafting Instruction

Martin Litton (see Chapter 3), Curtis Chang, Dick Shedd, Barry Dow, Chris Quinn and Mike Gagner of Great River Journeys (now Oars/Dories), Lewiston, Idaho; also Cary Hibbard. And Doug Lawrence, Boise, Idaho, and Les Bechdel of Canyons Incorporated, McCall, Idaho.

Equipment, Food

Doug Tims (and George Aragon and Mike McLeod) of the Maravia Corp., Boise, Idaho, for all their help, which extended far beyond the raft itself; Jack Nelson (and John Pitetti and Kami Inman) of Cascade Outfitters, Springfield, Oregon, from whom I got not only most of my rafting gear but also staunch long-term support; Ron Mattson of Cascade Frames/Fabrications, Eugene, Oregon; Dick Carter of Ultraflex Oars, Lake Oswega, Oregon; Tom Martin, Dave Geoffrey and Larry Curtis of Avon Seagull Marine, Irvine, California, for their interest and advice, beyond supplying my outboard motor; Ray Danielson and Michael Anderson, for last-minute pre-trip equipment adjustments.

Wayne Gregory of Gregory Mountain Products, Temecula, Calfornia (packs); Alex Tilley of Tilley Endurables, Don Mills, Ontario, Canada (hat); Joel Freeman of Freeman Industries, Tuckahoe, New York (TRAK soapless supersoap); Robert Shanebrook of Eastman Kodak (film); Takao Akatsu of A&F Corp, Tokyo (stove).

Dennis Korn of AlpineAire Foods, Nevada City, California, for his care in tailoring a healthy menu to my meticulous demands, supplying the bulk of it and forwarding supplementary items along my route; Belinda Sanda of Backpacker's Pantry, Redding, California, for her altruism in referring me to AlpineAire; also Ken Fontecilla of Wee-Pak Foods; and Janice Harrell, chief dietician, Community Hospital, Monterey, California, for her lucid professional advice.

Logistics

Bureau of Reclamation: Julian Rhinehart and Blaine Hamann, of course (see Chapter 18). At Fontenelle—Gary Butterfield, Ron Hale, Lee Mink and Ken McKowan. At Flaming Gorge—Tom Welstad, Janell Pershon, Joe Parker, Allan Pallison, Floyd Gale and Leo Ragino. At Hoover—Deborah

Sewell, Joe Kahl and Howard Carver. At Parker—Freddy Hoggatt. At Yuma—Ed Lohman, Bob Steele, Harold Pritchett and Jerry Power.

National Park Service: At Dinosaur—Dennis Huffman, Nick Eason, Jim McBrayer, Dave Martin and Mary Damm. At Canyonlands—Harvey Wickware, Danny Sims, Dave Stimson and Larry Frederick. At Grand Canyon—Richard Marks, Ken Miller, Butch Wilson, Tom Workman, and Paddy, the very helpful ranger at Phantom.

U.S. Post Offices: John Parra and Shirley Nether, Green River, Wyoming; Frank Judd and Marynell Snow, Jensen, Utah.

Also, in various places and modes: C. L. ("Chip") Rawlins of Logan, Utah; Linda Paulson of the Great Outdoor shop, Pinedale, Wyoming; Tom Curry of BLM, Pinedale, Wyoming; John Robey of USGS, Menlo Park, California; Luna Leopold; Christopher and Martha McKellar, who gave me post-hospital succor in Salt Lake City on my way to Pinedale; Howard and Anita Swann of Santa Cruz, California; Dee Holiday of Holiday River Expeditions; Joe Schwenk of Hite Marine, Utah; A. C. Krogh and Mrs. Shannon Peters of Mead View, Arizona; Todd, of Wilderness River Adventure, who transported me and mine to the foot of Glen Canyon Dam; Al Goff; Antonio Sandoval; Dennis Underwood; Tom Clotfelter; and Fred Nagel.

GENERAL—*Direct and Indirect Aid*

Drs. Richard King, Basil Allaire, Ada Koransky and Stephen Barkalow—for coping with Fletcheritis and several undeniably real medical afflictions.

Steve Jones of Boise, Idaho—for going out of his way to point me in some early right directions. Jim Ward of Adventure 16; Finis Mitchell; Harvey Butchart; and Mike Johnson.

Also the Ledger family, who took photos on Flaming Gorge Reservoir; Verlin Hatch, who did likewise on Powell Reservoir; Ray Hofsinger, boatman, Holiday River Expeditions, who did the same, and more, at Jones Hole Creek, Whirlpool Canyon; Tom Rickets, who helped at Jensen; and Gary Anderson (and also Edith and Bill) of Wahweap Marina, Lake Powell, who assisted well beyond the call of duty.

REALIZATION OF THIS BOOK

Once again, I stand in profound debt to my literary agent, Carl D. Brandt. From the idea's germ, through every slow and often painful succeeding stage, he proved to be a superb and tireless river-book doctor. His secretary, Margaret Maycumber, nurse-assisted. His son, Cameron Brandt, managing editor of *The World Paper,* read an entire early draft manuscript and offered sterling suggestions.

Only in retrospect have I recognized how much I owe to Gustav Mahler, whose symphonies—shiningly captured on CDs by Georg Solti and the Chicago Symphony Orchestra—revitalized me, evening after evening, through months and years of writing and rewriting.

RESEARCH

Robert L. Reese, USFS, Pinedale, Wyoming, for Wind River botanical facts; David Taylor of Berkeley, California, and Jeff Obrecht of Wyoming Game and Fish Department, for beaver information; Brad Dimock, Flagstaff, Arizona, for the transcript of Buzz Holmstrom's journal.

Bruce R. Schmidt, Chief of Fisheries, State of Utah, for details of fishery management below Flaming Gorge Dam; Glade Ross, Dinosaur NP, for historical material on Lodore School, etc.; Tom Walgenbach, Jean Grace and Dr. Mel Bristowe for advice on Ephemeridae.

Also, in their different fields, Brant Calkin, SUWA; Charles Cartwright, former Park archaeologist, Canyonlands NP; Joseph Pagnano, Sr.; David Lavender; Tom Moody; Loie Evans; Nicole Tostevin, Gregory K. Silber.

Dr. William H. Calvin, who, personally and through his book *The River That Flows Uphill,* directed me to much "memory" material, including Elizabeth Loftus's work.

And the staffs of several libraries, notably: Bullhead City Library, Arizona; Pat LeFaivre, head librarian, Sweetwater County Library, Wyoming; Dr. William Frank of the Huntington Library, San Marino, California; Joe Johnson et al. at Monterey City Library, California; Gail Knoles, Mary MacDonald, Sandy Palazzolo and Cindy Brinsmead of Carmel Valley Library, California.

ASSISTANCE IN PHOTOGRAPHIC AND OTHER MATTERS

Steve Myrick, Rob Mari, Anthony Barker, Kevin Campbell, Anita Williams, Sylvia Purcupile, Anne Larsen, Tony de Sugny, Veronica Tagg; and Cliff Kennedy, my long-time computer guru.

PUBLICATION

All the good people at Knopf who have gone a long way toward restoring my faith in publishing. Ashbel Green, my editor for many years, who shepherded the book, tirelessly, from germ to printer and beyond—supporting and mildly cajoling me as necessary, while always tolerating my idiosyncrasies. His assistant, Jennifer Bernstein, a paragon of cooperation and efficiency. Anthea Lingeman, the caring and expert designer. David Lindroth, who labored lovingly over the maps. And Melvin Rosenthal, production editor, who once again questioned and corrected—meticulously yet understandingly—my words and punctuation, and did everything possible, and then some, to nudge us toward unattainable perfection.

SOURCES QUOTED OR LEANED ON (*in order of appearance*)

A River No More: Philip L. Fradkin (Knopf, 1981)

Canyon Country: Julius Stone (Dutton, 1932)

The Wind in the Willows: Kenneth Grahame (first published in England, 1908)

Run, River, Run: Anne Zwinger (paperback: University of Arizona Press, 1984)

Sensitive Chaos: Theodor Schwenk (Rudolf Steiner Press, England, 1965)

"The Cataract of Lodore" (poem): Robert Southey

The Exploration of the Colorado River and Its Canyons: John Wesley Powell, introduced and edited by Wallace Stegner (paperback: Penguin, 1987)

River Rescue: Les Bechdel and Slim Ray (Appalachian Mountain Club, 1985)

Journal of Solo Trip Down the Green and Colorado Rivers: Buzz Holmstrom (privately published typewritten copy of his journal). Also an article by Robert Ormond Case: *He Shot the Colorado Alone* (*Saturday Evening Post*, February 26, 1938)

Through the Grand Canyon, from Wyoming to Mexico: Ellsworth Kolb (Macmillan, 1920)

Desert Notes: Barry Lopez (paperback: Avon, 1981)

"What Any Lover Learns" (poem): Archibald MacLeish

The Beatles, a Yogi, and the Search for Plants: Roger Di Silvestro (Audubon Engagement Calendar, 1995)

Solitude: A Return to the Self: Anthony Storr (paperback: Ballantine, 1989)

"An Essay on Man" (poem): Alexander Pope

Down the Colorado: Robert Brewster Stanton (University of Oklahoma Press, 1965)

"The Hollow Men" (poem): T. S. Eliot

The Place No One Knew: Eliot Porter (Sierra Club, 1963, 1966)

River Runners of the Grand Canyon: David Lavender (Grand Canyon Natural History Association, 1985)

The Journey Home: Edward Abbey (paperback: Dutton, 1977)

The Origin of Species: Charles Darwin (paperback: New American Library, 1958)

Affect and Accuracy in Recall: Studies of "Flashbulb" Memories:

E. Winograd and U. Neisser, editors (Cambridge University Press, 1992). Contains both "memory" studies quoted in my Chapter 19: Elizabeth Loftus on the Tony Conigliaro/Jack Hamilton case; and Ulric Neisser's *Challenger* surveys.

"Ozymandias" (poem): Percy Bysshe Shelley

Should Trees Have Standing?: Christopher D. Stone (paperback: Tioga Publishing Co., Palo Alto, Calif., 1988)

Religion Without Revelation: Julian Huxley (paperback: New American Library, 1957)

I, Fellini: Charlotte Chandler (Random House, 1995)

Photographic Credits

Photographs by author (sometimes with assistance, as mentioned or implied in text), with the following exceptions: page 270 by Anthony Barker; pages 272 and 279 by Kevin Campbell; and page 374 by Anita Williams.

A Note about the Author

COLIN FLETCHER was born in Wales and educated in England. After six years' World War II service in the Royal Marines, he went to East Africa in 1947, farmed for four years in Kenya and later surveyed and built a road over a virgin mountain in Southern Rhodesia (now Zimbabwe). In the 1950s, he crossed the Atlantic and prospected—among other pursuits—in northern and western Canada. In 1956, he moved south to California. Soon afterward he spent a summer walking from Mexico to Oregon across California's deserts and mountains. Later he became the first man known to have walked the length of Grand Canyon National Park within the Canyon's rim. Each of these feats generated a book: *The Thousand-Mile Summer* and *The Man Who Walked Through Time*. Mr. Fletcher continues to explore—and to write books: *The Complete Walker* (revised twice), *The Winds of Mara, The Man from the Cave,* and *The Secret Worlds of Colin Fletcher.*

A Note on the Type

The text of this book was set in a typeface called Times New Roman, designed by Stanley Morison (1889–1967) for *The Times* (London) and first introduced by that newspaper in 1932. Among typographers and designers of the twentieth century, Stanley Morison was a strong forming influence—as a typographical adviser to the Monotype Corporation, as a director of two distinguished publishing houses, and as a writer of sensibility, erudition and keen practical sense.

Composed by American-Stratford Graphic Service,
Brattleboro, Vermont
Printed and bound by Quebecor Printing,
Martinsburg, West Virginia
Maps by David Lindroth, Inc.
Designed by Anthea Lingeman